EMERGING WRITING RESEARCH FROM THE MIDDLE EAST–NORTH AFRICA REGION

International Exchanges on the Study of Writing

Series Editors: Terry Myers Zawacki, Magnus Gustafsson, and Joan Mullin

The International Exchanges on the Study of Writing Series publishes book-length manuscripts that address worldwide perspectives on writing, writers, teaching with writing, and scholarly writing practices, specifically those that draw on scholarship across national and disciplinary borders to challenge parochial understandings of all of the above. The series aims to examine writing activities in 21st-century contexts, particularly how they are informed by globalization, national identity, social networking, and increased cross-cultural communication and awareness. As such, the series strives to investigate how both the local and the international inform writing research and the facilitation of writing development.

The WAC Clearinghouse, Colorado State University Open Press, and University Press of Colorado are collaborating so that these books will be widely available through free digital distribution and low-cost print editions. The publishers and the Series editors are committed to the principle that knowledge should freely circulate. We see the opportunities that new technologies have for further democratizing knowledge. And we see that to share the power of writing is to share the means for all to articulate their needs, interest, and learning into the great experiment of literacy.

Other Books in the Series

Plane, Sylvie, et al. (Eds.). (2017). *Research on writing: Multiple perspectives.*

Lillis, Theresa, Harrington, Kathy, Lea, Mary R. & Mitchell, Sally (Eds.). (2015). *Working with academic literacies: Case studies towards transformative practice.*

Myers Zawacki, Terry & Cox, Michelle (Eds.). (2014). *WAC and second-language writers: Research towards linguistically and culturally inclusive programs and practices.*

Kirkpatrick, Andy & Xu, Zhichang. (2012). *Chinese rhetoric and writing: An introduction for language teachers.*

EMERGING WRITING RESEARCH FROM THE MIDDLE EAST–NORTH AFRICA REGION

Edited by Lisa R. Arnold, Anne Nebel, and Lynne Ronesi

The WAC Clearinghouse
wac.colostate.edu
Fort Collins, Colorado

University Press of Colorado
upcolorado.com
Boulder, Colorado

The WAC Clearinghouse, Fort Collins, Colorado 80523-1040

University Press of Colorado, Boulder, Colorado 80303

© 2017 by Lisa R. Arnold, Anne Nebel, and Lynne Ronesi. This work is licensed under a Creative Commons Attribution-NonCommercial-NoDerivatives 4.0 International.

Library of Congress Cataloging-in-Publication Data

Names: Arnold, Lisa R., editor. | Nebel, Anne L., editor. | Ronesi, Lynne, editor.
Title: Emerging writing research from the Middle East–North Africa region / edited by Lisa R. Arnold, Anne Nebel, and Lynne Ronesi.
Other titles: International exchanges on the study of writing.
Description: Fort Collins, Colorado : The WAC Clearinghouse ; Boulder, Colorado : University Press of Colorado, [2017] | Series: International exchanges on the study of writing
Identifiers: LCCN 2017008065| ISBN 9781607327035 (pbk.) | ISBN 9781607327042 (ebook)
Subjects: LCSH: English language—Rhetoric—Study and teaching (Higher)—Middle East. | English language—Rhetoric—Study and teaching (Higher)—Africa, North. | English language—Rhetoric—Study and teaching (Higher)—Foreign speakers.
Classification: LCC PE1068.M628 E46 2017 | DDC 808/.042071056—dc23
LC record available at https://lccn.loc.gov/2017008065

Copyeditor: Don Donahue
Design and Production: Mike Palmquist
Cover Image: Alexey Sergeev
Cover: Adapted from a design by Abdul Wasay Ahmad, AWA Design, Dubai
Series Editors: Terry Myers Zawacki, Magnus Gustafsson, and Joan Mullin

The WAC Clearinghouse supports teachers of writing across the disciplines. Hosted by Colorado State University, and supported by the Colorado State Univeristy Open Press, it brings together scholarly journals and book series as well as resources for teachers who use writing in their courses. This book is available in digital formats for free download at wac.colostate.edu.

Founded in 1965, the University Press of Colorado is a nonprofit cooperative publishing enterprise supported, in part, by Adams State University, Colorado State University, Fort Lewis College, Metropolitan State University of Denver, Regis University, University of Colorado, University of Northern Colorado, Utah State University, and Western State Colorado University. For more information, visit upcolorado.com.

Contents

Acknowledgments vii

Foreword ix
    Rula Diab

Introduction 3
    Lisa R. Arnold, Anne Nebel, and Lynne Ronesi

SECTION 1: COMPLICATING PREVALENT ASSUMPTIONS

1 Linguistic Superdiversity and English-Medium Higher Education in Qatar 27
    Anne Nebel

2 Global Spread of English in Academia and Its Effects on Writing Instruction in Turkish Universities 41
    Hacer Hande Uysal

3 Expanding Transnational Frames into Composition Studies: Revising the Rhetoric and Writing Minor at the American University in Cairo . 67
    James P. Austin

SECTION 2: CONSIDERING THE IMPORTATION OF WESTERN MODELS

4 Territorial Borders and the Teaching of Writing in English: Lessons from Research at the University of Balamand 85
    Samer A. Annous, Maureen O'Day Nicolas, and Martha A. Townsend

5 An Arabian Gulf: First-Year Composition Textbooks at an International Branch Campus in Qatar 115
    Mysti Rudd and Michael Telafici

6 Great Expectations or Great Outcomes? Exploring the Context of English Language Policy Transfer in Bahrain 133
    Aneta L Hayes and Nasser Mansour

SECTION 3: STRIVING FOR BALANCE ACROSS BORDERS

7 Rewriting Resistance: Negotiating Pedagogical and Curricular Change in a U.S./Kurdish Transnational Partnership 151
    Connie Kendall Theado, Holly Johnson, Thomas Highley, and Saman Hussein Omar

8 Integrating Writing Assignments at an American Branch Campus in Qatar: Challenges, Adaptations, and Recommendations 175
Ryan T. Miller and Silvia Pessoa

9 Hybrid Writing Positions within WAC/WID Initiatives: Connecting Faculty Writing Expectations and MENA Cultures 201
Amy Hodges and Brenda Kent

Section 4: Creating Student Space(s)

10 Literacy Narratives Across Borders: Beirut and Dearborn as Twenty-First Century Transnational Spaces 219
Lisa R. Arnold, William DeGenaro, Rima Iskandarani, Malakeh Khoury, Zane Sinno, and Margaret Willard-Traub

11 The Dance of Voices: A Study on Academic Writing at AUB 241
Najla Jarkas and Juheina Fakhreddine

12 Students Running the Show: Performance Poetry Night 265
Lynne Ronesi

Afterword 289
Michele Eodice

Contributors 295

Acknowledgments

The editors would like to acknowledge and thank the many teachers and students from the Middle East–North Africa region whose perspectives and work are addressed in this volume.

We sincerely thank Dr. Rula Diab and Dr. Michele Eodice for their reflections on the volume, as articulated in the foreword and afterword.

We appreciate the guidance of the International Exchanges on the Study of Writing series editors—Terry Myers Zawacki, Magnus Gustafsson, and Joan Mullin—as well as our anonymous reviewers, for their support in bringing this work to fruition. Additionally, we are grateful to Ashleigh Petts at North Dakota State University for her help with proofreading the manuscript. And thanks to Mike Palmquist, for his promotion of research, exchange, and open-access scholarship through The WAC Clearinghouse.

Finally, we are grateful to our own colleagues, friends, and families for their continued interest in and encouragement of our work.

Foreword

Rula Diab
LEBANESE AMERICAN UNIVERSITY (LEBANON)

Developing students' English writing skills in the MENA region has been a long-standing endeavor, in view of the region's various American-style universities, some of which are well established and date back to the 1800s and early 1900s, such as the American University of Beirut (AUB) and Lebanese American University (LAU) in Lebanon and the American University of Cairo (AUC) in Egypt. More recently, there has also been a steady proliferation of English-medium universities and international branch campuses (IBCs) in the area, especially in the Gulf, as demonstrated by the Education City in Qatar, which houses international branches of six American universities. Together, these universities provide a headquarters for research related to writing pedagogy in the MENA region, research which is beginning to make a name for itself in writing scholarship, as exemplified in this volume. Indeed, this timely volume presents a much-needed exploration of the various approaches to the teaching and learning of writing taking place at universities in this region, in addition to a discussion of the many challenges faced by writing program administrators and writing faculty in this linguistically, culturally, and ethnically diverse area.

We can better understand the exegesis for this volume by considering how conversations about writing programs and pedagogy have evolved in the region, particularly in the last decade. In October 2007, a symposium on MENA writing centers was held in Doha, Qatar, led by Dr. Michele Eodice and attended by more than fifty writing program administrators, writing center professionals, and writing faculty from the MENA region. As director of the AUB Writing Center at the time, I was fortunate to participate in this symposium and meet a large number of scholars and practitioners in the region interested in the learning and teaching of writing. The symposium provided a unique opportunity to network, discuss the importance of developing students' writing skills, and explore writing programs and centers at other universities. Participants discussed various topics related to second language writing in general and, in particular, issues that continue to confront those of us who are teaching in and managing writing programs in the MENA region. These issues—many of which are addressed in this volume—include the complex socio-cultural and sociopolitical dimensions of writing in this multilingual region, the various challenges related to implementing Writing Across the Curriculum/Writing in the Disciplines (WAC/WID) programs, as well as administrator, faculty, and student attitudes towards and misconceptions about teaching writing, writing programs, and writing centers.

One major and immediately tangible result of the Doha 2007 symposium was the establishment of a regional branch of the International Writing Centers Association (IWCA)—the Middle East North Africa Writing Centers Alliance (MENAWCA), which has since become an influential organization that encourages writing research and professional networking in the MENA region. Although this volume is not affiliated with MENAWCA, it can be seen as a response to the growing professionalization of writing pedagogy and research in the region, which has been encouraged in part by the series of biennial conferences sponsored by the organization since 2007. These conferences have provided space for regular conversations across national and institutional borders about the specific challenges and opportunities of writing pedagogy and program development in the region. The MENAWCA conferences in 2009 (UAE University, Al Ain), 2011 (American University of Sharjah), 2012 (College of the North Atlantic, Doha, Qatar), 2014 (Canadian University of Dubai), and 2016 (Sultan Qaboos University, Muscat, Oman) have explored a variety of themes, including the development of writing centers in the MENA region; situating and sustaining writing centers and serving the academic community by supporting student writing; creating a "writing culture;" and investigating the relationships between theoretical ideals and writing program, writing center, and writing classroom realities in the MENA region. These conferences were meaningful for me especially because I joined LAU and became the founding director of its writing center, which started operating in 2010. I had the opportunity to share my experience proposing and establishing the LAU Writing Center, and I outlined the challenges faced (Diab, 2009, February).

The main theme of the 2012 conference—about establishing a "writing culture"—stands out as a crucial one in the MENA region, which is addressed in this volume as well as in my own work: How do students and faculty view writing? How much writing are students doing outside the required writing classes? How dominant is plagiarism? How can students and faculty become more involved in WAC approaches? At the time of the MENAWCA conference, I was heavily involved in exploring such questions about how a "writing culture" could be fostered at LAU with the help of the new writing center and the English program. At the 2012 conference, I shared the proposed plans: offering services to the LAU community, namely individualized tutorials and group workshops on specific writing topics that help improve students' writing and emphasize the importance of WAC/ WID; planning to establish a formal WAC initiative, which would outline specific WAC policies and implement them in the curriculum as needed; and finally, proposing to expand writing center services by establishing another branch of the writing center in the second LAU campus in Byblos. We also planned to offer community outreach, such as conducting workshops for other universities and high schools in Lebanon to help them establish their own writing centers and train some of their teachers to run them (Diab, 2012, November). There were, of course, the usual obstacles to the above initiatives, such as funding and concerns of some disciplinary faculty regarding their responsibility in teaching writing in their disciplines, as well as the role of the writing center (Diab, 2012).

In this volume, several chapters connect with my own experience of negotiating institutional realities with the larger goal of developing a "writing culture." For example, Samer Annous, Maureen Nicolas, and Martha Townsend highlight a situation similar to ones I have encountered firsthand at more than one university in the region: they describe the challenges involved in teaching writing at multilingual English-medium universities where this teaching is not maintained or even valued across the curriculum. Their findings, reported in "Territorial Borders and the Teaching of Writing in English," suggest that disciplinary faculty do not believe that English skills such as writing can or should be reinforced in the disciplines, a common phenomenon at universities in Lebanon and the region. Annous, Nicolas, and Townsend's investigation of students' attitudes also reveals a similar apathy and misconception related to English writing across the curriculum. My own experience supports their conclusion that "territorial knowledge boundaries" can be extremely harmful to students' learning of English writing, especially in an EFL context. Similarly, but reporting from an IBC in Qatar, Ryan Miller and Silvia Pessoa explore faculty attitudes and expectations about writing. While acknowledging the need for adaptation to the particular local context, Miller and Pessoa argue that institutions such as theirs need a focus on writing and reading across the curriculum.

Several chapters in this book also address the socio-cultural and socio-political dimensions of writing and the teaching of writing in the MENA region, including student identity and multilingualism in the MENA-based writing classroom and faculty attitudes and expectations. For example, Lisa Arnold, William DeGenaro, Rima Iskandarani, Malakeh Khoury, Zane Sinno, and Margaret Willard-Traub argue that transnational exchanges can help to not only motivate students but also to suggest curricular and institutional change, a claim I wholeheartedly agree with and support. Their project, which involved students at AUB and the University of Michigan-Dearborn, opens up exciting avenues for transnational and international exploration and collaboration in writing scholarship. My own experience in Lebanon suggests that such exchanges are valuable for their exploration of students' linguistic identities in more than one context and culture. In Lebanon, for instance, there could be several factors contributing to students' perceptions of their linguistic, ethnic, and national identity (Diab, 2009); transnational exchanges can help students to not only explore others' identities but to also become more aware of their own. Aneta Hayes and Nasser Mansour, based on their qualitative study of teachers' perceptions of the influence of societal factors on the success of English-medium education in Bahrain, suggest that making certain modifications to the curriculum to make it better fit students' own socio-cultural context may sometimes be necessary. Amy Hodges and Brenda Kent interview faculty in the disciplines, namely engineering faculty, at an IBC, to examine the challenges they faced regarding the teaching and learning of writing. They argue that a professional tutor with teaching experience may be an appropriate support for WID courses in the MENA region. Such studies emphasizing the importance of recognizing and, when necessary, adapting to the particular local context when integrating or adopting foreign curricula should be taken into consideration, particularly in an EFL context.

I cannot think of anyone more suitable for undertaking the collection and editing of this timely volume than Drs. Lisa Arnold, Anne Nebel, and Lynne Ronesi. Their collective, rich, and varied experiences with writing instruction and writing program administration in Lebanon, Qatar, and the UAE, respectively, have enabled them to put together an insightful and thought-provoking collection of articles that will be of interest to both professionals in the region as well as globally. The above mentioned sociocultural and sociopolitical dimensions of writing in the MENA region, transnational and international collaborations, World Englishes and translingual approaches to writing pedagogy, and faculty attitudes and expectations are only some of the many important issues explored in this volume that will be of interest to researchers and practitioners worldwide.

Almost a decade after the 2007 symposium in Doha that resulted in the establishment of the MENAWCA, writing research in the MENA region has started to carve its place in writing scholarship, as exemplified in this volume. May this collection of articles be the first of many that will help to familiarize the rest of the world with writing research and practice in this richly diverse and complex area.

References

Diab, Rula L. (2009). Lebanese university students' perceptions of ethnic, national, and linguistic identity and their preferences for foreign language learning in Lebanon. *The Linguistics Journal, Special Edition, September 2009*, 101–120. Retrieved from http://www.linguistics-journal.com/2014/01/07/lebanese-university-students-perceptions-of-ethnic-national-and-linguistic-identity-and-their-preferences-of-foreign-language-learning-in-lebanon/.

Diab, Rula L. (2009, February). *Starting from scratch: Establishing a writing center at the Lebanese American University*. Paper presented at the Middle East North Africa Writing Centers Alliance (MENAWCA) Conference, Al-Ain, UAE.

Diab, Rula L. (2012). Faculty perceptions of a new writing center. *Academic Exchange Quarterly, 16*(4), 85–90.

Diab, Rula L. (2012, November). *Fostering a "writing culture" at the Lebanese American University: The role of the writing center*. Paper presented at the Middle East North Africa Writing Centers Alliance (MENAWCA) Conference, Doha, Qatar.

EMERGING WRITING RESEARCH FROM THE MIDDLE EAST– NORTH AFRICA REGION

Photograph by Alexey Sergeev. Used with permission.

Introduction

Lisa R. Arnold
NORTH DAKOTA STATE UNIVERSITY (US)

Anne Nebel
GEORGETOWN UNIVERSITY (QATAR)

Lynne Ronesi
AMERICAN UNIVERSITY OF SHARJAH (UAE)

A university student in the United Arab Emirates watches a Spoken Word channel on YouTube, and, feeling more confident, starts to draft a poem on his phone for a campus performance poetry event. A student in Beirut, Lebanon and another in Dearborn, Michigan reflect on the information gathered during their Skype call as they begin to compose a literacy narrative about their partner. In Doha, a student educated only in English since kindergarten who speaks Spanish and Arabic at home wonders what to write on a survey that prompts her for her "second language." Two faculty in Beirut struggle to facilitate an authorial research voice in English for students whose heritage languages are French and Arabic, while two colleagues in Qatar worry their students might not relate to the topics and perspectives in their assigned American textbooks. Long-term faculty in Cairo fear possible disenfranchisement when their department adopts a more U.S.-based curricular approach. Secondary school teachers in Bahrain who are obliged to employ Communicative Language Teaching to support student transition to western-style universities protest that the model's objectives are not shared by students, their parents, or society at large. In Turkey, faculty express concern that micro- and macro-level institutional and state language policies seem to shortchange instruction in academic writing both in English and in Turkish. Kurdish faculty in Iraq, involved by their administration in "yet another" partnership with an international university contest the relevance of western-based approaches, particularly student-centered strategies, given Kurdish institutional and cultural constraints.

These scenarios, detailed in the chapters of this collection, *Emerging Writing Research from the Middle East–North Africa Region*, represent some of the many situated and strategic writing initiatives at postsecondary institutions in the area we refer to as the MENA region. These few examples, along with the multifarious negotiations described in the following 12 chapters, serve to highlight how American "expertise" in writing studies does not always translate smoothly with(in) local institutional and community cultures of writing in the Middle East. Although events in the MENA region dominate world news, it is an area little understood by the rest of the world—certainly historically, politically, and culturally, but also within the discipline of Rhetoric and Composition. As Composition Studies and related disciplines make a "global turn" (Donahue, 2009; Hesford, 2006; Muchiri, Mulamba, Myers & Ndoloi, 1995), perspectives from the MENA region have only very recently been included in the discussion (Arnold, 2014; Golson & Holdijk, 2012; Ronesi, 2011, 2012; Zenger, Mullin & Haviland, 2014).

Consequently, there is an increasing need for research into post-secondary writing practices and pedagogy in the MENA region. This is particularly so as the MENA region has been the site of longstanding and revered institutions of American-style liberal arts institutions of higher education—in particular, the American University of Beirut in Lebanon (founded in 1866) and American University of Cairo in Egypt (founded in 1919)—as well as, in the last two decades, the location of a steadily growing number of English-medium universities and international branch campuses (IBCs), particularly in the Arabian (or Persian) Gulf States. Given the all too frequent perception of the MENA region as ideologically, politically, and culturally opposed to "the West," the curricular trajectory of these institutions, "in all [their] contradictory complexity" (Hall, 2014, p. 6) offers an important opportunity for examining the interactions between various cultures, different educational systems, and diverse faculty and students. Indeed, given prevailing assumptions about the East-West polemic, many of our readers may well wonder whether, and how, a mutually agreeable balance among stakeholders could ever be struck in these institutions.

The scholarship in this collection brings these exceptional collaborations and explorations to light and attests to the many strategic and thoughtful practices of teaching and learning writing that are taking place, as well as the varied challenges faced by writing faculty and administrators in the region. This scholarship needs to be shared globally, as it will shape how writing centers, writing programs, and Writing in the Disciplines (WID) and Writing Across the Curriculum (WAC) initiatives, in the region and outside of it, will respond to the increasing globalization of higher education, as well as to international discussions about World Englishes and other language varieties, and translingual approaches to writing and writing pedagogy. Further, insights from MENA writing studies have the potential to help composition and language scholars in North American and Europe expand their theorizing and practice in more globally informed directions.

Situating Writing Studies in the Middle East–North Africa (MENA) Region

To fully appreciate the chapters in this volume, it is important for readers to have some understanding about the MENA region. The World Bank designates the following countries as comprising the MENA region:

> Algeria, Bahrain, Djibouti, Egypt, Iran, Iraq, Israel, Jordan, Kuwait, Lebanon, Libya, Malta, Morocco, Oman, Qatar, Saudi Arabia, Syria, Tunisia, United Arab Emirates, West Bank and Gaza, and Yemen (World Bank, 2013)

However, by all accounts, the area understood as MENA has not been officially standardized. Citing religious and historical commonalities, Alan Weber (2010) describes MENA as "delineating regions where Islam is the dominant religion and which encompasses nations and peoples who were formerly part of an Islamic empire or Caliphate" (p. 16.2)—a definition which includes Turkey in the MENA region, as we did in this volume.

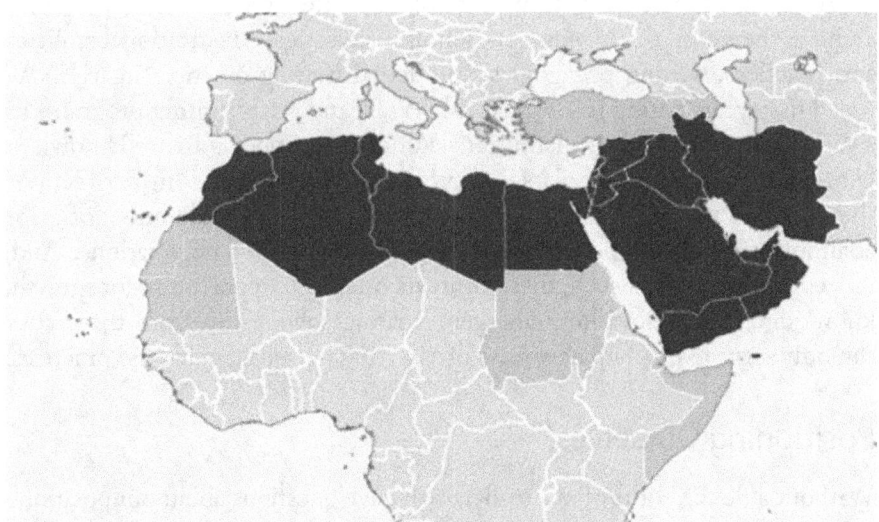

Figure 1. MENA (2011). Courtesy of Wikimedia Commons.

Even under this umbrella definition, the MENA region is one of extreme diversity. Economic disparity characterizes this region of 300 million, with some of the wealthiest countries in the world, such as the oil-rich Gulf States of Kuwait, Saudi Arabia, Qatar, and the United Arab Emirates, and resource-scarce countries such as Egypt and Yemen (World Bank, 2013). While Islam and Arabic are uniting features of most of the MENA countries, there is religious and linguistic plurality, and Arabic dialects very widely, as do traces of the linguistic and cultural practices of former British and French colonizers. The *lingua francas* of English and French today figure largely in the identity of many countries, the effects of colonization and globalization. MENA residents often negotiate a number of languages and dialects, and incorporate both local and global approaches and practices in their lives—a flexibility and accommodation people from predominantly monolingual contexts would find unfamiliar and challenging. As such, we understand the MENA region as a truly globalized one, in which historical and political realities have resulted in hybridity where different traditions, ideologies, rhetorics, and practices are navigated by its peoples—those whom Edward Said (1993) has referred to as "the political figures between domains, between forms, between homes, and between languages" (p. 332). Surpassing the notion of hybridity, MENA becomes a site of superdiversity (Vertovec, 2007), where increased flows of peoples, cultures and languages intersect and interact, aided by advances in technologies and communication systems, in ways yet to be fully explored or understood.

As such, negotiating within that complex site "in between" is the overarching theme of this volume, as scholars investigate institutional policies and practices, writing pedagogies, and actual writing practices in MENA-based first-year writing (FYW), WAC/WID, and other writing programs in a variety of postsecondary institutions. While these models are well known to U.S.-educated writing scholars and professors, the intricate "in-betweeness" these models occupy in a MENA context requires an abandonment of prior assumptions and are, perhaps, best viewed as constant negotiations. And, indeed, understood as such, these contexts offer rich opportunity for growth, knowledge, and innovation; emergent writing scholarship from these sites can only serve to open up new ways of assessing our pedagogies and practices.

Positioning Ourselves

Without a doubt, some of our readers will have questions about our positioning as editors, as well as the voices included (and not included) in this collection. From the beginning, we were well aware of our positions as relative "outsiders" in the MENA region—we are three Caucasian, American-born, and American-educated women who do not speak Arabic fluently. Simply put, we do not, and cannot, represent the vast majority of those who teach writing in higher education across the region. At the same time, we collectively have more than 28 years of experience living and working in the region. When we sent out the call for chapter proposals (CFP), we were all situated in the region—Arnold at the American University of Beirut as an assistant professor of English and writing program administrator (WPA); Ronesi at the American University of Sharjah as an assistant professor in the Department of Writing Studies; and Nebel at Georgetown University Qatar as an instructor of first year writing, Assistant Dean and Director of Academic Services. Arnold has an educational background in rhetoric and composition, Ronesi in TESOL and curriculum and instruction, and Nebel in applied linguistics.

We were each invested in pursuing the collection for a variety of reasons. Generally speaking, we wanted to do our part to overcome the dearth of published writing research in the MENA region by collecting diverse perspectives that could shed light on the state of writing research in the region. In addition, we wanted to facilitate a conversation across the region about how different writing faculty have responded to the challenges and opportunities of their institution's writing programs and how they are researching and theorizing writing practices in MENA. Much of Arnold's interest in developing the collection emerges out of her work as a WPA at AUB, where she collaborated with colleagues and students to develop a culture of writing through the creation of a permanent WPA faculty position, professional development activities, seminars, an annual celebration of student writing, and building a network of writing teachers across Lebanon. Ronesi's involvement in the collection is grounded in her experience with WAC/WID in Morocco and in the UAE, particularly with undergraduate writing initiatives such as writing centers and writing fellows programs, and a research focus on curricular adaptation and student negotiation and positionality. Nebel's interest in the project arises from her experience teaching first-year writing in the US, Europe, and the Middle East, and her research as an applied linguist in the analysis of complexity in writing development, as well as from her work establishing and directing a writing center and writing program in Qatar. Together, we were intrigued by the complexities and challenges of our contexts, and the potential of bringing together multidisciplinary insights on the research and practice of writing studies in MENA.

In spite of our positioning at three different institutions in three countries, one of the primary challenges of editing this collection occurred as we disseminated the CFP and solicited diverse perspectives in response. Notably, we found very few avenues for reaching out to and connecting with writing scholars and practitioners in the region; apart from international lists originating in North America or Europe, there is only the Middle East North Africa Writing Center Association (MENAWCA) and TESOL Arabia which aim to support regional connection and collaboration. There is yet no professional infrastructure specifically for MENA writing faculty. Consequently, our initial CFP was disseminated via various academic listserves in the MENA region, in Europe, and in the US, as well as through personal contacts. In response, we received 32 proposals representing only nine out of the 22 MENA countries noted in the previous section (for our purposes, we have included Turkey as a part of the region). After a year and a half of the review process—which included careful vetting of the proposals and multiple revisions of the chapters submitted following editorial and peer review—our collection represents voices from only seven countries (Lebanon, Turkey, UAE, Qatar, Egypt, Iraq, and Bahrain). What's more, many of the authors included in this collection are like us—not native to the region, its language, or culture, but with on-the-ground experience conducting research and building programs at local institutions.

We were not at ease with these limitations. During the process of reviewing proposals and chapter submissions and providing revision suggestions for authors, we struggled with recurring concerns that point to larger problems inherent to transnational work. As we distributed the CFP, we asked ourselves whose voices we were (not) hearing in the proposals submitted, and how we might locate and promote voices representative of the diversity of the MENA region. We wondered how professional situations and (lack of) resources or support may have prevented potential contributors from submitting a proposal. And as we vetted proposals and, eventually, chapter submissions, we often found ourselves uncomfortable with our role in determining who and what belongs in a collection such as this, when we were positioned as relative outsiders, culturally, linguistically, and educationally. By way of example, in a few instances, we had to make decisions about the viability of chapters whose research was not guided by an Institutional Review Board (IRB) or an institutional policy for research ethics. While seeking IRB approval is a standard part of such scholarship in the US and elsewhere, educational institutions in other countries often have quite different policies whose parameters may not be commensurate with U.S.-based IRBs, or, as in the case at some MENA institutions, no instituted provisions for ensuring ethical research practices. We wondered again and again how to negotiate between our cultural ideals of best practice in scholarship and standards and the practical realities of MENA-based research.

Additionally, international branch campuses (IBCs) of U.S. universities, which often recruit faculty from the US and abroad, are flourishing in the MENA region. And as transnational partnerships between foreign and Arab institutions and faculty are created to develop programs and curriculum, as well as to engage students, international faculty are exposed to the region through research collaboratives and in consultant capacities. As a result,

U.S.-oriented faculty may have been better positioned than their MENA counterparts to contribute to our volume.

Also, our own institutional positioning and educational backgrounds, in combination with our intention to publish the collection through a U.S.-based publisher, likely suggested to potential contributors that research based at English-medium, American-style universities would be the most appropriate for our volume. And finally, because of our own linguistic limitations, we accepted chapters only written in English—this decision may have discouraged some potential contributors from submitting proposals, especially those who do not work at English-medium institutions in the region.

We could not escape these factors, nor could we escape our conviction that this volume was needed, in spite of its (and our) limitations. We appreciate the reflective and critical eye that our authors have brought to bear on the complicated realities of this region. We recognize the many perspectives that remain un(der)represented in the present volume, and we hope this collection will be understood by our readers as a first glimpse, rather than a comprehensive representation, of writing research in the MENA region. Ultimately, we are proud of the strength of the final collection and for the perspectives that each contribution provides about the state of writing research for our readers in and outside of the region.

Locating MENA Writing Scholarship

At the 2012 Middle East–North Africa Writing Centers Alliance (MENAWCA) conference in Doha, Qatar, Terry Myers Zawacki delivered a keynote speech in which she urged attendees to pursue research about writing practices and pedagogies in the region. Published the same year, Thaiss, Bräuer, Carlino, Ganobcsik-Williams & Sinha's (2012) volume, *Writing Programs Worldwide: Profiles of Academic Writing in Many Places*, reports on writing programs at three MENA-based institutions: American University of Cairo in Egypt (Golson & Holdijk, 2012), American University of Sharjah in the United Arab Emirates (Ronesi, 2012), and Sabanci University in Turkey (Tokay, 2012). And recent studies by a number of MENA-based scholars—Gülşen (2012) on Turkish higher education, Rajakumar (2012) on Qatari female Facebook practices, and Zenger (2012) on Lebanese college students' use of digital media—highlight literacy practices in the region.

These publications and presentations signify growing interest in MENA-based writing scholarship. This increased activity demonstrates that the culturally and linguistically rich MENA contexts are emerging in English language scholarship as an exciting site for writing studies. Recent book chapters and conference presentations, as well as the responses to our own call for proposals, highlight the complex negotiations of identity, language, culture, institutions, and pedagogies within the MENA region and indicate the potential of making significant contributions to emerging bodies of scholarship.

The issues raised in recent MENA-based presentations and chapters intersect with themes that the chapters in this volume address. One strand of ongoing research examines the politics of language and its effect on institutions and practices (see Hayes & Mansour; Nebel; Ronesi; and Uysal, this volume). At the 2014 Writing Research across Borders (WRAB) conference, for example, a number of presentations by Algerian scholars highlighted the country's pluriliteracy and its manifestation in the educational system: Benali (2014) addressed the writing styles of Algerian student learners in French; Bounouara & Legros (2014) investigated whether student planning in Arabic and French produced a better persuasive essay in French; and Graoui & Chelli examined English as a foreign-language curriculum modification at Algerian high schools (Chelli & Graoui, 2014; Graoui & Chelli, 2014). Additionally, a chapter included in *International Advances in Writing Research: Cultures, Places, Measures*, edited by Bazerman, Dean, Early, Lunsford, Null, Roger & Stansell (2012), focuses on the political implications of Iranian academics writing in English (Riazi, 2012).

Along similar lines, scholars have begun to theorize the teaching of academic writing in linguistically diverse contexts, such as those found in the MENA region (see Hodges & Kent; Nebel; and Ronesi, this volume). Cox and Zawacki's (2011) special issue in Across the Disciplines on "WAC and Second Language Writing: Cross-field Research, Theory, and Program Development," and Zawacki & Cox's (2014) multi-authored volume, *WAC and Second Language Writers: Research Toward Linguistically and Culturally Inclusive Programs and Practices*, have made tremendous strides towards a foundation of research on L2 writers in U.S. university classrooms. Two of those studies—Ronesi (2011) and Zenger, Mullin & Haviland (2014)—consider L2 writers based at universities in the MENA region.

Another line of research found not only in this collection but also in various conference presentations and book chapters is related to the challenges and opportunities of conducting transnational partnerships and exchanges in the MENA region (see Annous, Nicolas & Townsend; Arnold, DeGenaro, Iskandarani, Khoury, Sinno & Willard-Traub; and Theado, Johnson, Highly & Omar, this volume). At the 2014 WRAB conference, for example, Karatsolis from Carnegie Mellon-Qatar joined scholars from the Massachusetts Institute of Technology and the Australian Council for Education in a panel discussion of the use of computers in writing assessment research (Perelman,

McCurry, Karatsolis & Lane, 2014). Also at WRAB, Gitsaki and Robby represented the Higher College of Technology in the United Arab Emirates at a round-table discussion focused on the intersection of writing, language, and new media across educational contexts (Hicks et al., 2014).

Additionally, a number of researchers have pursued questions related to the viability of importing western pedagogical, curricular, and programmatic models in the MENA region (see Annous, Nicolas & Townsend; Austin; Hayes & Mansour; Hodges & Kent; Jarkas & Fakhreddine; Miller & Pessoa; and Rudd & Telafici, this volume). At the 2014 WRAB conference, colleagues from Texas A&M-Qatar provided insights on interpreting western-style honor codes in light of Middle Eastern values and practices to an interdisciplinary and international discussion on ethos in writing and writing instruction (Johnson et al., 2014). At the same conference, along with American and Australian colleagues, Iskenderoglu-Onel & Ronesi highlighted WAC-WID challenges from their respective English-medium universities in Turkey and the United Arab Emirates (Tarabochia, Ronesi, Iskenderoglu-Onel & Chanock, 2014).

These chapters and presentations reveal a need to explore writing pedagogies, programs, and practices in the region, a need this collection addresses while also raising additional questions that point the way to further research. For example, chapters in this collection raise issues that resonate, explicitly and implicitly, with work in applied linguistics and translingual theories of writing (see Hayes & Mansour; Nebel; Ronesi; and Uysal, this volume). Scholars such as Blommaert & Rampton (2012), in their ethnographic studies of linguistic superdiversity, and Blommaert (2010), who explores the sociolinguistics of globalization, consider the linguistic consequences and realizations of today's unprecedented levels of diversity, which opens new frontiers for the study of writing in sites like MENA. Likewise, Yildiz's (2012) work on the "post-monolingual condition" takes up an interdisciplinary lens through which to view and interrogate the ideologies of mother tongue and bilingualism and to examine the tensions among the languages multilingual writers claim. This scholarship offers new directions for theorizing academic writing from diverse and evolving sites such as the MENA region.

Given these growing areas of research and the plethora of English-medium universities and IBCs—structured similarly, or connected directly, to universities in the US, UK, Canada, Australia, and others—in the MENA region, a volume dedicated to writing pedagogies and practices in this context was imperative. Moreover, the research highlighted above, particularly from the 2014 WRAB conference, suggests that scholars in the region are poised to study and theorize their context. As such, we anticipate that this collection will be the first of many to provide new lenses through which we can understand and learn from the diverse writing practices and pedagogies in the region and that it will spark interest in transnational collaborations.

Volume Overview

Collectively, the chapters included in this volume consider questions and themes that are familiar to those of us who teach, conduct research, and live in the MENA region. For example: How can we build a culture of writing at MENA institutions when many students and the regional population more generally do not recognize or value the rhetorical nature of writing? Through what methods might we persuade faculty across disciplines to take responsibility for ongoing writing practice and pedagogy in their classrooms? How should teachers, researchers, and administrators in the region respond to western writing studies scholarship and writing curriculum, such as textbooks and program design? What can we learn by examining how and why MENA-based writing faculty incorporate, extend, or ignore western scholarship and curriculum? How can teachers, researchers, and administrators make use of and identify potential resources for curriculum and program development in their immediate surroundings and with their own students in mind? How can we make use of existing ties across institutional, national, linguistic, and cultural borders to promote effective teaching and learning?

In view of these questions and considerations, we are eager to offer this volume to our local, regional, and international colleagues as a resource and a starting point. This collection has been divided into four sections, each containing three chapters. These chapters overlap in their exploration of four major themes: complicating prevalent assumptions in writing studies scholarship; questioning the viability and value of importing western programmatic and pedagogical models into the MENA region; negotiating national, cultural, institutional, and disciplinary borders while implementing change; and creating innovative spaces for student learning.

Section I: Complicating Assumptions

The three chapters included in this section highlight the ways in which writing programs, curriculum, and theories must evolve in response to the realities of globalization and linguistic diversity. Together, these chapters, representing Qatar, Egypt, and Turkey, complicate long-held assumptions in writing studies and applied linguistics as they demonstrate how the interaction of the global and the local demand critical responses by scholars, teachers, and administrators. These chapters also illustrate the challenges faced by institutions and educators as they negotiate the politics of language policy.

In "Linguistic Superdiversity and English-medium Higher Education in Qatar," Anne Nebel of Georgetown University Qatar introduces the volume with a theoretical overview of the complicated socio-linguistic landscape of the MENA region. Nebel begins with the changing global landscape of learning and scholarship in Qatar which has resulted from large-scale shifts in migration patterns and dramatically increased connectivity, creating a condition of extreme diversity. Against this background of "linguistic superdiversity," a concept developed by Jan Blommaert, Nebel reexamines vexed concepts and categories from writing studies, such as native speaker and second language learner, adopting a sociolinguistic framework which she argues can help scholars better understand and theorize writing studies in Qatar, the MENA region, and elsewhere in the world today. Challenging the monolingual ideology that still circumscribes writing scholarship and practice, she uses the example of Qatar to explore a post-monolingual paradigm for reimagining writing studies in a polycentric and transnational world.

The second chapter in this section, "Global Spread of English in Academia and its Effects on Writing Instruction in Turkish Universities," offers both an historical analysis of the state-level policies governing the role of English in tertiary education in Turkey and a contemporary exploration of how these macro strategies have impacted national scholarly outcomes and language instruction at two universities in Ankara. Author Hacer Hande Uysal, from Gazi University, provides close examination of the consequences of an imported monolingual ideology as realized in scholarly production over time, the positioning of Turkish versus English in the university curriculum, instructional methods, and ultimate language attainment. Uysal argues for greater critical awareness of Anglo-centric discourses and pedagogies and their hegemonies in order to preserve the value and place of the Turkish language in Turkish higher education and global scholarship. Uysal's chapter offers important insights on the political dimensions of writing at one MENA location, which has relevance to many others.

The final chapter in this section recounts the revision of a writing minor at the American University of Cairo (AUC) in an exploration of the internal and external influences that shaped its realization. In "Expanding Transnational Frames into Composition Studies: Revising the Rhetoric and Writing Minor at the American University of Cairo," James Austin of Fort Hays State University in the US (and formerly with AUC) investigates the development of a program that both drew from U.S.-based models and arose organically from local needs and expertise. Emphasizing the distinction between an exported approach as imposed and hegemonic and an imported approach which underscores the choices and agency of the local actors, the author urges the field to move beyond the entrenched binary thinking of local versus western to explore richer and more nuanced relationships and interactions with MENA sites of writing scholarship and practice. Further, Austin calls for the field to make use of more expansive and contextually sensitive frames from literacy studies in attempting to understand and engage new global educational environments. Austin's description of the process of curriculum revision at AUC provides an apt transition into the volume's second thematic section, which questions how western pedagogical and programmatic models can or should (not) be imported into MENA-region institutions of higher education.

Section II: Considering the Importation of Western Models

In this section, the three chapters consider the complexities of importing western pedagogical, curricular, and programmatic models in the MENA region. Speaking from their positions in Lebanon, Qatar, and Bahrain, the authors of these chapters suggest that student and faculty identity, as well as their beliefs about writing, must be considered when integrating western models of writing pedagogy or curriculum into MENA-based educational institutions. These contributions underscore the need for sensitivity to sociocultural realities when considering western models for MENA classrooms and programs, particularly as to how these models may discount the perceptions and practices about writing that local teachers, students, and the community hold. Ultimately, these chapters emphasize the value of critical reflection and engagement as teachers and administrators consider adopting western models across national, linguistic, and cultural borders.

The first chapter in this section, "Territorial Borders and the Teaching of Writing in English: Lessons from English at the University of Balamand," highlights the complexity of writing development at English-medium universities where the teaching of writing is not valued or sustained across disciplines. Two faculty members at the University of Balamand in Lebanon, Samer Annous and Maureen O'Day Nicolas, and one WAC scholar based in the US, Martha Townsend, analyze data from a review of the Faculty of Business' syllabi, interviews with faculty and students in the Faculty of Business and the Cultural Studies program, and Townsend's observations during her visit. They find that faculty and students, who often struggle with English in the multilingual context of Lebanon, share a sense of "territorial borders," which works against a productive transfer of writing knowledge or a sense of responsibility for writing pedagogy outside of the English department. Just as Arnold, DeGenaro, Iskandarani, Khoury, Sinno, and Willard-Traub's and Kendall Theado, Highly, Johnson, and Omar's chapters in later sections present a variety of challenges related to transnational exchange, Annous, Nicolas, and Townsend argue that the context of English-medium universities in multilingual contexts pose particular obstacles to the successful implementation of writing across the curriculum.

In the second chapter of this section, Mysti Rudd and Michael Telafici, based at Texas A&M-Qatar, explore the viability of American-authored textbooks and the development of writing curriculum at IBCs of American universities in their chapter, "An Arabian Gulf: First-Year Composition Textbooks at an International Branch Campus in Qatar." Noting the linguistic, cultural, and national diversity of the student body at their home institution and other IBCs in comparison to their U.S. counterparts, Rudd and Telafici draw on their own experiences and observations of teaching first-year composition at Texas A&M-Qatar, as well as surveys of students, to study the appropriateness of two textbooks commonly used in the US to teach composition—*They Say/I Say* (Graff, Birkenstein & Durst, 2012) and *Writing about Writing* (Wardle & Downs, 2011)—for their own IBC's first-year writing classes. While Rudd and Telafici see both benefits and drawbacks for the incorporation of either textbook, they leave readers with a set of questions and suggested practices that will prove valuable for writing faculty using any American-authored textbook at IBCs or other institutions of higher education with similar demographics.

In the third chapter of this section, "Great Expectations or Great Outcomes? Exploring the Context of English Language Policy Transfer in Bahrain," authors Aneta Hayes of Keele University and Nasser Mansour from Exeter University, both in the UK, investigate how societal factors have impacted the perceived viability and effectiveness of a western curricular and pedagogical model (Communicative Language Teaching) in Bahrain's secondary schools. The authors highlight the challenges perceived by teachers of negative student and society views of the value and practice of English language pedagogy and the obstacles these present to classroom learning and preparation for post-secondary success. Reporting on their qualitative study of teacher perceptions, Hayes and Mansour contribute to the debate on the effectiveness of imported pedagogies and ideologies in light of traditional societal views of education, and the associated methods of teaching and learning, in Bahrain. They argue that the perceptions of teachers reflect a juxtaposition common to many MENA countries, in that students' sociocultural context competes with general economic developments in the country. This juxtaposition, Hayes and Mansour contend, results in discordant readings—by teachers, students, and the local community—of the importance of curricular reforms.

Section III: Striving for Balance across Borders

The three chapters that comprise this section of the volume examine important social, cultural and political dimensions of negotiating institutional, disciplinary, national, and cultural borders, particularly when implementing curricular, pedagogical, or programmatic change. With a focus on universities in Qatar and the Kurdistan Region of Iraq, these chapters demonstrate that global-local negotiations and exchanges aren't always smooth or equal. These chapters present readers with the innovative responses to teaching, curriculum, and program design that emerged in the midst of change, and they offer openness and critical reflection as well as the willingness to negotiate, as stances that others in similarly complex situations might take.

The value, and difficulty, of faculty collaboration across borders is described in the opening chapter of this section, Connie Kendall Theado, Holly Johnson, Thomas Highley, and Saman Hussein Omar's "Rewriting Resistance: Negotiating Pedagogical and Curricular Change in a US/Kurdish Transnational Partnership." The four authors of this chapter report on the results of a government-sponsored University Linkages Partnership between the University of Cincinnati (UC) and Salahaddin University-Hawler (SUH), in the Kurdistan Region of Iraq. One of the goals of the partnership was to facilitate an exchange among faculty members at both universities to help shape the revision of the SUH English department's curriculum through monthly online discussions and in-person workshops at both universities. The contributors consider how initial moments of "passive resistance" to these exchanges by the SUH faculty—including a lack of participation on the part of SUH faculty and a pointed critique of the readings chosen by the UC team by the department chair—led to important reconsiderations of the partnership's structure, a more nuanced understanding of differing educational realities and expectations, and a deeper appreciation for the assumptions at play in any cross-cultural work.

In the section's second chapter, "Integrating Writing Assignments at an American Branch Campus in Qatar: Challenges, Adaptations, and Recommendations," authors Ryan Miller from Kent State University and Silvia Pessoa from Carnegie Mellon University (Qatar) consider the recent proliferation of IBCs worldwide—particularly in the MENA region—and provide a rigorous review of the research. Miller and Pessoa problematize the IBCs' role vis-à-vis the host country, the main institution, and the adaptation of curricula and instruction to accommodate the requirements of both. Culling data from a broader four-year longitudinal study of academic literacy development at an American IBC in Qatar (see Pessoa, Miller & Kaufer, 2014), Miller and Pessoa analyze interviews from 65 IBC faculty across the curriculum who had previously taught at the U.S. main campus or at other American universities. This analysis culminates in wide-ranging recommendations for designing writing instruction for IBCs.

The last chapter in this section, "Hybrid Writing Positions within WAC/WID Initiatives: Connecting Faculty Writing Expectations and MENA Cultures," makes a second compelling argument for considering how WID or WAC programs can be localized or hybridized within the MENA region. Like Miller and Pessoa, Amy Hodges and Brenda Kent draw on interviews from faculty at an IBC—their colleagues at Texas A&M University at Qatar—to determine challenges they faced in the writing component of their courses. Their analysis of 10 multilingual engineering faculty who teach writing-intensive courses determined that, while acknowledging the importance of writing in their discipline, the faculty did not feel it part of their responsibility to instruct students in the discourse of their discipline. That perspective, coupled with the IBC students' primary and secondary experience with more teacher-centered learning environments, led Hodges and Kent to argue for hybrid writing consultants—staff positions with the combined roles of tutor, teacher, and writing fellow—as a locally relevant way to communicate cross-cultural differences in writing expectations between faculty and students.

Section IV: Creating Student Spaces

In this final section, the three chapters feature qualitative research studies that explore the culturally sensitive approaches to the teaching and learning of writing at English-medium, American campuses in Lebanon and the United Arab Emirates. The American University of Beirut (AUB) and the American University of Sharjah (AUS) are campuses that are linguistically rich and superdiverse (see Nebel) and characterized by students with multiple and translingual—particularly oral—competencies. Highlighting faculty and student responses to the challenge of reconciling cultural, linguistic, educational, and institutional realities with American-style academic writing, these chapters showcase innovations and adaptations that intend to prepare students for writing both in their coursework and in the international arena. Notably, these campus-based responses reflect deep concerns about preparing students to enter transnational discourse communities and finding ways to create space in which students can organically engage in the learning of writing.

In "Literacy Narratives across Borders: Beirut and Dearborn as 21st-Century Transnational Spaces," writing faculty at the American University of Beirut and the University of Michigan-Dearborn describe a transnational collaboration in which first-year writing students interviewed their overseas peers about their literacy practices. Lisa Arnold, William DeGenaro, Rima Iskandarani, Malakeh Khoury, Zane Sinno, and Margaret Willard-Traub found that in the process of interviewing and writing literacy profiles of their peers, students became more aware of their locatedness—their rhetorical positioning in the world and in relation to others. And in the process, students entered and identified themselves within a transnational discourse community. While the authors noted a number of practical and intellectual limits of the project—including the logistics of the interview process across large time differences as well as the short duration of the assignment, which may have prevented students from arriving at complex understandings of their peers' and their own literacy practices—they argue that such transnational exchanges are valuable for their potential not only to motivate students, but also to inspire curricular and institutional change.

The section's next chapter, "The Dance of Voices: A Study on Academic Writing at AUB," focuses more specifically on a particular challenge in academic writing faced by student writers in the MENA region—that of authorial voice. Najla Jarkas and Juheinna Fakhreddine, based at the American University of Beirut, analyze the academic, personal, and reflective writing of 44 students in order to test their hypothesis that first-year composition students benefit from explicit instruction in developing their authorial voice. Jarkas and Fakhreddine suggest that although L2/3 students coming from the MENA region gradually learn to incorporate external voices into their texts through explicit instruction, they struggle with maintaining and interweaving an authorial voice in relation to other voices in argumentative writing.

The volume's final chapter ends on a celebratory note, portraying student learning through extra-curricular engagement. In "Students Running the Show: Performance Poetry Night," Lynne Ronesi at the American Univeristy of Sharjah chronicles how participating students, interviewed over the course of three semesters, situate a performance poetry night—an event known to most of them only through western-origin digital media—to accommodate their interest in engaging in multivocalic expression and community-building. Drawing from New Literacies research, Ronesi likens the development of the poetry event to the creation of an "affinity space" (Gee, 2004, 2005) where student diversity and creativity in writing can be appreciated even as the AUS writing curriculum focuses exclusively on academic English. Ronesi underscores the need for writing faculty to investigate student participation in out-of-classroom literacy practices to shed insight on novel and contextually appropriate approaches for supporting literacy development.

Here and Beyond

Our aspirations in editing this volume are several and can be outlined as follows: First, we want to make MENA-based writing research available to those who conduct research, teach, or administer writing programs in higher education within the region, so as to foster intra-regional dialogue and exchange about writing. Currently, there is a dearth of knowledge or discussion about how writing in English is taught and learned at the university level in the region, by whom, and with what approach(es). Additionally, we have very little knowledge about how writing programs have been theorized or evolved, or where these programs fit into different institutional structures throughout the region. This volume provides a starting point from which our current understandings and knowledge can be shared and built upon.

Second, this volume will foster international dialogue and exchange about writing by making MENA-based English-language writing research available to scholars outside the region. Scholarship in writing studies has, thus far, generally elided the MENA region, and the international writing community is largely unfamiliar with the region, its students, teachers, and scholars, and/or the unique linguistic, cultural, and political characteristics of the region that inform regional teaching and administrative practices. At the same time, the number of English-medium institutions of higher education in the region has grown considerably over the last two decades, and many of these institutions purposefully recruit western-trained faculty to teach within and administer their writing programs. The discipline must address the unique challenges and possibilities inherent to teaching and conducting research in the region, as long as the cross-national and cross-cultural exchange of scholars and practitioners continues.

While many writing scholars may not be cognizant of the MENA region specifically, a growing number have a vested interest in fostering and maintaining a well-grounded international perspective in line with best practices of teaching, research, and administration in writing studies. This is particularly true of practitioners, scholars, and administrators who work with international and multilingual MENA students outside of the MENA region. This collection makes MENA-based writing research available to those writing studies scholars who do not live or work in the region but who work with students or scholars from the region. These audiences will benefit from this volume in that it provides much-needed background knowledge about the diverse educational opportunities and experiences that individuals coming from this region may have had.

Finally, this volume provides a starting point from which teachers, administrators, and scholars can articulate gaps in knowledge about writing practices and pedagogy in the MENA region—a region rich in cultural, ethnic, and linguistic diversity with a long tradition of writing and rhetorical practice. We hope readers will feel driven to explore further the variety of questions and considerations that have emerged from this work, and, to that end, we suggest the following future avenues of inquiry, which range from practical to theoretical and cross the four section themes. To start: Our experience working on this volume suggests that MENA scholars would benefit from more networks and venues to inspire and consolidate research. What immediate steps can we take to respond to this need? And, how can MENA practitioners be encouraged and supported to engage in research and theorizing in their contexts? From a praxis perspective, this volume has revealed a number of pedagogical challenges and responses emerging from IBCs and from western-style standalone universities. For the IBCs, challenges and responses emerge as they adapt an already established and required curriculum to local needs. And for the latter, comprised of both U.S.-accredited universities and universities modeled on western curriculum, challenges and responses evolve as a result of practitioners and administrators having more latitude in developing "grassroots," locally-driven pedagogical approaches. Developing a research framework for both IBCs and standalone institutions that is grounded in this understanding would prove fruitful.

More considerations and questions emerge from the linguistic complexity highlighted in several of the chapters: How can scholars in plurilingual MENA contexts extend the work in applied linguistics and translingual theories of writing, particularly in developing language that can complicate vexed concepts such as "native speaker" or "second language learner." How can scholars accurately reflect the positionalities of individuals who negotiate life using more than one language? And just as pertinently, how do practitioners both honor and acknowledge student pluriliteracy and the translingual context, yet also attend to the needs of students at English-medium MENA institutions, who, by rights, should graduate with a level of English proficiency that is commensurate with that of their peers at western-style institutions? While we do not conflate a translingual approach with reduced rigor in writing instruction and assessment, from our perspective "on the ground," we can easily understand how the notion of theorizing translingualism into the curriculum might be perceived as a misguided "foreign luxury" at

MENA institutions, which justifiably seek to bring their students to a level of proficiency deemed adequate for university academic writing and a globally-oriented career (see for example Arnold, 2016). MENA scholars must consider the weight of English in a context where it cannot be taken for granted. Further, scholars must take pains to ensure that moves toward a translingual approach indeed support plurilingualism and promote linguistic proficiency and do not inadvertently result in a weakening of the high standards to which we need to hold our MENA students accountable. Further theorization of these questions and considerations is paramount.

As these questions suggest, the complex contemporary realities and socio-political histories of this region are fundamental to what we do as writing practitioners, and this collection speaks to how much more we have to learn. As such, this volume thus points toward the need for continued research and the value that accumulated data, representative of other positionalities and perspectives, will give us over time. Indeed, with more volumes such as this one, we can arrive at a more comprehensive understanding of writing research, administration, and pedagogy in the region. What's more, and perhaps just as importantly, this volume—and hopefully others like it—will give scholars and teachers based outside of the region a better understanding of the diversity of experience, language, and culture that is often collapsed under the "Middle East–North Africa" umbrella.

References

Arnold, L. R. (2014). "The worst part of the dead past": Language attitudes, policies, and pedagogies at Syrian Protestant College, 1866–1902. *College Composition and Communication, 66*(2), 276–300.

Arnold, L. R. (2016). "This is a field that's open, not closed": Multilingual and international writing faculty respond to composition theory. *Composition Studies, 44*(1), 72–88.

Bazerman, C. (2015). Creating identities in an intertextual world. In A. Chik, T. Costley & M. C. Pennington (Eds.), *Creativity and discovery in the university writing class: A teacher's guide* (pp. 45–60). Sheffield, UK: Equinox.

Bazerman, C., Dean, C., Early, J., Lunsford, K., Null, S., Rogers, P. & Stansell, A. (Eds.). (2012). *International advances in writing research: Cultures, places, measures*. Fort Collins, CO: The WAC Clearinghouse and Parlor Press. Retrieved from http://wac.colostate.edu/books/wrab2011/.

Benali, A. (2014, February). Pour une modélisation linguistique des modèles d'écriture des lycéens apprenants scripteurs. Paper presented at Writing Research Across Borders III Conference, Paris, France.

Blommaert, J. (2010). *The sociolinguistics of globalization*. Cambridge, UK: Cambridge

University Press.

Blommaert, J. & Rampton, B. (2011). Language and superdiversity. *Diversities, 13*(2), 1–21. Retrieved from http://unesdoc.unesco.org/images/0021/002147/214772e.pdf.

Bounouara, Y. & Legros, D. (2014, February). Planifier en arabe ou en français pour produire un texte argumentatif en FLE de meilleure qualité ? Presented at Writing Research Across Borders III Conference, Paris, France.

Chelli, S. & Graoui, H. (2014, February). Writing in English: Towards a genuine application in the competency-based approach. Paper presented at Writing Research Across Borders III Conference, Paris, France.

Cox, M. & Zawacki, T. M. (Eds.). (2011). WAC and second language writing: Cross-field research, theory, and program development [Special Issue]. *Across the Disciplines, 8*(4). Retrieved from http://wac.colostate.edu/atd/ell/index.cfm.

Donahue, C. (2009). "Internationalization" and composition studies: Reorienting the discourse. *College Composition and Communication, 61*(2), 212–243.

Gee, J. P. (2004). *Situated language and learning: A critique of traditional schooling*. New York: Routledge.

Gee, J. P. (2005). *Language, learning, and gaming: A critique of traditional schooling*. New York: Routledge.

Golson, E. & Holdijk, L. (2012). The Department of Rhetoric and Composition at the American University in Cairo: Achievements and challenges. In C. Thaiss, G. Bräuer, P. Carlino, L. Ganobcsik-Williams & A. Sinha (Eds.), *Writing programs worldwide: Profiles of academic writing in many places* (pp. 181–188). Fort Collins, CO: The WAC Clearinghouse and Parlor Press. Retrieved from http://wac.colostate.edu/books/wpww/.

Graff, G., Birkenstein, C. & Durst, R. (2012). *They say / I say: The moves that matter in academic writing with readings* (2nd ed.). New York: W. W. Norton & Co.

Graoui, H. & Chelli, S. (2014, February). Are you joking? I can't even write a sentence: An authentic approach to writing in English. Paper presented at Writing Research Across Borders III Conference, Paris, France.

Gülşen, T. (2012). The "popular" Turkish academy. In B. T. Williams & A. A. Zenger (Eds.), *New media literacies and participatory popular cultures across borders* (pp. 74–89). New York: Routledge.

Hall, J. (2014). Multilinguality across the curriculum: Research toward linguistically and culturally inclusive programs and practices. In T. M. Zawcki & M. Cox (Eds.), *WAC and second language writers: Research toward linguistically and culturally inclusive programs and practices* (pp. 5–14). Fort Collins, CO: The WAC Clearinghouse and Parlor Press. Retrieved from http://wac.colostate.edu/books/l2/.

Hesford, W. (2006). Global turns and cautions in rhetoric and composition studies. *PMLA, 121*(3), 787–801.

Hicks, T., Ehrensberger-Dow, M., Gitsaki, C., Kiesler, N., Massey, G., Perrin, D., Robby, M., Sharma, S. & Turner, K. (2014, February). Writing, language, and new media: Challenges and possibilities across educational contexts. Symposium presented at Writing Research across Borders III Conference, Paris, France.

Johnson, J., Warwick, N., Rudd, L., Seawright, L., Small, N., Folk, M., Gilewicz, N.

& Allard-Huver, F. (2014, February). Writing and the teaching of writing in the age of shifting ethos. Symposium presented at Writing Research across Borders III Conference, Paris, France.

Muchiri, M. N., Mulamba, N. G., Myers, G. & Ndoloi, D. B. (1995). Importing composition: Teaching and researching academic writing beyond North America. *College Composition and Communication, 46*, 175–198.

Perelman, L., McCurry, D., Karatsolis, A. & Lane, S. (2014, February). Automated essay scoring and its alternatives: Appropriate uses of computers in writing. Symposium presented at Writing Research across Borders III Conference, Paris, France.

Pessoa, S., Miller, R. T. & Kaufer, D. (2014). Student challenges and development in the transition to college literacy at an English-medium university in Qatar. *International Review of Applied Linguistics, 52*(2), 127–156. doi:10.1515/iral-2014-0006.

Rajakumar, M. (2012). Faceless Facebook: Female Qatari users choosing wisely. In B. T. Williams & A. A. Zenger (Eds.), *New media literacies and participatory popular cultures across borders* (pp. 125–134). New York: Routledge

Riazi, M. (2012). Producing scholarly texts: Writing in English in a politically stigmatized country. In C. Bazerman, C. Dean, J. Early, A. Lunsford, S. Null, P. Roger & A. Stansell (Eds.), *International advances in writing research: Cultures, places, measures* (pp. 449–466). Fort Collins, CO: The WAC Clearinghouse and Parlor Press. Retrieved from http://wac.colostate.edu/books/wrab2011/.

Ronesi, L. (2011). "Striking while the iron is hot." A writing fellows program supporting lower-division courses at an American university in the UAE. *Across the Disciplines, 8*(4). Retrieved from http://wac.colostate.edu/atd/ell/ronesi.cfm.

Ronesi, L. (2012). Profile of the American University of Sharjah (AUS). In C. Thaiss, G. Bräuer, P. Carlino, L. Ganobcsik-Williams & A. Sinha, A. (Eds.), *Writing programs worldwide: Profiles of academic writing in many places* (pp. 429–438). Fort Collins, CO: The WAC Clearinghouse and Parlor Press. Retrieved from http://wac.colostate.edu/books/wpww/.

Said, E. (1993). *Culture and imperialism.* New York: Alfred Knopf.

Tokay, D. (2012). A writing center journey at Sabanci University, Istanbul. In C. Thaiss, G. Bräuer, P. Carlino, L. Ganobcsik-Williams & A. Sinha. (Eds.), *Writing programs worldwide: Profiles of academic writing in many places* (pp. 417–428). Fort Collins, CO: The WAC Clearinghouse and Parlor Press. Retrieved from http://wac.colostate.edu/books/wpww/.

Tarabochia, S., Ronesi, L., Iskenderoglu-Onel, Z. & Chanock, C. (2014, February). Ways of working with students and faculty: A transnational conversation about WAC / WID. Symposium presented at Writing Research across Borders III Conference, Paris, France.

Thaiss, C., Bräuer, G., Carlino, P., Ganobcsik-Williams, L. & Sinha, A. (Eds.). (2012). *Writing programs worldwide: Profiles of academic writing in many places.* Fort Collins, CO: The WAC Clearinghous and Parlor Press. Retrieved from http://wac.colostate.edu/books/wpww/.

Vertovec, S. (2007). Super-diversity and its implications. *Ethnic and racial studies,*

30(6), 1024–1054.

Wardle, E. & Downs, D. (2011). *Writing about writing: A college reader.* Boston: Bedford St. Martin's.

Weber, A. S. (2010). Effectiveness of web-based learning in the Middle East and North Africa (MENA) region. *The International Journal of the Computer, the Internet and Management, 18*(1), 16.1-16.4. Retrieved from http://ijcim.th.org/SpecialEditions/v18nSP1/16_Full_Alan%20S.Weber.pdf.

Willard-Traub, M., Arnold, L., De Genaro, W., Iskandarani, R., Khoury, M & Sinno, Z. (2014, February). Learning literacies in 21st-century transnational spaces. Presented at Writing Research across Borders III Conference, Paris, France.

Williams, B. T. & Zenger, A. A. (2012). *New media literacies and participatory popular cultures across borders.* New York: Routledge.

World Bank. (2013). Middle East and North Africa. Retrieved from http://web.worldbank.org/WBSITE/EXTERNAL/COUNTRIES/MENAEXT/0,,menuPK:247619~pagePK:146748~piPK:146812~theSitePK:256299,00.html.

Yildiz, Y. (2012). *Beyond the mother tongue: The postmonolingual condition.* New York: Fordham University Press.

Zawacki, T. M. & Cox, M. (Eds.). (2014). *WAC and second language writers: Research toward linguistically and culturally inclusive programs and practices.* Fort Collins, CO: The WAC Clearinghouse and Parlor Press. Retrieved from http://wac.colostate.edu/books/l2/.

Zenger, A. A. (2012). Constructing local context in Beirut: Students' literacy practices outside of class. In B. T. Williams & A. A. Zenger (Eds.), *New media literacies and participatory popular cultures across borders* (pp. 33–43). New York: Routledge.

Section 1: Complicating Prevalent Assumptions

1 Linguistic Superdiversity and English-Medium Higher Education in Qatar

Anne Nebel
GEORGETOWN UNIVERSITY (QATAR)

This chapter problematizes several concepts and categories which persist in writing studies despite phenomenal changes in the global landscape of learning and scholarship. The author argues that these serve to perpetuate a monolingual ideology incongruous with today's polycentric, transnational, translingual world. New discourses of internationalization raise important considerations but don't fully engage the complexities of emerging global sites of learning and communication. Using a critical sociolinguistics frame, the author examines English-medium higher education in the State of Qatar, a site of "linguistic superdiversity," to pose new questions about how we theorize and do writing studies in today's globally connected world.

Keywords: linguistic superdiversity; critical sociolinguistics; linguistic landscape studies; monolingual ideology; postmonolingual ideology

The emergence of new global sites of English-medium higher education presents scholars in the field of writing studies the opportunity to re-examine the theories and practices that are transported and translated to new contexts, and also to reflect on their continued relevance at their origins. Recent work on internationalization in the scholarship and practice of college composition calls for a multilingual approach, the rejection of monolingualism, and the adoption of a translingual norm (Horner, NeCamp & Donahue, 2011). This is an important direction for the field, but while Horner, NeCamp, and Donahue (2011) advocate for a "translingual model of multilingualism emphasizing working across languages" (p. 270), their argument rests on a view of languages that has been problematized recently by scholars in sociolinguistics. Adopting a critical sociolinguistics frame, I argue that we need to begin to question several foundational concepts and categories in the theory and practice of writing studies in order to make sense of and learn from new global sites of college writing. Taking the example of English-medium higher education in the State of Qatar in the Arabian Gulf, as part of the Middle East–North Africa (MENA) region more broadly, I introduce a critical sociolinguistic perspective, derived largely from Jan Blommaert's (2012a, 2012b, 2013a, 2013b, 2015) recent and groundbreaking work, which can help writing studies rethink some of our translingual assumptions to better empower learners and scholars in the twenty-first century.

Qatar is a small, independent Arabian Gulf state adjacent to the United Arab Emirates. It has only one major city, its capital, Doha, home to the national university as well as numerous foreign institutions including American, British, Canadian, Dutch, and French (for detailed discussion of international branch campuses, see Miller and Pessoa, this volume). Because of its small size (roughly 11,000 km^2 or 4,000 m^2), centralized population, and educational sites in the capital, Qatar is generally used in global discussions to refer to Doha and all other areas of the country together. Qatar offers an important example of an emerging global educational site that resists some of the basic categories of mainstream writing studies, including the categories of first-language (L1) and second-language (L2) users of English, international, and foreign students. Owing to shifts in global migration forces and patterns, Qatar's population is now comprised of approximately 220,000 Qatari nationals and 1.5 million expatriates, creating a workforce that is nearly 95% foreign (Ibnouf, Doub & Knight, 2014). Foreign, however, has complex nuances in Qatar as well as in other Gulf societies, where long-term expatriate residents and their children cannot seek citizenship; consequently, they remain local but always peripheral and never integrated systematically (see Ahmad, 2012, for analysis of migrant labor in the Gulf; and Vora, 2015, for an interesting case study). This intense diversity is also evident in higher education as a microcosm of society in general.

On a positive note, this diversity results in a vibrant inter-mixing of peoples who connect and communicate across the invisible borders of their adopted and heritage cultures. It is not at all uncommon to encounter students at English-medium, U.S. universities in Qatar who use two different languages or dialects at home, another at primary or secondary school, and attend university in English. As a teacher of first-year writing in Qatar, and in my interactions with student writers across their college years in the MENA region, I have known many students with "native-like" American accents and fluency who taught themselves English by watching cartoons and had very limited formal instruction at school. Still, their language abilities and varying levels of literacy in other languages support their integration of English as a resource among others. Conversations outside classrooms reveal a fluidity born of the translingual realities of the twenty-first century (see also Ronesi, this volume). Successful communication is not simply a product of high levels of proficiency but an outcome of developing the competence to navigate multiple contexts and registers to meet a given need, whether to connect on Facebook, text a classmate, or write a paper in first-year composition. While the situation may appear similar to that of some campuses in the US, the multiplicity of linguistic resources drawn upon in global sites like Qatar surfaces a number of assumptions about how languages and their acquisition are understood in mainstream composition scholarship.

From this perspective, writing studies is well served by related theorizing within the field of applied linguistics, particularly from the subfields of second-language acquisition and sociolinguistics. A growing body of writing scholarship already engages with work in second-language writing or draws from sociolinguistics in general (for example, Canagarajah, 2002, 2005, 2012; Cox & Zawacki, 2011; Matsuda, 2013; Matsuda & Silva, 2014; Silva & Matsuda, 2012; Zawacki & Cox, 2011; and the *Journal of Second Language Writing*); however, this work tends to divide into the two distinct camps of "second language" and "translingual" writing research and theory, both claiming similar but different foci and both often stopping short of addressing the complexities and tensions that lie underneath the common categories of languages and writers (see Atkinson, Crusan, Matsuda, Ortmeier-Hooper, Ruecker, Simpson & Tardy, 2015, for an overview). Further, while the terms "native speaker," "first-language writer," "second-language writer," or "multilingual learner" are widely used to denote language differences in writing, the categories in use might actually constrain our understandings and obscure our view of the underlying ideology.

In this chapter, I will focus on the potential of a critical sociolinguistic frame, largely informed by the pioneering work of Jan Blommaert, for advancing understandings of writing in translingual global contexts like MENA. Taking Blommaert's (2013a) work in linguistic landscape studies as a starting point, I explore Qatar as a site of linguistic superdiversity and then discuss the implications of superdiversity on academic writing in English-medium higher education. Against this backdrop, I go on to problematize some current constructs, terminology and ideological assumptions in U.S. English writing studies, pointing toward the need to ask some different questions, to "rethink and unthink" the concept of first and second languages and the writers, international or other, who are identified with them. I suggest that these terms no longer serve us in writing studies, and that instead of helping the field move forward in a global era, they keep us stuck in old thinking that is tied to an ideology few sociolinguistic scholars would still espouse.

Critical Sociolinguistics and Writing in Global Contexts

Blommaert argues that critical sociolinguistics can help us reassess how we understand language in writing as part of "changing language in a changing society" (Blommaert, 2010, p. 2). Critical sociolinguistics takes us beyond traditional understandings of discrete languages in homogenous societies, where there are first- and second-language users, and promotes instead "a sociolinguistics of mobile resources, not immobile languages" (Blommaert, 2010, p. 102). This view moves us away from long-held ideas about what languages are and how people communicate through them, as well as how, where, why and by whom academic writing takes shape.

Indeed, a very useful approach to analyzing and understanding the dynamics of language use is found in linguistic landscape studies (LLS), which are "descriptive as well as analytical" in "documenting the landscapes of today's globalized cities" (Blommaert, 2013a, p. 1). LLS help make sense of the shifting and emerging terrain of linguistic varieties and their deployment in meaning making and can potentially move us away from viewing a physical space as localized and static, to a more dynamic space of cultural, political and social interaction and negotiation. LLS can also serve as a "diagnostic of social, cultural and political structures inscribed in the linguistic landscape" (Blommaert, 2013a, p. 3) and offer a means to more deeply understand and engage with complex, modern, human networks.

The LLS approach is particularly suited for making sense of Qatar, which in the past decade has experienced a 124% growth in its population (Ibnouf et al., 2014), as it advances in a visionary process of development. Strategically building its human capacity for a future that relies on knowledge production instead of a carbon-based economy (General Secretariat for Development and Planning, 2008), this small Gulf state in the MENA region now hosts seven premier U.S. universities on its Education City campus, which claim a collective faculty and student body "from 89 different nationalities with diverse backgrounds, cultures, religions, financial status, and citizenship" (Ibnouf et al., 2014, p. 47). The great diversity of these university student populations has often had an unanticipated impact on the program, the faculty and the learners themselves (see Hodges & Kent; Miller & Pessoa; Rudd & Telafici this volume) in ways that are just now being explored in Qatar as well as in similarly developing sites in MENA and elsewhere. This new scale of diversity that is being experienced is referred to as *superdiversity* and is discussed in detail in the following sections.

Superdiversity is a term first proposed by social anthropologist Steven Vertovec (2007) to describe a new level of diversity the world is currently experiencing—a diversification of diversity—brought about by shifting forces of migration and mobility. A multitude of social, economic and political forces brings people from a great range of origins to new locations, creating categories of migrants that resist traditional definitions and force new thinking about who moves where and why. The reasons for migration, the direction of movement and the rise of new modes of communication have allowed people to connect and stay connected where they would previously have experienced more fragmentation and disconnection. As a result, people continue to draw upon multiple social and linguistic resources, which they blend into new activities and interactions. That is, new patterns of migration and new possibilities of interconnectivity and intercommunication have created "a condition distinguished by a dynamic interplay of variables among an increased number of new, small and scattered, multiple origin, transnationally connected, socio-economically differentiated and legally stratified immigrants" (Vertovec, 2007, p. 1024). Such a shift in positioning and contact calls us to "reorient some fundamental approaches within the social scientific study of migration in order to address and to better understand complex and arguably new social formations" (Meissner & Vertovec, 2014, p. 542). Among the new social formations are contexts of learning in higher education where there is now a mixing of people who geographically, socioeconomically and linguistically might otherwise never have come together. Recognizing the challenges and opportunities of this phenomenon allows us to explore previously held constructs in a new and fluid space that should necessarily invite a shift in thinking to meet the complex characteristics of the context and time.

Qatar is now not only home to a minority of native nationals together with regional neighbors and long-term expat guests and workers from distant origins; it is fast becoming a "a world of 'postmigrants'" or "second-generation immigrants" who "do not so much mark the phenomenon of migration as that of the aftermath of it." (Yildiz, 2012, p. 170). Alongside still swelling numbers of migrant laborers who are often the focus of attention in the international press, new generations of postmigrants add increased diversity to the socioeconomic and sociocultural tapestry of Qatar. These "multidimensional shifts in migration patterns" (Meissner & Vertovec, 2014, p. 541) necessarily alter the linguistic landscape of the emerging superdiverse global sites. It is this linguistic superdiversity that is of importance in the discussion of writing studies in the MENA region. While the scale of the city of Doha and, indeed, the entire country is smaller than that of cities traditionally considered global hubs (like London, for example), Qatar has many of the features and "interrelated dimensions of globalization and global cities characteristics" (Block, 2008, p. 2) that, given the shifting dynamics of the region, are becoming more common in other areas of MENA as well.

Qatar, then, can be usefully seen as a site of superdiversity, a convergence of peoples, cultures, and languages, for varied and unpredictable reasons, that is at once dynamic and integrative *in situ*, as well as constantly and immediately connected to multiple points of origin through easily accessed digital technologies. The result is a vibrantly varied population that communicates across and among its constituents, orally and in writing, across numerous speech communities, for work, family, education, travel, social systems and services, or leisure enjoyment. The students who populate first-year composition courses at U.S. universities in Qatar are part of this "postmigrant" era; they are master navigators of their polycentric, transnational, and translingual world (Canagarajah, 2012).

As Blommaert (2013b) writes, superdiversity "denies us the comfort of a set of easily applicable assumptions about our object, its features and meanings" (p. 3). What assumptions do we make of the students in a U.S. composition course in the US versus those in the MENA region? In what ways do we leverage students' language rich backgrounds, their metacognitive awareness of language systems, and the ease with which they move between identities and spaces of their worlds?

In the US, for example, there is a tendency to divide composition students very broadly into the two categories of native speakers and second-language learners, categories which are likely not accurate in the first instance and which obscure the complexities of students' language and cultural experiences. For example, when we consider a student a native speaker of English (leaving aside the question of the validity of conflating speech and writing), we more likely mean a monolingual English user, someone we assume to have not just a tacit and intuitive facility with speaking and writing in English, but one who also shares a set of values, experiences, and knowledge about English that is consistent with the academy we work in, the materials we use, and the developmental pathways we anticipate our students will follow. Those are sizable assumptions. Further, in our U.S. writing classrooms, we often do not acknowledge the language other than English that our students bring to the classroom or make the effort to surface, value and draw upon other literacies and repertoires, or take advantage of the metalinguistic knowledge they may have from learning and using other languages. Rather, the monolingual paradigm continues to structure how we teach and understand our learners, as a number of U.S. scholars have pointed out (e.g., Horner, NeCamp & Donahue, 2011; Matsuda, 2006).

In Qatar, we cannot start from a position that assumes and privileges a shared understanding of and set of experiences with English (or even Arabic)—not cultural, educational, or linguistic. Given the great diversity, we have to assume there will be very little in common among the students in the ways they have learned and used English in their lives prior to studying at an English-medium university. We must begin from a new common starting point. As a class unfolds and the students learn more about each other, their rich, lived language experiences typically come to the fore, and a new space of hybridity is created where there is no one who represents the monolingual native speaker norm. In composition classes in Qatar and other MENA sites, superdiversity compels us to deconstruct the ideologies and practices behind traditional categories of learners.

Blommaert (2013a) poses two central questions about superdiversity:

> The interaction of these two forces—new and more complex forms of migration, and new and more complex forms of communication and knowledge circulation—has generated a situation in which two questions have become hard to answer: who is the Other? And who are we? The Other is now a category in constant flux, a moving target about whom very little can be presupposed. (p. 5)

When we pose these questions about who we are and who the writers are at English-medium, U.S. universities in Qatar, we find it difficult to provide simple answers: Who is the other? Who are we? Both of these seemingly essential categories shift into a new light when explored in the context of superdiverse sites like Qatar. Further, who is the second-language learner, the native speaker, the foreign student, the international student? The categories no longer easily apply.

In a recent writing class, for example, one of my students grew up speaking French with his mother, a regional dialect of Arabic with his father and siblings, Modern Standard Arabic at grammar school, and both French and English in high school. At an English-medium university in a third country, what category of writer and learner applies to him? Or to the half-Spanish, half-Egyptian student who has been in English-language schools since kindergarten but speaks Spanish and Arabic at home: is she a second language learner of English? In what ways would an ESL writing course respond to the complexities of her language knowledge and use? Student profiles such as the two examples here are in fact the norm and not the exception in MENA (see Annous, Nicolas & Townsend; Arnold et al.; Hodges & Kent; Jarkas & Fakhreddine; Miller & Pessoa; Ronesi; Rudd & Telafici, this volume). As identities and language profiles become ever more multi-layered, fitting complex and dynamic human beings into fixed categories of identity that describe a less-connected, less-mobile, less-global world of the past, seems not only improbable but totally unhelpful.

Asking such questions from within MENA about MENA students should push us to ask the same questions in other contexts, particularly in the US: What does it mean to be a first or second language writer in a world where heterogeneous identities are common and mobility and communication displace borders and distance? What is useful in labeling a language as a defined and discrete system when "languages" such as English, Arabic, and Spanish have so many varieties and dialects? We only need look to Arabic for an excellent example. Arabic is not simply diglossic, the two varieties being Modern Standard Arabic (MSA), which is debated and contested in the literature as a native language or mother tongue (Albirini, 2016), and a regional dialect, of which there are a great many varieties. Qatari, Lebanese, and Egyptian Arabic, for example, are distinctly different dialects, all equally different from MSA. Consequently, an Egyptian student who has moved to Qatar will not only know Egyptian Arabic, but will have learned English and MSA at school, possibly French as well, the Gulf dialect more generally, and the Qatari dialect, too. It becomes inaccurate to consider such a student in the English composition classroom a second-language user of English. Linear understandings of language acquisition are rapidly giving way to more dynamic views of development and use (Larsen-Freeman, 2012).

Linguistic Superdiversity and Its Implications for Writing Studies

If we adopt a critical sociolinguistic perspective, then we can start to see language and superdiversity "as a space of synthesis, a point of convergence or a nexus of developments" where new understandings are possible, and "[to] see complexity, hybridity, 'impurity' and other features of 'abnormal' sociolinguistic objects as 'normal'"(Blommaert, 2013b, pp. 2–3), as today's global renditions of yesterday's fixed forms. That is to say that sites like Qatar open a space for thinking differently about how we understand and respond to language in context in writing studies. Examining the rich linguistic diversity in English-medium higher education in Qatar, we may find, as Blommaert say, that:

> a space of theoretical work emerge[s] in which "exceptional" forms of language [are] increasingly seen as privileged

lenses through which a different gaze on all of language became possible. In other words: starting from exceptionally "unusual" language, "normal" language also [begins] to look different. (Blommaert, 2013b, p. 4.)

When we look more closely at what we might have traditionally categorized as "learner English" or "foreign student writing," we might start to understand writing of all varieties in a new light.

The concept of superdiversity also helps us understand that many writers in today's transnational world do not operate in one language as discrete and separate from the others that they use. Rather,

> [i]n a superdiverse context, mobile subjects engage with a broad variety of groups, networks and communities, and their language resources are consequently learned through a wide variety of trajectories, tactics and technologies, ranging from formal language learning to entirely informal "encounters" with language. (Blommaert & Backus, 2012, p. 1)

In arguing for "a mature sociolinguistics of writing," Blommaert challenges us to "unthink the unproductive distinction between 'language' and 'writing', to view writing as the object of sociolinguistic inquiry" (2012b, p. 1). To do so, we also need to ask new questions, starting with how we view language itself. Indeed, Jørgensen, Karrebæk, Madsen and Møller (2011), arguing from a sociolinguistic perspective challenge the widely held view that "'language' can be separated into different 'languages'" (p. 23), such as English or Arabic. They describe languages instead as "abstractions, they are sociocultural or ideological constructions" (p. 23). Like Blommaert, they call us to move away from a bounded view of languages that can be categorically separated into first and second (or third or fourth) languages and acknowledge instead the rich complexity of resources deployed in social communication. In the view of Blommaert and Rampton (2012, p.1), "languages have now been denaturalized, the linguistic is treated as just one semiotic among many"—in other words, static categories such as L1 and L2 cannot persist.

With regard to monolingual ideology that is called into critical view, Yildiz (2014), in her exploration of the postmonolingual condition of the twenty-first century, argues that:

> Recognizing the workings of the monolingual paradigm . . . requires a fundamental reconceptualization of European and European-inflected thinking about language, identity and modernity. For monolingualism is much more than a simple

> quantitative term designating the presence of just one language. Instead, it constitutes a key structuring principle that organizes the entire range of modern social life, from the construction of individuals and their proper subjectivities to the formation of disciplines and institutions, as well as imagined collectives such as cultures and nations. (p. 2)

When we choose to view language through a postmonolingual lens and to engage the tensions between monolingualism and multilingualism, as Yildez compels us to do, we can untangle the categories and concepts of first, second, foreign (etc.) language, so writing studies can more meaningfully engage in global contexts in a postmonolingual world.

This change in our viewpoint calls for a paradigmatic shift in writing studies: We need to move beyond clearly demarcated views of languages, fixed in a rigid order of acquisition along a linear path of development, toward a more dynamic understanding of situated language development and use, and view writing within this larger frame as an object of critical sociolinguistic inquiry that informs both the teaching and learning of writing.

As teachers and scholars of writing in post-secondary education, we can apply this thinking to our work by first expanding our awareness of ourselves and others, and opening our theorizing to cross pollination from related fields, applied linguistics and critical sociolinguistics among them. We can then critically examine the assumptions of the theoretical frameworks, curricula, textbooks, and assessment tools that have structured writing studies; the language and behaviors that shape our scholarship and practice, revisiting our vocabulary in light of new understandings and discarding terms that might be holding us back. For example, categories of writers such as "native speaker" and "ESL" have been left unexamined too long; they tie us to a past out of sync with today's reality and potentially create artificial dichotomies that can polarize our thinking. Reconsidering these terms will actually help us re-evaluate how we order and organize our thinking and our field. Many of the authors of the chapters that follow describe student bodies that already challenge and problematize these entrenched terms in their work in Lebanon (Annous, Nicolas & Townsend; Arnold et al.; Jarkas & Fakhreddine), the UAE (Ronesi) as well as others in Qatar (Hodges & Kent; Miller & Pessoa; Rudd & Telafici). Critically examining our work invites us to move away from old labels and the static categories they prescribe, and, in searching for new language to describe and develop the work of our field, we will undoubtedly come to new understandings. The place to begin evolving the paradigm is in the language itself.

Conclusion

Recent attention to internationalization in composition in North American higher education is causing the field of composition to reconsider monolingual assumptions in our pedagogy and scholarship (Horner, NeCamp & Donhue, 2011; Matsuda, 2006). Further, as Donahue (2009) points out, while our focus has been on how "the US experience is being internationalized," we need to consider how the "import/export focal points create blind spots," in how we understand the assumptions behind our own thinking and practice. As Zawacki and Habib (2014) argue, it is "time to re-examine our role as teachers of language ... and to consider what new or different questions we in writing studies should be asking about where and how we can attend to students' language development—cognitive and sociocultural, grammatical and rhetorical, linguistic (fluency and accuracy)—within the writing processes we're teaching our students to employ" (p. 651), as well as how "to generate new questions about the languaging and writing processes through which students acquire academic writing competence" (p. 655).

In Qatar, and in other MENA contexts, we find ourselves teaching, researching and doing our own writing in the context of superdiversity in a new transnational state: In our daily realities, our students move into a space they own together, unbound by first and second language distinctions, by communicating and writing in an English of higher education as part of a superdiverse context. How does a space like Qatar invite us to rethink and unthink the monolingual assumptions and constructs that dominate U.S.-based writing studies, whether at international branch campuses or locally operated extensions of American (or other) institutions?

As we consider a critical sociolinguistic frame in our rethinking and unthinking, we are challenged by Blommaert (2015), who asks whether "certain academic discourses [are] 'clearly' locked into one or another culture" thus providing "an implicit judgment of the legitimacy of voice" (p. 1). When we ask this question of writing studies, we should not be too surprised to find that U.S.-based discourses appear to enjoy this implicit legitimacy of voice, as evidenced in the content of textbooks and scholarly journals alike, whether discourses around student writers, pedagogies, or scholarship. We should not be surprised, either, that we still seem to be "locked" into a predominantly American culture of theorizing and doing composition studies, where the categories of L1, L2, native speaker, and so on continue to constrain both our thinking and our impact. Blommaert helps to expose the underlying monolingual ideology and the terminology and assumptions that hold us back from more meaningful international exchanges, as instances of multidirectional, transnational meaning making in a mobile and connected reality.

Along these lines, Yildiz (2014) challenges our rethinking and unthinking further with her question: "What is the relationship between language and identity today? According to the monolingual paradigm, there is one privileged language, the mother tongue" (p. 202). In complex and superdiverse sites like Qatar, the idea of "mother tongue," as I've argued, is problematic when hybrid realities call for much greater flexibility and fluidity in communication, and a "mother tongue" becomes just one of many resources. Yildiz's (2014) message is powerful for teaching writing in the superdiverse MENA region. As she says, "Recognizing the monolingual paradigm and its workings can be a step towards denaturalizing monolingualism as an unquestioned norm and standard according to which other linguistic configurations and practices are measured" (p. 206). For the MENA region, this means recognizing and moving away from the traditional monolingual assumptions of U.S. composition studies and developing instead a more locally situated but globally informed approach to the teaching of writing. There is much opportunity in thinking about superdiversity and a critical sociolinguistics of writing in Qatar and the MENA region, but also anywhere else where writing is taught, explored, practiced, studied, developed, and discussed; opportunity to question the language we use to organize and interpret the world of writers and writing. If we reflect on the lessons of Qatar and dare to unthink what no longer serves but constrains us, then we are poised to create "a new culture in our scholarship of writing" (Blommaert, 2015, p. 2). This new culture is one that will recognize and value the complexities of living, learning and communicating in a post-monolingual world and will reconfigure teaching and scholarship in this light.

References

Albirini, A. (2016). *Modern Arabic sociolinguistics: Disglossia, variation, codeswitching, attitudes and identity.* New York: Routledge.

Ahmad, A. (2012). Beyond labor: Foreign residents in the Gulf states. In M. Kamrava & Z. Babar (Eds.), *Migrant labor in the Persian Gulf* (pp. 21–40). New York: Columbia University Press.

Atkinson, D., Crusan, D., Matsuda, P. K., Ortmeier-Hooper, C., Ruecker, T., Simpson, S. & Tardy, C. (2015). Clarifying the relationship between L2 writing and translingual writing: An open letter to writing studies editors and organization leaders. *College English, 77*, 383–386.

Block, D. (2008). Multilingual identities and language practices in a global city: Four London case studies. *Journal of Language, Identity, and Education, 7*(1), 1–4.

Blommaert, J. (2010). *The sociolinguistics of globalization*. Cambridge, UK: Cambridge University Press.
Blommaert, J. (2012a). Citizenship, language, and superdiversity: Towards complexity. *Working Papers in Urban Language & Literacies, 95*, 1–5.
Blommaert, J. (2012b). Writing as a sociolinguistic object. *Tilburg Papers in Culture Studies, 42*, 1–28.
Blommaert, J. (2013a). *Ethnography, superdiversity and linguistic landscapes: Chronicles of complexity*. Bristol, UK: Multilingual Matters.
Blommaert, J. (2013b). The second life of old issues: How superdiversity "renews" things. *Tilburg Papers in Culture Studies, 59*, 1–8.
Blommaert, J. (2015). Commentary: "Culture" and superdiversity. *Tilburg Papers in Culture Studies, 127*, 1–3.
Blommaert, J. & Backus, A. (2012). Superdiverse repertoires and the individual. *Tilburg Papers in Culture Studies, 24*, 1–32.
Blommaert, J. & Rampton, B. (2012). Language and superdiversity. *Diversities, 13*(2), 1–21.
Canagarajah, S. (2002). *A geopolitics of academic writing*. Pittsburgh, PA: University of Pittsburgh Press.
Canagarajah, S. (Ed.). (2005). *Reclaiming the local in language policy and practice*. New York: Routledge.
Canagarajah, S. (2012). *Translingual practice: Global Englishes and cosmopolitan relations*. New York: Routledge.
Cox, M. & Zawacki, T. M. (Eds.). (2011). WAC and second language writing: Cross-field research, theory, and program development [Special Issue]. *Across the Disciplines, 8*(4). Retrieved from http://wac.colostate.edu/atd/ell/.
Donahue, C. (2009). "Internationalization" and composition studies: Reorienting the discourse. *College Composition and Communication, (61)*2, 212–243.
General Secretariat for Development Planning. (2008). Qatar National Vision 2030. Retrieved from http://www.qdb.qa/English/Documents/QNV2030_English.pdf.
Horner, B., NeCamp, S. & Donahue, C. (2011). Toward a multilingual composition scholarship: From English only to a translingual norm. *College Composition and Communication, 63*(2), 269–300.
Ibnouf, A., Dou, L. & Knight, J. (2014). The evolution of Qatar as an education hub: Moving to a knowledge-based economy. In J. Knight (Ed.), *International education hubs: Student, talent, knowledge-innovation models* (pp. 43–61). Dordrecht, NL: Springer.
Jørgensen, J. N., Karrebæk, M. S., Madsen, L. M. & Møller, J. S. (2011). Polylanguaging in superdiversity. *Diversities, 13*(2), 23–37.
Larsen-Freeman, D. (2012). Complex, dynamic systems: A new transdisciplinary theme for applied linguistics? *Language Teaching, 45*(02), 202–214.
Matsuda, P. K. (2006). The myth of linguistic homogeneity in U.S. college composition. *College English, 68*, 637–651.
Matsuda, P. K. (2013). Response: What is second language writing—And why does it matter? *Journal of Second Language Writing, 22*(4), 448–450.

Matsuda, P. K. & Silva, T. (Eds.). (2014). *Second language writing research: Perspectives on the process of knowledge construction.* New York: Routledge.

Meissner, F. & Vertovec, S. (2014). Comparing super-diversity. *Ethnic and Racial Studies, (38)*4, 541–555.

Rampton, B. (2013). Drilling down to the grain in superdiversity. *Tilburg Papers in Culture Studies, 48*, 1–28.

Silva, T. & Matsuda, P. K. (Eds.). (2012). *On second language writing.* New York: Routledge.

Vertovec, S. (2007). Super-diversity and its implications. *Ethnic and Racial Studies, 30*(6), 1024–1054.

Vora, N. (2015). Is the university universal? Mobile (re)constitutions of American academia in the Gulf Arab states. *Anthropology & Education Quarterly, 46*(1), 19–36.

Yildiz, Y. (2012). *Beyond the mother tongue: The postmonolingual condition.* New York: Fordham University Press.

Zawacki, T. M. & Cox, M. (2011, December 21). Introduction to WAC and second language writing. *Across the Disciplines, 8*(4). Retrieved from http://wac.colostate.edu/atd/ell/zawacki-cox.cfm.

Zawacki, T. M. & Habib, A. S. (2014). Internationalization, English L2 writers, and the writing classroom: Implications for teaching and learning. *College Composition and Communication, 65*(4), 650–658.

2 Global Spread of English in Academia and Its Effects on Writing Instruction in Turkish Universities

Hacer Hande Uysal
GAZI UNIVERSITY (TURKEY)

This chapter examines Turkish macro-level state policies of scholarly publishing from the 1980s when publications were mainly in Turkish, to the present when Turkish has lost its significance with regulations mandating that international publications be written in English as a prerequisite for academic promotion. Second, a field study explores the influences of the state publishing policies on both Turkish and English academic writing instruction in two major universities in Ankara (one Turkish- and one English-medium), focusing on three sub-policies of language-in-education policy implementation: access, curriculum, and materials and methodology. The results indicate that despite some conflicting micro-level planning and practices with state policies, the macro-level state policy has largely influenced the academic literacy practices at these universities as more courses aimed at developing English academic writing skills and Anglo-American research traditions are offered while academic writing in Turkish is neglected. English has gained a higher status and hegemony in scientific literacy, especially in the English-medium university, yet both Turkish and English writing instruction need to improve in quality.

Keywords: global spread of English; Turkish language policy; scholarly publication; academic writing instruction

The global spread of English in academia and scholarly publishing, and its political and pedagogical consequences, have been of interest in recent scholarship (e.g., Canagarajah, 2002; Flowerdew, 1999, 2000; Lillis & Curry, 2010; Philipson, 2008; Swales, 1997; Tardy, 2004). The spread of English in academia as the *lingua franca* of scientific publications has caused increasing pressure on academics around the world to write in English and according to

English norms. As written academic discourse in English is highly standardized and embedded in Anglo-American culture, and as Anglo-Americans are in gatekeeping positions in most international journals (Tardy, 2004), this imposition of English on scholars who are non-native speakers (NNS) of English has raised the issues of linguistic and cultural hegemony (Kaplan, 2001; Phillipson, 2006; Swales, 1997; Tardy, 2004). The diffusion of powerful cultural rhetoric, especially through academic writing instruction (Canagarajah, 1999), and the homogeneity caused by the elimination of other cultural rhetorics over time, has been a major concern (Kachru, 1995; Mauranen, 1993).

The pressures caused by the global spread of English in academia and in scholarly publications have also influenced governmental policy-making in many countries that aim to become a part of the global scientific community. However, although some studies have examined the spread of English language in state policies in local contexts (e.g., Uysal, Plakans & Dembovskaya, 2007), research investigating the spread of English specifically in scholarly publishing policies in local contexts is limited, and research looking into the interplay between macro-level government policies of scholarly publishing and micro-level academic writing instruction is almost nonexistent. Yet, as Baldauf (2005) suggests, macro-level policies often extend to micro situations such as educational practices, but applications at this level can also be independent and different from the macro-level policies. Thus, investigations at micro level are also needed "to better understand both policy implementation and solutions of micro-policy problems" (Baldauf, 2005, p. 964).

Therefore, to fill this important gap in the literature, this study explores this global issue through the example of Turkey. The study first historically examines the macro-level state policies of scholarly publishing in Turkey. Second, as studies of language policies in practice are needed (Ramanathan, 2005; Spolsky, 2004), and education is a critical vehicle for language spread (Kaplan & Baldauf, 1997), the impact of the state policies on micro-level practices of academic writing instruction is also explored in two major universities in Ankara, Turkey, focusing on three sub-policies of language-in-education policy implementation—access, curriculum, and materials and methodology (Kaplan & Baldauf, 1997, 2005).

Historical Background

Turkish Language and Literacy Planning in General

Turkey was founded as a democratic nation-state in 1923 after the collapse of the multinational Ottoman Empire. Due to its unique history and geopolitical location between Asia and Europe, Turkey has often faced struggles between opposing forces such as West and East, past and future, modernization and nationalism (Akarsu, 1999; Kinzer, 2001). This complexity is also reflected by unclear goals and contradictory practices in language planning and policy. For example, while English is offered as the only foreign language in most state schools, and the spread of English in education has been strongly encouraged as a means of modernization and westernization, English-medium education at secondary schools was eliminated in 1997 as it was seen as a threat to the purity and status of Turkish (Uysal et al., 2007, p. 197).

Nonetheless, the global spread of English has been strongly felt in Turkey, which has always turned its face to the West more than the East, having been the member of NATO and OECD, the Council of Europe, and OSCE, and a candidate for European Union membership (Eurydice, 2010). English became influential especially after World War II because of increasing contact and closer ties with the United States (Demircan, 1988). English was embraced to integrate Turkey with the west, to participate in international communication, and to achieve technological and economic advancement and modernization. In addition, due to the gatekeeping function of English in Turkey, internal motives such as gaining access to better education and career opportunities, higher living standards, and academic promotion also contributed to the spread of English (Dogancay-Aktuna & Kızıltepe, 2005).

The spread of English has also been promoted through national language-in-education planning in Turkey—an "expanding circle" context (Kachru, 1992).[1] For example, 99.95% of primary-school students and 91.94% of secondary-school students learn English as a compulsory foreign language (Tok & Arıbaş, 2008), and students start learning English in second grade. In tertiary education, the spread of English is even more strongly evident as English has increasingly become the medium of education in many universities. For example, while English-medium instruction (EMI) was offered in six universities in 1990, around 79 out of 165 universities currently offer education completely in English in all departments (100% English), or in some departments, such as Economics, Medicine, and Engineering, or through some courses in English (30% English) (ÖSYM, 2011). EMI has been a topic of hot debate for years. While some support EMI for providing opportunities for content-based learning and actual use of English (Alptekin, 1998; Bear, 1998; Sert, 2008), the majority oppose it, arguing that EMI reduces students' ability to understand concepts, leads to superficial content learning, threatens Turkish, and creates an elite class alienated from the realities of the society (e.g., Demircan, 1995; Kılıçkaya, 2006; Kırkgöz, 2005; Köksal, 2002; Sinanoğlu, 2002) (see also Hayes & Mansour, this volume, for a related discussion of the impact of societal pressures on English-language education in Bahrain).

With respect to Turkish language and literacy planning, first, the country went through an extensive language reform to realize a new national identity, language unity and modernization between 1920 and 1930 (Dogancay-Aktuna, 1995). Ottoman—the higher diglossic variety composed of Turkish, Persian, and Arabic based on Arabic script—was abandoned, and Turkish—the lower diglossic variety—was accepted with the Latin alphabet as the national language. As a result, even the small number of people who were literate in Ottoman became illiterate overnight, and the literacy rate in Turkish was only 6% in 1923 (Dogancay-Aktuna, 1998). However, due to meticulous governmental efforts, the average adult literacy rate has today increased to 88.7% (UNDP Report, 2009). Nevertheless, as literacy experiences in modern Turkish have been quite recent, Turkish literacy education still has serious problems, especially in regard to writing (Ayyıldız & Bozkurt, 2006; Göçer, 2010).

Turkish Macro-level Scholarly Publishing Policies

In this section, state policies of scholarly publishing and factors behind these policies are discussed according to the changes in views and tendencies with regards to scientific publications in Turkey. This historical analysis is done based on published literature, regulations/laws, policy documents from the related Turkish state institutions, and Eurydice (2010) as data sources.

A Brief Historical Look at Scholarly Publishing Policies (1981–Present)

Until the 1980s, Turkish universities were basically teaching-oriented, and scholarly publishing was not a part of academic duty for many academics. However, in 1981, with the centralization and restructuring of all Turkish higher education institutions under the supervision of the Higher Education Council (HEC), principles of the Anglo-American university system in terms of education, research, and general university structure, which highlighted the importance of research and publishing, were adopted. This change gave rise to a new understanding within the long-established teaching-oriented Turkish university culture (Ak & Gülmez, 2006; Ardınç, 2007). However, in this period, publications were still mainly in Turkish and in national journals; additionally, many publications lacked proper citations, which often resulted in plagiarism (Ardınç, 2007; Pazarlıoğlu & Özkoç, 2009).

Later, international publications started to gain momentum, especially in the disciplines of the Natural Sciences and Medicine after the 1993 economic incentive program for international publications initiated by the Turkish Scientific & Technological Research Council (TUBITAK) through its sub-unit Academic Network & Information Center (ULAKBIM). This was followed by individual university's initiations of economic incentives and rewards for international publications (Arıoğlu & Girgin, 2002). These incentives never covered national publications in Turkish; thus, in a way, local and Turkish publications were discouraged. In this period, the general writing tendency was simply to translate Turkish articles into English before submitting them to international journals (Ardınç, 2007), so academic writing instruction in English was not a priority.

Between the years 1996 and 1999, international publications started to gain priority over Turkish. Overall, a 26% of increase was monitored in publications in The Institute for Scientific Information (ISI) database (Başkurt, 2007). However, the increasing quantity of the articles published in this period was negatively correlated with their quality as manifested by the decrease in citation statistics between 1993 and 1999 (Arıoğlu & Girgin, 2003). Thus, to increase the quality and standards of international publications, in 1997, TUBITAK excluded conference proceedings, reports, and opinion articles from the incentive program and limited the applications to research articles published in journals in the ISI database. This led to an increase in research articles along with a dramatic decrease in theoretical or opinion articles (Arıoğlu & Girgin, 2002, 2003). During this period, the importance of acquiring writing skills in English was understood, and ethical concerns regarding plagiarism were also raised with increasing western influence in academia (Ardınç, 2007).

With participation in the Bologna Reform Process (1999), Turkey undertook steps for integration, such as standardization, academic quality assurance, and accreditation in tertiary education in line with the European standards (HEC, 2010). These integration attempts with Europe and with the global scientific world resulted in developing new standards for academic promotion, research, and publishing. Hence, for the first time, criteria for academic promotion were established by the regulation of the Inter-University Council (IUC, 2000). With this regulation, proficiency in a foreign language and publications in journals indexed in the ISI database became mandatory requirements for associate professorship in most fields. In addition, international publications were endowed with twice as much value as national publications.

With the new publishing criteria and promotion policy of HEC, academic performance started to be associated solely with the number of international publications in the ISI database. Overall, a steep increase in international publications was observed between 1981 and 2010. While Turkey was 45th among world countries with only 439 international publications in 1980 (Ak & Gülmez, 2006), Turkey became 18th with 24,821 publications in 2008, and the total number of Turkish publications in ISI databases was 197,346 by 2010 (Akıllı et al., 2009, TUBITAK-ULAKBIM, 2011). In this period, concerns regarding the situation of Turkish as the language of science were also raised (e.g., Ergenç, 2001; Kılınç, 2001).

Academic Literacy-in-Education Practices in Turkish Universities

To explore any connections between macro-level state policies and micro-level implementations, academic literacy-in-education planning and practices in two major state universities in Ankara were investigated. The focus of research was on the three main sub-policies in language-in-education planning related to implementation—access, curriculum, and materials and methodology—due to their direct relevance to the research goals (Kaplan & Baldauf, 1997; 2005). The two universities selected represent different orientations and perspectives. Gazi University (GAZI)—a Turkish-medium university—was established in 1926 with a more traditional, nationalistic, and teaching-oriented view. It is one of the most populous universities in Turkey with more than 77,000 students. The Middle East Technical University (METU), on the other hand, was established in 1957 around a U.S.-university model with 100% English-medium education. It is a more elite and research-oriented university with around 26,000 students.

Methodology

Data Collection

The methods used included document collection and analysis, and interviews were also conducted to confirm and validate the findings. First, to understand how access and curriculum policy are impacted by the implementation of macro-level state policies, courses with an academic writing component were identified by looking at curricula in all departments in both universities and the HEC's course descriptions. Second, these courses were examined in detail based on the syllabi, textbooks, and assessment rubrics obtained from university websites or from instructors and students. Finally, to supplement information derived from the documentary sources and to establish cross-validation and triangulation (Merriam, 1998), face-to-face semi-structured interviews with key informants were conducted in both universities.

The participants constituted 40 students from various departments (24 students from GAZI and 16 students from METU) who had already taken the writing/research courses in their particular university and 16 instructors (nine instructors from GAZI and seven instructors from METU) who had taught at least one course with an academic writing component in either GAZI or METU. The participants were selected on a voluntary basis through several campus visits to the Schools of Foreign Languages, English Language Teaching, and Turkish Education programs in both universities, and to the Department of Modern Languages at METU. Semi-structured interviews were chosen as a method because they provide reliable and comparable qualitative data through two-way communication (Cohen & Crabtree, 2006). In the interviews, questions were asked regarding: class hours devoted to writing; genres and writing features taught; level of writing; textbooks used; main objectives; and teaching approaches and methods. Notes were taken during the interview and, when necessary, additional questions were asked later via e-mail (See Appendix 1 for interview questions).

Data Analysis

Kaplan & Baldauf's (1997; 2005) policy descriptions for access (who learns what and when), curriculum (how much time is allocated to writing instruction in the curriculum, what are the objectives of teaching/learning), and materials and methods (which materials and methodology are employed) were used as a framework of guidance in data analysis. For example, the documents were analyzed according to the amount of time allocated to teaching and practicing academic writing in classes; the course objectives were analyzed according to the writing genres covered and the level of writing done (e.g., writing paragraphs vs. research papers). The content of the course materials, rubrics, and syllabi were also analyzed according to the presence or absence of certain Anglo-American writing features, such as plagiarism, linear deductive organization, topic sentences, and cohesive markers. This analysis highlighted the western influence on academic writing instruction as well as source awareness, and the value attached to academic writing and these writing features (Krippendorff, 2004). Then, the notes taken during the interview were read to determine whether or not they confirmed the findings of the document analysis and also to understand in depth the methodology and practices used in writing classes.

Results

Access Policy

Upon examination of HEC's course descriptions and curriculum in all departments in both universities, it was found that a variety of compulsory and elective courses involving Turkish composition and research skills, as well as English academic writing, are available for students. Academic writing courses in METU and GAZI in both Turkish and English are similar at the lower undergraduate level but vary at the upper undergraduate level. Recently, some new academic writing courses have been introduced, especially at graduate level, and additional support for English academic writing (such as writing centers) has also been on the rise in both universities. The courses with an academic writing component in Turkish and English in the two universities can be seen in table 2.1.

In preparatory classes, where students are immersed in English for at least 20 hours a week for a full academic year before they start their undergraduate studies, it was found that academic writing is offered only in English in both universities. Yet, it is important to note that preparatory English education is compulsory for the 30% English (some programs at GAZI, such as economics and engineering) and 100% English-medium departments (all programs at METU) (HEC 2008).

During the first-year undergraduate studies, compulsory general English or English for Academic Purposes courses (EAP I & II) are also taught in both universities for two semesters. Again in the first year, English majors in English language teaching (ELT) programs are required to take an integrated Advanced Reading and Writing (ARW) course for three hours a week for two semesters. Likewise, in the first year of the undergraduate studies, a common compulsory Turkish or Turkish Composition class is offered to all students for two semesters in both universities. These first-year Turkish and English courses are similar at both universities, as these are required courses by the HEC for all departments in all universities in Turkey (HEC, 2008).

In upper-level courses at the undergraduate level, on the other hand, more differences are observed between the two universities as METU offers more opportunities for academic writing, particularly in English, to a wider student population than GAZI. For example, in the second and third years, compulsory and elective courses targeting acquisition of English academic writing and research skills are available in METU for all programs. In addition, while the research methods courses are offered in Turkish for all majors includ-

Table 2.1. Courses with an academic writing component in GAZI and METU

Medium	GAZI	METU
Intensive English Preparatory Class (two semesters)		
English	Compulsory for the 30% English-medium programs and English majors since 1996.	Compulsory for all departments since 1961.
Undergraduate		
English	**1:** General English for two semesters (C). **1:** Advanced Reading &Writing for two semesters only for English majors (ELT) (C) **2:** General English for two semesters (C)	**1:** English for Academic Purposes I & II (EAP) for two semesters (C) since the foundation of the university. **1:** Advanced Reading &Writing for two semesters only for English majors (ELT)(C) **2:** Research Methods (C) for a semester. **3:** Advanced Writing & Research Skills (C) for English majors. **3 or 4:** Writing Term Papers (E). *(Not opened for the last 2 years).*
Turkish	**1:** Turkish I: Composition (C) or **2:** Turkish I & II **2:** Research Techniques (C) for a semester.	**1:** Turkish Written Communication or **3:** Turkish I & II (C)
Graduate		
English	Ph.D. Writing for publication course in ELT program (E) since 2011.	MA or MS Research Methods for some departments (C). Ph.D. Research Methods (C)
Turkish	Ph.D. Research Techniques (C) Academic Writing I & II (since 2011) Creative Thinking and Writing in Arts Education (E) Academic Writing in Biology (E)	
Additional Support for English Academic Writing		
	A weekend course for academic faculty on English scientific writing for one semester in Fall 2010. An English Academic Writing Center since 2015.	An English Academic Writing Center since 2001

Coding: **C**: *Compulsory* | **E**: *Elective* | **1**: *1st year course* | **2**: *2nd year course* | **3 or 4**: *3rd or 4th year course*

ing English majors in GAZI, the same courses are offered in English in METU. At the graduate level, several new graduate courses aimed at teaching advanced academic writing skills have been introduced in both universities. Moreover, there has been a recent increase in additional academic writing support in English, such as writing centers both in METU and GAZI and a weekend English scientific writing course in GAZI.

This significant increase in the variety of academic literacy courses at the graduate level and in the amount of additional support for English academic writing took place especially after 2000 when international publications in English became a prerequisite for academic promotion and started to be seen as the number one indicator of academic success in HEC's policies. This indicates that the macro-level state policies might have influenced the academic literacy-in-education planning and instruction in both universities. Yet, it is also important to note that while these opportunities all target English academic writing in METU, Turkish writing instruction has remained stable over the years.

Curriculum Policy

Time Allocated to Academic Literacy Education

Time is an important prerequisite for the development of academic writing skills, which involve complex linguistic, cognitive, and socio-cultural factors. Building academic writing skills requires a long time and intensive practice to be able to use the language accurately and appropriately; to employ skills and strategies related to the writing process such as generating ideas, drafting, organizing, revising, and editing; as well as to establish social skills such as developing awareness of writing conventions, genre-specific features, and audience expectations in a particular context. Acquisition of these skills in L2 entails even more time and practice, as it means socialization into a new discourse community that is likely to have different writing conventions and audience expectations. Therefore, the amount of writing instructional time is critical in any academic writing instruction, particularly L2 academic writing instruction.

When we look at the situation in Turkish universities, despite the variety of the writing courses and the rise in the number of new academic writing opportunities in both universities, as listed in Table 2.1, a detailed examination reveals problems with class time devoted to academic writing in practice. First, it was found that some planning by both the HEC and universities resulted in the elimination of certain academic writing courses, which thus caused serious limitations in classroom hours. For example, as reported in the Department of History booklet, the first-year EAP I & II in METU, which is currently four hours a week for two semesters, used to be ten hours a week before the mid-1980s, but as the HEC increased the student quota, which brought about a serious shortage of instructors, the number of hours for these ten-credit Freshman English courses had to be decreased to four. Similarly, the first-year ARW I & II courses, which are offered for English majors in ELT programs, is currently three hours a week for two semesters (a total of six credit hours). However, from the interviews with the instructors, it was understood that these courses were introduced to the curriculum in 2006 by combining three separate academic literacy courses—Advanced Reading Skills and Advanced Writing Skills for two semesters, and a second-year Academic Writing course for a semester (a total of 15 credit hours)—into one. As the number of classes and class hours allocated to academic literacy was restricted, academic literacy-in-education for English majors was negatively affected. This indicates a contradiction with the HEC's own publishing policies, which, on the one hand, necessitate higher-order academic literacy skills for academic success and international publishing, and, on the other hand, decrease the number of academic writing courses and cut the class hours.

Second, it was found that writing is generally embedded in the preparatory and first-year general English or EAP courses but often neglected when compared to other language skills. The preparatory teachers in GAZI stated that, for the students who are not English majors, only around 10% of the total class hours (around one to two hours of the total 20–25 hours per week) are devoted to writing. All teachers said that writing is not given priority in their classes and it is often left behind other skills; therefore, students do not have enough opportunities to practice and produce effective academic papers. GAZI instructors said they lecture about writing one week and let the students write for one hour in class the next week. That is, the students may only write for one hour every two weeks. Some instructors also mentioned that the students are not motivated to write in English because they do not write, but instead they take tests, in future English courses. Because writing is not central in university education in general, reading, grammar, and vocabulary, which often appear in tests, are given the utmost priority in English classes. At METU, the situation seems a little better than it is in GAZI. For example, the instructors said that teaching writing is an essential part of the program from the very beginning of the academic year because students are asked to write paragraphs in the preparatory class exit exam. The classes comprise around 20% writing (three to five hours of the total 15–25 hours of English course per week), and students not only learn about writing rules but also practice writing in class every week.

In the first-year English classes at METU, around one hour in a four-hour-a-week EAP class is allocated to writing. Instructors said they try to attend to all skills equally and spend time on writing in class every week, but by writing for one hour a week, their students can only achieve basic-level writing in English. The instructors at GAZI stated that English is three hours a week, but writing is almost non-existent in the first-year English classes, especially for students who have not attended the preparatory classes. In the second year, nonetheless, they said the situation becomes better as they can allocate 20–30% of the course hours to writing. In the first-year ARW course for English majors, METU instructors stated that they distribute course time equally between reading and writing, but GAZI instructors maintained that approximately 70% of the class time is devoted to reading, while writing sections in the book are often given as homework for students because they do not have time to deal with writing in class. All instructors at GAZI complained that the integrated reading/writing course is ineffective when compared to previous separate reading and writing courses, and they claimed that the integration of both meant that neither reading nor writing could be taught adequately. Overall, all instructors and most students stated that the integrated Academic Reading and Writing course does not allow them to learn and practice higher-level academic writing skills such as the development of logical argument, or writing well-organized, cohesive, and coherent paragraphs and essays, due to time constraints.

In the second-year Research Methods course, which is three hours a week in both universities, some writing instruction on research reporting is included in the syllabus; however, the time allocated to writing in these classes largely varies according to the instructor and departments. For example, while some students said they actually wrote a research paper and received feedback between drafts in the Research Methods course, other students said they never wrote a research paper, but only took tests on research methods. In METU, in the third year, there is an additional Advanced Writing and Research Skills course for three hours a week for English majors. All students stated that they found this course very helpful as instructors attend to each individual writing assignment and provide feedback both in and out of classroom time whenever needed. However, instructors claimed that the course hours are not adequate for providing a sufficient knowledge base about both research and writing skills at the same time, and thus teachers have to make personal sacrifices such as arranging extra office hours to help students with their writing. One instructor said they need more time because students come to classes with no previous knowledge of academic writing and scientific thinking skills in Turkish, which could then be transferred to English.

Turkish Composition or Turkish I & II classes are only two hours a week for all programs for two semesters, and writing is only covered for one semester as part of a curriculum that includes not just writing but some content on language in general (see the next sections for a detailed description). Therefore, when compared to the academic English writing instruction especially in METU, Turkish writing instruction at the undergraduate level seems to fall short for developing students' Turkish academic writing skills.

The graduate courses are all three hours a week for either the fall or spring semester. While the general research methods courses have been offered for almost three decades, specific writing courses targeting academic writing, including thesis writing and writing for publishing purposes, have been more recently introduced to the curriculum in various departments, especially at GAZI. Moreover, some additional support for English writing in the form of writing centers has also been offered at both universities. The writing centers at METU and GAZI offer one-on-one tutorial sessions for 45 minutes to graduate students and academic faculty by appointment. According to the writing center director of METU, approximately 300–350 sessions are held in one semester to offer help with English academic writing. Because the writing center has just been opened at GAZI, such statistics are not yet available. At GAZI, a weekend course on English scientific writing was also offered in 2010 for three hours a week for eight weeks during the fall semester for graduate students, research assistants, and faculty.

Objectives of the Courses (Targeted Genres and the Levels of Writing)

In preparatory classes and the first-year English courses, English academic writing at the paragraph level and the essay level is offered. While EAP I mainly includes paragraph writing with just an introduction to essay writing, EAP II includes academic essay writing and incorporates a documented argumentative and a reaction-response essay in its syllabus. The ARW I & II courses for English majors at both universities also have a similar focus. While the former teaches mainly paragraph-level writing with an introduction to essay, the latter includes essay-level writing and an introduction to all types of essays.

While academic English writing practices were found to be limited to paragraph and sometimes to essay-level writing at the undergraduate level, the situation for Turkish is worse, as almost no Turkish academic writing instruction exists. Although Turkish composition courses are given for two semesters, writing is only taught for one semester, as the other Turkish composition course focuses on oral presentation skills and Turkish speaking skills. Moreover, the greater part of these courses comprises units about language, culture, and grammar. Although language, culture, and grammar are topics all closely related to writing, these issues are presented as lectures in isolation, not combined with or integrated into writing instruction. Most students from various programs claimed that they have not written in these courses, but instead they only learned theoretical information through lectures about writing, including information about how to write in genres that were generally nonacademic, such as petitions, letters, tales, and poetry. Some students also asserted that their instructors mostly focused on Turkish grammar, spelling, and punctuation, rather than making them practice actual writing. This situation is likely to have dire consequences, especially for students of the Turkish-medium programs (mostly social sciences and humanities) at GAZI, as this means these students do not practice academic writing in either Turkish or English, while students in 30% English (hard sciences) at GAZI and 100% English programs at METU experience at least some form of academic writing in English at the undergraduate level.

As for the research courses, it was found that despite its existence in the syllabus, instruction on writing about or reporting on research comprises a small portion of the classes, and sometimes students even finish these courses without practicing any writing or submitting a research paper. Despite their variability, research methods courses at both the undergraduate and graduate levels generally focus on basic research methods and techniques, such as statistical sampling procedures, writing hypotheses, controlling variables, data collection, data evaluation, test reliability/validity, and quantitative and qualitative research methods, including surveys, case studies, correlation studies, and statistical analysis with SPSS program. Thus, only a small part of these courses deals with writing issues such as plagiarism, reviewing the literature, and reporting the research results. Moreover, as stated by the instructors and students, only some of these courses at the undergraduate level require in-class writing or a written final project, and teacher feedback on drafts is often either limited or nonexistent. It was also found that in some classes, students only received theoretical instruction on writing and did not have any chance to write in or out of the class; instead, many students had multiple-choice or short-answer exams that asked them about research design and academic writing skills, such as statistical methods, referencing, or APA style.

A few elective courses at METU and GAZI (mostly for English majors) were found to have a deeper focus on scientific academic writing; however, these courses do not have a large impact, as they are limited in number and student access. However, at the graduate level, some graduate courses and additional activities target longer and more scientific writing of research papers, theses and dissertations, and even scientific articles, in harmony with the goals of the state policies.

Materials and Methodology Policy

English and Turkish Instructional Materials

The analysis of materials in this part of the study demonstrates that English and Turkish academic writing textbooks and instruction differ in ways that are important to consider in relationship to how English and Turkish are valued in university courses and in scholarly publishing. Specifically, there are striking differences in the content and emphasis of textbooks (e.g., general versus academic) as well as in course assessment practices.

With respect to English academic writing, it was found that except for the books required in the first-year EAP I & II courses at METU, and ARW courses in the ELT programs at both universities, all books are written and published by western authors and publishers. For example, in the METU preparatory classes, *Lifelines* and *Q: Skills for Success* series by Oxford University Press, and the *Top Notch* series by Longman Pearson, with many supplementary books written by both foreign and Turkish authors, are used. In the preparatory classes at GAZI, *Speak Out* as well as some writing books, such as *Fundamentals of Academic Writing* and *Strategic Writing* by Pearson, and *Reading and Writing Unlock* by Cambridge, are required. Similarly, the first- and second-year general English courses at GAZI follow *English for Life* and the *Q: Skills for Success* series by Oxford University Press. In the writing component of these courses, the focus is on English writing rules regarding paragraph and essay writing such as deductive organization, cohesion, coherence, unity, thesis statements, and topic sentences (see also Rudd & Telafici, this volume, for an appraisal of English-language writing textbooks in Qatar).

Common locally produced books are also used in EAP I & II in METU and ARW courses in both universities. These books include all four language skills; yet, while all these skills are covered in EAP I & II, in ARW only the reading and writing parts are covered. The names of the books are *Academic Survival Skills I & II*, published by Black Swan (Ankara). These books are written by Turkish instructors working in the Modern Languages Department at METU and are published by a local publisher; however, these books follow Anglo-American conventions of academic discourse. For example, the first book presents topics related to expository and reaction paragraph writing, as well as conventions regarding paragraph writing, such as: introducing explicit main ideas and topic sentences; supporting ideas; different patterns of organization (narration, description, process analysis, etc.); supporting techniques (e.g., examples & illustrations, data, facts, statistics, testimony, etc.); unity and coherence; and cohesive devices (with a list of transitions). In addition, the book provides an introduction to essay writing with rules regarding choosing and narrowing down a topic; making outlines; parallelism; coordination and subordination; formal writing style; hedging and tentativeness; introductory strategies; writing the body of the essay; conclusion strategies; unity and coherence; revising and editing strategies; writers' techniques and purposes for writing (to inform, to persuade, etc.); and considering audience, point of view, tone, register, and style.

The second book provides guidelines regarding how to write a research-based documented argumentative essay and a reaction-response essay. First, some knowledge base is introduced about basics of doing and writing research, such as identifying and selecting relevant sources; referencing and citing according to APA; borrowing ideas (summarizing, paraphrasing, direct quoting); plagiarism; and strategies of avoiding writer's block. Then conventions related to argumentation and argumentative writing are presented through various topics, such as writing an argumentative thesis; preparing a pro-con chart; refuting the counterarguments; outlining; unity and coherence; avoiding logical fallacies; analyzing and synthesizing opinions; and avoiding sexist language.

Turkish writing books have content that is quite different from the English academic writing books mentioned above. While English books are academically oriented, technical, detailed, and rule-based, Turkish writing books seem to have devoted considerable space to discussing more general issues about language, culture, civilizations, and history, rather than writing itself. In addition, a considerable part of the writing content focuses on genres of non-academic writing and creative writing. Writing instruction differs from English especially in terms of the emphasis given on certain writing topics addressed and the number of writing activities or exercises for practice. Moreover, although the writing rules seem to overlap with English at first sight, they are explained in a very general manner. Many specific details in global writing rules in English, such as cohesive markers, hedging, subordination, strategies related to the writing process, and paragraph structure (e.g., topic sentences) are either missing in the Turkish books or very superficially explained; instead, the focus seems to be more on sentence-level grammar rules and punctuation in writing.

For example, first it was found that some Turkish classes use no textbooks; yet, two textbooks were mentioned in the interviews for other Turkish classes. These were *Türkçenin sırları (The Mysteries of Turkish)* (Banarli, 2013), which focuses only on Turkish language instruction (sentence-level grammar), and *Üniversiteler için Türkçe I Yazılı Anlatım (Turkish I: Written Composition for Universities)* (Yakici, Yucel, Dogan & Savas, 2006). For the purposes of this research, the latter book on writing was analyzed. The first three units out of the six of the Yakici et al. (2006) textbook covers general topics, such as definitions of language, and the relationships between language and culture and culture and civilization. In the fourth unit, some theoretical knowledge about writing is introduced, such as topic selection; narrowing and development of the topic; the importance of words and sentences in composition; planning compositions; main ideas; use of imagination; types of expression (narration, description, definition, explanation, exemplification, persuasion, and comparison); point of view (creative writing and non-fiction opinion writing); textual analysis of written genres such as formal writing (petition, meeting or event records, meeting decision writing, report, job letter, CV, advertisement, memorandum, legal texts); creative writing (tale, fairy tale, poetry, short story, novel, drama); and opinion writing (article, criticism, essay, memoir, diary, travel writing, letter, interview, presentation). In the final unit, information about writing a bibliography, note taking and summarizing techniques are given. However, the focus then turns to sentence- and word-level language instruction rather than writing. For example, 25 Turkish grammar and spelling rules are explained one by one, and then common word- and sentence-level language problems and common mistakes in Turkish are listed under 27 categories, including wrong spelling; wrong use of apostrophe; parallelism; wrong use of idioms and proverbs; unnecessary verbs, and so on. These are followed by punctuation and abbreviation rules.

As understood from course syllabi, textbooks and interviews, one striking finding was that Turkish courses include and emphasize mostly non-academic genres that do not adequately address the academic writing needs of the students, as can be seen in the list of genres above. For example, while the book devotes 56 pages to creative writing such as fairy tales and writing poems, the essay is explained in a half page followed by some example essays, for a total of ten pages. Moreover, essay writing is explained in general terms mostly related to language style and personal voice when compared to English books, in which more specific and detailed rules on essay writing are given. Overall, creative writing, as well as some formal genres such as legal petitions and job letters, seem to be given priority over academic texts in Turkish classes. This suggests that some cultural factors may be at work, as suggested by contrastive rhetoric research that discusses differences in writing education across cultures (e.g., Kadar-Fulop, 1988; Li, 1996; Liebman, 1992; Liu, 2005; Uysal, 2008). Another reason for the difference might be the low importance given to writing in the higher education system in Turkey, as students reported they do not write much in Turkish composition classes or in their departmental courses, and instead often take short-answer or multiple-choice tests. Academic writing is not central to Turkish universities or in assessment procedures, which is reflected in academic writing education as well.

English L2 and Turkish L1 Teaching Approaches and Methods

There is considerable variation in teaching approaches and methods across English and Turkish language writing instruction at Turkish universities. In terms of teaching methods, scholars agree that learning L2 writing is an overwhelmingly difficult process involving very complicated factors; therefore, no single teaching approach will suffice (Blanton & Kroll, 2002). Instead, all approaches to second language instruction should be blended together as each of these reflects a valuable and indispensable part of the second-language writing construct (Silva, 1990). That is, the product approach focusing on lexical-syntactic features, controlled or guided composition focusing on discourse-level textual features; the process approach focusing on the underlying recursive and exploratory writing processes of the individual; the contrastive rhetoric approach focusing on the L1 cultural influences on writing; and the genre approach focusing on the social aspects of writing, such as writing according to the descriptors of various genres and expectations of audiences in specific contexts, should be used in a complementary manner. However, these approaches can be used selectively and some writing features may gain importance over others according to the purpose of the writing instruction. In the case of EAP classes and in any writing for publishing purposes, particularly for ESL/EFL students, product-oriented controlled or guided composition and genre approaches are often dominant. Thus, in academic ESL/EFL writing classes, the emphasis is often too much on the final product and the mastery of English academic writing conventions following strict models and formulas. Some scholars have expressed concern that this kind of instruction may lead to restriction in creativity inherent in writing (Hyland, 2003). Others have suggested that strictly following Anglo-American writing norms could result in assimilation into L2 cultural literacy or the elimination of individual voice and diversity in writing (Canagarajah, 1999; 2002; Kachru, Y. 1997). Instead, some recent critical approaches recommend the maintenance of individual and cultural voice by representing one's identity and code-mixing L1 rhetoric with English writing conventions even in academic or scientific writing (Canagarajah, 2006a, 2006b; Curry & Lillis, 2004; Harwood & Hadley, 2004).

With these concerns and recommendations in mind, we note that Turkish university instructors employ a product-oriented methodology with a limited reflection of genre and process approaches as students are getting familiarized with the conventions of certain paragraph and essay types, and often students write one or two drafts before the final product in the preparatory, first- and second-year English, EAP, and ARW courses. Due to the time constraints, this first draft is often done at home and feedback is provided by the teachers on these texts in either written form or by showing the papers through an overhead projector or computer to the class and going over the problems in crowded classes. In ARW courses, an integrated reading-writing language teaching approach is also adopted. However, although this is a highly advocated approach to academic writing as it provides students with both content knowledge and familiarity with rhetorical structure and conventions (e.g., Canagarajah, 2002; Hyland, 2000), in the Turkish context, as reported by the instructors, this approach was not successfully implemented due to the restricted class hours (see also Miller & Pessoa this volume for related discussion of writing classes in U.S. universities in Qatar).

The third-year Writing Term Papers course at METU also uses foreign sources, which include the *APA Publication Manual* and *Writing the Research Paper: A Handbook* (Winkler & McCuen, 1999). On the other hand, the third-year Advanced Writing and Research Skills course at METU and the other research courses do not use a particular textbook but follow photocopied materials generally based on foreign sources. Besides research techniques and statistical knowledge, these courses have more in-depth content for research writing regarding APA style, quoting, summarizing, paraphrasing, and synthesizing, avoiding plagiarism, argument fallacies, citations, and referencing. In these classes, students receive one-on-one written and oral feedback in all steps of their writing of the research papers, and they write multiple drafts in and out of the classes thanks to personal efforts of the instructors. In the graduate writing courses at GAZI, again no specific textbook is used. The courses are based on lectures, readings, textual analysis of the targeted genres such as theses and dissertations (Academic Writing I & II), and research articles (e.g., the Academic Writing for Publishing Purposes course). Additionally, writing samples of academic writing are provided through a genre-based process approach, in which students are given feedback on their writing and are allowed to write multiple drafts after considering audience expectations and genre requirements.

As for the teaching approach for Turkish composition, the interviews revealed that most of these courses' content is presented through lectures and oral presentations "teaching about writing," rather than practicing actual writing. Thus, writing is often not practiced in classes, and students are at best asked to write only in exams, reflecting a product approach. In Turkish textbooks, no tasks for actual writing practices are provided, which confirms the students' accounts. The parts of the textbook related to writing are organized by presenting a brief introduction to certain genres, which is followed by sample model texts.

Discussion and Conclusions

The increasing spread and dominance of English in global academia and research publishing is strongly evident in the Turkish context. English seems to have become a "lingua academica" (Phillipson, 2008) in Turkey because, besides functioning as the medium of instruction in more universities, it has also become the widely accepted language of science and research publications. The historical analysis of Turkish state policies demonstrates a continuous encouragement and even imposition of English as the language of science and research publishing as a means to integrate with Europe and the global scientific world. Accordingly, Anglo-American academic values of "publish or perish" seem to be adopted through a shift of focus from teaching to research and from national to international publications in English. The consequences of the state policies are most obvious in the steep increase in the number of publications in the ISI database, which has become an important indicator of one's academic success.

The reflections of the state policies are also manifested in micro-level literacy-in-education practices, as more courses aiming to develop English academic writing skills and additional support through writing centers started to be offered at universities, while academic writing in Turkish is extremely neglected. With such a weak infrastructure of Turkish academic literacy instruction, English is likely to gain an even higher status and hegemony in scientific literacy in the near future. As a result, given the dominance of English in Turkish academia through both top-down government policies and literacy-in-education practices, more planning and policy is needed to preserve a place for Turkish in the academic domain and in academic writing instruction.

In addition, English academic writing and research courses, whether they use local or foreign sources, mainly promote Anglo-American writing norms, logic, and research traditions; this promotion points to the diffusion of a powerful cultural rhetoric through academic instruction in the Turkish context, which is similar to other contexts as suggested by Canagarajah (1999). Although effective instruction in English rhetorical and scientific conventions is needed for participation in the Anglo-centric discourse community, more critical pedagogical approaches have recently been suggested. These approaches involve awareness-raising about the complexities and sociopolitical issues surrounding English academic writing, and code-mixing with L1 writing for rhetorical creativity and diversity instead of rhetorical homogeneity (Canagarajah, 2006a, 2006b; Curry & Lillis, 2004; Harwood & Hadley, 2004). Yet, these recent trends have not made their way into academic literacy instruction in Turkish universities.

At the same time, it should be noted that English academic writing instruction also seems to suffer from various problems, such as inadequate class hours and product-oriented teaching approaches in both universities. For example, the number and classroom hours of some English and English academic writing courses decreased over the years, which contradicts macro-level state policies. For that reason, writing cannot be practiced much in classes, and students do not write multiple drafts and receive feedback from teachers or peers between drafts. In addition, writing in English does not go beyond essay writing, and it is often neglected among other language skills.

Moreover, considering the general characteristics of the Turkish educational system and academic culture at the tertiary level, in which students are given lectures and assessed through tests instead of being assigned papers or portfolios, writing is often not central and not practiced in other departmental courses. Therefore, these limited literacy-in-education practices in both English and Turkish seem to fall short in preparing future academics to publish in prestigious international journals and to compete in the global scientific world. Hence, attempts should be made both to increase the classroom hours and quality of academic writing instruction in both Turkish and English in future planning and practice.[2]

Notes

1. National language planning is possible because education in Turkey is highly centralized. While primary and secondary education is under the responsibility of Ministry of National Education, tertiary education is supervised and coordinated by the Higher Education Council.
2. This research is part of a larger project about the effects of Turkish state publishing policies on: 1. Turkish scholars' publishing behaviors in Turkish vs. English (Uysal, 2014a); 2. University practices of research, publishing, and promotion (Uysal, 2014b); and 3. Academic writing instruction. This chapter reports on the third part of the research on writing instruction at Turkish universities. This research was supported by Gazi University Individual Research Grant (BAP) 04/2012-26.

References

Ak, M. Z. & Gülmez A. (2006). The analysis of international publication performance of Turkey. *Akademik Incelemeler [Academic Investigations]*, *1*(1), 25–43.
Akarsu, F. (2000). Transition and education: A case study of the process of change in Turkey. In K. Mazurek, M. Winzer & C. Majorek (Eds.), *Education in a global society: A comparative perspective* (pp. 315–329). Boston: Allyn and Bacon.
Akıllı, E., Büyükçınar, Ö., Latif, V., Yetgin, S., Gürses, E. A., Saraç, C. & Demirel, İ. H. (2009). *Türkiye Bilimsel Yayın Göstergeleri II 1981–2007 Türkiye Ülkeler Gruplar [The publication indicators of Turkey (II) 1981–2007, Turkey, Countries, Groups.]* Ankara: TUBITAK.
Alptekin, C. (1998). Learning a foreign language does not mean losing Turkish. In A. Kilimci (Ed.), *Anadilinde cocuk olmak: Yabanci dilde egitim [Being a child speaking in the mother-tongue: Education through foreign languages]* (pp. 34–37). Ankara: Papirüs Publications.
Ardınç, F. N. (2007). Türkçe yayın ve akademik yükseltme kriterleri [Turkish publications and academic promotion criteria]. In O. Yilmaz (Ed.), *Sağlık Bilimlerinde Süreli Yayıncılık* (pp. 35–38). Ankara: Tubitak-Ulakbim.
Arıoğlu, E. & Girgin, C. (2002). 1974–2001 döneminde ülkemizde bilimsel yayın performansının kısa değerlendirilmesi [The evaluation of scientific publication performance of Turkey between 1974–2001]. *Science & Utopia Journal, 95,* 62–66.
Arıoğlu, E. & Girgin, C. (2003). Ülkemizin yayın sıralamasına eleştirel bir bakış [A critical look at the publication rankings of Turkey]. *Science & Utopia Journal, 105,* 38–41.
Ayyıldız, M. & Bozkurt, Ü. (2006). Edebiyat ve kompozisyon eğitiminde karşılaşılan sorunlar [The problems faced in literature and composition education]. *Turkish Education Sciences Journal, 4*(1), 45–52.
Baldauf, R. B. (2005). Language planning and policy research: An overview. In E. Hinkel (Ed.), *Handbook of research in second language teaching and learning* (pp. 957–970). Mahwah, NJ: Lawrence Erlbaum.
Banarli, S. (2013). *Türkçenin sırları.* İstanbul: Kubbealtı Nesrıyat.
Bear, J. (1998). Yabanci dilde egitim [Education in foreign languages]. In A. Kilimci (Ed.), *Anadilinde çocuk olmak: Yabanci dilde egitim [Being a child speaking in the mother-tongue: Education through foreign languages]* (pp. 73–76). Ankara: Papirüs Publications.
Blanton, L. L. & Kroll, B. (Eds.). (2002). *ESL composition tales: Reflections on teaching.* Ann Arbor, MI: The University of Michigan Press.
Canagarajah, A. S. (1999). *Resisting linguistic imperialism in English teaching.* Oxford, UK: Oxford University Press.
Canagarajah, A. S. (2002). *Critical academic writing and multilingual students.* Ann Arbor, MI: University of Michigan Press.
Canagarajah, A. S. (2006a). Negotiating the local in English as a lingua franca. *Annual Review of Applied Linguistics, 26,* 197–218.

Canagarajah, A. S. (2006b). The place of world Englishes in composition: Pluralization continued. *College Composition and Communication, 57*(4), 586–619.
Cohen, D. & Crabtree, B. (2006). *Qualitative research guidelines project.* Princeton, NJ: Robert Wood Johnson Foundation.
Curry, M. J. & Lillis, T. (2004). Mulitilingual scholars and the imperative to publish in English: Negotiating interests, demands, and rewards. *TESOL Quarterly, 38*(3), 663–688.
Demircan, Ö. (1988). *Dünden bugüne Türkiye'de yabancı dil [Foreign languages in Turkey from past to present].* İstanbul: Remzi Kitabevi
Demircan, Ö. (1995). Yabancı öğretim diliyle nereye? [Where to go with foreign language as the medium of education?]. *Ögretmen Dünyası, 182*, 19–20.
Dogancay-Aktuna, S. (1995). An evaluation of the Turkish language reform after 60 years. *Language Problems and Language Planning, 19*(3), 221–249.
Dogancay-Aktuna, S. (1998). The spread of English in Turkey and its current sociolinguistic profile. *Journal of Multilingual and Multicultural Development, 19*(1), 24–39.
Dogancay-Aktuna, S. & Kiziltepe, Z. (2005). English in Turkey. *World Englishes, 24*(2), 253–265.
Ergenç, I. (2001). Bilim dili ve ana dil (Language of science and the mother tongue). *Bilim ve Ütopya, 80*, 12–13.
Eurydice. (2010). Organization of the education system, Turkey 2009–2010. Retrieved from http://www.etf.europa.eu/webatt.nsf/0/60E61005D5CC5AD1C12 57AA30025212F/$file/Organization%20of%20the%20education%20system%20 in%20Turkey%202009.2010.pdf.
Flowerdew, J. (1999). Problems in writing for scholarly publication in English: The case of Hong Kong. *Journal of Second Language Writing, 8*(3), 243–264.
Flowerdew, J. (2000). Discourse community, legitimate peripheral participation, and the nonnative English speaking scholar. *TESOL Quarterly, 34*(1), 127–150.
Göçer, A. (2010). Writing education in Turkish education. *The Journal of International Social Research, 3*(12), 178–195.
Harwood, N. & Hadley, G. (2004). Demystifying institutional practices: Critical pragmatism and the teaching of academic writing. *English for Specific Purposes, 23*, 355–377.
HEC-The Higher Education Council. (2008). The regulation on the conditions of teaching foreign languages and English-medium education in tertiary education. *Official Gazette* No: 27074. Retrieved from http://www.yok.gov.tr/.
HEC. (2010). *The Higher Education System in Turkey.* Bilkent, Ankara. Retrieved from http://www.yok.gov.tr.
Hyland, K. (2003). *Second language Writing.* Cambridge, UK: Cambridge University Press.
IUC-Inter-university Council. (2000). Doçentlik sınav yönetmeliği. [Regulation for the associate professorship exam]. *Resmi Gazette*, No. 24157.
Kachru, B. B. (1992). Teaching world Englishes. In B. B. Kachru (Ed.), *The other tongue: English across cultures* (pp. 355–365). Urbana, IL: University of Illinois Press.

Kachru, Y. (1995). Contrastive rhetoric in World Englishes. *English Today, 41*, 21–31.

Kachru, Y. (1997). Cultural meaning and contrastive rhetoric in English education. *World Englishes, 16*, 227–350.

Kadar-Fulop, J. (1988). Culture, writing, and curriculum. In Purves (Ed.), *Writing across languages and cultures: Issues in contrastive rhetoric* (pp. 25–50). Thousand Oaks, CA: Sage Publications.

Kaplan, R. B. (2001). The dominance of English as a lingua of science: Effects on other languages and language communities. In U. Ammon (Ed.), *The dominance of English as a lingua of science: Effects on other languages and language communities* (pp. 3–26). New York: Mouton de Gruyter.

Kaplan, R. B. & Baldauf, R. B. (1997). *Language Planning: From practice to theory.* Clevedon, UK: Multilingual Matters.

Kaplan, R. B. & Baldauf. R. B. (2005). Language-in-education policy and planning. In E. Hinkel (Ed.). *Handbook of research in second language teaching and learning* (pp. 1013–1034). Mahwah, NJ: Lawrence Erlbaum.

Kılıçkaya, F. (2006). Instructors' attitudes towards English-medium instruction in Turkey. *Humanizing Language Teaching, 8*(6), 1–16.

Kılınç, A. (2001). YÖK bilimde Türkçeye karşı mı? [Is HEC against Turkish in science?] Retrieved from http://mimoza.marmara.edu.tr/~avni/dersbelgeligi/dil/Ahmetkilinc.htm.

Kinzer, S. (2001). *Crescent and star: Turkey between two worlds.* New York: Farrar, Straus &Giroux.

Kırkgöz, Y. (2005). Motivation and student perception of studying in an English-medium university. *Journal of Language and Linguistic Studies, 1*(1), 101–123.

Köksal, A. (2002). *Yabancı dilde öğretim: Türkiye'nin en büyük yanılgısı [Education in foreign languages: Turkey's biggest mistake].* Ankara: Öğretmen Dünyası.

Krippendorff, K. (2004). *Content analysis: An introduction to its methodology.* Thousand Oaks, CA: Sage Publications.

Li, X. M. (1996). *"Good writing" in cross-cultural context.* Albany, NY: State University of New York Press.

Liebman, J. (1992). Toward a new contrastive rhetoric: Differences between Arabic and Japanese rhetorical instruction. *Journal of Second Language Writing, 1*, 141–165.

Lillis, T. & Curry, J. M. (2010). *Academic writing in a global context.* London: Routledge.

Liu, L. (2005). Rhetorical education through writing instruction across cultures: A comparative analysis of select online instructional materials on argumentative writing. *Journal of Second Language Writing, 14*(1), 1–18.

Mauranen, A. (1993). *Cultural differences in academic rhetoric.* Frankfurt: Peter Lang.

Merriam, S. B. (1998). *Qualitative research and case study applications in Education.* San Francisco: Jossey-Bass Publishers.

ÖSYM. (2011). *Student selection and placement examination list of preferences book.* Ankara: YÖK.

Pazarlıoğlu, M. V. & Özkoç, H. (2009). The econometric analysis of international publications of Turkey between 1983–2004. *Sosyal Bilimler, 7*(2), 45–58.

Phillipson, R. (2006). English, a cuckoo in the European higher education nest of languages? *European Journal of English Studies, 10*(1), 13–32.

Phillipson, R. (2008). Lingua franca or lingua frankensteinia? English in European integration and globalization. *World Englishes, 27*(2), 250–267.

Ramanathan, V. (2005). *The English-Vernacular divide: Postcolonial language politics and practice.* Clevedon, UK: Multilingual Matters.

Sert, N. (2008). The language of instruction dilemma in the Turkish context. *System, 36,* 156–171.

Sinanoğlu, O. (2002). *Bye-Bye Türkçe.* Ankara: Otopsi Publications.

Silva, T. (1990). Second language composition instruction: Developments, issues and directions in ESL. In B. Kroll (Ed.), *Second language writing research insights for the classroom* (pp. 11–23). New York: Cambridge University Press.

Spolsky, B. (2004). *Language policy.* Cambridge, UK: Cambridge University Press.

Swales, J. (1997). English as tyrannosaurus rex. *World Englishes, 16*(3), 373–382.

Tardy, C. (2004). The role of English in scientific communication: Lingua franca or Tyrannosaurus rex? *Journal of English for Academic Purposes, 3,* 247–269.

Tok, H. & Arıbaş, S. (2008). Teaching foreign languages during adaptation process to European Union. *İnönü University Education Faculty Journal, 9*(15), 205–227.

TUBITAK-ULAKBIM. (2011). *Turkish Publication Statistics.* Retrieved from http://www.tubitak.gov.tr/tubitak_content_files/english/sti/statistics/TR_STI60.pdf.

UNDP-United Nations Development Program Reports. (2009). Retrieved from http://data.un.org/Search.aspx?q=literacy+rate+turkey.

Uysal, H. H. (2008). Tracing the culture behind writing: Rhetorical patterns and bidirectional transfer in L1 and L2 essays of Turkish writers in relation to educational context. *Journal of Second Language Writing, 17*(3), 183–207.

Uysal, H. H. (2014a). English language spread in academia: Macro-level state policies and micro-level practices of scholarly publishing in Turkey. *Language Problems and Language Planning, 38*(3).

Uysal, H. H. (2014b). Turkish academic culture in transition: Centre-based state policies and semi-peripheral practices of research, publishing, and promotion. In K. Bennett (Ed.), *The Semi-periphery of academic writing: Discourses, communities, and practices* (pp. 165–189). London: Palgrave Macmillan.

Uysal, H. H., Plakans, L. & Dembovskaya, S. (2007). English spread in local contexts: Turkey, Latvia, and France. *Current Issues in Language Planning, 8*(2), 192–207.

Winkler, A. & McCuen J. K. (1999). *Writing the research paper: A handbook.* Boston: Cengage.

Yakici, A., Yucel, M., Dogan, M., Savas, Y. (2006). *Üniversiteler için Türkçe I Yazılı Anlatım (Turkish I: Written Composition for Universities)* (3rd ed.). Ankara: Gazi Kitabevi.

Appendix 1: Interview Questions

Instructors

1. How many hours of ---- class do you teach per week?
2. How much of your classes do you award to teaching and actual practicing of academic writing?
3. What writing genres and types do you cover in your classes?
4. What is the level of writing done? Do you practice writing academic essays or research papers?
5. What are the specific objectives of your course? For example, what writing features do you teach and emphasize in classes?
6. What textbooks do you use in your classes?
7. What are the main approaches and methods you employ while teaching writing?

Students

1. How much actual writing practice did you do in ---- class?
2. What kind of writing did you do in that class? (For example, essay, letter ...)
3. What levels of writing did you do? For example, did you write paragraphs, essays, research papers ...?
4. What were the goals of that class? For example, what specific rules for writing did you learn in --- class?
5. Which textbooks did you use in ---- class?
6. How did the teacher teach writing in ---- class?

3 Expanding Transnational Frames into Composition Studies: Revising the Rhetoric and Writing Minor at the American University in Cairo

James P. Austin
FORT HAYS STATE UNIVERSITY (US)

> This chapter examines U.S.-based approaches to curricular revision of the Rhetoric and Writing Minor at the American University in Cairo (AUC) through analysis of faculty interviews and relevant artifacts. Through this analysis, and consideration of AUC's development in the context of changes in Egypt, the chapter argues that U.S.-based curricular approaches satisfied various local needs among AUC's writing faculty and students. These findings complicate claims within international composition studies, which are concerned with non-reflective export of U.S. linguistic, pedagogical and program models into international sites. This chapter calls for expanding the perspective of U.S.-based approaches to composition studies to include paradigms from transnational literacy studies.
>
> Keywords: transnationalism; composition studies; literacy studies; international writing programs

In recent years, the global presence of universities styled after U. S. institutions of higher education has increased such that, as of June 2015, there were more than 270 international branch campuses (IBCs) operating in other countries (Lane & Kinser, 2015), an increase from more than 200 in 2011, 162 in 2009 and 82 in 2006 (Lawton & Kastomitros, 2012). Many of these IBCs are versions of universities originating in the US. Additionally, more than 65 IBCs are located in the Middle East, primarily in the United Arab Emirates and Qatar. (See Miller & Pessoa, Telafici & Rudd, and Hodges & Kent, this volume, for discussion on IBCs.) This influx of IBCs correlates with an increase in new standalone universities with U.S.-based orientations, such as the American University of Kuwait and the American University of Sharjah (See Ronesi; Jarkas & Fakhreddine; and Annous, Nicolas & Townsend this volume, for discussions of standalone universities.).

For U.S.-based IBCs or standalone "American Universities," writing unit development often presents challenges for local WPAs who seek to reconcile distant approaches with local needs and practices. This development has raised concern among some composition scholars with international foci. In their study of African universities in the 1990s, Muchiri, Myers and Ndoli (1995) counter assumptions about the universality of writing instruction by describing infrastructural and other material challenges for writing students in Kenya, Tanzania, and Zaire. Schaub (2003) critiques the "insularity" of composition studies when describing the challenges he experienced as a WPA at the American University in Cairo in the 1990s. Donahue (2009) expresses concern over the non-reflective export of U.S.-based rhetoric and composition models abroad, calling for "deep intercultural awareness [and] familiarity with other systems and contexts" (p. 236) as part of the internationalization of U.S.-based writing research.

The call to integrate U.S.-based approaches to rhetoric, composition and writing with practices in other countries been taken up meaningfully within recent scholarship. In his introduction to *Writing Programs Worldwide: Profiles of Academic Writing in Many Places*, Thaiss (2012) seeks to "honor the variety and rich complexity of persons, languages, traditions, geographies, conditions, and purposes that both inspire and constrain the writing pedagogies and research" (p. 6) of the forty-plus international writing programs profiled in the volume. The purpose, he claims, is to learn "how an institution . . . conceives of the needs of its students in regard to learning a discipline, 'writing,' that in basic ways crosses all disciplines and aids learning in all of them" (2012, p. 6). He cites the Bologna Process in Europe and the emergence of the Internet as an open source for the exchange of curriculum as factors driving transnational approaches to writing research and program administration. Martins (2015) builds upon this scholarship in his introduction to *Transnational Writing Program Administration*. He renews calls for approaches that are able to transcend a "narrow, . . . privileged, Western view" (2015, p. 5) of composition, thereby moving beyond unidirectional flows of U.S.-based approaches to writing programs and pedagogies into non-U.S. sites. This includes repositioning writing programs to meet "context-specific educational, curricular, and cultural needs and interests" (Martin, 2015, p. 7) in ways that reflect ongoing practices and offer collaborative approaches for developing programs.

In this chapter, I will contribute to this scholarship by describing the development of a writing unit at the American University in Cairo (AUC), which has distinct historical, linguistic, and educational features. By examining a period when the Department of Rhetoric and Composition purposefully expanded curricula and adopted ideologies germane to U.S.-based approaches for its rhetoric and writing minor, I will argue that, while the process generated tension among international and national faculty, the largely U.S.-based approach to program development served departmental needs and student interests while responding to exigent institutional circumstances. As I will show, the new curriculum allowed students access to literacy knowledge that could be deployed across a range of Egyptian professions with international reach (such as business and non-governmental organizations). The students also benefited from approaches to creative nonfiction practiced in the US that seemed to address a submerged need for public discourse in Egypt. Faculty discovered meaningful opportunities for professional development and career advancement that had the potential to alter departmental roles and career trajectories. For the department, this turn represented an opportunity to maintain autonomy in a university undergoing significant academic reorganization.

Moreover, this study reveals findings which, on the surface, seem paradoxical: while the adoption of U.S. approaches to a writing curriculum served the needs of an English-language, U.S.-styled department and institution located in Egypt, it also served Egyptian needs. These findings will complicate concerns within the field about the importation of primarily U.S.-based pedagogies and practices to writing programs in institutions in other countries.

To provide historical context, I describe AUC's evolution into a U.S.-styled institution through ideological, political and economic changes within Egypt, resulting in developments which also gave rise to a writing unit purposefully aligned with composition studies from the United States. Next, I account for the ways in which the development and revision of the rhetoric and writing minor benefited the department, faculty and students to show that, while tensions over curricular changes often correlated to national and/or disciplinary affiliations, the purposes driving the revision coalesced with locally-determined departmental needs and student interests—needs and interests focused largely on English-language literacies associated with U.S.-based approaches. Next I describe the way in which extra-departmental factors accelerated aspects of the curricular revision as an example of the ways in which international writing programs must account for institutional realities.

The significance of these findings will then be treated in the context of composition scholarship to demonstrate that perspectives from transnational literacy studies are useful in accounting for the unique and complex interactions between global and local contexts such as the one studied throughout this chapter.

Personal Connections to the Department of Rhetoric and Composition

I have a personal connection to AUC, the Department of Rhetoric and Composition and the developments with the rhetoric and writing minor I address in this chapter. In 2006, I came to work in what was then known as the Writing Program at AUC, just as the unit was poised to break from the Department of English and Comparative Literature and establish an autonomous campus presence. This development corresponded with curricular changes. For instance, standardized syllabi and adjudication committees, which had been in place to protect the program from accusations of inconsistency and poor student writing development, were phased out. Faculty were encouraged to propose novel ways to teach extant composition offerings and develop new, upper-division offerings that could become part of a proposed minor. With another faculty member, for example, I proposed a creative nonfiction workshop class, which received an enthusiastic response from Egyptian students and is still offered more than six years after I returned to the United States.

This was an exciting period for me. Just two years removed from my MFA program, I was now living in Cairo, working with warm, enthusiastic students, and I was becoming increasingly involved in helping this writing unit during its transition. I understood that the stakes were high, not only for the Department of Rhetoric and Composition, but for writing units everywhere that sought autonomy within the academy. I wanted to be a part of this new department's success. Once the minor was approved and students began enrolling, I proposed to my chair a separate administrative position to address the specific needs of the minor. She agreed and appointed me as the coordinator of the minor. Soon, I was working closely with departmental faculty and administrators from Egypt and the United States with backgrounds in business, grant writing, rhetoric and composition, creative writing, cultural studies, and other fields.

As I coordinated the rhetoric and writing minor, I was struck by the concern among some faculty about the direction of the department. I noticed that these concerns often ran along national lines or were expressed by those with significant institutional experience. Later interviews reconfirmed the concerns of several constituencies. These ranged from a group that resisted vetting their syllabi to those who resisted making any kinds of changes that might be suggested. As one instructor reported during our interview, this resistant faculty did not identify with rhetoric and was uncomfortable with its inclusion in the curriculum.

Because of these moments of resistance, I found myself questioning what we were doing. Was it in the best interests of everybody in the department to make these new transitions to U.S.-based approaches to rhetoric, composition and writing? Who would be affected by these changes? What had motivated these changes in the first place? These questions arose many times during the year I coordinated the rhetoric and writing minor. Some of my colleagues were concerned that they might be sidelined simply because of their kind of expertise or national affiliation. Was this turn simply another iteration of western ideological imperialism that would marginalize Egyptians or others who lacked specialized training in U.S.-based approaches to rhetoric and composition?

While my involvement with the rhetoric and writing minor provided valuable experience and prompted many questions, I was too embedded within the context to find meaningful answers. Moreover, I was not yet aware of transnational literacy studies scholarship. This scenario, and my resulting unanswered questions, drove my decision to return to the US to pursue doctoral studies in the field; this choice allowed me to develop the tools and insights to learn about the complex international politics of English and western education, the ways in which international writing programs function within these larger histories and present dynamics, and the relationship between what I had observed and experienced at AUC with what I was beginning to read in rhetoric and composition scholarship.

During my studies, I came to understand that the curricular revision at AUC was richer and more complex than what might be perceived as western imperialistic hegemony in the guise of rhetoric and composition. I discovered that binary ways of thinking about the interaction of western ways of knowing with non-western sites and people could not fully account for the development of this institution, the Department of Rhetoric and Composition, and the rhetoric and writing minor. What I seek now are more nuanced ways to consider, in their full richness and complexity, the interplay of U.S.-based approaches to program development with non-U.S. institutions, faculty and students.

Situating Revision: The Development of AUC and the Writing Unit

In their history of the AUC writing unit in *Writing Programs Worldwide: Profiles of Academic Writing in Many Places*, Golson and Holdijk (2012) note that sequenced writing courses were first developed at AUC in the 1950s, at the height of pan-Arab nationalism. Interestingly, AUC had been granted a waiver to policies that had otherwise shuttered foreign-language schools in Egypt (Murphy, 1987). Given that the initial establishment of sequenced writing courses occurred simultaneously with the exodus of English in educational institutions elsewhere in the country, it is likely that the university perceived a need to train its own students in English language and literacy practices, especially because, during the same period, AUC's English Language Institute was established. This development also suggests that the university saw English language and writing education as a significant part of its mission, and that Egypt, even at the height of Nasserite Arab nationalism, considered it worthwhile to maintain an English-language university in the country.

When Anwar Sadat realigned Egyptian ideologies and economic policies in the 1970s in ways that benefitted English in Egypt, thereby increasing the local significance of an AUC education, the writing unit began to align itself with developing U.S.-based *episteme*. Locally trained faculty in TESOL or literature began teaching in the unit, resulting in a mixed department of Egyptian, American, and British faculty that remains today. The unit began drawing upon emergent scholarship in composition studies throughout the 1970s and 1980s before formally aligning itself with the WPA Learning Outcomes within the field of rhetoric and composition in the early twenty-first century, "to better reflect current U.S. practices and to allow for easier integration with the credit-hour structure" (Golson & Holdijk, 2012, p. 184). This movement ultimately resulted in unit independence from the Department of English and Comparative Literature and the establishment of the rhetoric and writing minor, which appeared in the university catalog in 2009 and offered emphasis areas in academic, business and technical, and creative writing.

Both the history provided by Golson and Holdijk and informant interviews reveal that U.S.-based approaches to writing at AUC were enabled through local developments and invited by local actors. In most cases, these local actors were not rhetoric and composition scholars, but an international mix of faculty trained in TESOL, cultural studies, applied linguistics, creative writing, and literature. In this respect, aspects of the U.S.-based approach were *imported* into Egypt, not *exported* from the United States. This distinction is crucial. As AUC developed more purposefully into a U.S.-styled educational site, the writing unit also evolved by taking on the qualities of the U.S.-based approach. According to interview findings, this helped shield the unit from institutional critique and resulted in a curricular revision of the lower-division program. These developments also provided the foundation for future changes, such as hiring rhetoric and composition scholars from the United States and creating the rhetoric and writing minor. The fact that

U.S.-based approaches were used in this localized manner strongly suggests that U.S.-based approaches can be appropriated by local actors when there is a historical tradition of the U.S.-styled university and when its writing unit serves national, institutional and/or student needs. Throughout this chapter, I detail evidence that supports my call for more expansive frames that can account for the kinds of interactions non-U.S. faculty and students had with the U.S.-based approach.

Methods and Data Collection

For this study, which had full approval from the IRB at AUC, I interviewed eight faculty who were employed by the Department of Rhetoric and Composition during the curricular revision period. I used Skype as the interface and Audacity for recording. I requested interviews with faculty who were directly involved with the revision to the rhetoric and writing minor, or who had developed and taught courses that would have been impacted by the revision. These faculty represented a mix of Americans and Egyptians, came from many different educational backgrounds, and possessed many kinds of writing and literacy expertise. However, they are not intended to be fully representative of the nationality, educational background and areas of expertise among the department. For example, there was a significant faction of British faculty who were not interviewed for this study, but their involvement in this aspect of departmental operations was negligible. Other Egyptian faculty who taught primarily lower-division composition courses were also not interviewed, as they were not involved in teaching or developing upper-division courses that would have been included in the minor and thereby impacted by the minor's revision. Some Egyptian and American faculty members who were involved with aspects of the curricular revision were asked to participate, but they either declined or did not respond to the request. While their firsthand accounts are not included in this chapter, their involvement in the revision was often described through other interviews and the artifacts submitted by those who participated.

During the hour-long interviews, I asked participants about their role in the department and in regard to the revision of the rhetoric and writing minor during the 2009–2010 academic year. They were also asked to comment on what they considered to be the most significant activities and dynamics that arose during the revision period. These interviews were then coded to generate a coherent timeline for the period under study, and to establish the positions and activities of interview participants and others mentioned during the interviews. Following this, the interviews were coded for dominant themes regarding the impact of the revision on faculty and students. Brief follow-up interviews were sometimes used to address questions that arose after the initial coding.

I also asked the interview participants to provide artifacts relevant to the study, which I used to augment and support interview findings. These artifacts ranged from personal (such as e-mails among faculty members addressing questions, concerns and disagreements) to public (a departmental self-study; a departmental memorandum; a draft of the original rhetoric and writing minor; a PowerPoint presentation for the university provost). Participants were aware that artifacts would be used within the study; however, anonymity is protected when these artifacts are mentioned. Several of these artifacts were used to account for the kinds of roles assumed by faculty members and the ways in which role changes and other kinds of interactions impacted faculty during the revision.

Additionally, I used the archival website *The Wayback Machine* to locate the 2009 and 2010 version of the catalog for the rhetoric and writing minor on the Internet so that changes in the mission and learning outcomes for the minor could be compared from one year to the next. This comparison not only helped establish the ways in which the minor had been revised to reflect an increased focus on U.S.-based approaches, but was used alongside primary sources to demonstrate ways in which changes extended from local practices and served local needs.

Intersections: U.S.-Based Curriculum and Student Needs

The most significant findings in my study concern the changes that occurred in the Department of Rhetoric and Composition as a result of the revision of the rhetoric and writing minor. In this section I describe the ways in which a U.S.-based approach to this curricular revision intersected with the professional, creative and cultural needs of students, through my informants' experiences of the benefits to their students.

An American faculty member with long ties to the region and the international business community in Egypt described courses that he had originally developed following the adoption of WPA First-Year Outcomes and through collaboration with international faculty and businesses in Egypt. He explained the rationale for these courses during an interview:

> I had also worked a lot on USAID projects in Egypt, and in Tunisia and Morocco and Libya. I knew that the skills that we needed the local hires to have were completely absent.

They were lacking. I saw [business and technical writing courses] as an opportunity to equip the students at AUC with the necessary skills to advance themselves quickly into management positions in the private sector.... When these students would graduate and go to work for companies, they would write and say, "Exactly what you were teaching me is exactly what I need."

Indeed, the revision to the rhetoric and writing minor provided occasion to extend this teaching approach, maintaining focus on the production of "business and science/technical communications" while also analyzing the "norms and conventions" of the business, science and engineering fields, according to an archived version of the revised minor's academic catalog (The American University in Cairo, 2010). During interviews for this study, some departmental faculty who had taught these business and technical writing courses prior to the revision recounted their earlier concern that curricular revisions—and a new "jargon" of rhetoric—would disrupt successful collaborations among the department, other institutional constituencies, and outside business contacts. These informants expressed relief that the revision did not result in these types of disruptions but, rather, the establishment of disciplinary language in the catalog, alongside an applied focus allowing students to develop literacy abilities relevant to professional communication within Egypt.

Additionally, an American faculty member with an MFA reported during her interview that she developed a creative nonfiction workshop, which became an important cornerstone of the creative emphasis and provided Egyptian students a disciplined, public forum to address personal and cultural dilemmas in a society that prefers acquiescence to norms. Drawing from her experience as a student, this faculty member reported developing a "pedagogy and process that arose from creative writing workshops that began in Iowa," a reference to the University of Iowa's seminal MFA program in creative writing. According to this informant, the approach included practicing the elements of creative nonfiction and implementing a pedagogy where students shared work for class discussion. In such a "workshop" approach, the authors listen without interjecting, while the class, under the instructor's guidance, discusses the merits of the work.

This faculty member reported surprising results using this approach, as she found students were willing to write about and discuss topics not typically seen in Egyptian public discourse. For instance, she said that, when one student wrote about his atheist beliefs, she was initially concerned that she would have to "protect" this student from critique by his Muslim and Coptic Christian classmates, some of whom were devout. Instead, she observed the seriousness and curiosity of these students during the discussion, which focused on the merits of the writing and not disagreements with the student's ideology. She said she learned that these young Egyptians were eager for opportunities to acknowledge and discuss complex religious, ideological and cultural dilemmas that were not typically addressed in Egyptian society. Based on the perceptions of these two informants, it appears that courses in business, technical and creative writing, developed and taught by U.S. faculty and similar to courses one might find in the United States, met emerging professional, creative and cultural needs for Egyptian students.

As part of the U.S.-based revision of the minor, the department chair, a scholar in rhetoric and composition hired from the United States, established a weekly rhetoric and composition proseminar. While the proseminar was open to all departmental faculty, it was specifically meant to provide faculty members with backgrounds outside rhetoric and composition the opportunity to learn about the foundations and development of the U.S.-based approach to the discipline. For Egyptian faculty with training in literature or TESOL or for American faculty with MFA degrees, the proseminar was an opportunity not only to learn about the discipline, but to gain purchase in an evolving department and develop new abilities that could be reflected in teaching and other departmental activity.

Despite these expanded opportunities, my study revealed continuing concerns about the way in which revisions to the minor would impact faculty. According to one American faculty member involved with curricular revisions, one concern focused on the possibility of "disenfranchisement" among long-term faculty: "There was a lot of suspicion coming in, like, 'are these recommendations saying that I'm not legitimate or that I should teach this? Am I about to be disenfranchised with regard to the upper division?'"This concern overlapped with the apprehensions of those faculty members who reported being uneasy with the "jargon" accompanying the new approach. Another American faculty member with long ties to the region "heard directly" that "people who had been in the department a long time [but whose backgrounds were not in rhetoric and composition] were uncomfortable with change, and maybe felt a little bit threatened," as the new policy gave preference to a narrow band of faculty who were not just educated in the United States, but who also had the appropriate kind of training relevant to the new direction. While those faculty members with long ties to AUC were warranted in their concerns, their concerns must be considered within the context of the extra-departmental institutional factors that were accelerating the pace of the disciplinary turn in the minor.

Extra-Departmental Institutional Concerns: An Issue of Time

In addition to the departmental changes that came about as a result of revising, two recurrent concerns surfaced during the period under study: the speed with which the rhetoric and writing minor was revised and the manner in which its reorientation with U.S.-based approaches was emphasized. Yet, while these concerns might suggest that the turn toward U.S. approaches represented the very sort of development transnational composition scholars have cautioned against, there was another kind of localized, extra-departmental dynamic driving the speed and direction of the program's revision: the activities of a new provost with an agenda for significant restructuring of academic schools and departments. This agenda generated significant anxiety among faculty throughout the campus and specifically within the Department of Rhetoric and Composition. Some were concerned about layoffs, significant pay cuts, large increases in teaching load, or loss of access to professional development opportunities at the university. Anxiety that the university might disinvest in the Department of Rhetoric and Composition also hovered over the revision of the minor, which further drove the decision to implement U.S.-based approaches with the hope that such a move would quickly legitimize the nascent department.

One of the significant developments that also impacted their decision making involved differences in the ways in which the new provost communicated with faculty. Interview participants reported that the provost convened an unusually high number of faculty committees designed to offer recommendations to the provost's office. Because of this, it was difficult for department administrators to address concerns directly to the provost, as had been the case under different administrations; instead, these concerns were remediated into formal committee recommendations which never appeared to be acted upon. This created the additional, perhaps unintended, consequence of distancing faculty from the chief academic officer. It also exacerbated existing anxiety because faculty were unable to establish a rapport with the provost and were unclear about the ways their departments might be impacted by large-scale changes.

At the same time, other conversations about the ethos and makeup of the Department of Rhetoric and Composition were happening in committees and faculty configurations across the campus. Several interview participants claimed that the purpose and history of rhetoric and composition as a standalone discipline was not well known on the AUC campus, a problem that was initially addressed by at least one faculty member through conversations on the campus shuttle and during faculty committee meetings. Still, according to this faculty member, there was "pressure about what we were, and should we be a part of Core [Curriculum, which manages institutional requirements], [or] should we be added on to ESL." Also at this time, emerging concern about the size of the department—during the period under study, there were more than 40 full-time faculty in the department—led to preliminary discussions about ways to embed writing instruction within other departments, which would thereby abandon the department's mission to establish the U.S.-style Department of Rhetoric and Composition within the institution. According to interview participants, the provost would often mention Columbia University as an example of a successful institution without a standalone writing department. For some informants, these discussions indicated that either the provost was unfamiliar with the technical and scholarly aspects of the changing department and did not fully appreciate the needs and interests of writing students at AUC, or that the resources needed to develop the department would be redeployed in a vast academic reorganization.

The department responded in several ways. In order to help establish the history and development of the U.S.-based approach to the discipline, and thereby justify the autonomy of departmental status, the department invited the provost for a formal visit. During this visit, several faculty members offered a presentation that summarized unit history and the discipline of rhetoric and composition in the US to argue for the unique role of rhetoric and composition at AUC and in Egypt. Their purpose was to underscore the important kind of work done within this department, to offer a vision for the future, and to place this work on par with other departments. Indeed, according to one prominent faculty member, much activity was devoted to "trying to figure out how [the department] can become equal with other departments."

One of the major ways through which the department addressed concerns over its status was through accelerating the timeline for the adoption of U.S.-based approaches to the minor. Some informants said they had assumed that "the unit itself would have at least five years, if not ten, to grow into itself," which would have allowed the department the opportunity to evolve organically and to articulate its ethos and local purpose through its programs and other activities. While unforeseen complications and tensions would have inevitably arisen during this assumed process of organic development, the department nevertheless would have had time to develop into an entity that borrowed from the US while also drawing upon the eclectic intellectual, scholarly and creative expertise of faculty in order to meet emerging institutional and national needs. Indeed, the intention to move slowly was clear early on, from the 1990s when the AUC writing unit sponsored a weeklong visit by a U.S. composition scholar (whose recommendations were not adopted by the university faculty) to a visit from a major U.S. scholar in 2009. While these visits represented formal contact between established scholars and approaches from the United States and AUC, the goal was always to integrate U.S.-based approaches in a way and time deemed acceptable by the department.

However, the perceived need to quickly achieve equal status with other departments resulted in an accelerated time frame for revising the rhetoric and writing minor. This accelerated process resulted in turn in a focus on the qualifications needed to teach courses in the minor, which, for the period of my study, gave priority to U.S.-based faculty with the appropriate background.

The pressure applied by AUC's provost and the resulting accelerated revision of the rhetoric and writing minor offer two significant insights. First, this situation underscores the ongoing need for context-sensitive scholarship to account for the many kinds of localized developments that have an impact on the way in which U.S.-based approaches are taken up within non-U.S. sites. Through systematic attention to these kinds of localized factors, including the unique history of each institution, the field can account for many dynamics that drive the establishment and development of writing units outside the US that are based on U.S. models.

Second, while composition scholars have expressed concern about the unidirectional flow of U.S. perspectives, which may indicate a lack of collaborative will or possibly an imperialistic spirit, it is clear that institutional and national dynamics also influence the ways in which writing programs develop. Horner and Trimbur (2002) allow for the "significance of historically and institutionally immediate circumstances in what is . . . appropriate to a . . . set of institutional arrangements, made in a particular set of circumstances" (p. 623). In this AUC circumstance, then, a deliberately U.S.-styled, English-language institution modeled after universities in the United States nevertheless serves a range of Egyptian purposes, as I've suggested.

Reframing International Writing Program Development within Transnational Literacy Studies

As stated in the opening of this chapter, scholars dating back two decades have critiqued the imposition of western practices and infrastructure onto non-U.S. educational sites where writing is taught. These scholars (Donahue, 2009; Martins, 2015; Muchiri, Myers & Ndoli, 1995, Schaub, 2003; and others) have argued that context sensitivity can help avoid the non-reflective export of a U.S. version of composition studies and writing program development. Likewise, critiques by scholars in composition studies, such as Canagarajah (2006), Matsuda (2006), and Horner and Trimbur (2002), have called for translingual pedagogies and the inclusion of World Englishes in our writing classrooms. These arguments highlight the largely unidirectional flow of U.S.-based pedagogies and practices associated to programs outside the US, and the ways in which such pedagogies and practices may result in inappropriate writing pedagogies, curricula, and programs. Given these arguments, the findings for this study offer another possibility: that English-only education and U.S.-based approaches can serve local interests in non-English sites, especially in those with histories and configurations similar to AUC.

The findings described in this chapter might cause us to reconsider some of the arguments from transnational composition studies around the uncritical exportation of U.S. pedagogy to other global contexts. In particular, our field needs to account more fully for global-local interactions that are neither strictly unidirectional nor wholly collaborative; that is, we need more expansive frames within composition studies to account for the full richness of global-local interactions of people and approaches to literacy that inform the development of writing programs outside the United States (see Annous, Nicolas & Townsend; Nebel; Theado, Johnson, Highley & Omar; this volume).

A related field with such expansive frames is transnational literacy studies, a rich sub-field of New Literacy Studies that builds upon Brandt and Clinton's (2002) call to transcend the local-distant binaries that had narrowed the perspective of New Literacy Studies scholarship. According to Warriner (2009), recent work in literacy studies has moved away from primary attention to local literacies and has begun to consider the many ways in which local and distant contexts interact through differing views of, and uses for, literacy across borders. Warriner states that this turn developed as the anthropological fields of transnationalism and transmigration began to consider "local practices and processes" alongside macro-level "global flows" of transnational human and ideological movement (2009, p. 160). The synergistic upshot of these parallel developments is such that the focus of literacy studies on social practice became combined with work into the "influences, processes and 'by-products' of globalization and migration" (Warriner, 2009, p. 161) to gain insight into the complex and idiosyncratic nature of global literacies that manifest locally. This, she argues, can break both fields from the binary patterns that have limited their ability to capture the myriad interactions of, and uses for, local-global intersections in literacy.

Also within this field, Luke (2004) has called for increased attention to the relationship between literacy and formal institutions, such as schools, that impact the attitudes of many people toward literacy—both what it is and what it is useful for. Luke is concerned that educational contexts, as producers of "official" literacy, may encourage homogeneity in an era of internationalized global-local interaction. Because of this, he calls for "stud[ies] of local literacies . . . to engage increasingly with how the local is constituted in relation to the flows and 'travelling cultures' of globalization" (2004, p. 332). In the case of AUC, the Department of Rhetoric and Composition, and the development of the rhetoric and writing minor, I have argued that the writing instruction and curriculum in the Department of Rhetoric and Writing at AUC, which is based primarily on a unidirectional flow of a U.S.-based approach, *is* local, inasmuch as this configuration of locality was mediated through the adaptation of the university to local political, social, economic and ideological changes in Egypt.

I conclude this chapter with a call for composition studies to draw from theory and research in transnational literacy studies, so that the field can more fully account for the many ways in which U.S.-based approaches, pedagogies, and ideologies interact with many kinds of local environments in increasingly global educational configurations. There is a need for such scholarship, given the dynamism of globalized higher education, and the role that U.S. institutions are playing in the development of global universities throughout the Middle East–North Africa region and the world. Two important needs would be served by such scholarship. First, the field will be in a stronger position to account for many possible kinds of local-global interactions of U.S.-based approaches with non-U.S. sites. Second, those with interest in the field outside the United States, or who are working to develop writing programs in other countries, can utilize a more expansive perspective to consider for themselves how best to construct writing programs that incorporate U.S.-based approaches while also accounting for the historical and present exigent circumstances of the nations and institutions in which they are working.

References

The American University in Cairo (2010). "Rhetoric and writing minor." Retrieved from http://catalog.aucegypt.edu/preview_program.php?catoid=20&poid=3026&returnto=839.

Brandt, D. & Clinton, K. (2002). Limits of the local: Expanding perspectives on literacy as a social practice. *Journal of Literacy Research, 34*(3), 337–356.

Canagarajah, S. (2006). The place of World Englishes in composition: Pluralization continued. *College Composition and Communication, 57*(4), 586–619.

Donahue, C. (2009). "Internationalization" and composition studies: Reorienting the discourse. *College Composition and Communication, 61*(2), 212–244.

Golson, E. & Holdijk, L. (2012). The Department of Rhetoric and Composition at the American University in Cairo: Achievements and challenges. In C. Thaiss,

G. Bräuer, P. Carlino, L. Ganobcsik-Williams & A. Sinha (Eds.), *Writing programs worldwide: Profiles of academic writing in many places* (pp. 181–188). Fort Collins, CO: The WAC Clearinghouse and Parlor Press. Retrieved from http://wac.colostate.edu/books/wpww/.

Horner, B. Trimbur, J. (2002). English only and US college composition. *College Composition and Communication*, *53*(4), 594–630.

Lane, J. & Kinser, K. (2015). Branch campus listing (updated June 3, 2015). Retrieved from http://www.globalhighered.org/.

Lawton, W. & Katsomitros, A. (2012). *International branch campuses: Data and developments*. Retrieved from http://www.obhe.ac.uk/documents/view_details?id=894.

Luke, A. (2004). On the material consequences of literacy. *Language and Education*, *18*(4), 331–335.

Martins, D.S. (2015). Transnational writing program administration: An introduction. In D. S. Martins (Ed.), *Transnational writing program administration* (pp. 1–20). Logan, UT: Utah State University Press.

Matsuda, P. (2006). The myth of linguistic homogeneity in US college composition. *College English*, *68*(6), 637–651.

Muchiri, M. N., Mulamba N. G., Myers, G. & Ndoli, D. B. (1995). Importing composition: Teaching and researching academic writing beyond North America. *College Composition and Communication*, *46*(2), 175–198.

Murphy, L. R. (1987). *The American University in Cairo, 1919–1987*. Cairo: American University in Cairo Press.

Schaub, M. (2003). Beyond these shores: An argument for internationalizing composition. *Pedagogy*, *3*(1), 85–98.

Thaiss, C. (2012). Origins, aims, and uses of writing programs worldwide: Profiles of academic writing in many places. In C. Thaiss, G. Bräuer, P. Carlino, L. Ganobcsik-Williams & A. Sinha (Eds.), *Writing programs worldwide: Profiles of academic writing in many places* (pp. 5–22). Fort Collins, CO: The WAC Clearinghouse and Parlor Press. Retrieved from http://wac.colostate.edu/books/wpww/.

Warriner, D. (2009). Transnational literacies: Examining global flows through the lens of practice. In M. Baynham & M. Prinsloo, (Eds.), *The future of literacy studies* (pp. 160–180). London: Palgrave Macmillan.

Section 2: Considering the Importation of Western Models

4 Territorial Borders and the Teaching of Writing in English: Lessons from Research at the University of Balamand

Samer A. Annous
UNIVERSITY OF BALAMAND (LEBANON)

Maureen O'Day Nicolas
UNIVERSITY OF BALAMAND (LEBANON)

Martha A. Townsend
UNIVERSITY OF MISSOURI (US)

This chapter reports on a qualitative, multi-phase project undertaken at the University of Balamand (UOB), a private university north of Beirut that uses English as a medium of instruction (EMI). Two UOB researchers sought to discover whether writing skills taught in required English courses were transferring to subsequent EMI courses. Data from a syllabus review, interviews with teachers and students, and corroboration by an external consultant in Writing across the Curriculum reveal that even though UOB was an early adopter of EMI in the MENA region, the university needs to consider much more critically the complex implications of that linguistic decision.

Keywords: territorial borders; business; writing-across-the-curriculum; qualitative research; English as a medium of instruction (EMI)

With globalization and the internationalization of education, using English as a medium of instruction has become widespread in tertiary education (Coleman, 2006; Gill & Kirkpatrick, 2013). Many studies have highlighted the challenges faced by university students writing in English as a second or other language (L2). Evans and Morrison (2011) reported that writing is the most challenging aspect of university study. When writing in a second or additional language, university students are struggling to develop both their proficiency in the target language and their writing strategies and skills (Astroga, 2007; Hyland, 2007). Research also suggests that L2 students require additional support in their language development beyond the language classroom (Bacha, 2012; Cox, 2011; Zamel, 1995). Zamel (1995) warns that "it is unrealistic and ultimately counterproductive to expect writing and English as second or other language programs to be responsible for providing students with the language, discourse and multiple ways of seeing required across disciplines" (p. 518).

Students in English-medium universities are required to develop their academic writing in order to "participate in their disciplines and to demonstrate their learning to readers in these disciplines" (Hyland, 2013, p. 241). "Knowledge domain" is an important factor that impacts the writing of students and leads them to use "more sophisticated strategies and the production of better-structured texts" (Crossley, Roscoe & McNamara, 2014, p. 187). Although the value of knowledge domain and writing in the discipline has been highlighted by many researchers, many colleges and departments still do not consider teaching writing as their responsibility and often place a high value on content coverage only (Clughen & Connel, 2012; Zhu, 2004). Research has also shown that many professors feel territorial and possessive about their area of expertise (Becher & Trowler, 2001; Pawan & Ortloff, 2011; Zhu, 2004).

As is the case with most students in Lebanon, students at the University of Balamand have diverse writing experiences in English depending on their school training. (See also Jarkas & Fakhreddine; and Arnold, DeGenaro, Iskandarani, Khoury, Sinno & Willard-Traub, this volume, for the English writing experiences of Lebanese students.) In general, English-educated students study in English, so they are usually more exposed to different genres before joining college. French-educated students, on the other hand, study English language as a subject, and writing in English is not generally emphasized. However, when it comes to discipline-specific college writing, both groups of students still face problems as they try to adapt to new forms of academic writing. Although this challenge is also faced by native speakers of English, it is intensified for L2 students.

UOB follows a genre-based model for the teaching of academic writing, in which students from different disciplines are required to take two English courses that focus on writing extended texts. Students are expected to demonstrate critical thinking, linguistic accuracy, appropriate use of in-text citations, plus skill in summarizing and paraphrasing. However, there is no evidence that the skills acquired in these two courses are transferred to their major courses or whether professors in the different disciplines require their students to apply these writing skills in their discipline-based courses. In fact, the writing ability of UOB students has been a major cause of frustration for both teachers in the different disciplines and teachers of English.

This chapter reports on qualitative research conducted at UOB by Annous and Nicolas to assess the degree to which UOB's curriculum supports students in improving their writing in English. This chapter also reports on observations made by Townsend during a consultancy visit to UOB to determine whether embedding more writing in English in content courses might become a viable means of teaching students to learn to write in English. Annous and Nicolas are longtime UOB teachers of composition and other courses; they are also teacher trainers in the English-language-teaching graduate program. Townsend is a U.S.-based practitioner, researcher, and advocate of writing-across-the-curriculum (WAC) and writing in the disciplines (WID), whose work Annous and Nicolas had encountered during the early phase of their research.

By way of grounding Annous and Nicolas' study and Townsend's observations, which corroborate their findings, we (the three of us) first sketch a brief history of language use and instruction in the MENA region to situate the context in which UOB's students and faculty work. We follow with the methodology, findings, and discussion of Annous and Nicolas' research and, after that, observations from Townsend's visit, along with cautious recommendations for how to begin implementation of WAC in this environment. We believe the lessons we have learned have implications for other English as a medium of instruction (EMI) institutions in the MENA region.

MENA's and Lebanon's Rich Linguistic History

The MENA region is linguistically diverse. Comprised of eighteen Arab countries plus Israel and Iran, which together occupy an area larger than Europe and have a population greater than the US (Dagher & BouJaoude, 2011), the region's linguistic history is culturally vibrant. But this history and vibrancy create significant challenges for EMI institutions that hold high standards for their students. With the spread of Islam in the seventh century, Arabic became the dominant language in the Middle East, North Africa, and the Iberian Peninsula. With colonization in the late-nineteenth and early-twentieth centuries, French and English became "prestige" languages in the Arab world. After Arab independence from France, Britain, and Italy, Arabic became the official language of the new Arab states, but bilingualism remained very common in many countries, especially among the elite and urban communities. English is the *lingua franca* of expatriates who make up the majority of the population in some Arab Gulf countries, such as the United Arab Emirates and Qatar. Most important, English has become a symbol of modernity, technology, and education throughout the region (Joseph, 2013). Many of the MENA region's new universities, especially in Lebanon, Jordan, and the Arab Gulf states, use English as their medium of instruction.

One of the distinctive features of the Lebanese educational system is its mosaic of schools, which consists primarily of three types: a) state schools managed by the Ministry of Education; b) religious schools under the auspices of local or foreign Christian and Muslim authorities and missionaries; and c) non-religious private schools. Some of the latter are thought of as national because, although private, they follow the government curriculum, while others follow a distinctly foreign curriculum. The private confessional schools and schools founded by missionaries, mainly Jesuit and Protestant, are the most dominant schools in Lebanon because of their historical roots dating to the nineteenth century. Most state and private schools in Lebanon use French or English as their medium of instruction.

American and British missionary schools introduced English to Lebanon in the nineteenth century. Although Lebanon was a French colony from 1920 to 1943, and French and Arabic were the official languages of Lebanon under the French mandate, English continued to survive as a major language in private schools. The 1950s oil boom in the Arab Gulf increased the number of students enrolled in EMI schools throughout the region. Lebanon also became a regional hub for Arabs who wanted to learn (in) English.

Historically, private universities in Lebanon have attracted students from all over the Arab world. Prior to the Lebanese civil war (1975–1990), Lebanon had only four private universities in addition to one state university, the Lebanese University. Established in 1866, the American University of Beirut (AUB) was the first institution to provide higher education in the region. The Lebanese American University (LAU), formerly known as the Beirut College for Women (1949–1973) and Beirut University College (1973–1994), was, like AUB, established by American Presbyterian missionaries. Both AUB and LAU adopted EMI because of their historical connection with American missionaries. Beirut Arab University, affiliated with Alexandria University in Egypt, used English and Arabic curricula. Saint Joseph University used French because of its ties to French Jesuit missionaries. Lebanese University, established in 1951, used mainly French and Arabic as its languages of instruction.

After 1990, postwar Lebanon witnessed the establishment of more than thirty universities and colleges, the majority of which use English as the medium of instruction (EMI). The biggest universities in Lebanon were founded by confessional groups, with the Christian Maronites establishing Notre Dame University and the Holy Spirit University of Kaslik; the Shi'a Muslims establishing the Islamic University; and the Greek Orthodox Church founding the University of Balamand. The majority of these universities use EMI and most of the French-medium universities also offer programs in English, especially in the fields of engineering, science, and business. Many of the newly established for-profit universities use "American" or "international" in their names to attract local and international students. Lebanon is now among the top thirty host countries in the world for international students (World Bank Report, 2011). Over 11% of UOB's students are international who are seeking to study in English-medium programs.

Lebanon and the Circles of English

The Lebanese Constitution of 1990 states that Lebanon has an "Arab identity and belonging" and that Arabic is the national language of the country (Constitution Project, 2014). Moreover, the 1997 Ministry of Education curriculum reform emphasized the effective and efficient use of the Arabic language. The language-in-education policies followed by private and public schools and universities, however, contradict the constitution and the curricular reform. Using English or French as a medium of instruction has been a distinctive feature of higher education in Lebanon for more than a century; it would be nearly impossible to change this tradition. Recent studies have shown that students and educators perceive foreign languages, English in particular, as more useful than Arabic for future careers (Diab, 2000; Shaaban & Ghaith, 2002; Zakharia, 2010).

Kachru (1992) presents a persuasive model that divides the world's users of English into three circles: inner, outer, and expanding. The inner circle refers to English-speaking countries such as England, the United States, and Australia, in which English is considered the "native" language (English as the native language, or ENL). The outer circle consists of former colonies of ENL countries, such as India and Nigeria, where English is considered a "second" language (English as a Second Language, or ESL). The expanding circle comprises all other countries, such as China, Japan, and Russia, where English has become important in business, science, technology, and education. English in these contexts is considered a foreign language (English as a Foreign Language, or EFL). According to Xiaoqiong and Xianxing (2011), EFL students usually study English to communicate with nonnative speakers in the outer and expanding circles where English is used for functional purposes such as finding a job, pursuing academic studies, and communicating with professional contacts.

In some contexts, the lines between the outer and expanding circles have become fuzzy (Berns, 2005). Lebanon, in particular, can be situated between the outer (ESL) and the expanding (EFL) circles. In fact, English in Lebanon is used as a second language in EMI schools and universities and as a foreign language in the community because it is not usually spoken outside the classroom (Bacha & Bahous, 2011; Nicolas & Annous, 2013). English is taught as a subject in French-medium schools and is used as a medium of instruction in EMI schools.

Consistent with the British Council's report, cited below, the adoption of EMI in Lebanon has not been sufficiently or critically explored. Characteristics that should be considered when designing EMI programs include the proficiency level of students and content teachers, the dominant language on campus and in the community, and the international students and staff. As Doiz, Lasagabaster, and Sierra (2013) warn, "the implementation of EMI programs has to be carefully planned, providing highly qualified teachers (both in content and language), as well as students with the necessary English proficiency. Yet this has not always been the case" (p. 216).

Context for the University of Balamand

UOB is a private university of 5,500 students located 75 kilometers north of Lebanon's capital, Beirut. It was founded in 1988 by the Antiochian Greek Orthodox Church as an EMI institution even though one of the founding faculties (schools), the Fine Arts Faculty, was a French-medium constituent (Lebanon's strong relationship with France under the French Mandate has influenced terminology in our system of higher education; thus, schools of specific disciplines are referred to as "Faculty"). The Fine Arts Faculty continues to use French as the medium of instruction, and some of the disciplines in the Faculty of Arts and Social Sciences (FASS) have both French and English tracks. The Faculties of Engineering, Science, Medicine and Business are exclusively English medium. The university is located on a mountain overlooking the Mediterranean Sea with the country's second largest city, Tripoli, visible on the coast slightly to the north. The mountainous elevation secludes UOB and its population from urban interaction, which has implications for students' language use, a phenomenon we address later.

That UOB is an EMI institution is not surprising. Research conducted by the Oxford University Department of Education and the British Council (Dearden, 2014) shows that "a fast-moving shift" is occurring worldwide from EFL to EMI. The shift is occurring at all levels of education, from university to secondary and primary. As the British Council report shows, however, little empirical research has been done to show how, why, and when EMI is introduced and delivered. More importantly, the consequences of EMI on teaching, learning, assessment, and teachers' professional development are likewise understudied.

In recent history, many Lebanese living in urban communities have grown up speaking both Arabic and French. For the last thirty years or so, the use of English has increased such that younger generations who are bilingual in Arabic and French are also incorporating English into their linguistic repertoire. This phenomenon, however, creates a challenging literacy conundrum. Many younger Lebanese who are *orally* communicative in multiple languages find themselves unable to produce adequate *written* communication in any of the languages they speak.

Even though Lebanon is a small country, the various linguistic abilities of its population tend to pool in certain areas. In the north, where UOB is located, Arabic is the default language. UOB's student body is primarily Arabic speaking; English is a second or even third language for many students. On UOB's campus, one is more likely to hear students speaking Arabic, or a mixture of Arabic and English, rather than English alone. Arabic is commonly used when interacting in the surrounding community.

UOB's undergraduate students typically range in age from 18 to 22. Placement into the first of two required English composition courses is based on scores from an external exam such as the TOEFL or SAT I. If students do not score at UOB's admission level (490 on the SAT I written portion and 600 on the paper-based TOEFL or 100 on the iBT TOEFL), they are placed in one of five remedial levels. UOB instructors are primarily native Arabic speakers who are fluent in English. A large majority of instructors hold postgraduate degrees from American institutions in the US. Only a small number are native English speakers.

Annous and Nicolas have first-hand knowledge of UOB's English-language curriculum. As long-time instructors at UOB, we (Annous and Nicolas) have been closely involved in designing the curriculum, and we teach many of the seven courses (two required and five remedial) that comprise the Composition and Rhetoric sequence. Our knowledge of what students are asked to do versus what they are able to do is the driving factor behind the research reported here. Our responsibility for students' ability to write in English, and our vested interest in their success, have led us to want to inform policy decisions that affect the skills students demonstrate upon graduation.

Since UOB operates within the expanding circle of Kachru's English-language model (EFL), UOB students need a customized approach to the acquisition of English. Students' attainment of a competitive level of English requires that they receive assistance in transferring language skills to a variety of contexts. We (Annous and Nicolas) hoped our investigations would help us understand how our students are using English in UOB's EMI curriculum, some of which occurs in UOB's Cultural Studies program, but most of which occurs in the curriculum of students' major course of study. We also wanted to know what kinds of writing skills were being taught or reinforced in the EMI courses.

Methodology

To that end, we conducted a three-stage, multi-method study consisting of syllabi review, one-on-one interviews with instructors in the Faculty of Business, and one-on-one interviews with instructors and a student focus group in the Cultural Studies program. The FASS dean also commissioned an external expert observational visit, which occurred between stages one and two. Overall, we sought to discover whether English writing skills are transferring to EMI courses in the students' course of study and if not, why not. We wanted to be able to make data-driven decisions regarding how best to nurture students' acquisition of writing skill.

As a young, private teaching institution, UOB has not yet established a formal Institutional Review Board (IRB) to guide research procedures. In lieu of IRB guidelines, we needed institutional permission to conduct our research, and so approached the FASS dean, to whom we report, for permission to undertake the research. The dean supported the project and secured the necessary permission from other faculties, which granted us access to the data sources. The FASS dean also supported our request to bring in Martha Townsend, whose research on WAC we had become familiar with, for an exploratory visit to ascertain UOB's readiness for a WAC initiative.

The Participants

The participants included a total of ten students and fourteen instructors, all of whom were interviewed by both of us. The instructors' participation was solicited through an informative email. Six Business and eight Cultural Studies instructors were interviewed. Four out of the fourteen faculty respondents (approximately 29%) hold master's degrees; all others hold doctoral degrees. The students' participation was solicited by Annous, when he visited the EMI Cultural Studies classrooms to explain the project and invite volunteers to participate in a focus-group interview. This method resulted in a random sample of ten students from four different EMI Cultural Studies courses. All participation was voluntary and participants were assured of anonymity.

The interview data has been kept confidential, and we have preserved the anonymity of all participants.

Three Stages of Research

We began our study with a review of syllabi from all thirty of the Faculty of Business (FOB) courses taught in the Spring 2011 semester (see Appendix A). A content analysis was conducted on all the syllabi based on the syllabus review strategy developed by Ridley and Smith (2006). Since English is the *lingua franca* of international business, we assumed that written communication in English would be central to the business school's curriculum. We also assumed that students would be encouraged to transfer the writing skills they had acquired in UOB's English composition courses to their business courses. We began with this unobtrusive review, thinking that if the syllabi included explicit writing assignments and/or writing-to-learn activities, we could infer that the FOB was promoting writing in English beyond the required English composition classes.

The syllabus review generated stage two of the investigation. We designed an in-depth, semi-structured interview protocol to inquire about FOB instructors' thoughts about students' use of English and the instructors' role in developing students' writing skill and awareness of discipline-specific conventions. For this stage, we conducted one-on-one interviews with six instructors (see Appendix B), two of whom hold master's degrees and four of whom hold doctoral degrees. Both of us were present during the interviews, which we tape-recorded. The typed interview transcripts were subjected to member checking (Cohen & Manion, 1994), and we used an inductive matrix process (Miles & Huberman, 1994) for our transcript analysis.

The third stage of our study, which investigated general education courses offered by the Cultural Studies program at UOB, consisted of two parts: one-on-one interviews with nine instructors who teach in the program (see Appendix C), and a focus-group interview with a random sample of ten students (see Appendix D). This third stage thus added the important component of student perspectives to our work. For both sets of participants, the questions were designed to reveal the instructional methodologies used by instructors, including whether feedback was given to the students on their writing. The questions were also intended to reveal whether instructors nurtured written English through any pedagogical strategies, such as pre-writing instruction or feedback on output. Further, the questions probed instructors' and students' opinions about how these courses contribute to improving proficiency in written English.

We jointly conducted hour-long instructor interviews using a semi-structured protocol with eight instructors who teach the required EMI Cultural Studies courses. Interview transcripts were member checked (Cohen & Manion, 1994), and an iterative process identified emergent themes, discussed below.

Annous conducted the student focus-group interview while Nicolas took notes, observing from outside. Here again, a semi-structured interview protocol was used. The focus-group interview was also recorded so we could refer to the raw data during the analysis. Students were given the choice of speaking in either Arabic or English. Several chose to speak only in Arabic, while some used both Arabic and English, which reflects the bilingual characteristics of the UOB population; several of the students spoke only in English when addressing the questions but even these students resorted to Arabic when the discussion escalated. A random sample of ten students who represent all four courses and all class levels comprised the focus group. Themes were extracted from the focus group interview through an inductive process and then combined with the instructor interviews in order to triangulate findings (see Appendix F).

Findings and Discussion

Stage One: FOB Syllabus Review

The syllabus review led us (Annous and Nicolas) to infer two very different outcomes. First, FOB instructors seem unaware of the potential of using writing as a learning strategy. Second, FOB instructors seem to lack awareness of their responsibility to train students in the writing conventions of their discipline.

The review showed that only nine of the thirty syllabi from courses offered that spring (less than one-third) mention writing of any kind. Appendix E displays those courses and shows how writing was reported as either an intended learning outcome or as an activity in the course. The table reveals that three of the courses that mention writing do not clearly state what the writing activity is. The remaining six syllabi mention an essay or report but nowhere on the syllabus is there any description of the writing requirements or the writing process. It is possible that the FOB instructors could have distributed more detailed assignment guidelines during the semester, apart from what the syllabi indicate (although our further findings, below, do not suggest this was the case). Finally, the syllabi also do not mention whether author stance or audience perspective are stressed (Nicolas & Annous, 2013).

Stage Two: FOB Teachers' Perceptions

The iterative analysis of our in-depth, semi-structured interviews with the six FOB instructors generated five themes. These themes reveal the business instructors' opinions regarding writing in English in their classes and their attitudes toward nurturing students' English written skills in business genres. All five themes include respondent triangulation; in other words, more than one respondent needed to express a similar point of view for a theme to be generated (Miles & Huberman, 1994). The themes that emerged from this stage are:

1. FOB teachers do not believe it is their responsibility to teach or focus on language acquisition in any of the languages students use;
2. The FOB relies heavily on use of students' first language (spoken Arabic);
3. The teaching methodologies and assessment employed in FOB do not include WID tasks;
4. FOB teachers place a singular focus on subject content to the exclusion of building skill in writing; and
5. A cohesive environment that would enable the FOB and the Department of English to work toward a common goal of graduating students who are competent writers in English does not seem to exist (Annous & Nicolas, 2015).

These findings suggest that UOB is not fully preparing its English L2 students for work in an English-speaking world. The teachers in stage two of the study strongly and explicitly express a belief that students' ability to communicate in written English is not their responsibility and, furthermore, that the students have such poor language skill that the instructors are obliged to resort to Arabic in order to cover the necessary content. One respondent characterized students' English language use as "catastrophic." When probed to explain the perceived lack of language skill, participants largely blamed the prevailing culture students live in, with one saying, "This culture is not a reading culture; students do not read enough, and that's why their language suffers."

The respondents asserted a position that language and the ability to write in English is something separate from their subject domain. The interview transcripts contain numerous comments, such as "I do not feel that my courses are the place to correct language" and "I feel the grade should reflect how well they understood finance only."

This approach to tertiary education in an Arabic-speaking context that has adopted an EMI model of education seems to indicate isolated silos of knowledge that do not serve a student body that needs to cultivate skills required for international competitiveness. The university thus appears to have cultivated what educational theorists Becher and Trowler (2001) refer to as academic "territorial borders." Becher and Trowler (2001) posit that, within tertiary educational institutions, different academic "tribes" function in separate territories having different knowledge distinct from other academic tribes in the same institution. This seems to us to be the position espoused by the FOB participants. They claim that it is not their job to teach English-language communication skills, and they also claim they do not have the knowledge to do so.

This finding echoes that reported in the British Council study mentioned earlier: "EMI teachers firmly believed that teaching English was not their job. They did not consider themselves responsible for their students' level of English. . . . They did not see themselves as language teachers in any way" (Dearden, 2014, p. 6). As one of the professors interviewed for that report says, "I'm not interested in their English, I'm interested in their comprehension of [the subject being taught]" (p. 6).

With the extent of the FOB instructors' beliefs thus revealed, we realized that we needed to investigate a different program that had further-reaching implications for the entire UOB student body. The Cultural Studies curriculum, consisting of four courses, is required of every student at UOB (except for the Fine Arts students who take a different sequence of courses). After re-establishing permission through the FASS dean to conduct additional research, this time in FASS, we set out to investigate the general education courses offered by the Cultural Studies program to learn to what degree English-writing skill development is integrated into that program.

Stage Three: Students' and Instructors' Perceptions of Writing in the Cultural Studies Program

The third stage of the project expanded the focus of the investigation to include communication skill in English in general. This investigation clearly revealed information germane to the development of students' writing skill in English. The series of four required Cultural Studies courses addresses early civilization; religious studies; key philosophers, including Arab philosophers; and contemporary thinkers. We assumed that, as with EMI courses required throughout all UOB degree programs, the Cultural Studies courses would be fostering essential skills in written English.

We constructed a matrix for each emergent theme that included supporting data (see Appendix F for examples of the matrices). Twelve themes emerged from the transcripts, which we then clustered by related themes to determine our primary findings (Miles & Huberman, 1994).

Inherent in the findings from this stage of research is that the required Cultural Studies courses do not nurture students' ability to communicate in written English. The data revealed that ineffective feedback on student writing, as well as an absence of a pedagogical focus on writing, contribute to the lack of enhancement of written skill in these courses. Furthermore, students seem to believe that the courses' only value is in increasing their general knowledge base. Students were unaware that these courses could serve any other purpose, such as skill development in written English. One student sarcastically commented that, "Since our English skill is not better even after we take the two required English courses, then why would a Cultural Studies teacher be able to help us with our English?" Other students in the focus group disputed the contention that *no* improvement is achieved in the English writing courses, but they did concur that the Cultural Studies courses do not nurture their ability to a significant degree. A consensus was reached that students who come from EMI high schools already know English, so they "really don't learn anything new" at university, whereas students who come from French-medium high schools probably do improve their English through the English courses and the Cultural Studies courses simply by having to use it, by being exposed to the language.

Students also claimed to have learned the content and ideas taught in these classes but felt they could not express themselves adequately in English on written exams on the content knowledge. This claim suggests that students do not feel capable of handling the content of a cultural or philosophical nature in English, or at least they lack confidence in their ability to express their viewpoints on these topics in written English. In other words, they felt they could handle *oral* class discussions on difficult topics, but when it came to expressing their ideas *in writing*, they suffered from a lack of confidence and a lack of skill. This finding also speaks to the methodology of the courses. According to the students, not all instructors are clear about the writing conventions students should use in exams. Students claimed that even such essential assignment parameters as length and genre are unclear. Students were very expressive when revealing this last point. One young woman said that the only feedback one instructor ever gave was "more length," so she wrote a "recipe" in the middle of her answer the next time to add length, which she claimed the instructor did not even notice. Another student, sounding very irritated, explained that no matter how hard he tried to address the "few comments" he received from his instructor on exams, he always achieved the same grade, as if the instructor did not notice the differences.

The interviews with the Cultural Studies instructors revealed a remarkably similar point of view to the instructors in the business school regarding their role as university professors. (See also Hodges & Kent, this volume, for discussion on instructors' responses to teaching writing in their discipline.) Most of the respondents expressed a position that they "are not English teachers, after all." One respondent was quite adamant about this point, saying, "We don't teach how to write essays; we assume [students] have learned this in their English classes. It's not our responsibility to teach them this as Cultural Studies teachers." However, three of the instructors on this program also teach English and two of them emphasized their role in linking language skill to the discipline. One said, "I go very deeply in this [how to write], like verb choice, and [I] go into the essence of language . . . We analyze the language in the text and mistakes they make in their essays and explain linguistic problems they're facing. I give feedback on speech and writing." But the third instructor, who also teaches some English courses, agreed with the majority of respondents by saying, "I'm not into teaching them how to write an essay, because I think they know it."

We (Annous and Nicolas) believe that the data suggest that the concept of academic territorial borders exists not only among the FOB instructors but also among both the instructors in the Cultural Studies curriculum and their students. The implications of this finding are quite far-reaching: If students unconsciously view their academic work as occurring from within academic territorial boundaries, then they will be less inclined to transfer skills and knowledge beyond these boundaries. Since the instructors confine their instruction within disciplinary borders, they will not promote student interaction with new or existing knowledge, nor will students initiate the process. As a result, students could think that the proper way of learning in tertiary education is within, rather than across, academic borders and boundaries.

Further, the findings from this stage of the study indicate that the methodologies practiced in UOB's required Cultural Studies courses neither reinforce students' acquisition of written English skill nor nurture other important literacy skills (such as reading), which would also contribute to better writing. UOB needs to be explicit about the purpose these courses serve in every major program. Certainly, the message—intended or not—transmitted to students is that the expansion of their general knowledge is the purpose of the courses; that the content knowledge these courses contain is of paramount importance; and that no other benefit can be derived from the courses. At the same time, the message being transmitted to teachers is that they do not bear any responsibility for students' acquisition of written skill in this

EFL/EMI context. The same message permeates the FOB curriculum. In both of these cases, the message is that *content* is the most important aspect of university study and students need to do whatever is necessary to learn it. In other words, the message being sent through the adherence to disciplinary borders with emphasis on content is that all other skills associated with academic work, particularly the acquisition of effective written skill in English in an EFL environment, is secondary or even isolated to a particular "tribe." The potential for UOB's required Cultural Studies courses to add to students' written skill in English is, therefore, lost.

The findings from this third stage of the research corroborate the findings from the first two stages. Taken together, the three stages suggest a situation whereby a tertiary educational institution functioning in an EFL environment has juxtaposed an EMI model onto a firmly established institutional structure that promotes "silos" of knowledge. We conclude that Becher and Trowler's (2001) concept of "knowledge territory" permeates the university. Instructors identify with a discipline and its content and do not acknowledge the role writing plays in the discipline or in the learning process. This phenomenon is not unique to UOB and can be found elsewhere (Bacha & Bahous, 2008; Pawan & Orloff, 2011; Plutsky & Wilson, 2001). Territorial knowledge boundaries are clearly detrimental to students' development, especially in written English communication in an EFL context.

A WAC Expert's Observations on Writing in English at UOB

Annous and Nicolas had already conducted the stage-one syllabus review before I (Townsend) visited. Annous and Nicolas' knowledge of UOB's culture and the fact that WAC is relatively uncommon outside the "inner circle" of English countries, led them to believe that UOB's composition instructors and administrators needed to know what WAC is and does if the institution were to consider implementing any form of WAC philosophy or pedagogies. They asked if I would prepare a presentation titled "What Is WAC? And Why Should Today's University Implement It?" to be delivered jointly to faculty and students enrolled in English 203, UOB's second required composition course.

Over three separate class periods, 300 students, their instructors, and assorted administrators gathered in a lecture hall to hear my talk, in which I attempted to convey in the least pedantic manner possible the idea that what students learn in composition classes should carry over to subsequent classes as well—a problem that also vexes educators in the US. For the most part, students responded as would U.S. students in any similar forced lecture setting—with a combination of polite tolerance mixed with boredom, confusion, and curiosity.

As part of my interactive presentation, I asked students to prepare some informal writing, which I collected. I responded to some of the students' questions and comments during the presentation itself. Others I replied to in a letter that I wrote to students in return, conveyed to them via their instructors. I hoped that my letter would invite students and instructors alike to continue a conversation I tried to start with my presentation. I wanted to show them that informal writing has value. I wanted to let them know that American students ask the same questions about writing and that those questions do have reasonable answers. I wanted to suggest that staying after class to ask more questions and sharing one's writing with a complete stranger (as some had done after my presentation) can be signs of intellectual curiosity. And finally, I wanted to support the studying I knew they would soon be doing for their upcoming, in-class final exam.

Whether my letter accomplished any of these goals is unknown. But I believe that demonstrating the use of informal writing, both to students and to instructors, was important. And in writing back to them, I had hoped to reinforce that pedagogy. One student did email me later, sending along some writing she was proud of, which I interpreted as one of several signs during my visit that, with encouragement, UOB students *can* take pleasure in written discourse. In retrospect, I believe that while my presentation served some good, it actually provided a better lesson for WAC consultants who are doing international consulting. My attempting to describe the characteristics that undergird strong WAC programs for administrators, while at the same time trying to convince students to carry forward their new knowledge of writing, was simply too much, too soon, for too many audiences.

In addition to my three large-lecture presentations, I also met individually and in groups with scores of UOB instructors and students in settings that ranged from department meetings, class observations, one-on-one coffee breaks, over meals, and in individuals' offices. I sat in on a high-school teacher's oral defense of her master's degree. I met with American colleagues who were then working with the Writing Center at the American University of Beirut. And I engaged in nonstop conversation and analysis with the American friend who was then teaching at UOB and who housed me during my visit. Each conversation informed my thinking about the possibility of implementing some version of WAC; each conversation added to the layers of complexity that were, at that time, not yet informed by stages two and three of Annous and Nicolas' research.

Following my visit, I submitted a six-page report to the dean, summarizing six key observations. On the positive side of the equation, I reported that, "Most professors and administrators with whom I spoke were curious and interested—even energized—about the potential for Balamand's adapting WAC theory and pedagogies to enhance teaching and learning in the curriculum" (unpublished letter, June 6, 2011). I also acknowledged the skepticism many raised about the seeming futility of teaching English composition and using WAC pedagogies. I conveyed my impression of a group of instructors deeply divided between wanting to do a good job in serving UOB's students but who, at the same time, were discouraged by students' apparent ennui, lack of interest in their English classes, and a willingness to sacrifice academic integrity to pass those courses.

I reported seeing "the potential for building alliances with professors at the American University of Beirut," with whom I had met before leaving Lebanon. They reported encountering many of the same issues that UOB faces and seemed interested in discussing mutual concerns with colleagues at their neighboring institution. Building alliances with other universities in Lebanon and the region seems to be the most productive way for all institutions to achieve better outcomes. I also identified an American colleague who was doing work on WAC with a university in Saudi Arabia, who could participate in the establishment of relevant guidelines, given his experience with WAC in the Arab world. I encouraged the dean to forge contacts and connections in the region, noting that WAC's international presence has increased in recent years and that UOB had the potential to become a leader in the region.

My report highlighted four other key conclusions: First, I wrote that UOB seems to lack a writing culture. Here, I was referring to the fact that virtually all the students I spoke with, in my presentations and in classes, reported doing little to no writing anywhere except in the required composition courses. By that time, Annous and Nicolas' syllabus study had already shown "no evidence" of writing in the FOB curriculum. My own conversations with instructors corroborated what students were telling me. Many students, in fact, had simply said they "do not need" writing in their careers.

Second, I reported that students are resistant to writing in general. They were unaware of the potential for writing to help them form thoughts and ideas. They had never considered asking their professors about the professors' own writing habits. When I asked them to write informally during my presentation, they had groaned audibly and had to be encouraged to get out paper and pen. In response to my prompt "What does 'writing' mean to you?" this student's remark was typical: "It is just work to do to have good grades and to pass my English course." In response to my prompt "What is one question *you* have as a result of my talk today?" students wrote such things as: "Why should I pay all these [sic] money for writing?" and "Why are these classes obligatory?" A sizable number replied that they had no questions for me. Overall, the student responses I collected indicated that they see writing as a set of "skills" to master, rather than seeing writing as a way of knowing and as a means to an end that can enrich their personal and professional lives.

Third, I noted that plagiarism is a dominant theme. Throughout the week, numerous instructors had discussed with me the degree to which students' trilingualism understandably complicates their learning to write in English. When they write, UOB students focus on correctness, especially grammar and citation format, rather than on conveying ideas and arguments. Instructors reported needing to act as "police" when grading student papers, while students adopt a "catch me if you can" attitude, with a foregone conclusion that academic dishonesty is the norm. Composition instructors require that virtually all writing be done in class, so that plagiarism is forestalled. Convinced that most students would pay for outside-of-class papers to be written for them, virtually all instructors and administrators agreed that the writing-in-class policy is necessary. Not allowing students to write outside of class because of the fear that students will have someone else do their writing for them severely limits the kind and quality of in-class writing that can be assigned.

Finally, I noted that, "These issues notwithstanding, many of the writing-related phenomena I observed at UOB exist in the US as well." I reassured the dean that American students are not as knowledgeable about writing as we wish they would be; that our curricula are not perfect; and that we, too, struggle with plagiarism in our classrooms. I noted that it takes an entire four- or five-year undergraduate degree program in higher education for most students to become "good" writers—and that their growth in writing continues on into graduate school if students pursue graduate degrees.

I followed my 2011 UOB-specific observations to the dean with four pages of observations about WAC in general (e.g., WAC is *primarily a faculty development* initiative; transition to WAC takes time; instructors need continual support). And I offered a set of three specific recommendations that UOB might consider, elaborating on how each might be enacted:

1. Appoint a FASS WAC liaison.
2. Create a FASS WAC council to advise and assist the liaison.
3. Initiate efforts to secure one, and possibly two, Fulbright visiting professors with WAC expertise as soon as practicable.

At the time I wrote these recommendations, all three seemed reasonable and within the realm of possibility. The FASS dean was open to suggestions for addressing what he realized were genuine issues for UOB students. Having had a successful track record of bringing Fulbright faculty to campus, it was the dean who inquired about the possibility of Fulbright faculty with WAC expertise coming to help begin a WAC initiative. UOB instructors' interest was such that it could have been built upon. Momentum was noticeable. And while student resistance was high, there were signs that not every student shared that resistance. Everyone involved seemed to believe that a significant culture shift with regard to writing was both desirable and possible. Although these recommendations seemed plausible when written in 2011, political instability in the region since that time prohibits enacting the final one. The U.S. Department of State has discontinued the Fulbright program in Lebanon until further notice. Moreover, since I offered these recommendations, FASS has undergone a change in administration and UOB has begun accreditation procedures. Consequently, the momentum towards WAC implementation has halted and all programs are being evaluated in light of accreditation requirements.

Conclusion

Our chapter provides a critical look at a particular context in one EMI learning environment. The lessons could possibly have ramifications for other EMI learning environments in Arabic-speaking contexts. By knowing how, or even whether, writing in English is taught or reinforced in EMI courses, we now better understand the reasons why many students fail to exhibit effective writing skills in English during their university studies and after. Through the research conducted thus far, we (Annous and Nicholas) are also now better able to arrive at conclusions about implementing curricular reforms or policy recommendations, including the possibility of WAC, through a systematic process that would hopefully lead to UOB graduates having effective skill in written English.

The three stages of our evaluation of the institutional context have led to some major findings: Instructors are generally unaware of the role writing can play in the teaching/learning process. Writing is not utilized in the disciplines as a learning tool. Content mastery, at the expense of any other important and arguably related skill, especially in an EMI context, seems to be of the highest value for most instructors, regardless of the discipline. Students seem to believe that they come to our EMI institution only to learn information without realizing the major skills they might learn in class, such as persuasive writing, critical thinking and public speaking. Our research reveals that students seem to have a predetermined idea that universities are made up of independent silos of knowledge where disciplinary border crossing is not even considered. We all now believe that the acquisition of effective written skill in English should be an explicit learning objective across disciplinary borders for EMI institutions like UOB that operate in non-English speaking contexts.

The ultimate challenge that UOB faces, along with many other institutions in similar contexts, is that many instructors in EMI tertiary educational institutions operating in the outer and expanding circles of English may be non-native speakers of English who lack the confidence and competence to deal with students' language acquisition. When being hired, instructors' competence in English must be foregrounded. For existing instructors at EMI institutions who are striving to improve students' English communicative skill outcomes, training and ongoing support must be provided by knowledgeable experts in the field. As the British Council's report (Dearden, 2014) shows, too little professional development is currently provided for EMI instructors. This situation is unacceptable. To reiterate Doiz, Lasagabaster, and Sierra's (2013) warning, "[T]he implementation of EMI programs has to be carefully planned, providing highly qualified teachers (both in content and language), as well as students with the necessary English proficiency" (p. 216).

Collaboration between the English department (or whichever unit houses the writing program) and instructors in other disciplines is crucial to breaking down academic territorial borders. The thirty-year history of WAC in the US shows that regular, ongoing faculty development workshops can be an effective way to bring discipline-based faculty into conversation with one another (Fulwiler, 1981; Russell, 1991; McLeod & Soven, 2006). At the University of Missouri (Townsend's home institution), for example, it was a collective complaint about student writing from faculty in many disciplines that led the university's Dean of Arts and Science to create a cross-disciplinary committee in 1984 to address the problem (Townsend, Patton & Vogt, 2012). That committee became the university's Campus Writing Board, which still meets monthly to guide fellow faculty and Campus Writing Program staff toward the improvement of student writing. UOB chose English as the medium of instruction to meet the challenges of globalization and the demands of internationalized education. UOB was one of the first universities established in Lebanon during the region's shift to EMI; now, the university needs to consider much more critically the complex implications of its linguistic decision.

References

Annous, S. & Nicolas, M. O. (2015). Academic territorial borders: A look at the writing ethos in business courses in an environment in which English is a foreign language. *Journal of Business and Technical Communication, 29*(1), 93–111.

Astroga, M. C. (2007). Teaching academic writing in the EFL context: Redesigning pedagogy. *Pedagogies: An International Journal, 2*(4), 251–267.

Bacha, N. (2012). Disciplinary writing in an EFL context from teachers' and students' perspectives. *International Journal of Business and Social Science, 3*(2), 233–256.

Bacha, N. & Bahous, R. (2008). Contrasting views of business students' writing needs in an EFL Environment. *English for Specific Purposes, 27*(1), 74–93.

Bacha, N. & Bahous, R. (2011). Foreign language education in Lebanon: A context of cultural and curricular complexities. *Journal of Language Teaching and Research, 2*(6), 1320–1328.

Becher, T. & Trowler, P. R. (2001). *Academic tribes and territories: Intellectual enquiry and the culture of disciplines* (2nd ed.). Buckingham, UK: SRHE and Open University Press.

Berns, M. (2005). Expanding circle: Where do we go from here? *World Englishes, 24*(1), 85–93.

Clughen, L. & Connell, M. (2012). Writing and resistance: Reflections on the practice of embedding writing in the curriculum. *Arts and Humanities in Higher Education, 11*, 333–345.

Cohen, L. & Manion, L. (1994). *Research methods in education* (4th ed.). London: Routledge.

Coleman, J. (2006). English-medium teaching in European Higher Education. *Language Teaching, 39*, 1–14.

Constitution Project (2014). Lebanon's constitution of 1926 with amendments through 2004. Retrieved from https://www.constituteproject.org/constitution/Lebanon_2004.pdf.

Cox, M. (2011). WAC: Closing doors or opening doors for second language writers? *Across the Disciplines, 8*(4). Retrieved from http://wac.colostate.edu/atd/ell/cox.cfm.

Crossley, S., Roscoe, R. & McNamara, D. (2014). What is successful writing? An investigation into multiple ways writers can write successful essays. *Written Communication, 31*(2), 184–214.

Dagher, Z. & BouJaoude, S. (2011). Science education in Arab states: Bright future or status quo? *Studies in Science Education, 47*, 73–101.

Dearden, J. (2014). English as a medium of instruction—A growing global phenomenon: Phase 1. Interim report presented at Going Global 2014. British Council 2014/E123. Retrieved from https://www.britishcouncil.org/sites/default/files/english_as_a_medium_of_instruction.pdf.

Diab, R. (2000). Political and socio-cultural factors in foreign language education: The case of Lebanon. *Texas Papers in Foreign Language Education, 5*(1), 177–187.

Doiz, A., Lasagabaster, D. & Sierra, J. (2013). Future challenges for English-medium instruction at the tertiary level. In A. Doiz, D. Lasagabaster & J. Sierra (Eds.), *English-medium instruction at universities: Global challenges* (pp. 213–221). Bristol, UK: Multilingual Matters.

Evans, S. & Morrison, B. (2011). Meeting the challenges of English-medium higher education: The first-year experience in Hong Kong. *English for Specific Purposes, 30*, 198–208.

Fulwiler, T. (1981). Showing, not telling, at a writing workshop. *College English, 43*(1), 55–58.

Gill, S. K. & Kirkpatrick, A. (2013). English in Asian and European higher education. In C. Chapelle (Ed.), *The Encyclopedia of Applied Linguistics*. Oxford, UK: Blackwell.

Hyland, K. (2007). Genre pedagogy: Language, literacy and L2 writing instruction. *Journal of Second Language Writing, 16*, 148–164.

Hyland, K. (2013). Faculty feedback: Perceptions and practices in L2 disciplinary writing. *Journal of Second Language Writing, 22*, 240–253.

Joseph, J. (2013). Signs of belonging: Culture, identity and the English language. In H. McIlwraith (Ed.), *Perspectives on English in the Middle East and North Africa* (pp. 53–72). London: British Council.

Kachru, B. (1992). Teaching world Englishes. In B. Kachru (Ed.), *The other tongue: English across cultures* (pp. 355–360). Urbana, IL: University of Illinois Press.

McLeod, S. & Soven M. (2006). *Composing a community: A history of writing across the curriculum*. West Lafayette, IN: Parlor Press.

Miles, M. & Huberman, A. (1994). *An expanded sourcebook qualitative data analysis*. Thousand Oaks, CA: Sage.

Nicolas, M. O. & Annous, S. (2013). Assessing WAC elements in business syllabi. *Business Communication Quarterly, 76*(2), 172–187.

Pawan, F. & Ortloff, J. (2011). Sustaining collaboration: English-as-a-second language and content-area teachers. *Teacher and Teacher Education, 27*, 463–471.

Plutsky, S. & Wilson, B. (2001). Writing across the curriculum in a college of business and economics. *Business Communication Quarterly, 64*(4), 26–41.

Ridley, D. & Smith, E. (2006). Writing across the curriculum works: The impact of writing emphasis upon senior exit writing samples. *Research & Practice in Assessment, 1*(1), 1–5.

Russell, D. (1991). *Writing in the academic disciplines, 1870–1990: A curricular history*. Carbondale, IL: Southern Illinois University.

Shaaban, K. & Ghaith, G. (2002). University students' perceptions of the enthnolinguistic vitality of Arabic, French and English in Lebanon. *Journal of Sociolinguistics, 6*(4), 557–574.

Townsend, M., Patton, M. & Vogt, J. (2012). Uncommon conversations: How nearly three decades of paying attention allows one WAC/WIC program to thrive. *Writing Program Administration, 35*(2), 127–159.

World Bank (2011). *Internationalization of higher education in MENA: Policy issues associated with skills formation and mobility*. Washington, DC: World Bank. Retrieved from http://documents.worldbank.org/curated/en/2011/01/15155739/internationalization-higher-education-mena-policy-issues-associated-skills-formation-mobility.

Xiaoqiong, B. & Xianxing, J. (2011). Kachru's three concentric circles and English teaching fallacies in EFL and ESL contexts. *Changing English: Studies in Culture and Education, 18*(2), 219–228.

Zakharia, Z. (2010). Language-in-education policies in contemporary Lebanon. In O. Abi-Mershed (Ed.), *Trajectories of education in the Arab World: Legacies and challenges* (pp. 157–184). New York: Routledge.

Zamel, V. (1995). Strangers in academia: The experiences of faculty and ESL students across the curriculum. *College Composition and Communication, 46*, 506–521.

Zhu, W. (2004). Faculty views on the importance of writing, the nature of academic writing, and teaching and responding to writing in the disciplines. *Journal of Second Language Writing 13*, 29–48.

Appendices

Appendix A: Business courses included in the syllabi review

Course code and title	Brief description (abbreviated from the syllabi)
1. ACCT210: Financial Accounting I	"This course studies the accounting reports produced for financial decision making."
2. ACCT211: Financial Accounting II	"Its overall aim is to familiarize students with the different types of business organizations with an emphasis on partnerships and corporations."
3. ACCT202: Survey of Accounting and Finance	"This is a remedial course for non-business MBA candidates."
4. BUSN210: Business Communication	"A thorough introduction to business communication concepts and theories. Participants in this course will gain knowledge in written and oral skills and engage in a business class communication experience."
5. BUSN220: Managerial Economics	"This course introduces the student to the various methods used by companies in decision making taking into consideration the resource constraint."
6. BUSN221: Global Economy	"[This course will] present a comprehensive, up-to-date, and clear exposition of the theory and principles of international economics."
7. BUSN230: Strategic Management	"[This course] focuses on how firms formulate, implement, and evaluate strategies, by highlighting different issues such as the organization"s mission and vision."
8. BUSN240: Business Law	"[This course] introduces the students to the fundamental concepts of civil and commercial law."

Appendix A—*continued*

Course code and title	Brief description (abbreviated from the syllabi)
9. ECON201: Survey of Economics	"[This course offers an] introduction to the field of economics and its principles, both at the micro and macro levels."
10. ECON211: Microeconomics Theory	"[This course offers an] introduction to microeconomics concepts and analysis."
11. ECON212: Macroeconomics	"Macroeconomics is the study of the behavior of the economy as a whole. The three major goals of macroeconomics are good level of growth, price stability and low unemployment rate."
12. ECON247: Intermediate Macroeconomics	"[This course] will introduce and develop the main techniques and models used in macroeconomic theory."
13. ECON293: History of Economic Thought	"[This course] will trace the evolution of economic thinking throughout history."
14. FINE220: Managerial Finance	"[This course is] an introductory course where students acquire knowledge about basic concepts and methods used in finance."
15. FINE230: Financial Institutions	"[This course] examines how financial markets (such as those for bonds, stocks and foreign exchange) and financial institutions (banks, insurance companies mutual funds, and other institutions) work."
16. FINE241: Investment	"[This course] examines the theoretical issues and quantitative techniques of the financial management of the firm."
17. HOSP200: Introduction to Travel, Tourism and Hospitality	"[This course provides] a comprehensive overview of the world"s largest and fastest growing business called the tourism and hospitality industry."
18. HOSP213: Restaurant Management and Purchasing	"This course identifies the elements involved in operating a successful restaurant."
19. HOSP224: Service Management	"[This course] will address the distinct needs and problems of service excellence mainly in the hospitality and tourism industry."
20. HOSP225: Rooms Division Management	"This course introduces the student to the hotels" rooms operations."
21. HOSP230: Conventions, Special Events and Catering	"[This course] provides students with an understanding of the convention and meetings market."
22. HOSP231: Hospitality Purchasing	"[This course will] promote an understanding of the managerial aspects of the hospitality purchasing activity. Emphasis is placed on strategic selection and procurement considerations based on item need, value and supplier information."

Appendix A—*continued*

Course code and title	Brief description (abbreviated from the syllabi)
23. HOSP236: Housekeeping Management	"[This course is] designed to provide students with both classroom theoretical principles of professional housekeeping knowledge, as well as on-hand competencies and skills."
24. HOSP240: Yield Management	"This course focuses on managing the hotel's demand-side decision in order to maximize revenue and occupancy vis-à-vis the market and the competition."
25. MGMT 220: Principles of Management	"[This is an] introductory course covering the fundamental principles of management, including objective setting techniques, operational planning and the control process."
26. MGMT 230: Organizational Behavior	"[This course]deals with the impact of individual and team values, attitudes, perception, needs, motivation, leadership, communication, power politics, conflict, and work design on organizational behavior."
27. MGMT291: Business Ethics & Professional Responsibility	"[This course] introduces students to ethical concepts, helps them apply these concepts to business decisions and identify moral issues involved in the management of specific problem areas in business."
28. MRKT220: Principles of Marketing	"[This] course is designed to introduce students to the basic terminology, concepts and practices of contemporary marketing as applied in a variety of contexts."
29. MRKT291: Advertising and Promotion	"[This course provides an] emphasis on elements and process of developing effective advertising programs using integrated marketing communications."

Appendix B: Interview protocol—FOB instructors

1. Knowledge of writing-across-the-curriculum strategies
   - How would you define writing-across-the-curriculum strategies?
   - Can you describe some characteristics of writing-across-the-curriculum strategies?

2. Writing activities in business courses
   - Do you include writing assignments?
   - What are the written assignments?

3. General opinion about students' ability to communicate in English
   - Do you allow Arabic to be spoken?
   - Do you ever have to resort to Arabic to ensure understanding?

4. General evaluation of students' written performance
   - Are you satisfied with your students' writing? What are the problems?
   - Do you assess students' writing?
   - Is the quality of students' writing part of the grading criteria?
5. Willingness to incorporate writing activities in the future
   - What do you envision the role of a writing center should be?
   - Can you itemize some of the challenges you face when incorporating writing activities?

Appendix C: Focus-group interview protocol—CVSQ students

1. Describe a typical CVSQ session? What are the methods that the professors use? What are the typical activities?
2. What are the difficulties you are facing in the CVSQ courses?
3. What is your general perception of the CVSQ courses?
4. How do you rate your English language skills? Reading? Writing? Speaking? i.e. are you confident in your English language skills?
5. To what extent you think the CVSQ courses help you develop your writing skills in English? Reading skills?
6. Do you receive any feedback on your writing? If yes, what kind of feedback? Are you satisfied with the kind of feedback you are receiving?

Appendix D: Interview protocol—CVSQ instructors

General methodology that could foster/hinder student communication

1. Describe a typical class session:
2. How do you begin (propose a question, begin a lecture, etc.)?
3. Any group work, student presentation of an idea or topic, etc.?
4. What language are students allowed to use in class?
5. Do you find you need to use Arabic?
6. Do you correct Arabic use and/or translate to English if need be?
7. Class exercises are mentioned on some of the course content tables and in course evaluation for some courses on the syllabi; what is the nature of these exercises?
8. Are they written or oral?
9. Multiple choice or short answers?

Discipline-specific strategies
1. Do you teach the conventions of your discipline?
2. Written conventions such as verb choice, style etc.
3. If not, how do students know about what is conventional or acceptable in this discipline?

Evaluation of students' communicative skill
1. For any written work you require of your students, are language and higher-order concerns like organization and development part of your grading rubric?
2. If no, why not?
3. If yes, are students trained by you on your expectations in this area?
4. What kind of written genre do you require?
5. How much is the written product usually weighed in the final evaluation?
6. Do students receive any training on this genre in class?
7. Do you have a pre-prepared grading rubric for written assignments? Do students know these criteria ahead of time?
8. Do you require presentations?
9. If so, how are they evaluated? What criteria do you look for?
10. If not, why not, any reason not to require a presentation?
11. On tests, midterm and final, do you assess students' language skill as part of the grade?
12. Do students know that their language is part of the final grade?
13. What about organization of paragraphs and development of ideas?
14. When class participation is counted in the final evaluation breakdown, how is it measured?
15. What type of participation (debate, discussion, etc.)?
16. Do you keep physical track of a student's participation in discussion for final evaluation?
17. Is critical thinking considered a goal of this course?
18. Is it listed as an Intended Learning Outcome (ILO)?
19. If so, how is this skill measured? Through what kinds of assignments or activities?

General perceptions of students' communication ability in English
1. How would you rate your students' overall language competence?
2. Writing, reading, speaking?
3. In your opinion, how can students' language skills be nurtured and developed?

Appendix E: Business courses that included some reference to writing in the syllabus review

Major	Course	Writing Type	Weight	Additional comments
Accounting	Intermediate Financial Accounting	Essays/reports/research project	10%	Writing is mentioned in the ILOs*
				Writing is a Certified Public Accountant exam requirement
Accounting	Managerial Accounting	Essays	N/A	
Accounting	Auditing	Reports and team projects	30%	Writing is mentioned in the ILOs.
				Writing skills are formally mentioned in the assessment section.
Hospitality	Hospitality Purchasing	Project	25%	Writing is indirectly mentioned in the ILOs: "to develop and document policies."
Management	Organizational Behavior	Book Review	20%	
Management	Business Ethics & Professional Responsibility	Cases/Assignments	55%	Not clear what the written work is
Marketing	Advertising & Promotion	Portfolio	25%	
		Case Study Analysis	15%	

*ILO: Intended Learning Outcome

Appendix F: Stage 3 samples of matrices arrived at through the data analysis

The primary findings matrices were arrived at through a clustering process. Matrices of individual themes were created, and then those themes were clustered together to arrive at the three primary findings that are presented first. Examples of individual theme matrices are provided below the primary findings:

Primary Finding 1, with supporting themes

The methodology of the cultural studies courses does not promote skill/literacy enhancement, explicitly or implicitly.

- "Inconsistent and ineffective group work"
- "Lack of research designed activities"
- "Use of L1 in class"
- "Uneven or ineffectual feedback given to students"

Primary Finding 2, with supporting themes

Neither students nor teachers believe these courses serve to nurture English writing skills.

- "Purpose of CS is not language skill acquisition"
- "Purpose of the courses is to develop critical thinking"
- "Content courses/content coverage as the primary ILO"

Primary Finding 3, with supporting themes

Either students fail to understand the importance of reading for the development of their communicative skill or the readings do not lend themselves to this function due to their level of difficulty.

- "The texts are too difficult for the students."
- "Students generally do not read the assigned readings and/or do not understand what they've read."
- "Students rely heavily on Spark notes for comprehension".
- "This is not a reading culture."

Following are a sample of the matrices for the themes that informed the Primary Findings. P# refers to data from a professor and the number of the interview, and FG identifies data from the student focus group.

Matrices of data for two of the themes in Primary Finding 1:

Theme: Inconsistent and ineffective group work

- "In small groups they could take the discussion anywhere. I want the discussion to be purposeful." P3
- "Rarely use group work because there is a lot of material to cover—lecture and class discussion." P1
- "No group work—sometimes discussion but not always." P4

- "All lecture and discussion." P5
- "What happens in class depends on the 'doctor,' if there is group work or lecture." FG

Theme: Uneven or ineffectual feedback given

- "I tried to do what the teacher wanted me to on the next exam but I got the same grade." FG
- "We don't know how grades are arrived at and how we can improve." FG
- "Some professors just want length, so you can write a recipe in the middle of your answer and they'll never know since they don't read closely anyway." FG
- "Instructors are interested in content: how much we know. They should ask us direct questions and we give direct answers (not require essay answers on exams)." FG
- "I give feedback on speech and writing." P2
- "I offer feedback on short assignments and presentations." P3
- "Why do I have to worry about their English skills? Do I have to become an English teacher?" P1
- "I will underline language errors." P4
- "I have a reputation for pointing out mistakes." P5
- "I give group feedback after the first exam and then I mark the language pretty extensively." P7

Matrices of data for two of the themes in Primary Finding 2:

Theme: Instructors' academic role

- "I am not teaching English; it's not my purpose in these classes." P7
- "I will try to teach them words, but [teaching students how to write] is not my job". P1
- "Maybe the English courses need to be tougher. English department needs to fail more." P8
- "These are not English courses after all." FG

Theme: Instructors claim that the development of ideas and critical thinking are the aims of their courses.

- "We are interested in educating them in opinions and ideas and history." P7
- "Critical thinking is the absolute objective." P5

5 An Arabian Gulf: First-Year Composition Textbooks at an International Branch Campus in Qatar

Mysti Rudd
TEXAS A&M UNIVERSITY (QATAR)

Michael Telafici
TEXAS A&M UNIVERSITY (QATAR)

The two case studies presented in this chapter explore the cultural complexities of adopting American-authored textbooks and materials to teach first year composition (FYC) at an international branch campus in Qatar. Through surveys, observation and student writing, the authors investigate the extent to which their students engage with the American textbooks each has adopted—They Say, I Say with Readings (Graff, Birkenstein & Durst, 2012) and Writing about Writing (Wardle & Downs, 2011). To foster culturally sensitive adaptation of FYC content and promote student-centered pedagogy, the authors posit guidelines for localizing the content of FYC courses for English as Additional Language students.

Keywords: pedagogy; composition; FYC; IBC; textbook adoption

As of March 2015, there were roughly 250 International Branch Campuses (IBCs) open or in development or planning scattered across the globe. Ninety of these are IBCs of American universities, over twice as many as the second most common home country, the United Kingdom (Cross-Border Education Research Team, 2015). In the Middle East–North Africa (MENA) region alone, 56 IBCs from various home countries currently operate, with the vast majority of these hosted by Gulf Cooperation Council (GCC) countries, a dozen of which are U.S.-based institutions. What is also noticeable is the flow of importing countries and exporting countries. Taken together with the United States, Canada, the United Kingdom, Australia, and Ireland, Anglophone home institutions account for 60% of all IBC home institutions, compared to zero for the GCC (Cross-Border Education Research Team, 2015). This is just one facet of the global inequality of the provider-consumer network in international education (Altbach, 2010; see also Hodges and Kent; and Miller and Pessoa, this volume, for additional studies on IBCs in the MENA region).

Along with this proliferation of IBCs of American universities in the MENA region in the last fifteen years, the American college curriculum requirement of first-year composition (FYC) has also been exported. Depending on the particular branch campus and the major/degree offered, additional FYC courses are sometimes added to the branch campus curriculum in order to accommodate English as an Additional Language (EAL) learners (for additional discussions of how required composition has been implemented, successfully and unsuccessfully, within MENA-based universities, see also Annous, Nicolas, and Townsend; Arnold, DeGenaro, Iskandarani, Khoury, Sinno, and Willard-Traub; Austin; Jarkas and Fakhreddine; Miller and Pessoa; and Uysal, this volume). At Texas A&M at Qatar (TAM-Q) where we teach, these prerequisite courses for FYC are frequently taught by TESOL-trained (Teachers of English to Speakers of Other Languages) teachers. Although the number of semesters of required FYC-type courses is extended to meet the needs of the learners of English as an additional language enrolled at TAM-Q, more often than not, the textbooks adopted for FYC remain the same as those of the home campus. This is not an unusual practice, as the lifting of an entire curriculum and its transplantation to an international branch campus is a common occurrence among the "crossborder curriculum partnerships" that include IBCs (Waterval, Frambarch, Driessen & Scherpbier, 2014). Agreements for IBCs in Education City in Doha, Qatar dictate that the home institutions recreate programs at the host institution that replicate the curricula of the home campus as much as possible. The replication of home campus requirements includes the qualifications of the faculty, the standards for student admission, the sequence of courses required in the degree plan, and, sometimes, even the textbooks to be used. But adoption of particular textbooks endorsed by the home campus does not ensure a good fit for the students enrolled at the local host institution. In this chapter, each of us takes a closer look at the concerns raised by both teachers and students and share the conclusions we have come to based on our separate experiences of adopting Americentric textbooks to teach FYC to engineering majors at TAM-Q.

By reflecting on the usefulness of the textbooks we've adopted for our TAM-Q FYC courses, we hope to encourage FYC teachers across the MENA region to participate in examining both the value and the appropriateness of adopting western textbooks to teach EAL learners in the Middle East. At the end of this chapter, we offer a set of questions MENA writing teachers might use to reflect on the textbooks and materials they use to teach FYC. We then share our developing strategies for localizing the content of our TAM-Q FYC courses. Our ultimate goal is to foster critical reflection among teachers and deep listening for students so that culturally sensitive practices are realized in the teaching and evaluation of FYC in transnational contexts.

Methodology and Research Questions

To investigate the usefulness and appropriateness of the adoption of specific U.S. textbooks and materials to teach FYC at TAM-Q, we focused on the composition textbook that each of us has used for more than two semesters: Telafici has adopted the department-recommended *They Say/I Say: The Moves that Matter in Academic Writing with Readings* (Graff, Birkenstein & Durst, 2012), and Rudd has adopted *Writing about Writing* (Wardle & Downs, 2011). We address the following questions:

1. By focusing the FYC curriculum on U.S. authors, whose voices and what views are potentially marginalized? When preparing students to "find a way of entering a conversation with others' views" (Graff, Birkenstein & Durst, 2012, p. 4), whose views and values are being privileged?

2. To what extent do our students engage with the readings and assignments included in the textbooks each of us uses?

As a framework for exploring these questions, we looked to the guidelines for teaching FYC as recommended by two U.S.-based organizations: the National Council of the Teaching of English (NCTE) and the Council of Writing Program Administrators (CWPA). We relied on their descriptions of "best practices" in the field to determine to what extent we, as American instructors teaching at an American university in the Middle East, are following these guidelines and to what extent we should be following them. We also found several of the NCTE position statements (especially those on Second Language Learners and Second Language Writing) to be particularly useful frameworks for our case studies since these feature the perspectives of our EAL students. Many of the NCTE position statements argue for being inclusive of students' home languages and experiences, dating back to 1972 when the resolution that became known as SRTOL (Students' Right to Their Own Language) was first drafted by the Executive Committee of NCTE (Larson, 1974). Consequently, NCTE's emphasis on making room for students' experiences and home languages in the classroom speaks to us as writing teachers who want to value and empower our TAM-Q EAL students.

Our methods foreground the voices and views of our former students as they respond to our questions about the reading and writing assignments promoted by the FYC textbooks we have each adopted. As teacher-researchers, we also draw upon our own experiences of teaching from these textbooks, observing our students' responses to assignments and engaging in informal discussions with former students about the usefulness of these texts. We have also conducted anonymous surveys on textbook satisfaction and reading preferences in our FYC courses. Through these venues, our students have made their voices heard. From the student perspectives gained from these data, we discuss the usefulness and appropriateness of adopting two textbooks, *They Say, I Say with Readings* and *Writing about Writing*, to teach FYC to engineering students at a Middle East branch of our institution.

Exploring the Local Context for Our FYC Courses

If the understanding and application of rhetoric are objectives in most FYC courses (Council of Writing Program Administrators, 2008), then FYC teachers need to practice what we preach. Engaging students halfway across the world, who may or may not ever study or live in the US, requires student-centered teachers to adapt both their materials and their strategies. Linguistic imperialism—a system in which "the dominance of English is asserted and maintained by the establishment and continuous reconstitution of structural and cultural inequalities between English and other languages" (Phillipson, as cited in Canagarajah, 1995, p. 591)—is not simply a case of uneven valuation of what is written and how, but also what is read and what students are allowed or encouraged to write about.

First, we provide some detail on the local context: We teach in Qatar, a country whose broader national goals include creating an "[educational] system [that] will also encourage analytical and critical thinking . . . [one that] will promote . . . respect for Qatari society's values and heritage, and will advocate for constructive interaction with other nations" (Qatar National Vision, n.d.). Qatar Foundation, our umbrella sponsoring organization at Education City, is considered a driving "engine" within this national vision (Qatar Foundation, n.d.). While our FYC courses seek to foster analytical and critical thinking, we use readings and writing assignments from U.S.-based textbooks to allow students to practice these skills, directly affecting what students think and write about—hence our concern with using American texts in our branch campus in Qatar.

According to the Council of Writing Program Administrators' Outcomes Statement (2008), "Students should ... integrate their own ideas with those of others ... [and] understand the relationships among language, knowledge, and power." Further, NCTE (2009) states that teachers of second language writers should:

> [reflect] on how writing assignments may tacitly include *cultural assumptions or tacitly rely on knowledge of culturally-specific information* [emphasis added]. Writing instructors should also gain experience designing writing assignments with second language students in mind, considering topics that are culturally sensitive to second language writers and including directions easily understandable to multiple audiences.

Given these best practices, we wonder if the cultural assumptions and culturally-specific readings and writing assignment suggestions in our U.S. textbooks would be problematic for our student population, which at TAM-Q hovers at 50% Qatari nationals with very few U.S. students (Kent, personal communication, February 18, 2015).

As teachers with considerable combined experience working with international students, we are aware of the problems of teaching only an Americanized view. Yet as teachers who work without the security of tenure, we are also sensitive to program expectations for teaching from a departmentally sanctioned textbook. Thus, we both found ourselves teaching U.S. textbooks to our majority Arab FYC students, while steeling ourselves for the possibility that they might reject these books because they would not be able to relate to the views and topics. The students' feelings about these texts in response to our questions, however, proved complicated to interpret, as self-reported views can belie what lies below the surface. Our findings are described in the following case studies, the first narrated by Rudd and the second by Telafici.

Case Study #1 Conducted by Mysti Rudd
Rudd's Reasons for Adopting Writing about Writing (WAW)

When I first began teaching FYC at TAM-Q in Fall 2012, I was told that all of the English teachers in our department were expected to adopt the recommended common FYC text: *They Say / I Say: The Moves that Matter in Academic Writing with Readings* (*TSIS*) (Graff, Birkenstein & Durst, 2012).

In addition to the recommended text, however, every teacher was allowed to adopt other textbooks alongside *TSIS*. I chose to assign the shorter edition of *TSIS* (245 pages rather than 701 pages) that did not include an anthologized section of readings. For the readings that students were assigned to summarize and respond to, I adopted *Writing about Writing: A College Reader* (*WAW*) by Elizabeth Wardle and Doug Downs (2011).

I chose *Writing about Writing* (*WAW*) because I had been intrigued by Downs and Wardle's (2007) article "Teaching about Writing, Righting Misconceptions: (Re)Envisioning 'First-Year Composition' as an Introduction to Writing Studies" because I was familiar with many of the articles authored by American composition scholars; in addition, the suggested assignments, such as literacy narratives and discourse community ethnographies, convinced me that the *WAW* approach to teaching FYC would not be that different from other textbooks with readings. There were, however, some major differences in the genres, length, and reading level of the articles anthologized. A common criticism of adopting *WAW* is that the readings are too difficult for FYC students, particularly first-generation college students or students at open-access institutions. Yet I also knew that relying on a formal textbook such as *WAW* could add to my authority in the FYC classroom, since I was already familiar with the articles anthologized in the book. I was concerned about establishing my authority in the TAM-Q classroom because I sensed that I would need to make significant changes from being a teacher who had previously taught students in the US to becoming one of the few female professors (13 out of 81) teaching Arab engineering students in Doha's Education City.

Even though colleagues in my department cautioned me against adopting *WAW* because they believed it would be too difficult for the English academic language learners enrolled as engineering majors, I was determined to test this argument for myself. Rather than risk underestimating my students, I believe in holding high expectations for all of my students and then encouraging them to go beyond what they previously believed they could achieve. I hoped that the difficult reading level of the articles in *WAW* would cause my TAM-Q students to strive to achieve understanding. From the moment I decided to adopt *WAW*, however, I also planned to ask my students about its continued use in subsequent semesters.

It was not long before I began to receive feedback from students on *WAW*. After the reading assignment I gave the first day of the first semester, a conscientious student stopped by my office to exclaim, "Do you know how long it took me to read the assignment for tomorrow's class?" And before I could venture a guess, he replied, "Eight hours! It took me eight hours to read the

30-page introduction to the textbook!" As a seasoned teacher of FYC, I had suspected that the assigned reading would be challenging to these first-year students for whom English was a second or even third language (after Arabic and French), but I had also been advised by our program chair to make the course as rigorous as if I were teaching it at the home campus in College Station, Texas. And, during faculty orientation, we were informed that Sheikha Mozah, the Emir's wife and the visionary responsible for establishing the group of branch campuses in Qatar known as Education City, had mandated that the curriculum for students at the host institution mirror the curriculum of the home institution. On the other hand, I was warned by my local colleagues that our Arab engineering students at TAM-Q did not like to read. But just because many of my students didn't want to read didn't mean that they didn't need extensive practice in reading academic articles. I reasoned that future engineers needed to be careful and analytical readers and so, for the first time in my 15-year history of teaching FYC, I expected my students to spend as much time completing their reading assignments as they would drafting their writing assignments.

Due to the *WAW* reading load, I anticipated resistance, and I did indeed receive some complaints about the workload on end-of-semester teacher evaluations. However, I was surprised by the number of positive comments that my students made on the textbook satisfaction survey I distributed at the close of each semester, which I share in the next sections.

Findings from the Textbook Satisfaction Survey

To gather perspectives from my FYC students on my adoption of *WAW* and whether I should adopt it for subsequent semesters, I conducted a textbook satisfaction survey in Spring 2014. I administered this survey during the last day of class in each of my FYC sections, asking students to fill the form out anonymously. Of the 25 students who were asked to complete the survey, 22 placed their surveys in an envelope in the back of the classroom, which was then sealed, handed to the department secretary, and not delivered to me until grades had been posted for the semester. The survey was intended to elicit narrative responses as it asked open-ended questions, beginning with "What was your impression of WAW at the beginning of the course?"

First Impressions of WAW: Boring, Big, and Scary!

The most common adjectives chosen by survey respondents to describe their general reaction to the adopted textbook were *boring*, *scary* and *big*. I perceived these to be negative comments, as were the comments "not joyful" and "confusing," but these judgments were not as negative as the one by the survey respondent who simply had one word to describe the textbook: *dreadful!* Commenting on his first impression of *WAW*, another survey respondent wrote, "I thought it was very fluffy, but I hadn't even gone through it yet, just judging a book by its cover."

Some counted the pages of the readings and concluded that the articles were "too long" or "too hard." One student even admitted that her first response to *WAW* was the thought, "I am not going to read the articles." Not all of the survey respondents' first impressions of *WAW* were negative, however, as three respondents thought the book looked "professional" or "academic." One survey respondent claimed that *WAW* was her "first book that actually looks like a college book," adding, "And by first college book, I mean a black and white book with too many words and so little images." Only one survey respondent admitted to being curious about the contents of *WAW*.

Student Responses on the Usefulness of Assigned Readings from WAW

By the end of a semester, my students had been assigned to read as many as 20 *WAW* articles. When asked on the survey to name the articles that they found to be useful, nearly half of the respondents (10 out of 22) named the first long article assigned, "Helping Students Use Textual Sources Persuasively" by Margaret Kantz, originally published in *College English* in 1990. This finding is not surprising to me, as my FYC syllabus allots more class time for the study of this article than any of the other articles in *WAW*. Some of my students admitted to reading this article three times before they could understand it enough to write a coherent summary. But I wondered if it was not just the length of the article (16 single-spaced pages) but also the reading level that they struggled with.

But more than that, I suspect that Kantz's (1990/2011) proposition that texts (and by extension, authority) can and should be challenged is a radical concept for many of my Qatari students. In subsequent class discussions, at least one of my engineering students every semester has invariably brought up Kantz's (1990/2011) statement that "the only difference between a fact and a claim is how they are received by an audience" (p. 76). Many of my students find this claim unsettling, sometimes stating outright in the middle of class, for example, that "Gravity is a fact, not a claim!" At TAM-Q, I continue to assign Kantz's article because I believe that engineers, in particular, can benefit from questioning the bias of source material as they learn to question positivist approaches to the challenges facing us.

Final Impressions of WAW: "It Made Me a Better Reader"

When asked, "In what ways did your impression of the textbook *Writing about Writing* change by the end of the course?" only three students responded negatively, stating that their views hadn't changed, and that they found the textbook "still hard and the wording is difficult." The majority of students (16 out of 22), in contrast, shared mostly positive comments about their changed perceptions of the text, saying, for example:

- [The textbook] was not as boring as I thought, and it still impresses me and is not like an ordinary textbook.
- At the end of the course, when I have read most of [WAW's] articles, I had really important concepts that would influence my writing.
- I felt the hard words and complexity of [WAW] really made me a better reader. Sitting for two hours reading through a complicated text had to do something to my reading abilities.
- I stopped viewing this book as something difficult to comprehend. I began to understand that by multiple readings the concepts become comprehendible.
- My impression of the book changed when I saw my writing and reading skills improve.
- At the beginning of the course, I didn't think that the concepts of the book will stick in my mind and will change my writing. But now that I studied it, I believe that this book taught me about writing more than I learned in my 12 years of school. I also believe that I'll use this book as a reference for my writing in the future.

Because many of my students seemed burdened by the reading load plus the level of difficulty of the assigned readings, I expected the survey respondents to overwhelmingly recommend that I discontinue teaching from this text. Instead, the survey results showed the opposite to be true. Of the 22 survey respondents, 15 recommended that I adopt WAW for future sections of the course. Only one student registered an unequivocal "no," another two said they didn't know, and four fit in the "yes, but" category, qualifying their response with advice for adapting the curriculum for the subsequent semester. Here are the suggestions of those who responded with a qualified yes:

- I think there should be an explicit introduction of the book itself and what it contains.
- Yes, but it should be relied on less, where some articles are somewhat useless to me."

- Yes, but the content of the book could [be reduced]; you could pick some articles and give them as handouts.
- Yes, it is a challenging book to get around; however, with addition to the research journal and in-class discussion, everything will become clear.

Based on these answers, it is clear to me that if I do persist in adopting *WAW*, I must introduce the purpose of the book better, reduce the readings assigned, and maybe even invite previous students to talk about the course with current students in order to allay their fears of a text that most label as *big*, *boring*, and *scary* at first glance. But I am also wary of adhering too closely to the results of the satisfaction survey. More than anywhere I have ever taught, learning in the classroom in Qatar seems to be dependent on the relationship created between teacher and student. If students come to respect me and my teaching of FYC and believe that I deeply care about their learning, then they are likely to accept any text I adopt. But with that respect comes a responsibility to keep listening and learning from my students. If I expect my students to be open-minded and adaptable, then I too must leave my "comfort zone" of Americentric readings. Why, after all, should my students at IBCs have make most of the cultural accommodations?

Case Study #2 Conducted by Michael Telafici

Telafici's Considerations for Adoption of *They Say, I Say with Readings (TSIS)*

In Fall 2013 I taught my first FYC course at TAM-Q. While Rudd assigned *WAW* in addition to *TSIS*, I assigned the longer version of *TSIS* only. During the summer previous to that term, I obtained a copy of *TSIS* to begin planning my syllabus. What I found (not surprisingly, and quite reasonably, considering the text's intended audience) was a potentially useful book that contained cultural allusions well beyond what my previous four years of teaching experience in our English Foundation Program had taught me regarding what our TAM-Q students know about American culture and socio-economics.

I also noted that of the 44 readings in *TSIS*, only one reading was about the Middle East ("Reforming Egypt in 140 Characters?" by Dennis Baron), and even that one was not written by someone from the Middle East. In an attempt to remedy the lack of Arab-authored readings provided by *TSIS*, I consulted with Arab faculty at other Education City branch campuses to get ideas for sources. Sources offered included *qifanabki.com* (a Levantine site), *arablit.wordpress.com* website (also almost exclusively from Egypt, Iraq, the Levant—i.e., the traditional literary form). I was also pointed towards *jadaliyya.com*, an ostensibly pan-Arab news/commentary site, but whose Arabian Peninsula page front matter contained the goal "to provide an open and collaborative space for the production of knowledge *on a region that has largely escaped critical engagement*" (Jadaliyya.com, n.d [emphasis added]), so even local open source material seemed to be sparse.

However, there can be some advantages to using an American text, such as compensating for the limited number of Gulf/Qatari sources in English. American sources can also help students avoid politically difficult topics such as the volatile situation in many Arab countries during the Arab Spring as well as heightened political tensions even between Gulf States. The difficulty I faced in choosing topics or sources for student essays was informed by my past experiences with Qatari students who were explicit in their desire to portray their government and culture only in a very stable and positive light. Adopting *TSIS* could allow me to avoid topics that students in previous semesters were clearly uncomfortable discussing in class, often to the point of non-participation.

As a result, I decided to adopt *TSIS with Readings*. One potential difficulty avoided, but another created: in this context the NCTE (2009) dictum mentioned previously creates a tension between, on the one hand, reading materials that contain "cultural assumptions or tacitly rely on knowledge of culturally-specific information" (i.e., Americentric topics) and, on the other hand, "consider[ation] of topics that are culturally sensitive to second language learners." The latter rules out topics that may be perceived as not respecting local cultural and religious norms.

However, I also felt it important to gauge students' receptiveness to the text's readings, without prejudicing them either toward or against western or Arab sources, and to inquire into their previous reading material/habits. In my section of 16 students, all but one were native Arabic speakers, all had attended secondary school in Qatar, eleven were Qatari nationals, and five were residents of Qatar but nationals of another country. All were functionally bilingual. An in-class questionnaire, given at the beginning of the term, posed questions regarding their secondary school reading texts as well as their favorite books and authors. Based on their survey answers, I made two allowances regarding their first assignment:

1. Students would be free to choose topics and sources for essays (either from TSIS or not)
2. Students would analyze their chosen source for essay one (a rhetorical analysis).

Of all 16 sources selected by students for essay one, only one was written by an Arab author. This could, of course, be due in large part to the preponderance of English information on the internet, but data shows that even in the MENA region, most locally produced information is in English (Graham, Hogan, Straumann & Medhat, 2014). Throughout the remainder of the semester, students were free to choose their own sources for the remaining two major essays, but we used the readings in *TSIS* for class exercises and discussions, along with some open-source materials.

Findings of Survey: Student Reactions to TSIS

Toward the end of the semester, I administered a brief anonymous survey of students' perceptions of the class as a whole, containing three statements regarding the readings in *TSIS*, which the students rated on a five-point Likert scale (see Table 5.1).

Table 5.1: Results from survey questions on reading selections (n=16 students)

I find the essay topics in the book interesting	
Strongly Agree	15.4%
Agree	38.5%
Neither Agree nor disagree	23.1%
Disagree	23.1%
I wish we used the readings from They Say / I Say more	
Strongly Agree	7.7%
Agree	38.4%
Neither Agree nor disagree	30.8%
Disagree	23.1%
I wish the book had readings by authors from the Middle East	
Strongly Agree	15.4%
Agree	38.5%
Neither agree nor disagree	38.5%
Disagree	7.7%

It is noteworthy that while just over half agreed or strongly agreed with the statement "I wish the book had readings by authors from the Middle East," an equal percentage found the essay topics in the book interesting," and nearly half "[wished] we used the readings . . . more." Even though I surveyed a small sample of students (N=14), only one was not a native Arabic speaker, so I was surprised by the lack of interest in Arab sources.

How much of the predominance of English/western sources (of which *TSIS* is one example) are the students even aware of? Again, not wishing to prejudice my students, I gave them 10 minutes in class to look through the readings list in the table of contents in *TSIS*, then look at the readings themselves, confer with their peers in small groups, and develop a list of "noticeable patterns" in the readings and/or authors. During our class discussion, all student groups noted patterns of education/expertise in authors, which may suggest their interest in the rhetorical ethos of these sources. However, I was struck by the fact that not a single student in a classroom of local students on the Arabian Peninsula mentioned the fact that only one reading was about the Middle East.

The Use and Utility of TSIS: Notes from the "Field"

Americentric writing can affect student interactions and general comprehension. While exposure to new vocabulary is obviously encouraged in college, exactly what vocabulary students are exposed to and to what degree this exposure can be generally useful is a concern. During a class reading, only two of my students understood references to *The Sopranos* and *American Idol* contained in *TSIS*' introduction; such references are not only lost on our students, but these texts could be potentially insulting to Muslim and Gulf mores.

While I have taught students who have written about the popular U.S. television series *Breaking Bad* and violent video games, other less globalized facets of U.S. culture are not as well known, or even understood at all, or not even relevant to the majority of our students, especially the roughly 50% of all TAM-Q students who are native Qatari citizens. As a result, using the given *TSIS* readings for an all-class discussion involved more priming and vocabulary checking than would normally be required. In other words, I often found that when using American texts, we spent more class time attending to the cultural awareness and vocabulary needs of my students before we could begin "the meat" of teaching composition and rhetoric.

To give one example, a reading cluster in *TSIS* is titled "Is Higher Education Worth the Price?" Qatari students receive sponsorship from a Qatari company that includes full tuition payment and guaranteed employment upon graduation, so interest rates (forbidden in Islamic banking practices anyway) and Pell Grants are both unknown and irrelevant to these students' experiences or interests. It might not be surprising, then, that several students incorporated a much safer reading cluster, "Is Fast Food the New Tobacco?"

into essays on fast food and its effects on youth and adolescent health both worldwide and in Qatar. After all, Qatar has Burger King, but not Pell Grants.

What is the argument, then, for the overall utility of *TSIS* at TAM-Q, regarding both chapter content and readings? Other items in the previously mentioned survey (see Table 5.1) also revealed that fewer than one in three students reported having ever analyzed an essay, which argues *for* using the chapters of *TSIS*, as their coverage of both analytical and writing skills and the rhetorical "moves" are maybe even more useful for second language learners than for native speakers. For example, in several student conferences, students had difficulty determining which views were an author's and which were widely held or opposing views, a technique which is covered in chapter five of *TSIS*. I cannot definitely determine whether in all these instances an EAL issue caused the problem, but in one case, a student's misunderstanding was found to be based on an idiomatic difference between Arabic and English phrases that the student and I discussed in detail. In this case, since *TSIS* deals with explicit templates and signal phrases, the book could be at least as useful to EAL students as to native speakers, if not more so.

On the other hand, an over-reliance on templates/formulae is often cited as a *bête noir* of our English faculty in both formal and informal meetings. Students who have learned to introduce successive body paragraphs with a simple "firstly, secondly, thirdly" formula in our English Foundation program have been noted to struggle in developing more particular and relevant transitions between paragraphs. Adherence to templates and formulae do not necessarily prepare students to develop arguments or analyze sources. Criticism of using *TSIS* to teach FYC in American contexts has been published in *CEA Forum* by Amy Lynch-Biniek (2009) as she points out that adherence to templates can encourage students to bypass critical thinking, but the scholarship on using *TSIS* to teach FYC at IBCs is nonexistent.

The Verdict on Using TSIS to Teach FYC at an IBC: Some Answers, More Research Questions

Altogether, the ambivalent survey responses to the existing readings, the limited desire for more Middle Eastern readings, and the students' own selections of almost exclusively non-Middle Eastern favorite authors in the survey beg several further questions:

1. Do our students want to resist our textbooks and assignments but decide it is simply easier to accommodate? The only documented resistance in the three successive sections of FYC I have taught has been

four student essays arguing that Arabic is under attack by the emphasis on English in Qatar.
2. Are they accommodating because they are in an English class in an American university and therefore expect texts to be written by western authors in English rather than by Middle Eastern authors in English?
3. Does using western sources and topics allow Qataris to avoid writing and discussing delicate local social and political issues?

Perhaps to take advantage of this "safe distance" created by writing about western topics, one student wrote an essay on the hijab in the western world (not its use in the Muslim world), and another student wrote about women's rights without a single direct mention of Qatar. Another FYC student wanted to write about wasta (nepotism or favor-giving in Arabic) in Qatar, but did not find enough sources in English. So, his choices were to use the Arabic sources (which I can't read) and possibly have them translated (web translation is notoriously inaccurate—I have even taught lessons using double-translation and Google Translate with my students to prove this point to them), or switch topics. It is interesting to consider how many accommodations and/or adaptations like this may be happening as students choose their writing topics—or for that matter—how long accommodations like this have been happening.

Another measure of the possible hegemony of English sources was evident in the in-class questionnaire item that asked students to "name [their] favorite books and/or authors" without mentioning English or Arabic specifically. While two students answered that they had neither favorite authors nor books, of 22 authors named, only one was Arab—the great Egyptian Nobel laureate Naguib Mahfouz—and of the 25 books mentioned, only two were by Arab authors. It should be noted that the Arab author and books were mentioned by the same student (who also offered eight of the favorite book mentions). Leading the list of favorite authors (tied at three mentions) were Charles Dickens and J. K. Rowling, followed by William Shakespeare (two mentions). Based on the survey results, our students displayed a decidedly Anglophone/Anglophile bent in their reading before they even encountered FYC and *TSIS*.

Navigating the Gulf of Local Language and Content in Our FYC Classrooms

In order to approximate the best practices (as outlined by NCTE) of localizing and contextualizing the practice of teaching FYC to English Language

Learners in a global context, each of us individually and then together have considered the following reflective questions:

- How can I adapt materials to the local context?
- How can I meet curricular requirements and respect local notions of ethos?
- How can I be more inclusive of local voices in the readings I assign in FYC?
- How can I inform myself about local voices and views, considering many of these can be unwritten or published in different languages?
- How can I use western readings/texts as opportunities to encourage mutual intercultural curiosity?
- How can I invite the students' home cultures into the FYC classroom?
- How can I be an advocate for localizing the teaching of FYC at my university?
- How can I create consensus among my colleagues in moving towards a more inclusive and culturally sensitive FYC curriculum?
- How can I privilege the voices and views of my students in the FYC classroom?

By pondering these questions that have neither permanent nor finite answers, we aim to critically reflect on our current FYC practices and to constantly strive to be responsive to our local context and the needs of the students who populate our classrooms.

Although a reflective practitioner is never finished with the work of localizing and contextualizing the teaching of writing, we have made a few "baby steps" in our endeavors to create culturally inclusive classrooms at TAM-Q. To counter the absence of Middle Eastern texts and sources and to invite the home cultures of our students into the FYC classroom, we have begun to adapt our FYC teaching practices in the following ways at TAM-Q:

- We allow students to use non-translated Arabic sources for their researched papers.
- We encourage students to conduct and record oral histories and ethnographies of their family and friends in their mother tongues.
- We expand our notions of texts to include non-print formats such as photographs, interviews, videos, commercials, and advertisements, inviting students to bring examples of these texts to class.
- We incorporate more discussion of assigned readings and invite students to contribute to the curriculum by suggesting class readings.

- We address the confluence of power, language, and identity by assigning and sharing digital narratives that chronicle students' various journeys, both academic and otherwise.
- We encourage students to share their projects with the larger community via websites and journal publications and to invite friends and family to their presentations.
- We encourage students to invite friends and family to their presentations.

As we make room for these practices and widen our definition of "texts," there will necessarily be less time in our courses and room in our FYC curriculum for the Americentric readings we have previously been assigning. Only by moving out of our comfort zones of relying solely on teaching with American texts will we as FYC teachers be able to more effectively localize our practice, better serve our students, and follow the rhetorical principles that we teach.

References

Altbach, P. G. (2004). Globalisation and the university: Myths and realities in an unequal world. *Tertiary Education and Management, (10)*1, 3–25. Retrieved from http://dx.doi.org/10.1080/13583883.2004.9967114.

Canagarajah, A. S. (1995). [Review of the book *Linguistic imperialism* by Robert Phillipson]. *Language in Society, 24*(4), 590–594.

Council of Writing Program Administrators. (2008). WPA Outcomes Statement for First-Year Composition. Retrieved from http://wpacouncil.org/positions/outcomes.html.

Cross-Border Education Research Team. (2015). Branch Campus Listing. Retrieved from http://www.globalhighered.org/.

Graff, G., Birkenstein, C. & Durst, R. (2012). *They say/I say: The moves that matter in academic writing with readings* (2nd ed.). New York: W.W. Norton & Co.

Graham, M., Hogan, B., Straumann, R. K. & Medhat, A. (2014). Uneven geographies of user-generated information: Patterns of increasing informational poverty. *Annals of the Association of American Geographers, 104*(4), 746–764.

Jadaliyya (n.d.). Arabian Peninsula. Retrieved from http://arabianpeninsula.jadaliyya.com/.

Kantz, M. (2011). Helping students use textual sources persuasively. In E. Wardle & D. Downs (Eds.), *Writing about writing: A college reader* (pp. 74–91). Boston: Bedford St. Martin's.

Lynch-Biniek, A. (2009). Filling in the blanks: They say, I say, and the persistence of formalism. *CEA Forum, 38*(2). Retrieved from https://web.archive.org/.web/20130131120128/http://www2.widener.edu/~cea/382lynchbiniek.htm.

Larson, R. L. (1974). Resolution on Language. *College Composition and Communication*, 25(3). Retrieved from http://www.ncte.org/library/NCTEFiles/Groups/CCCC/NewSRTOL.pdf.

National Council of Teachers of English (2009). CCCC Statement on Second Language Writing and Writers. Retrieved from http://www.ncte.org/cccc/resources/positions/secondlangwriting.

Qatar Foundation. (n.d.). About. Retrieved from http://www.qf.org.qa/about.

Qatar National Vision 2030. (n.d) Retrieved from http://www.mdps.gov.qa/en/qnv1/pages/default.aspx.

Texas A&M University at Qatar. (2014). *2014–2015 University catalog*. Doha, Qatar. Retrieved from http://www.qatar.tamu.edu/wp-content/uploads/documents/records/catalog/14_15_catalog.pdf.

Wardle, E. & Downs, D. (2011). *Writing about writing: A college reader*. Boston: Bedford St. Martin's.

Waterval, D. G. J., Frambarch, J. M., Driessen, E. W. & Scherpbier, A.J.J.A. (2014). Copy but not paste: A literature review of crossborder curriculum partnerships. *Journal of Studies in International Education*, 19(1), 65–85.

6

Great Expectations or Great Outcomes? Exploring the Context of English Language Policy Transfer in Bahrain

Aneta L Hayes
KEELE UNIVERSITY (UK)

Nasser Mansour
EXETER UNIVERSITY (UK)

> This chapter addresses English language education and writing pedagogy in secondary schools in Bahrain and explores the impact of societal factors on the operational delivery of education programs that have been borrowed from another country. The authors draw on data from focus groups held with teachers from 10 secondary schools in order to gain a better understanding of how a new teaching policy is indigenized by people on the ground. The chapter concludes that Communicative Language Teaching (CLT) borrowing in Bahrain presently reflects merely the government's great expectations, with real outcomes suffering from a time-lag. The authors argue that the students' personal context competes with general economic developments in the country, resulting in discordant readings of the importance of the new reforms.
>
> Keywords: English-language education; socio-cultural frameworks; teacher perceptions; transition to higher education; Bahrain

International policy borrowing is a topical issue in the Middle East, as importing educational successes observed in other countries is seen as a "quick fix" to internal dissatisfaction, negative external evaluation, economic competition, and globalization (Phillips & Ochs 2004), all of which have affected the region to a varying extent in different countries (see also Uysal, this volume). The growth of policy borrowing in culturally diverse states, however, raises questions about its viability in the socio-cultural context surrounding the pedagogic culture in the target community. At the time of this writing, we, the authors, were involved in a three-year long study, researching the transition of Bahraini students to western-style universities whose national education context was just being transformed as a result of changes to English language education, based on the success of a Communicative Language Teaching (CLT) program in Singapore. The issues that were raised in the study about the role of socio-cultural frameworks of schools in such transitions prompted us to focus on the perceptions of secondary English language teachers. The teachers participating in this research provided insights into how a new policy became indigenized and adapted in the country's education system. The aim of this chapter, therefore, is to present teacher perceptions regarding the impact of the socio-cultural context on the potential for successful CLT implementation in schools in Bahrain (for other discussions of faculty perceptions on curriculum implementation in the MENA region, see Annous, Nicolas & Townsend; Austin; Hodges & Kent; Miller & Pessoa; Theado, Johnson, Highly & Omar, this volume).

This chapter draws on focus group data with secondary teachers, but before turning to our focus group findings, we begin with a discussion of the latest English teaching and writing pedagogy initiatives in Bahrain. These initiatives have been introduced with dual aims of increasing students' opportunities to study in foreign universities, either in the region or worldwide, and of creating an education system that can support the county's transition to the knowledge economy. The socio-cultural context and specific intricacies of secondary education in Bahrain, however, present an interesting narrative system for the development of these reforms. We thus review relevant literature on the impact of societal factors in the "target" culture on the operational delivery of programs that have been borrowed. We suggest that, particularly in our example, an analysis of community, parental, and student influences on English language education and writing pedagogy is essential if we are to understand why international transfers of programs become indigenized in a particular way, which, in turn, may cause some of the concerns about the levels of student preparedness for university writing in English. Next, we explain our research, our methods, and describe our participants. After the discussion of findings, we offer an analysis of how the voices of our teachers helped us develop a more advanced understanding of what happens to programs and pedagogies that are not locally situated.

Background to English Education and Writing Pedagogy in Bahrain

The history of education in Bahrain indicates that the country's first schools were developed with an emphasis on the mastery of "pre-packaged" knowledge in certain subjects to respond as quickly as possible to the growing demand for literate people who could acquire information quickly to teach and work in offices (Shirawi, 1989). M. K. H. Quaddummi (1995) explains that this view on education is the reason why rote learning and inculcation became culturally ingrained methods of teaching. The focus on "usable" knowledge also indicates that education has traditionally been positioned as an important chain in the country's economic development, with very early investment in other sectors than just the oil industry. The role of education supporting the economy became particularly prominent in the early 2000s when the country began preparations for the transition to the knowledge economy, urging significant reforms of the education sector. For secondary schools, as well as the primary and intermediate sectors, this meant undergoing changes under the umbrella of National Education Reform Initiatives (NERI) whose aims, *inter alia*, were to graduate students with professional qualifications to a degree level and emphasize practical skills and English language development applicable to the labor market (Bahrain Economic Development Board, 2008).

The intricacies surrounding the secondary system in Bahrain and the national schools in particular, however, beg the question of the relevance of reforms focused on preparing future university students and citizens able to fill the gap in the labor market. Students who usually populate national secondary schools come from expatriate families who were brought to Bahrain on government employment contracts to work in military and police sectors. The jobs in these sectors have been occupied by members of these families for generations, which historically and politically have been "reserved" for them. Nowadays they have also come to symbolize membership and belonging to a particular community. What, among other things, characterizes these communities is a very instrumental and pragmatic approach towards school and education, particularly the English language, which was commonly claimed by the parents to be unnecessary for their children who were preparing to continue their jobs in the government sectors, where Arabic is used (Abdulmajeed, 1995). This may suggest that students will prefer the inculcation methods culturally developed in Bahrain, as the context in which their future career prospects are located is likely to shape views that education is valuable when it facilitates a quick completion of the secondary certificate, which, in turn, also facilitates the transition to the careers occupied by their parents. Arabic is also the primary language the students use at home and at school, and the fact that education in national schools is delivered in Arabic makes English an additional "outlier." While this might be more relevant for boys than for girls, female students may also be attracted to traditional pedagogies, as they offer opportunities for higher grades and status (Hayes, Mansour & Fisher, 2015). Such national attitudes are thus likely to cause some tensions between the new purposes of education linked to the economic vision for Bahrain and the more traditional, "domestic" views. If the new pedagogies are not relevant for the students, what does this then mean for the teachers? What decisions will teachers make and how will they position themselves to tailor their ways through the new reforms?

While researching the transition issues in the broader study, we uncovered important themes about expectations and reality in conversations with our teachers. We report below how CLT, being an approach emphasizing classroom interaction and paying little attention to grammatical accuracy (Richards & Rodgers, 1986), is viewed to be affected by the pre-existing arrangements in the national education system in Bahrain. Following CLT, students are expected to interact with others in the classroom, either in group or pair work, but also in writing. This interaction involves completing tasks that are mediated through language and involves negotiation of information and information sharing. For example, asking for directions and asking supporting questions to make sure individuals take the correct route involve exchanges of information regarding the local area. Broadly speaking, assessment is therefore based on evaluating levels of communication and students' competence in achieving the objectives within the constraints of their language proficiency (Richards, 2006). The teachers in our study noted that this differs from nationally set assessment arrangements in Bahrain that require high levels of mastery of knowledge and error-free competence. We explore this "mismatch" below.

The government in Bahrain introduced CLT at all levels of education in 2005 to shift English language pedagogy in the country from discrete language items to developing students' communication skills in English, self-expression, and thinking (Al-Baharna, 2005). Supporting this shift was a new genre-based writing pedagogy introduced in 2002 (Bax, 2006), grounded in the idea "that a more systematic approach to teaching of these skills could benefit from a more systematic approach to the kinds of *texts* included in the syllabus" (Bax, 2006, p. 321) The genre-based approach contained many CLT elements, as it focused on developing skills for communication. It was believed that the focus on genres provided a systematic approach to English teaching whereby teachers could focus on one area of writing at a time (e.g., writing a story or a letter of complaint), which would enable them to better support the students in advancing their skills as they could focus on one text at a time (Bax, 2006).

The findings that we report below give insights into the implementation of CLT that were perhaps unexpected by the policy makers, particularly in relation to the assumption that teachers were going to simply adopt the new pedagogies, or at least actively seek ways of their adaptation that would remain faithful to CLT. These insights are theorized below in the context of literature that places negotiations of school processes in the center of interactions between individuals and their socio-cultural contexts.

Theoretical Background

While being initially focused on the intercultural transition of students in Bahrain—that is, how students were negotiating their journeys from one culturally specific education setting to another—we focused our literature search on factors that affect this transition. Some studies discuss the impact of national culture on students' levels of adaptation to the new teaching and learning environment (e.g., Druzhilov, 2011; Jin, 2011; Serpell, 2007) and how students themselves experience the new learning environment, negotiating the influences from the past to adapt to the new teaching and social conditions in their host universities (e.g., Marginson 2014; Sovic, 2009). Other literature reminds us of the role of school in shaping particular student identities that may or may not have the required attributes to then progress to higher education (e.g., Mavor 2001). However, we were surprised to find that the effects of student aspirations on teachers' work and how the teachers subsequently position themselves to strike a balance between student and government goals is not discussed as a factor in transitions. This gap prompted us to theorize the findings we present below in the context of literature pointing to teacher decision-making, which we argue in the conclusion indicates that choosing policy to facilitate transition to higher education cannot simply be based on matching the pedagogy with the skills requirements at university. There is a chain of important decisions that are made prior to teachers undertaking new skills development.

This chain of decisions can be best explained by analytical perspectives that acknowledge the impact of socio-cultural factors surrounding teachers' school lives (e.g., Mansour, 2013). The context of the "target" country must therefore be considered, as its potential effect on the indigenization process is likely to determine how much of the borrowed model will retain its original elements (Phillips & Ochs, 2004). We noted in the research that the intricacies of the secondary context in Bahrain that we described above acted as powerful discourses affecting decisions of teachers regarding CLT, resulting in subjective interpretations of the best ways of tackling the conflict between the students' and the government's objectives. Research conducted elsewhere has shown similar outcomes and pointed out that societal beliefs underscoring the purpose of education and, subsequently, specific school structures, create a dynamic narrative for potential developments of the new policy (e.g., Das, Shaheen, Shrestha, Rahma & Khan, 2014; Li & Baldauf, 2011).

Furthermore, literature suggesting that teachers are not always willing to negotiate the established structures in light of the changing conditions of their work was particularly helpful in contextualizing our outcomes (e.g., Comber, 2011; Street, 2009). It has shown that how teachers respond to the new teaching agendas is contingent upon the perceived relevance of these agendas for students' needs and the values they place on education (Comber & Nixon, 2009) as well as whether complying with the new teaching policies may have reputational consequences for the teachers themselves (Hayes, 2016). Janks (2014), for instance, explains that attitudes towards policy and willingness to adopt it are developed based on the perceived social effects of engaging with it, particularly in terms of supporting parental aspirations regarding their children's future job prospects. Such insights helped to contextualize the teacher decision-making process that was revealed in this study with regard to what may cause delays and modifications to the intended outcomes of policy borrowing. We argue that these modifications and outcomes invariably have an impact on what skills are actually developed at school level, challenging the idea that policy borrowing is a "quick fix" and a guarantee for their development.

Methods and Participants

We report in this chapter on data from teacher focus groups. We chose focus groups as the approach to data collection because we were interested in the views of people who have shared similar experiences with CLT implementation (Stewart, Shamdasani & Rook, 2007).

English teachers from 10 secondary schools across five governorates in Bahrain took part in this study. Governorates refer to five districts into which Bahrain is split which have their own councils. Schools in each governorate were randomly selected. The total number of English teachers employed in these 10 schools was 85 and the total number of teachers included in all focus groups was 60. The teachers who were included in the study were all working full-time, all native speakers of Arabic, and of Bahraini, Egyptian, Jordanian, or Tunisian origin. Their teaching experience varied from one to more than 12 years and the age range was between 21 and 60 years old. All teachers had a teaching degree.

One focus group session was held in each school. During the focus groups, we inquired about the general pedagogy of teaching English, the context of English teaching practice in Bahraini schools and the challenges of implementing the present curriculum. The teachers were also asked to elaborate how they thought the context of their teaching practice influenced students' transition to university. All focus group questions can be found in the Appendix.

All focus groups were audio-recorded and transcribed in full. The focus group questions were written in English and Arabic but the discussions were conducted in English. On average, the sessions lasted between 40–60 minutes. To code the data, schools were randomly assigned a letter from A-J, and teachers were given numbers. So, for example, a response coded Teacher1B was from the teacher who spoke first in school B. All data were sent back to participants for validation, and no comments with corrections were returned.

Data were analyzed using the Constant Comparative Method (Glaser, 1965) to identify whether any differences or similarities existed in the English teaching practices across the participating schools and in teacher perceptions on their role in transition. This involved breaking data into units and coding them to develop categories. These categories were constantly evaluated as they were compared among different focus groups (Glaser, 1965). Constant comparisons were also used because, in interpretive research, comparing among different participant groups develops greater confidence in the findings through using multiple sources of evidence (Andrade, 2009). Segments of transcribed texts were coded with key concepts that summarized their content, and these concepts were then grouped together based on similarities. For example, text segments coded "easy to get marks on assessment projects," "memorizing model answers," "copy and paste," "not transferable to university," were grouped under the larger category of "assessment." Analysis was undertaken by each researcher individually and then compared to develop a set of overlapping themes. Below, we present only findings relevant to teacher perceptions regarding the effects of the school context on CLT. They are grouped under two themes: a) Great Expectations and b) Policy Rejection?

Findings

Great Expectations

Teachers drew comparisons between what was expected when the new curriculum (CLT) was implemented and what was really happening in their classrooms. As explained earlier in this chapter, the rationale for the new curriculum was to shift the focus of language teaching from "coverage" of the material to CLT, but according to the majority of teachers, this did not happen because:

> The curriculum is too long, we never have the time to teach them, we only perform lessons, that's all. We never teach. There are a lot of things in the book [all agree]. And if you're not going to deliver the whole thing, the students will also lose it [referring to what might be tested in the exam] and they won't trust the book any more. (Teacher 1E)

This type of comment, which was representative of many teachers, elucidates how the teachers were making sense of the new English teaching reform in light of traditional understandings of learning.

But it was also indicated that the expectations of the current curriculum could not be met because the decision about CLT was not adequate to the context in which it was being implemented, as this teacher noted:

> In my opinion, it's not bad [the curriculum]: the problem is not with the book though because even if you bring a simple book you can still make use of it. It's the system, people around you, administration, Ministry of Education, the department of curriculum, the administration in the school, you know, the whole thing. And the students' level, some of them you can't teach what they want you to teach. (Teacher 5G)

The comment from Teacher 5B highlights the incoherence of the decision to implement CLT, further suggesting that the new vision for English language education for Bahrain has not been accompanied by similar changes in domestic values and social developments. This was reflected in many conversations with our teachers who referred to aspects of teaching and learning as well as the socio-cultural intricacies surrounding secondary education in Bahrain.

First, a lot of teachers displayed contradictory views on language development to those promoted by CLT, as explicit focus on grammar was seen by the teachers as essential. For example, Teacher 1D said: "The directive is not to teach grammar. Grammar must come through texts. But it doesn't work [teachers all agree]. They must know the rules. They don't know the tenses." Second, the teachers also seemed to feel that students would not learn effectively when involved in communicative tasks when there is no teacher control. As one teacher explained:

> This approach [CLT] gives them new opportunities, shows them that there are other ways of teaching than those by means of which they have been taught so far. [But] if they

see the teacher who is serious and authoritarian, they will follow. (Teacher 2H)

The need for the teachers being in control of the classroom was perceived as resulting from students' understandings of learning but also teachers' own experiences, which indicated that:

> With the communicative approach, they make a big noise and they don't learn. Or some of the students work, the others copy from them and then that's it. They need something that would allow the teacher to control the class more. (Teacher 5D)

Whether these comments were grounded in teachers' own beliefs about learning that might have been shaped by their own socio-cultural context could not be concluded from the research. What was, however, evident is that teachers' choices to follow the traditional methods were informed by the interplay of students' career aspirations, communal attitudes that shape them, as well as national understandings of competence and the value of good grades. Details of this finding are provided in the second part of this results section.

Here, however, the teachers cited below explain the impact of familial connections and political settlements, which highlights the point made earlier regarding the incoherence of the government's decision to invest in education preparing for the transition to knowledge-based jobs. Teachers explained that students do not have aspirations to work in these jobs, suggesting that the new reforms have not been accompanied by relevant societal changes. For example:

> Here in the region, we have one big problem, students are not motivated because they go for the military jobs. They are not motivated to become a doctor or an engineer, and so on. Their motivation for learning is low because of this. The government makes it very easy for the students here in the Gulf to take military jobs, in military institutions, so why should they bother? (Teacher 3A)

A teacher in another school continued, noting that:

> The highest motivation for most of the students is to go and work as a soldier. They want to get their certificates and then go and serve in the army. They don't care . . . So they just sit in class, do nothing, they get their marks and in the end they get their certificates. (Teacher 2I)

The very pragmatic attitude towards education underscored by the objective of "getting their certificates" seems to then translate into very instrumental strategies, enabling students to meet course requirements with minimum effort. The teachers commented that as a result of this attitude, students "copy and paste from the Internet or they submit it in a foreign language" (Teacher 3B).[1] Also, "they pay a stationary [a little corner shop] to do it for them" (Teacher 1B).

There was a general sense among the teachers that such strategies were enabled because "for examining the writing topics, the questions are always from the book" (Teacher 8C). This also suggests a deeper paradigmatic issue, reflecting that necessary structural changes have not yet taken place to support the implementation of the borrowed policy. The teacher quoted below explains that the old system of preparing assessments by the Ministry of Education advisors who tend to rely on the content of the book results in facilitating the traditional forms of learning based on inculcation. This reliance contradicts the objectives of the new policy, suggesting that if CLT is to become successfully implemented:

> We don't want the examinations to concentrate only on the book. We want to encourage the students to read outside the book. The exam people, they don't go outside the book. For examining the writing topics, the questions are always from the book, we don't want this, we [should] teach the skill, how to describe, we don't want the exam paper to focus only on this. (Teacher 8C)

The comments in this section indicate that the new CLT policy has mainly been developed at the surface level and at present only reflects the government's great expectations. They also point to a complex interplay among factors related to teacher beliefs, student aspirations and structural changes in need of revisiting, all of which are predicted by the teachers to be a barrier to their fulfillment. The section below presents the results of this interplay, suggesting that teacher ambivalence and positioning in the borrowed system may be linked to socio-cultural and survival reasons that have subsequently led to an informal rejection of CLT.

Policy Rejection

One of the most significant themes that emerged in the research, pointing to an informal rejection of policy, was that the teachers did not actively seek ways of implementing CLT within the constraints of the "target" culture.

Rather, they reported subjugation to student and parental pressures. Because there have been no structural changes to the ways exams are designed and administered, and because "the students only study for the final exam [and] they don't want extra information" (Teacher 1A), the teachers explained that they continue to facilitate exam preparation through traditional ways of memorization.

> They take the model writing from the teachers. They just need the model for the exam. Yes, we provide them with the model writing . . . They hate you when you try to help them and explain what should be done first and then next, they don't like that, just direct monotonous way of teaching. That's it. (Teacher 3B)

It was also concluded that some teachers may have not actively sought to implement the new strategies because a number of participants indicated their support for teaching methods that can facilitate traditionally understood forms of competence, built through accuracy and certified by high marks. For example:

> All Arabs think in this way, you see. All of them want to get high marks and they stick to the written topics they will be examined in, so they study them carefully, by heart, to get high marks. But from my point of view, *that's their right*. (Teacher 2J)

The students' needs and teachers' own beliefs thus seemed to have informed decision-making that might have led to an informal rejection of CLT. The teachers in this study explained that they did not seek ways of trying to implement the new teaching pedagogy because they experienced a lot of resistance from the students and their parents. In refusing to implement the new pedagogy, they avoided negative evaluations of their own professionalism:

> They have model answers and they learn by heart. But, to be frank, it's not only the teacher, it's not the teacher's choice to do that. In the past, the ministry used to give us the topic that will be on the exam and we used to give them a piece of writing and they learnt it by heart. And the teacher who doesn't do this will be blamed by the students and the parents. (Teacher 1E)

Another teacher added:

> ... if you want to come up with ideas that are more creative and when the students can express themselves clearly, the newspapers will write that this is irrelevant and prevents the students' progress. So there are a lot of complaints about teachers. (Teacher 4F)

Negative evaluations seemed to be a big concern for teachers. Often, a sense of defense of their professionalism could be noted in conversations through comments which highlighted that teachers were prepared to teach CLT through their training but chose not to because they were deterred by the context:

> We've been through our training and we know about different methods, but when you try to apply them here, it does not match, some students cannot work with those methods. (Teacher 2D)

The decision-making process presented above was one of the most significant themes that emerged in the broader research to which the findings in this chapter are linked. We felt that it was important to present them here because they point to the limitations of our original approach to investigating transitions. Even though the findings presented here do not tell us much about the actual transition of students, they point to teacher decision-making, and the socio-cultural influences on which these decisions rest, as an important undercurrent in policy borrowing, a process that is often initiated to facilitate transitions. We expand on this point in the concluding remarks below.

Concluding Remarks

We presented in this chapter teacher perceptions regarding the impact of the context of schools in Bahrain on the potential for CLT implementation. We also showed that the socio-cultural context and specific intricacies of secondary education in Bahrain present a dynamic narrative system that was seen by the teachers to affect this potential. We found teacher choices and the undercurrents of their decision-making particularly interesting as the conversations revealed how the teachers position themselves in a borrowed education system, to strike a balance between student and government goals. Exploring teacher perceptions also gave us a more advanced understanding of what happens to programs and pedagogies that are not locally situated, suggesting answers to global questions of why policy transfers may not lead to the outcomes for which they are intended (see also Uysal, this volume). In our case, teacher sense-making had an impact on the outcomes of policy that was implemented in Bahrain to facilitate transition to higher education, suggesting that decisions to borrow a program cannot be simply based on matching the pedagogy with the skills requirements at university and assuming that this will provide a "quick fix" to the existing problems, when, simultaneously, the new teaching policy may be rejected by teachers in schools. Further developments of the research suggest that the perceptions of the type of skills needed at university were also inadequate (Hayes, Mansour & Fisher, 2015).

It seems that the socio-cultural intricacies of the secondary context in Bahrain acted as a powerful discourse affecting decisions of teachers regarding CLT. This then resulted in individual interpretations of the best ways of acting and taking decisions to continue to teach in traditional ways. Such teacher behavior also points to deeper issues related to the political incoherence of borrowing policy to improve life chances of young people in the country in a socio-political context where these life chances are not something that students aspire to. The conversations with teachers revealed that this incoherence is created by a lack of aspiration to do knowledge-based jobs, not implementing relevant structural changes in the national assessment system, and negative teacher evaluations by parents or in the national press that point to very traditional understandings of education still held in Bahrain.

While these conclusions concur with the literature regarding teacher choices (e.g., Comber & Nixon, 2009; Das et al., 2014; Janks, 2014; Li & Baldauf, 2011), as well as broader skepticism towards developments such as CLT in the Arabian Gulf (Aydarova 2013; Bahgat 1999), they also point to the negative role that policy borrowing may play in national developments aiming to support students' transition to higher education. It seems that such policy borrowing resulted in decisions by teachers not to implement new CLT approaches or undertake new skills development initiatives, which in turn affected the operational success of the curriculum changes proposed under NERI. This study revealed a complex chain of decisions involving students, parents, and teachers as well as those responsible for national assessments, all of whom are likely to have an impact on the government's strategy to improve students' transition to higher education.

The findings reported here suggest that hopes underlying CLT borrowing in Bahrain at present merely represent the government's great expectations. The great outcomes, on the other hand, that the change in pedagogy, particularly in terms of writing, is expected to bring about may suffer from a time-lag, before domestic and social developments catch up with the speed of education reform in Bahrain. We argue that what causes these delays is related to the fact that students, parents, and teachers who are subject to the new education reforms cannot fully appreciate their objectives, as they still internalize approaches to learning and teaching through nationally held beliefs about education. These beliefs, particularly for students, seem to be reinforced by the political and employment settlements that were created by the nation-state a long time ago but that are still held in high regard by the locals, despite the overall global progress that the country has made (Bahrain Education Board, 2008). For teachers, the socio-cultural context seems to be informing their pedagogical decisions. We conclude that the students' personal and educational context competes with general economic developments in the country, resulting in discordant readings of the importance of the new reforms. We also believe that the juxtaposition of global economic developments with traditional career opportunities and practices towards achieving education competence is relevant to many MENA countries. We therefore hope that much could be made of our research in future work.

Note

1. The teachers explained in the focus groups that students pay little attention to the projects they submit and when they copy from the Internet, they do not notice that the material is not in English.

References

Abdulmajeed, M. Y. (1995). Motivational and socio-cultural contexts of learning English as an international foreign language: A case study of fresh college students in Bahrain (Unpublished doctoral dissertation). University of Wales, Cardiff.

Al-Baharna, S. S. (2005). *Assessment for teaching and learning: A manual for assessing English language learning for secondary.* Bahrain: Ministry of Education.

Andrade, A. D. (2009). Interpretive research aiming at theory building: Adopting and adapting the case study design. *The Qualitative Report, 14*(1), 42–60.

Aydarova, O. (2013). If not "The best of the West," then "Look East": Imported teacher education curricula in the Arabian Gulf. *Journal of Studies in International-al Education, 17*, 284–302.

Bahgat, G. (1999). Education in the Gulf monarchies: Retrospect and prospect. *International Review of Education, 45*(2), 127–136.

Bahrain Economic Development Board. (2008). *Bahrain vision 2030: The Bahrain economic vision 2030: From regional pioneer to global contender.* Retrieved from http://www.bahrainedb.com/en/about/Pages/economic%20vision%202030.aspx#.VZ5f6ou4nHg.

Bax, S. (2006). The role of genre in language syllabus design: The case of Bahrain. *International Journal of Educational Development, 26*(3), 315–328.

Comber, B. (2011). Changing literacies, changing populations, changing places—English teachers' work in an age of rampant standardisation. *English Teaching: Practice and Critique, 10*, 5–22.
Comber, B. & Nixon, H. (2009). Teachers' work and pedagogy in an era of accountability. *Discourse: Studies in the Cultural Politics in Education, 30*, 333–345.
Das, S., Shaheen, R., Shrestha, P., Rahma, A. & Khan, R. (2014). Policy versus ground reality: Secondary English language assessment system in Bangladesh. *The Curriculum Journal, 25*, 326–343.
Druzhilov, S. A. (2011). The two-level system of higher education. *Russian Education & Society, 53*(9), 34–46.
Glaser, B. G. (1965). The constant comparative method of qualitative analysis. *Social Problems, 12*(4), 436–445.
Hayes, A., Mansour, N. & Fisher, R. (2015). Adopting Western models of learning to teaching science as a means of offering a better start at university? The impact of socio-cultural factors. In Mansour, N. (Ed), *Science education in the Arab Gulf states: Visions, sociocultural contexts and challenges* (pp. 169–189). Rotterdam: Sense Publishers.
Hayes, A. (in press). Deconstructing the magnetic properties of neo-liberal politics of education in Bahrain. *Globalization, Societies and Education*.
Janks, H. (2014). Globalisation, diversity, and education: A South African perspective. *The Educational Forum, 78*, 8–25.
Jin, W. (2011). Culture differences and English teaching. *English Language Teaching, 4*(2), 223–230.
Li, M. & Baldauf, R. (2011), Beyond the curriculum: A Chinese example of issues constraining effective English language teaching. *TESOL Quarterly, 45*, 793–803.
Mansour, N. (2013). Modelling the sociocultural contexts of science education: The teachers' perspective. *Research in Science Education, 43*, 347–369.
Marginson, S. (2014). Student self-formation in international education. *Journal of Studies in International Education, 18*(1), 6–22.
Mavor, S. (2001). Socio-culturally appropriate methodologies for teaching and learning in a Portuguese university. *Teaching in Higher Education, 6*(2), 183–201.
Phillips, D. & Ochs, K. (2004). Researching policy borrowing: Some methodological challenges in comparative education, *British Educational Research Journal, 30*(6), 773–784.
Quaddummi, M. K. H. (1995). *Textual deviation and coherence problems in the writings of Arab students at the University of Bahrain: Sources and solutions* (Unpublished doctoral dissertation). Nottingham University, Nottingham.
Richards, J. C. & Rodgers, T. S. (1986). *Approaches and methods in language teaching.* Cambridge: Cambridge University Press.
Richards, J. C. (2006). *Communicative language teaching today.* Cambridge: Cambridge University Press.
Serpell, R. (2007). Bridging between orthodox Western higher educational practices and an African sociocultural context. *Comparative Education, 43*(1), 23–51.
Shirawi, M. (1989). *Education in Bahrain: Problems and progress.* Oxford: Ithaca Press.

Sovic, S, (2009). Hi-bye friends and the herd instinct: International and home students in the creative arts. *Higher Education*, 58(6), 747–761.

Stewart, D. W., Shamdasani, P. N. & Rook, D. W. (2007). *Focus groups: Theory and practice*. London: Sage.

Street, B. (2009). What is meant by local literacies? *Language and Education*, 8, 9–17.

Appendix: English Language Teachers— Focus Group Questions

1. Can you tell me how you teach English?
2. Can you tell me about what influences the way you teach English?
3. Do you face any problems with teaching English? How would you solve these problems?
4. How do you feel about the reforms concerning the English curriculum and the changes in methods of teaching? How do you implement the curricular requirements and the new methods of teaching?
5. You are a qualified English teacher. How does your training apply to your current teaching situation?
6. Would you like to elaborate on the problems your students face with learning English? What in your opinion should be done to solve the problems students face?
7. How about students' transition to university? What do you know about the requirements/ language demand at university?
8. What in your opinion should be done to respond to the linguistic requirements at university? Are they considered in the design of the curriculum?

Section 3: Striving for Balance Across Borders

7 Rewriting Resistance: Negotiating Pedagogical and Curricular Change in a U.S./Kurdish Transnational Partnership

Connie Kendall Theado
UNIVERSITY OF CINCINNATI (US)

Holly Johnson
UNIVERSITY OF CINCINNATI (US)

Thomas Highley
UNIVERSITY OF CINCINNATI (US)

Saman Hussein Omar
SALAHADDIN UNIVERSITY-HAWLER (IRAQ)

In this chapter, the authors describe the benefits accruing to cross-institutional collaborations between U.S. and Kurdish university faculty engaged in curricular reform at a Kurdish institute of higher education (IHE) in Iraq. Discussion centers on resonant examples from the partnership's online forums where resistance not only played a positive role in negotiating pedagogical change but also resulted in richer understandings of how western pedagogies are perceived in a Kurdish cultural context. In examining contradictory points of discourse in our online disciplinary community, this chapter both complicates the idea of resistance in transnational partnerships and calls into question the presumed portability of western pedagogies for non-western university faculty and their students.

Keywords: transnational partnerships; higher education; English studies pedagogy; local knowledge; online discourse

Paradoxically, local knowledge can motivate conversations between different localities, answering questions that transcend one's own borders. It is when we acknowledge the localness of our own knowledge that we

> have the proper humility to engage productively with other knowledge traditions. The assumption that one's knowledge is of sole universal relevance does not encourage conversation. It is possible to develop a pluralistic mode of thinking through which we celebrate different cultures and identities, and yet engage in projects common to our shared humanity.
>
> —*Suresh Canagarajah (2002b), Reconstructing Local Knowledge*

The Power of Example

In his June 3, 2014, editorial, "Iraq's Best Hope," American journalist Thomas L. Friedman dubbed Kurdistan the "unsung success story of the Iraq war," citing the American University of Iraq—Sulaimani (AUIS) as an example of the progress being made in an otherwise militarily and politically troubled Iraq (para. 3). "It was the Kurds," Friedman observes, "who used the window of freedom we opened for them to overcome internal divisions, start to reform their once Sopranos-like politics and create a vibrant economy that is now throwing up skyscrapers and colleges in major towns of Erbil and Sulaimani" (para. 4). More, he suggests, it is through the continued success of universities like AUIS to bring an "American-style" college experience to its students that Iraq will find its "best hope" for the future. "The power of example," Friedman remarks, "is a funny thing. You never know how it can spread" (para. 11). Americans should still hope, he advises, "that our values will triumph where our power failed" (para. 5).

Friedman's advocacy for more American universities in Iraq as a means of spreading western knowledges and "teaching the values of inclusiveness" (para. 5), which he views as absent from former Iraqi Prime Minister al-Maliki's political agenda, is certainly a standpoint resonant with those who believe that the US must develop cross-national understandings with Iraq through humanitarian, rather than military, action. What Friedman's U.S.-centric standpoint potentially undercuts, however, is precisely that which Suresh Canagarajah's (2002b) epigraph calls our attention to: It is only when westerners fully recognize the localness of their own knowledge traditions that they can hope to engage colleagues working in other regions of the world in meaningful dialogues about "projects common to our shared humanity" (p. 257), like the ongoing development of higher education in Iraqi Kurdistan.

In this chapter, we describe the benefits accruing to cross-institutional collaborations between U.S. and Kurdish university faculty while challenging the U.S.-centric perspective Friedman advocates about the presumed portability of western knowledges and pedagogies into Kurdish institutions of higher education. We take for our starting point two guiding premises: The first is that all knowledge is inherently "local" (Canagarajah, 2002b); that is, community-specific, value-laden, discursively constructed and, thus, necessarily collaborative in nature (see Canagarajah, 2002a, pp. 54–55). The second is that transnational partnerships established between U.S. and Middle East–North Africa (MENA)-region university faculty for the purposes of facilitating educational reform are best served by adopting practices that "envision not just changing the *content* of knowledge, but the *terms* of knowledge construction" (Canagarajah, 2002b, p. 251, emphasis in original). Taken together, these premises suggest that, while transnational partners can never merely shed their localness or the biases that attend any one person's situated ways of knowing, we can nevertheless work toward the more "pluralistic mode of thinking" that Canagarajah envisions as both the cornerstone and the consequence of collaborative cross-cultural exchange (for discussion of other transnational partnerships, see Arnold, DeGenaro, Iskandarani, Willard-Traub & Sinno; Austin; and Miller & Pessoa, this volume).

Our goals for this chapter are admittedly modest. For, despite recent advances in global communication networks that now enable interaction across geographic, cultural, and institutional boundaries in ways that weren't possible before the Internet, university partnerships to increase transnational awareness and cross-cultural exchange between the US and Iraq have been left largely unexplored. As a result, little scholarship on the current state of the Iraqi higher educational system exists (Lawrence, 2008; Mazawi & Sultana, 2010; Ninnes & Hellsten, 2005; Suárez-Orozco, 2007), and research focused extensively on institutions of higher education in Iraqi Kurdistan is virtually non-existent. In pursuing the partnership activities described in this chapter and, later, in choosing to write collaboratively about them, we recognize our interpretations and articulations of these experiences as necessarily partial and bounded—which is to say, imperfect—keenly aware of the work that lies ahead.

Still, Friedman may well be right to suggest that the power of example is a "funny thing" in its ability to "spread." With those words in mind, we offer these examples of our shared experiences negotiating curricular reform at one university in Erbil, Kurdistan, in hopes of provoking larger-scale and longer-term collaborations with international colleagues throughout the MENA region. Our chapter begins with a discussion of the context within which our university partnership originated, and then moves to three vignettes that illustrate our contention that the notion of resistance in transnational collaborations needs to be rewritten to include recursive periods of silence, contact, and negotiation that are both contradictory and healthy; that is, a positive force necessary for educational reform. We follow these vignettes with a discussion of what we have learned from our experiences together and what new understandings might be possible in the future.

The University Linkages Partnership

In 2010, the University of Cincinnati (UC) received a multi-year sub-contract award for a U.S.-Iraq University Linkages Partnership (ULP) granted through the U.S. Embassy-Iraq/U.S. State Department. The ULP project itself was unique in that it represented our two nations' commitment to sustained cross-cultural and cross-institutional exchanges on critical subjects, like literacy learning and English education pedagogies. Four U.S. universities partnered with four Iraqi universities and completed the first iteration of the project: Ball State University and Tikrit University; Oklahoma State University and Basrah University; the University of Kentucky and Kufa University; and the University of Cincinnati and Salahaddin University-Hawler (SUH), located in the northern Iraqi region of Kurdistan.

Founded in 1968, SUH is the oldest and largest university in Iraqi Kurdistan, housing 12 colleges that align similarly with university structures in the US. SUH's colleges include engineering, education, art, agriculture, fine arts, and Islamic Studies, and enroll roughly 26,000 undergraduates and over 900 graduate students. Degree plans, however, are quite different from the typical semester system employed in the US. For example, SUH undergraduate students follow a four-year curriculum set by the Ministry of Higher Education and many required courses are offered on a yearly basis. Students are assigned to colleges based on their performance on national tests, a policy that contributes to what SUH faculty perceive as their students' lack of engagement with their respective degrees. After university life, most students are assigned lifelong jobs that can likewise result in a mismatch between the graduates' interests and their allotted occupations. These differences, among others, were part of the landscape our faculty partnership navigated over the course of the project.

Each partnership was expected to address a set of goals that had been negotiated by the ULP leadership at their initial June 2010 meeting in Baghdad, a site selected by the funding agency for its presumably "neutral" location. Ironically, Baghdad was not a neutral location for either American or Kurdish citizens in the summer of 2010, a full six months prior to the final draw-down of U.S. troops in Iraq. Given just three days to build rapport and plan initiatives around the grant's expected goals, ULP leadership faculty from both Iraq and the US began an enterprise that would last three years.

Holly,[1] a UC faculty member in the Literacy and Second Language Studies (LSLS) program who authored the grant proposal, traveled to Baghdad to dialogue with three SUH department heads from the Colleges of Basic Education, English, and (Business) Administration and six SUH faculty representatives about activities designed to meet the broader ULP objectives, including curriculum development and the inclusion of more student-centered teaching practices in Iraqi institutions of higher education. After the Baghdad meeting, Holly flew to Erbil to discuss the proposed partnership activities with faculty in the SUH English Language and Literature departments who would be directly involved in the grant. It was at this Erbil meeting that Saman, a professor of English literature who later became Chair of the SUH English department, joined the project as the fourth SUH department head representing the College of Languages. Upon her return to Cincinnati, Holly invited Connie—a faculty colleague in LSLS—and Tom—a new LSLS doctoral student—to join the UC team as facilitators for the English-education piece of the partnership.

In August 2010, our UC-SUH partnership began working on the goals negotiated in Baghdad. Among other general aims, like the development of a career center in Erbil and curricular reform in SUH's departments of finance and economics, UC and SUH English-education faculty identified specific objectives for our collaboration, including the revision of SUH English literature curricula to include classroom opportunities for project- and problem-based learning, writing-to-learn activities, formative assessment practices, and e-learning teaching techniques, as well as the establishment of exchange opportunities between SUH and UC students and faculty. To address these shared goals, partnership faculty identified two main activities: (1) the creation of a Blackboard learning community as a means of facilitating monthly online meetings, promoting focused discussion of theoretical and pedagogical scholarship, and exchanging teaching resources and materials with one another; and (2) a series of workshops, held both at UC and SUH, to demonstrate and practice instructional approaches, co-create and revise course syllabi, classroom materials, and assessment instruments, and further promote the cross-cultural exchange of pedagogical knowledge and disciplinary perspectives on English Studies education.

In addition to thirty online meetings held monthly across three consecutive academic years (2010–2013)—the first year of which serves as the main focus for this chapter—nine extended site visits lasting one to two weeks per trip were also completed over the course of our partnership: Seven visits to SUH by a total of seventeen UC faculty members and graduate students, and two visits to UC by a total of twenty-three SUH faculty members, graduate students, and university administrators. These visits variously centered on any number of professional activities, including the redesign of six English literature courses (e.g., syllabi, teaching materials, and rubrics), co-teaching classes together in person and via digital video conferencing, providing peer teaching observations, practicing classroom-based technologies, and drafting conference proposals, to name just a few. There was also time allotted for sight-seeing and side-trips, shared meals on campus, at restaurants, and in each other's homes, informal hallway conversations with students and their teachers, pick-up soccer games, singing, story-telling, movie-going, and photo-taking. A jointly organized conference was held at SUH at the end of the project period, where partnership faculty and graduate students shared research via poster sessions and presentations. Several UC-SUH faculty partners have continued to present together at international conferences, and to seek publication opportunities for the work we accomplished (see Beckett & Muhammad, 2014).

These accomplishments as they evolved over time notwithstanding, it is important to acknowledge that, from the outset, our collaboration met with a kind of passive resistance from SUH faculty perhaps best described as polite disinterest in the UC team's initial attempts to organize the Blackboard site and settle on topics for our online discussions. As Saman would later disclose, SUH administrators had a long history of signing multiple memorandums of understanding (MOUs) with different international academic institutions. Moreover, the majority of these MOUs did not thrive and collaboration never occurred, often because the faculty members who were expected to collaborate had not been involved in the writing of those agreements or because of monetary issues connected to unwieldy centralized funding systems and bureaucracy. Given this history, the idea of another partnership, this time with an American university, was understandably greeted with a less-than-enthusiastic response by SUH faculty.

Unaware of this history, the UC team pursued the goals of the partnership as planned and, as a result, the Kurdish faculty gradually began to view this project as different from previous MOUs; that is, as not only possible but also worthwhile for a number of reasons. For instance, Saman explained that the dream of travelling abroad had long seemed out of reach for many Kurdish faculty, as, for decades under Baathist rule, the country had been cut off from the international community. Since the agreement included not only online discussions but also faculty exchanges, SUH faculty were intrigued by the chance to gain first-hand experience in an American university setting. Also appealing was the fact that UC faculty would travel to Erbil and work with SUH faculty and students for extended periods of time, as this demonstrated the Americans' commitment to reciprocal learning and growth. Additionally, Kurdistan's Ministry of Higher Education had been working for several years to redevelop existing college-level curricula, so the idea of curricular revision was already a topic familiar to SUH faculty. Academic benefits aside, the potential for establishing strong personal relationships with each other was also a key motivator for SUH and UC faculty members alike.

Points of Contradictory Discourse

During the first year of the grant, American and Kurdish faculty members met exclusively online in preparation for a two-week series of workshops to be held at UC the following summer. The U.S. instructors had not met their online partners, and the Kurdish partners had only met Holly, UC's project leader. Brought together in an online environment unknown to the Kurdish faculty but familiar to the Americans, the initial balance of power weighed heavily on the UC side in terms of structuring online interactions using Blackboard technology. Less well understood by either side, however, was the looming presence of local knowledge (Canagarajah, 2002b) and the role those knowledges would play in our discussions, especially in terms of conditioning our responses to one another.

The contradictory nature of our partnership became apparent in our attempt to become a discourse community through this online environment that first year. John Swales (1990) has argued that discourse communities vary in degree, but that all should meet criteria that include: (1) a common public goal worked toward together; (2) a discursive forum accessible to all participants; (3) a forum that provides information and feedback while working toward the goal; (4) a developed expectation/genre/convention for how informational exchanges should proceed; (5) a discourse that tends to become increasingly specialized through shared and specialized terminology; and (6) a critical mass of experts in the group as novices enter. Many of these criteria were met through the online discussion board structure developed by the American partners, but issues of accessibility, the use and meaning of specialized language, and the types of feedback expected became noticeable challenges for the new partnership, especially in light of the wide range of diverse expertise and local knowledges expressed by all of the participants.

While Swales' (1990) criteria for defining the characteristics of effective discourse communities provide a useful model, these standards leave little room for contending with acts of resistance on the part of the discourse community's members. To help us better understand how resistance can function productively within discourse communities, we turned to Roz Ivanič's (1998) arguments for re-envisioning acts of resistance as "alignment with—or even 'accommodation to'—less privileged discourses" rather than being viewed as oppositional in nature (p. 93). Drawing on the work of theorists who take a critical stance on the social nature of any discourse community (Bizzell, 1992; Chase, 1988; Harris, 1989), Ivanič writes:

> The point is that resistance is not resistance for its own sake. It is motivated by a commitment to represent the world in a way which accords with the writer's values, by a refusal to be colonized by the privileged world views and discourses of privileged others, and by a desire to open up membership of the academic discourse community. (Ivanič, 1998, p. 93)

Further informing our interpretation of resistance as it played out across our online interactions is Canagarajah's (2002a) assertion that discourse communities "live always with indeterminacy, heterogeneity, and conflict" (p. 68). This particular mix of indeterminacy, heterogeneity, and conflict, Canagarajah suggests, is especially evident in discourse communities comprised of specific disciplinary groups, like the English-education learning community our partnership was working to establish: "Rather than focusing on shared common characteristics like language, values, knowledge, or genres of literacy for the constitution of the discourse community," he explains, "we should focus on an open-ended and dynamically changing circle of scholars who have to respond constantly to the conflicts shaping their activity from within and without their circle" (2002a, p. 68). A critical understanding, then, for recognizing the positive role resistance played within our disciplinary discourse community has been Canagarajah's notion of "perpetual tension"—between "established discourses being challenged and new discourses struggling for dominance," as well as between "privileged subjects and resisting/aspiring subjects with competing claims of knowledge" (2002a, p. 69). Such conflicts, or what we observed as points of contradictory discourse happening in our online exchanges, are not only to be expected, but are best viewed as the "engines of new knowledge/discourse creation" (Canagarajah, 2002a, p. 70).

What follows are three vignettes that illustrate critical junctures in our online discussions during the first year of the partnership. While resistance presents differently and in varying degrees in each vignette—silence in the first scenario, skepticism and competing assumptions about student learning and institutional realities in the second, and the clashing of instructional paradigms and the role of teachers in the third—what appears as a kind of linear progression over time is as much the result of our drafting this chapter together as it is the result of chronology. In truth, our recognition of and appreciation for the role resistance played in our partnership was much more episodic in nature, not unlike the progression of all learning and professional growth.

Nonetheless, our understanding of transnational partnerships has changed on account of these online interactions, as has our collective understanding of resistance and the generative role it can play in them. Periodic and recursive instances of silence, contact, and negotiation within the process of partnership development are necessary and healthy for strong cross-cultural affiliations to emerge and survive, and may be especially needed in transnational endeavors where cultures are vastly different. By learning to accommodate these contradictory points of discourse within our extended online dialogues, our theoretical perspectives have likewise been changed, inviting us to reconsider the collaborative practice of transnational educational research, where so often the local participants are considered the "other." And while the various acts of resistance highlighted here could be read as merely oppositional in nature, evidencing only difficulty in collaborating across cultural borders, for us, these vignettes represent instead earnest attempts on the part of the Kurds and the Americans alike at "opening up our understanding of what is happening elsewhere to adapt, resituate, [and] perhaps decenter our contexts" (Donahue, 2009, p. 215) toward productive ends. As our partnership developed, we could not help but notice the positive effect resistance within our collaborative efforts produced. Our co-authoring process, in its ability to foster reflection, encourage conversation, address (mis)perceptions, and clarify meaning, has also shaped our understanding of these cross-institutional and cross-cultural dynamics, as well.

Vignette One: Breaking Silences, Making Common Ground

Like many new relationships, our partnership began in fits and starts throughout the Fall of 2010. Blackboard technology created confusions for first-time SUH faculty users—how to log in, how to navigate the site, how to post and respond to discussion board threads—and these confusions were compounded by bureaucratic "red tape" on the UC side—how to establish guest Blackboard accounts for non-UC faculty and how to enable SUH faculty full access to UC library systems and electronic databases, again without benefit of UC faculty status. Spotty Internet connectivity and the lack of an IP address for SUH further complicated our efforts.

Aiming to alleviate confusions and answer questions in a more personal, face-to-face virtual environment, the UC team invited the SUH team, 15 literature faculty, to attend an "Orientation to Blackboard" meeting in September, using Adobe Connect technology. Possibly due to the Kurds' skepticism about the viability of the ULP MOU that had been struck in June, or perhaps, and more simply, due to the UC faculty's misunderstanding of SUH's academic calendar (first-year and returning students have different start dates), the orientation attracted just two SUH faculty members. Thirty minutes into the meeting, we lost connectivity and thus, we were forced to abandon the call.

October brought renewed hope, as most of the technological and bureaucratic issues had been resolved by that time and all of the SUH literature faculty had returned to campus. To facilitate the asynchronous discussions on the Blackboard site, the UC team created a schedule of monthly meetings across the first year, October 2010 through June 2011, and posted it to the site. Each meeting was scheduled to last three consecutive days, beginning on a Monday morning (Erbil time) and concluding on a Wednesday evening (Erbil time), with all participants posting as their time allowed within the three-day window. Pre-selected readings and an accompanying audio PowerPoint slide show to guide online conversations were posted by the UC faculty two weeks prior to the start of each monthly meeting. The readings included both theoretically- and pedagogically-oriented pieces, authored by North American theorists, with topics ranging widely (e.g., reading process theory, reader response theory, strategies for struggling readers and writers, responding to and evaluating student writing, teaching with technology).

While October's meeting only drew the participation of the same two SUH faculty members who had attended the Adobe Connect meeting the month before, the conversation was congenial and focused, with 20 total postings exchanged between the two SUH faculty, and the two UC participants charged with leading these exchanges, Connie and Tom. November's online meeting showed a slight increase in both total posts (28) and in the number of SUH participants (from two to three). By December, total postings had grown to 51, and the number of SUH faculty participants had doubled (from three to six). Additionally and importantly, December's discussion threads were noticeably more interactive, with SUH faculty responding to each other's posts with increasing frequency instead of mainly replying to UC faculty posts, as had been the case before.

Given the steady increase in participation and Blackboard postings, which the UC faculty regarded as burgeoning SUH faculty buy-in, our partnership's prospects looked promising. Ten days after the close of December's meeting, however, we received the first real push-back from an SUH faculty member—our co-author, Saman, Chair of the English department and leader of the SUH English literature team—who had not participated in the Blackboard conversations until that point in time.

"Dear colleagues," he began, "as you know, a few people from my team have been participating in the discussion forums. However, some members of the team, including myself, have not taken part in the discussion so far due to some reasons." The first reason, Saman explained, was rooted in their perception that they were being treated differently than their SUH colleagues who were participating in another Blackboard learning community focused on English-language education. "It seems that our colleagues from the language team," he observed, "have sent you an email in which they have provided a list of the topics they find as priorities for the discussions, and that the discussions are made on such basis as we were told." Continuing on, he wrote, "We, from the literature team, would also like to do the same," following up this comment with a list of five "challenging issues facing our teachers," including: (a) large class sizes; (b) how to play the role of a "guide" instead of "lecturer;" (c) teaching techniques for college literature teachers, specifically; (d) strategies for motivating underprepared students; and (e) ways to counter institutional bureaucracy that can negatively affect faculty efforts.

The second reason Saman shared was related to the first, although more pointedly aimed at the readings UC faculty had pre-selected for discussion. "We think that the articles you posted online," he remarked, "are more of arid theoretical issues than being directly related to the observations we have about our teaching as far as our system is concerned." To mitigate the force of his complaint, Saman continued, "This of course does not mean that our teachers have not benefitted from them as we all agree that teaching and learning are universal and they involve both theory and practice." "However," he concluded, "I and other members from my team who have seen the announcements posted online, apart from the teachers who have had reflections on them, believe it will be more fruitful and more practical to deal with the issues we have suggested above."

This event, Saman's explanation of his own and the majority of his colleagues' silence, represented a critical juncture in our nascent partnership. For all of the UC team's planning, the perception from the SUH faculty was that we had created exactly that which we were consciously trying to avoid: A UC-centered Blackboard space used mainly for "exporting" western texts (Donahue, 2009) and arguably aimed at changing the "content" of SUH faculty knowledge, to borrow Canagarajah's (2002b) language, instead of working to change the "terms" of knowledge construction within our discourse community. In turn, many Kurdish faculty members felt silenced by the structure the UC faculty had imposed on them. The pre-selected readings, "arid" theoretical texts as opposed to practical ones that spoke to the contexts of SUH English literature classrooms and students, evidenced a presumed lack of interest on the UC faculty's part for the real-world challenges the Kurdish faculty faced. More, the central promise undergirding our partnership had been unwittingly broken; namely, that SUH faculty priorities would constitute the basis of our online conversations. Saman's tone was as gracious as it was firm: "We are very grateful for your cooperation," his closing line read, adding that "we look forward to having a rich, fruitful, and long-lasting partnership." A future-oriented comment, to be sure, but a future that would unfold along a different path than the one we were currently traveling.

More than a mere act of resistance, Saman's posting served as an invitation to revisit the ostensibly shared objectives for our partnership to ensure they more accurately represented the "common public goal worked toward together," which Swales (1990) suggests is characteristic of effective discourse communities. Saman's posting also pointed toward the unexamined privileging of western theoretical knowledges conveyed by the pre-selected readings, which implicitly worked to position the UC faculty as "experts" and consequently—although unintentionally—foreclosed the relationship of SUH faculty participants to the UC faculty. Instead of derailing efforts, Saman's post provoked a collective re-examination of the ways in which local knowledges, western and non-western, were influencing the shape and trajectory of our emerging partnership—it was the critical first step, we discovered, in establishing actual, viable common ground.

Vignette Two: Building Critical Self-Consciousness, Negotiating Community Membership

According to Ivanič (1998), resistance can be read as reflecting an individual's "desire to open up membership" of a discourse community (p. 93). Working to increase opportunities for meaningful contact within our online discussions, this "opening up" dynamic translated into periodic instances of negotiation, especially with regard to the partnership's growing awareness of our local ways of knowing as university professors with expertise in English-education pedagogy and reading theory. The following vignette highlights how both Kurdish and American views on instructional practices and institutional contexts were introduced to each other through negotiating meaning around the reading and discussion of Louise Rosenblatt's (1978) scholarship on transactional theory. In this article, Rosenblatt posits readers and texts in a mutually reciprocal relationship to advance her argument that readers transact directly with texts, instead of authors, and thus call into question traditional theories about authorial intention and the locus of textual meaning.

While Rosenblatt's (1978) article provided the ostensive frame for our discussion of reading process theory, what we discovered in this particular online discussion was the mismatch in our working conditions and the nuanced differences in our culturally specific uses of language, which ultimately helped us expand our discourse community's membership by allowing us to address the "context bound, community specific, and nonsystematic" (Canagarajah, 2002b, p. 244) knowledges that each side of the partnership brought to the conversation. By explicitly attending to our own meaning-making processes, the group became more critically self-conscious of the local cultural knowledges—academic and geographic—we had previously assumed were more globally understood. In addition, the participants' increasing self-consciousness allowed us to more fully embrace Patricia Bizzell's (1992) notion of the power discourse communities possess to "shape world views" (p. 226), including the world views of those whose varied local knowledges reflect differing assumptions about pedagogy, student learning, and the role of English education in U.S. and Kurdish college contexts.

Rosenblatt's (1978) transactional theory resonated with the Kurdish professors' background as highly trained English literary scholars. Nevertheless, this article was still, as one SUH participant, Mr. Karwan, remarked, "A challenging paper to read . . . I had difficulty understanding it." He then went on to explain the meaning he was able to make of the text, while also pointing out the places where his understanding was less clear. Mr. Karwan's response was not necessarily surprising or even overtly resistant in and of itself, as Rosenblatt's discussion of efferent and aesthetic stances toward a text, coupled with abstract theories and concepts like semiotics and the "linguistic-experiential reservoir," is difficult for many who first encounter her theory. However, Karwan's willingness to state his confusion about these new concepts despite his attempts to reconcile them with his own deep knowledge of reading theory and pedagogy initiated a shift in the SUH faculty's online interactions—from mostly trading "academic" interpretations of the texts we were reading to demonstrate their understanding to questioning the texts' meanings and, by extension, their relative value for or applicability to SUH English literature classrooms. Just as importantly, this shift opened up space for dialogue in which each participant could draw upon his/her own teaching experiences to reconsider the usefulness of Rosenblatt's theory for Kurdish students.

Karwan was the first SUH faculty member to post to this thread and, as a well-regarded teacher and scholar, the timing of his post was undoubtedly consequential as well. Another SUH participant, Ms. Kani, joined the discussion by not only sharing her understanding of reading process theory and how it connected to Rosenblatt's (1978) work, but also by bluntly questioning its practical application in Kurdish classroom contexts that rely heavily on a teacher-centered instructional model of lecturing. In response, the UC faculty shifted the conversation to address reading strategy use within a more student-centered instructional approach, and connected these strategies contextually to explain the expectations U.S. university teachers have for teaching academic reading. Ms. Kani replied that Iraqi university faculty members also expect students to read in particular ways, too, and these ways of reading were modeled by SUH faculty through lecturing and recitation. "Keep in mind," she wrote, "the great challenges we face. Not only that students have to deal with the complexity of content and style of literary texts, they are also confronted with linguistic and aesthetic ambiguities in the second language context." Despite these real challenges, Ms. Kani was open to exploring new strategies that allowed for greater student connections to the required canonical texts, stating, "I hope that it will be useful. I'll try using it in my classes."

Another reminder of the context-specific challenges SUH literature faculty confront occurred in dialogue with Mamosta (the Kurdish word for "teacher") Sherko. Aiming to better understand how SUH literature classrooms functioned, Connie asked about the amount of time the Kurdish professors typically use for teaching a given text, noting that "we normally schedule 2–3 weeks—or 6–9 classroom hours—to complete a book, sometimes less." Mamosta Sherko was skeptical of that timetable, and explained that his students need 50 classroom hours to complete a short literary work like Miller's (1976) *Death of a Salesman* owing to several time-based obstacles he faced, including hours of his own personal time spent translating English into Kurdish for his students. In the course of this exchange, Sherko also explained a decidedly local phenomenon the SUH faculty call "casual holidays," where SUH classes are arbitrarily and unexpectedly canceled for varying lengths of time. "Casual holidays (a chronic disease) in Iraq creates obstacles in our syllabi," Mamosta Sherko wrote. "No one knows an exact time-table of holidays," he explained, "for example we hadn't expected that the 14th and 15th of this month to be holidays; we are informed just six hours before." Sherko's mention of SUH's casual holidays revealed an institutional reality and curricular planning constraint previously unknown to the UC partners. As a result, the group was able to negotiate alternate ways of structuring course syllabi, like the creation of a series of recursive and moveable learning modules rather than SUH's more typical linear curricular model, to better account for these periodic and unanticipated disruptions of the academic calendar.

Although the exchange of local knowledges was becoming more robust throughout this discussion thread, membership in the online discourse community itself still evidenced a dialectic resembling a "teacher-student" relationship rather than a "colleague-colleague" relationship, a tension that was exacerbated by the use of salutations. For example, most of the Kurdish participants used the title of "professor" when addressing the UC participants, which positioned the Americans as "experts," and they often responded to each other with evaluative comments like, "From all that you have written here, [Sherko], I would say you understood the paper's main arguments very well." These kinds of comments further positioned the Kurds as "students." The use of salutations may seem a minor aspect of the partners' interactions; however, it was a critical piece of locating and accommodating power within the online exchanges.

While the UC faculty's use of first names when responding to comments ostensibly aimed at opening up membership, they eventually recognized the Kurdish expectation of using more formal salutations. This accommodation was apparent, for example, in a posting in which Connie wrote, "Dear Karwan (or do you prefer Mr. Karwan?)." Such acts of critical self-consciousness about the power connected to the use of first names by the UC faculty or the use of positioning titles by the SUH faculty became an ongoing feature of our online conversations. For instance, Ms. Kani, once addressed by her first name, adopted the more casual U.S. salutation style in her future postings, phrasing that was also taken up by other Kurdish faculty members as the partnership progressed. Connie and Tom also took up the use of "Dr." and "Mr." or "Mrs." in their postings addressing the SUH faculty. As dialogue continued, we noticed that all of the participants' postings became less formal and specific cultural patterns in conjunction with salutations likewise became more sporadic.

The more informal use of salutations and growing partnership did not mean that participants did not continue to hold to other cultural and academic values. What the blending of cultural norms in respect to naming or identifying ourselves to one another allowed was movement away from polite correspondence among strangers to increased engagement about the topics and values that mattered to all participants, which included clashes over what was and was not yet possible in respect to student-centered pedagogy.

Vignette Three: Attending to Context, Negotiating Pedagogical Perspectives

While collectively, our growing recognition of the contradictions and overlaps between local knowledges across the partnership enabled us to negotiate new understandings that would count as relevant knowledge within our discourse community, the Kurdish faculty's resistance to wholesale adoption of western perspectives on literary analysis produced both increasingly synthesized and culturally relevant pedagogies best suited to SUH students and faculty. This next vignette centers on a thread surrounding a discussion of a chapter from Robert Scholes' (1985) book, *Textual Power*, where the SUH faculty's resistance to Scholes' critique of New Criticism was both noticeably strong and ultimately productive. This thread was particularly lively, with 51 total exchanges among eight participants. As a result of these exchanges, previously entrenched standpoints began to merge into new and discourse-community-specific understandings about what kinds of pedagogies might, or might not, be relevant for the study of western literary texts within the context of a Kurdish college classroom.

Scholes' (1985) acknowledgment of the role a reader's cultural knowledge plays in making textual meaning was received as incompatible with the New Criticism approach (Richards, 1930) embraced by the majority of the Kurdish professors. In short, they considered the role of the reader in meaning-making to be largely irrelevant, asserting instead that meaning resides in the text and that, as a result, teaching students the skill of "close reading" in literary analysis should remain the primary objective of literary study. For example, in his response to Scholes' theory, Dr. Ahmed wrote, "True that every reader, more or less, responds to a text with several natural reactions the moment they perceive a familiar situation or attitude. Yet, in my opinion, students should be sparing in their very subjective reflections at large." Saman agreed with Ahmed in his post to this thread, noting that while moving away from strictly teaching close reading skills was "absolutely essential," objectivity is critical for competent literary analysis, remarking that: "I agree with T. S. Eliot's view that poetry, for instance, is impersonal. It is the text that writes the author, not the other way round." Although both Dr. Ahmed and Saman acknowledged the reader's presence in the act of reading, the production of textual meaning was understood as inevitably outside of any individual reader's control.

The discussion of instructor roles and responsibilities also resulted in a clash between teaching paradigms favored by the SUH and UC faculty. Scholes' (1985, p. 30) suggestion that an instructor should facilitate rather than prescribe student interpretations of textual meaning was a particularly thorny assertion that met with resistance from a number of SUH faculty. All of the SUH faculty participants remarked that the complexity of English literature was a central challenge for their Kurdish students' comprehension of textual meaning, particularly with regard to "deciphering" the cultural codes embedded in western canonical texts. In turn, they reasoned that teacher-centered instructional approaches, where the professor is positioned as the "expert" literary critic, were essential to student learning. For example, Saman observed that "students can produce readings if the way is paved for them by the teacher . . ., beginning learners of English literature should not start with a text which has such a level of complexity that requires senior students to understand it." Other Kurdish professors supported the necessity of teacher-centered classrooms, with Dr. Ahmed noting that "the teacher . . . can hint at several clues and triggering remarks that enable the students [to] uncover and unlock certain implied and covert thematic motifs, symbols and inferences." Ahmed's remarks also underscore his affinity with New Criticism.

Pushing back on the SUH faculty's claims for teacher-centered pedagogies, the UC participants suggested that students could be afforded more responsibility for scaffolding their own learning, as opposed to relying on the teacher's interpretive processes for the discovery of meaning. For example, in her response to complaints about minimizing teacher control over explicating textual meaning, Connie wrote: "It's not so much that U.S. teachers don't focus on 'close readings' of texts—they still do, of course—but that they also often embed these close readings within larger classroom discussions of the historical, social, and political contexts within which a text is both 'produced' by a particular writer and 'consumed' by various groups of readers, as a way to emphasize any text's potential for being interpreted in multiple—even competing—ways." When Dr. Ahmed questioned the amount of class time allowing students to compose their own interpretations would take, Tom suggested using small discussion groups to facilitate conversations and Connie suggested using short in-class writing assignments. Ahmed's response was both polite and resistant: "I read your ideas thoroughly . . . and will try to apply them in my classes. What I am worried about is again, TIME. I am afraid I am not convinced by your 5-minute activities" (emphasis in original). Connie's reply was equally polite and equally resistant: "Yes, absolutely, time is indeed always an issue. Fair enough, too, that you're not completely convinced that an in-class writing exercise might only take 5 minutes to do. Hmm . . . I see that I'll have to work harder to persuade you." She then offered to post examples of this kind of writing assignment to the Blackboard site so they might continue the conversation later.

A little later in this thread, Tom suggested that one way to encourage multiple interpretations and increase student control over the production of textual meaning might be to pair the canonical western texts SUH faculty were required to teach with local Kurdish texts as a means of discovering how cultural codes operate in all literary texts. Several SUH faculty participants agreed with this idea in principle but rejected it in practice. For example, Saman remarked that "one problem we face as teachers of English literature is the problem of culture." However, he continued, "We are supposed to do *pure* (emphasis in original) English literature . . . at our departments of English. Thus, there is no room for local literature." In a separate post to one of his SUH colleagues, Saman further warned, "I think too much focusing on local literature is dangerous . . . if it causes us to divert from the main topic which is about teaching our students English literature."

This series of exchanges between SUH and UC faculty highlights the kind of "perpetual tension" that Canagarajah (2002b) suggests exists in all disciplinary discourse communities. As this thread demonstrates, both groups alternately resisted the claims expressed by the other. These acts of resistance, however, were not merely oppositional in nature or effect; rather, they served productively as a means of negotiating alternate and context-specific pedagogies that could account for Scholes' (1985) theory without usurping SUH faculty knowledge or control of their classrooms.

With regard to guiding student interpretations of western literary texts, the group went on to negotiate approaches that both acknowledged the SUH faculty's preference for New Critical pedagogies while incorporating in-class writing activities that fostered student connections with local knowledge. For example, Cross and Angelo's (1988) "one minute paper," a short writing assignment that invites students to respond to two text-based questions at the end of class, was adopted by SUH faculty as a means of encouraging students to "talk back to" and connect with literary texts while still using close reading skills to provide specific support for their interpretations and critiques. Similarly, pre-reading writing activities, like Elbow's (1995) "entering the text" strategy, which invites students to speculate about the thematic elements of a literary work in connection with personal experiences before reading the assigned text itself, appealed to the SUH faculty's interest and formal training in literary aesthetics.

The negotiation of instructor roles and responsibilities also resulted in alternate and more context-appropriate pedagogical approaches. While the SUH faculty held fast to "paving the way" for student interpretation through structured, teacher-led questioning strategies, they were open to integrating periodic small-group exercises in the form of literature circles (Peterson & Eeds, 2007) as a means of modeling academic reading and comprehension practices through peer collaboration. Even the relatively heated discussion about whether to use local Kurdish texts in SUH English literature classrooms brought about a blended approach that cautiously acknowledged the importance of teaching local texts while honoring the SUH's institutional expectations for teaching "pure" English literature. Here, SUH faculty decided that English literary works were only to be paired with English translations of local texts and used only sparingly with more advanced students whose grasp of basic literary analysis was already in evidence.

Merging pedagogical preferences and practices produced new instructional approaches that better suited SUH's teaching contexts. The SUH faculty's reluctance to submit wholesale to western pedagogical knowledges prompted a re-examination of Scholes' theory within our online discourse community, deconstructing and then reconstructing (Canagarajah, 2002b, p. 252) Scholes' perspectives to more fully address the Kurdish teaching and learning context.

Rewriting Resistance in Transnational Partnerships: An Invitation to Praxis

We return to Ivanič's (1998) understanding of resistance, which itself suggests somewhat conflicting notions of retaining one's values and refusing to be colonized while evincing a desire to open up membership in a discourse community. Throughout the first year of our partnership, we found ourselves increasingly called upon to "accustom ourselves" to these kinds of contradictions emerging in our online discussions rather than pursue a "theory that seeks to abrogate them" (Bizzell, 1992, p. 235). While not all contradictions can be "attended to at every moment," as Bizzell suggests, their presence ultimately "helps ensure the community's viability in the face of changing demands from other discourse communities and changing conditions in the material world" (1992, p. 235). The contradictory points of discourse we encountered in our online disciplinary community thus should not only be expected but welcomed as invitations to reexamine our purposes and goals as transnational partners.

In essence, the partnership invited both Americans and Kurds to confront the "global turn" in educational research and to examine how the internationalizing of English Studies curricula and pedagogy has become—and continues to be—a highly contested arena of research (Canagarajah, 2013; Horner & Kopelson, 2014; Horner, Lu & Matsuda, 2010). Cut off from the international research community for three decades under Saddam Hussein's regime, SUH faculty are rightly invested in marshaling educational change, an investment that benefited our partnership immeasurably. However, and as we learned, the very question of curricular and pedagogical revision in any university context always becomes: In what ways, and for whose reasons?

As the partnership unfolded into subsequent years, many SUH literature faculty found that, when employed over time, the strategies discussed in our online forums were beneficial for student learning and for expanding their own pedagogical repertoire. Still, instances of resistance persisted, especially with a small group of SUH faculty who considered student-centered strategies largely ineffective given the Kurds' institutional and cultural constraints, including large class sizes, meager budgets for new materials, and concern about how changing instructional practices would affect student preparation for required annual examinations. This particular group of SUH faculty also voiced concern that their local strategies might not be viewed as "correct" in the eyes of the UC partners, despite assurances to the contrary. In preparing this chapter, Saman speculated that such feelings of inferiority, as Canagarajah (2002b, p. 247) points out, may have been due to an abiding assumption that "the local [SUH] finds representation only according to the purposes and forms permitted by the powerful [UC]," an assumption that proved particularly difficult to dislodge.

That local knowledges are too often dismissed as inferior in comparison with knowledges from the west is a phenomenon well understood by the Kurdish faculty. At issue is the way western perspectives have been ideologically equated with the "global," as opposed to being understood as necessarily context-bound and thus unavoidably interested, as all local knowledges inevitably are. Our partnership was not immune to the effects of this persistent and troubling ideological bias, where "western" is regarded as interchangeable with "global." On this point, Mr. Karwan's observation is telling:

> Globalization, welcomed or unwelcomed, has posed many challenges to us in our communities and our classrooms. The traditional issues of power and control, the "voices" of teachers and students, the curriculum, [and the] school structure itself has dramatically changed. New trends [are] not only changing teacher-student relationships but the entire education system in this country.

Karwan was not alone in his concern about the effects of globalization for Kurdistan or the effects our partnership would have for SUH classrooms, and this question served as an important contextualizing feature for our collaborations. In fact, as Saman reported, many SUH faculty simultaneously admired the U.S. educational system yet also ignored the reality that, despite challenges in the Kurdish educational system, Kurdistan claims a strong academic and intellectual history that already validated their own and their students' potential. In Saman's words, SUH student potential needs only to be "triggered to get them more involved in classroom activities."

For those of us who acknowledged that resistance can be written into the process of negotiation, the partnership allowed for "cultural synthesis," a process Paulo Freire (1970/2001) asserts does not deny differences between opposing world views as, by its very nature, synthesis requires interaction between competing standpoints. Cultural synthesis, however, does deny the imposition of one world view over and above any other, demanding instead that competing knowledges are held in a dialectic relationship with one another to make space for transformative action. Through our sharing of local knowledges, the online community we created became this kind of "third space" (Gutiérrez, 1999) for critically examining our learning, a unique social and discursive arena that provided an avenue for praxis (Freire, 1970/2001), which in turn moved us beyond dialogue toward critical reflection about current realities and possible futures.

Current Realities, Possible Futures: Where our "Best Hope" Resides

In her 2009 article, "'Internationalization' and Composition Studies: Reorienting the Discourse," Christiane Donahue cautions that the U.S. perspective on educational change in other regions of the world is "highly partial . . . and largely export-based" (p. 214). More, she argues that laying claim to "unique knowledge, expertise, and ownership" of educational practices not only "present[s] the United States to the world as a homogenous nation-state with universal courses" but also results in "'othering' countries that have different, complex, and well-established traditions . . . as somehow lacking or behind the times" (2009, pp. 213–14). The challenge for U.S. researchers, Donahue explains, lies in resisting the "us-them" paradigm the current discourse on internationalizing higher education advances by "thinking about where our work fits into the world rather than where the world's work fits into ours" (2009, p. 214).

While the SUH-UC partnership provides just one example among many transnational collaborations in the MENA region, we believe our partnership contributes meaningfully to the larger paradigmatic shift Donahue (2009) envisions as necessary for reorienting the discourse on internationalizing higher education toward more pluralistic and egalitarian ends. Rewriting resistance into the process of negotiating curricular and pedagogical change at SUH not only served as the critical first step toward building authentic partnership relations but also became the enabling belief supporting our efforts across the three years. The challenge Donahue issues—to think more completely and less proprietarily about where western knowledges might "fit" into the world—engenders the "proper humility" that Canagarajah (2002b) reminds us is central to "answering questions that transcend one's own borders" (p. 257). Both stances are rooted in the kind of productive resistance our partnership learned to recognize, accommodate, and welcome.

It is easy to fall prey to the "us-them" binary Donahue (2009) describes. As one SUH faculty partner remarked over tea the morning Connie and Tom arrived at Salahaddin in Fall 2012, "it's not just ocean and land that stand between us." Indeed, there is plenty—the media, the war, world politics—we agreed, to keep us apart. These external "realities" notwithstanding, we also agreed there was much to support our collaboration: The relative stability of the Iraqi Kurdistan region that, at the time, allowed easy travel to and from Erbil; our shared commitment to extended visits on each other's campuses to work in classrooms together; our dedication to our professional growth; and our burgeoning friendships with one another. Like others who work in transnational partnerships, these realities were the ones that mattered most.

In reflecting on our work and in writing this chapter together, we are persuaded by Friedman's (2014) claim that academic success in Kurdistan is largely unsung. Our experiences bear witness to that perspective. But his claim that the values that will "triumph" in Iraq are somehow values America owns and so can export to other lands is deeply flawed. For, what our "discovery of difference" scholarship, as Donahue (2009, p. 214) might call it, affirms is that the values toward which America aspires—freedom, equality, safety, peace—are Kurdish values as well. Concern for the effects of globalization and for what internationalizing higher education means in the MENA region are shared concerns, if only for the simple but often overlooked reason that we live in one world. We are all staked in these transformations. In these future possibilities as well as our current realities, we are, as we have always been, each other's "best hope."

Note

1. We have chosen to use first names in the text, both ours as authors and our SUH colleagues as participants; using last names felt counter to the work we accomplished in the transnational partnership, in that the use of first names is deeply tied to the broader arguments we make about engaging productively across cultural borders. Kurdish forms of academic address regularly use titles, like Dr. or Mrs., in front of first names instead of last names (the more common form of academic address in the US); we see this Kurdish practice as critical for building trust and community in the partnership—which was also an important lesson for the U.S. participants about decentering our own contexts by attending to acts of resistance.

References

Beckett, G. & Muhammad, H. A-Q. (2014). Reflections on the University of Cincinnati and Salahaddin University Linkage Work. *Procedia—Social and Behavioral Sciences, 116*, 4372–4374.
Bizzell, P. (1992). *Academic discourse and critical consciousness*. Pittsburgh: University of Pittsburgh Press.
Canagarajah, A. S. (Ed.). (2013). *Literacy as translingual practice: Between communities and classrooms*. New York: Routledge.
Canagarajah, A. S. (2002a). *A geopolitics of academic writing*. Pittsburgh: University of Pittsburgh Press.
Canagarajah, S. (2002b). Reconstructing local knowledge. *Journal of Language, Identity, and Education, 1*(4), 243–259.
Chase, G. (1988). Accommodation, resistance and the politics of student writing. *College Composition and Communication, 39*, 13–22.
Cross, K. P. & Angelo, T. A. (1988). *Classroom assessment techniques: A handbook for faculty*. Ann Arbor, MI: National Center for Research to Improve Postsecondary Teaching and Learning.
Donahue, C. (2009). "Internationalization" and composition studies: Reorienting the discourse. *College Composition and Communication, 61*(2), 212–243.
Elbow, P. (1995). Breathing life into the text. In A. Young & T. Fulwiler (Eds.), *When writing teachers teach literature: Bringing writing to reading* (pp. 193–205). Portsmouth, NH: Heinemann Boynton/Cook Publishers.
Freire, P. (1970/2001). *Pedagogy of the oppressed*. New York: Continuum Press.
Friedman, T. L. (2014, June 3). Iraq's best hope. *New York Times*. Retrieved from http://www.nytimes.com/2014/06/04/opinion/friedman-iraqs-best-hope.html?_r=0.
Gutiérrez, K. (1999). Rethinking diversity: Hybridity and hybrid language practices in the third space. *Mind, Culture, and Activity, 6*(4), 286–303.
Harris, J. (1989). The idea of community in the study of writing. *College Composition and Communication, 40*, 11–22.
Horner, B. & Kopelson, K. (Eds.). (2014). *Reworking English in rhetoric and composition: Global interrogations, local interventions*. Carbondale, IL: Southern Illinois University Press.
Horner, B., Lu, M-Z. & Matsuda, P. K. (Eds.). (2010). *Cross-language relations in composition*. Carbondale, IL: Southern Illinois University Press.
Ivanič, R. (1998). *Writing and identity: The discoursal construction of identity in academic writing*. Philadelphia: John Benjamins Publishing Company.
Lawrence, Q. (2008). *Invisible nation: How the Kurds' quest for statehood is shaping Iraq and the Middle East*. New York: Walker Publishing Company.
Mazawi, A. E. & Sultana, R. G. (Eds.). (2010). *The world yearbook of education 2010: Education and the Arab world: Political projects, struggles, and geometries of power*. New York: Routledge.
Miller, A. (1976). *Death of a salesman*. New York: Penguin Books.

Ninnes, P. & Hellsten, M. (Eds.). (2005). *Internationalizing higher education: Critical explorations of pedagogy and policy.* Dordrecht, NL: Springer.

Peterson, R. & Eeds, M. (2007). *Grand conversations (updated edition): Literature groups in action.* New York: Scholastic.

Richards, I. A. (1930). *Practical criticism: A study of literary judgment.* London: Kegan Paul, Trench, Tubner & Company.

Rosenblatt, L. (1978). *The reader, the text, the poem: The transactional theory of the literary work.* Carbondale, IL: Southern Illinois University Press.

Scholes, R. (1985). *Textual power: Literary theory and the teaching of English.* New Haven, CT: Yale University Press.

Suárez-Orozco, M. M. (2007). *Learning in the global era: International perspectives on globalization and education.* Berkeley, CA: University of California Press.

Swales, J. (1990). *Genre analysis: English in academic and research settings.* Boston: Cambridge University Press.

8 Integrating Writing Assignments at an American Branch Campus in Qatar: Challenges, Adaptations, and Recommendations

Ryan T. Miller
KENT STATE UNIVERSITY (US)

Silvia Pessoa
CARNEGIE MELLON UNIVERSITY (QATAR)

> Recently, many western institutions have established international branch campuses (IBCs) in many parts of the MENA region. However, to be successful, IBCs must adapt to the needs of the context in which they operate. This chapter investigates challenges and adaptations in integrating academic writing across the curriculum at a branch campus of an American university in Qatar. Interviews with 65 faculty across disciplines highlight faculty perceptions of students' challenges with writing, and adaptations faculty make in response. Based on their findings, the authors make recommendations for adapting writing instruction for English-medium universities in the Middle East, especially at IBCs.
>
> Keywords: international branch campus; transnational education; curriculum adaptation; academic writing; faculty perspectives

Western Universities Going Global[1]

In today's increasingly globalized world, a recent trend in higher education has been the establishment of branch campuses of western universities worldwide. These campuses are beneficial to western universities as a means of gaining international recognition and additional revenue, and to the host country in preparing graduates to compete in today's highly competitive knowledge-based global market (Wilkins & Huisman, 2012). In particular, a number of Middle East nations have invited western universities to establish branch campuses. Worldwide, over 240 international branch campuses (IBCs) have been established, with approximately one third of these located in the MENA region (C-BERT, 2014; Miller-Idriss & Hanauer, 2011). Although English often has no official status in the host country, the vast majority of these branch campuses use English as the medium of instruction (Wilson & Urbanovic, 2014; see also the other chapters in this volume).

An important issue for these branch campuses is how to adapt to the institutional structures, expectations, and needs of the host country (Wilkins & Huisman, 2012). Scholars as well as national and international bodies have recommended that IBCs make adaptations that take the local context into account, while also delivering a quality of education that parallels the home institution (e.g., Smith, 2010; UNESCO/OECD, 2005). These simultaneous and sometimes competing demands can present challenges for faculty and students (Shams & Huisman, 2011).

Academic language, particularly in writing, has been found to be especially challenging for students at English-medium universities because much of the focus of learning is on content knowledge rather than on the language through which that content is learned (Doiz, Lasagabaster & Sierra, 2013; Evans & Morrison, 2011; Sonleitner & Khelifa, 2005).

In this chapter, we investigate challenges that students and faculty encounter in integrating writing assignments across the curriculum at an international branch campus of an American university in the Middle East. We begin, however, with a general background on IBCs to highlight some of the issues and challenges of teaching at international branch campuses that have been found in previous research. We then describe the study from which we draw our data, a four-year longitudinal study of literacy at a branch campus of an American university in Qatar, and the specific data that we focus on in this chapter, interviews with faculty at this campus. Our results illustrate a number of faculty perceptions of student challenges, faculty challenges with integrating writing assignments into their curricula, and adaptations that faculty make as a result of these challenges. Lastly, we make recommendations for integrating writing assignments at international branch campuses, specifically those in the Middle East (see also Hodges & Kent; Rudd & Telafici, this volume, for related discussion of student writing and writing assignments at IBCs).

International Branch Campuses

In recent years, higher education has become increasingly international; not only are more and more students studying abroad, but universities themselves are also expanding overseas through the establishment of IBCs. IBCs are satellite campuses established by educational institutions in a source country to deliver its educational programs in a host country (Naidoo, 2009). Although IBCs are not a new phenomenon—the University of London set up degree-granting programs at colleges outside of the UK in 1858 (Lane & Kinser, 2014)—the prevalence of IBCs has increased dramatically in the last 15 years due to changes in policies in many countries aimed specifically at attracting IBCs (Lane, 2011). Of the over 240 IBCs currently operating, the most prevalent source countries are the US, Australia, and the UK (Becker, 2009), and the Middle East is host to nearly one third of IBCs worldwide (Miller-Idriss & Hanauer, 2011). Despite their increasing prevalence, little research exists on IBCs in general (Altbach, 2007), let alone in the MENA region.

IBCs can be beneficial to the source institution as a way to gain international recognition and can benefit the host country by preparing graduates to work in increasingly knowledge-based developing economies (Wilkins & Huisman, 2012). In Qatar, the government is well aware that the nation's gas reserves will not last forever and has invested in IBCs as part of its effort to develop human capital, as outlined in the 2030 National Vision (General Secretariat for Development Planning, 2008).

Although many IBCs enjoy favorable economic conditions, with the cost of building construction and many other operational costs being shouldered by local partner organizations or governments (Becker, 2009; McBurnie & Ziguras, 2007), IBCs, often new, lack many of the human, material, and knowledge resources that have been built up over decades or centuries at the institution's main campus, making it more difficult to implement successful curricula at an IBC (Armstrong, 2007). IBCs have also been criticized because they could divert resources away from the source institution's main campus (Wilkins & Huisman, 2012) and because of concerns of academic freedom in some host countries (Wilhelm, 2011). In addition, some research has found instances of lowered quality of education at IBCs (Poon-McBrayer, 2011; Wilkinson & Yussof, 2005). Comparisons between main campuses and IBCs routinely question whether IBCs perform at a high enough level, and some have questioned the feasibility of conducting high-quality academic programs away from an institution's main campus (Dobos, 2011; O'Neill, 2012).

At many IBCs, quality is controlled by having faculty from the source institution's main campus develop curricula and syllabi, which are then delivered by faculty at the IBC (Dobos, 2011; Pyvis, 2011). However, this can be problematic, as there are often substantial differences between the context of the main campus and the IBC, necessitating appropriate adaptation and contextualization. Although international and national bodies, such as UNESCO and the New England Association for Schools and Colleges (NEASC), recommend that IBCs provide the same quality of education as at the source institution's main campus, they do not specify that curricula be identical (Smith, 2010), with the NEASC's guidelines specifying that "where possible and appropriate [curricula should be] adapted to the culture of the host country, while reflecting American educational values and practices" (as quoted in Smith, 2010, p. 801).

The issue of adaptation at IBCs is hotly contested, both in the literature and in practice. While many agree that adaptation must occur, an important question is to what extent and in what ways to adapt curricula. At IBCs in the Gulf States, staffing and curricula are often adapted to take account of local religion, culture, and values, and to reflect employment demands in the host country (Wilkins & Huisman, 2012). If such adaptations are not made, IBCs could lose credibility with the local community (Shams & Huisman, 2012). In addition, by not adapting, IBCs may risk imposing cultural colonialism through indiscriminate use of home-country ideas, theories, and practices (Wang, 2008). At the same time, if curricula are adapted too much for the overseas market, students at IBCs may find the education unauthentic (Willis, 2004). After all, many students enroll in IBCs in order to receive the same qualification as at the main campus, as well as knowledge about international issues, rather than a purely localized version (Wang, 2008; Zimitat, 2008).

Thus, in their adaptations to curricula and instruction, IBCs often need to find a balance between home and host contexts (Dunn & Wallace, 2004; Smith, 2010; Waterval, Frambach, Driessen & Scherpbier, 2014; Willis, 2003). Faculty at IBCs often feel pressure to construct curricula that "serve two masters," the source institution and the host country (Dobos, 2011, p. 32). IBCs need to offer curricula that are equivalent to those at the main campus while still taking into account local culture and values, and offer both accessibility to a global job market as well as a design for a local job market (Khondker, 2004; Leask, 2008). To be successful, IBCs must integrate the specific host culture where the university is located in ways that benefit students' future working opportunities (Hoare, 2012; Khondker, 2004; Miliszewska & Sztendur, 2011). By doing so, students are not only better prepared for finding a career after graduation, but learning is improved as students are better able to relate content to their own experiences and social contexts (Ziguras, 2008).

Adaptations at IBCs can take many forms. In order to help students relate to course content, textbooks may need to be altered to increase local relevance, or faculty may need to construct examples that are relevant to the local context (Debowski, 2005; Dunn & Wallace, 2006; Gribble & Ziguras,

2003). Some research has found that students at IBCs may have learning styles associated with the host culture, and which may differ substantially from students at the university's main campus (Eaves, 2011; Hefferman, Morrison, Basu & Sweeney, 2010). For example, IBCs may have expectations of student-centered or teacher-centered instruction or processes of questioning or critical thinking that differ from the host culture (Zimitat, 2008). Hefferman, Morrison, Basu & Sweeney (2010) found that students at an Australian university's IBC in China were more global learners; based on this, they recommend that instructors in that context adapt their instruction by first presenting the "big picture" of a lesson in order to establish the context and relevance of the subject matter before presenting individual steps, describing applications of concepts and "what-if" scenarios, allowing students to generate alternative solutions, and using more group work and guest speakers. To date, however, there has been little research conducted on adaptation of curricula and instruction at IBCs in the Middle East.

Teaching Challenges at IBCs

For faculty, teaching at an IBC can present a number of challenges for which they receive little formal preparation (McBurnie & Ziguras, 2007). In the Gulf region, some of these challenges may be institutional, such as differing ideas of mixed gender classes, shared governance, and academic freedom (Noori & Anderson, 2013). Others may be in terms of classroom management (Crabtree & Sapp, 2004); for example, Sonleitner and Khelifa (2005) note that "western-educated" faculty teaching in the UAE may have implicit expectations that only one person should speak at one time, while their students may feel that it is appropriate for several people to have simultaneous conversations. Faculty at IBCs may face particular challenges due to language issues, as few faculty have knowledge of the local language (McBurnie & Ziguras, 2007), and many students may have additional challenges because they are completing their studies in a second language (Coleman, 2006; Hughes, 2008). Technical and academic language, particularly in writing, can be especially challenging for students at English-medium universities (Evans & Morrison, 2011; Gerson, 2010, cited in Wilkins & Urbanovic, 2014).

In the Middle East, in particular, students often have challenges with English reading and writing. Some researchers have described an emphasis on oral communication over written communication in the Middle East (e.g., Meleis, 1982; Wilkins, 2001), which may result in an imbalance between students' oral and written skills. Due to frustration with students' reading and writing performance, some faculty have reported not being able to cover as much material as in their home country (Sonleitner & Khelifa, 2005). Although academic reading and writing can be challenging for students in the Middle East, there have been very few reports of faculty experiences with, and responses to, these challenges (see also Hodges & Kent, this volume).

A better understanding of the writing challenges that faculty encounter and the ways that they address these challenges will give us insights into a quickly growing segment of higher education. Much of the existing understanding of second language writing has come from the experiences of second language writers studying at universities in the major Anglophone countries, often in intensive English programs. Ortega (2009, p. 250) points out that "we should take great care to avoid the pitfall of treating teachers, writers, and writing contexts across studies as belonging to an undifferentiated, homogeneous contextual class," and that although labels such as *English as a foreign language* are useful, such labels "should not blind us to the great diversity [they] hide." As more and more universities expand into the Middle East by opening IBCs (and more local universities adopt English as the medium of instruction), it is important to better understand how writing instruction is implemented in these contexts.

The Study

In this study, we examine faculty perceptions about students' challenges with writing at an English-medium branch campus of an American university in Qatar, and whether and how they adapt their teaching as a result of those challenges. Our data are drawn from a larger four-year longitudinal study of academic literacy development at the institution. In the larger study, we followed the class of 2013 at the institution (N=85) examining their writing experiences, challenges, and development throughout their four years of college, and also conducting interviews with the faculty who taught them. At the beginning of the study, this IBC had been in Qatar for five years and had a student body of 350 students. At the time, there were three majors offered: business administration (48% of the students), computer science (31%), and information systems (21%). In addition to courses in their major, students took required and elective courses offered in a variety of subjects such as history, psychology, and architecture. In their first year, all students took a two-course sequence in academic reading and writing to help them acclimate to university-level literacy demands.

The students (male 47%, female 53%) are quite linguistically and culturally diverse: 63% consider Arabic, and 14% consider English, one of their native languages, and among the students, seventeen different native languages were reported. TOEFL and IELTS scores were generally high, with averages of 97 and 6.5, respectively. Most students are from the Gulf region, the greater Middle East, India, Pakistan, or Bangladesh, while a smaller number of students are from North Africa, Europe, or North America. Of the students in the study, 55% attended English-medium secondary schools, 20% both Arabic and English-medium, 10% Arabic-medium, and the remaining 15% in other languages. Approximately 20% of students attended a one-year transitional program in Qatar between high school and university.

While the larger study was multi-faceted and employed a variety of data collection methods (see Pessoa, Miller & Kaufer, 2014), in this chapter we focus on interviews with faculty with some reference to interviews conducted with students to better contextualize our findings and discussion. In total, one of the authors conducted 60 one-hour semi-structured interviews with faculty members. Most interviews were individual, though some were group interviews with faculty teaching in the same discipline. The interviews were conducted in the authors' or faculty participants' offices. Upon obtaining consent, interviews were audio and video recorded and subsequently transcribed verbatim for analysis. The purpose of the interviews was to obtain an understanding of 1) the literacy demands of the faculty's discipline in general and the specific courses they taught, 2) the faculty's perception about the students' academic strengths and challenges, and 3) the faculty's approaches to address students' needs and potential adaptations to their curriculum (see the appendix for the interview protocol). Because our focus was on the content of the interviews rather than the linguistic or textual features of the discourse, the transcripts were analyzed using thematic analysis, in which transcripts are reviewed recursively to identify themes (Duff, 2008; Richie, Spencer & O'Connor, 2003).

In total, 75 faculty members taught the students in the larger study, of whom we were able to interview 65. The faculty came from a variety of disciplines, including computer science, business administration, information systems, history, psychology, and English. The majority of the faculty interviewed are male and hold a doctoral degree from the US. Approximately half of the faculty come from the US and speak English as their native language, and the rest come from a variety of countries in the Middle East, North Africa, Europe, and Asia, and speak a variety of languages. In general, they have extensive experience teaching undergraduate students in the US and internationally, with only a few having taught mostly graduate students. More than half have been teaching at this IBC for more than three years with a few having been at the IBC from its inception in 2004. More than half of the faculty have experience teaching in the US, and about half of the faculty have extensive experience teaching at the institution's main campus in the US.

In the following section, we present the findings of the study, focusing on faculty perceptions of student writing challenges, what the faculty do to address the needs of the students, and adaptations that faculty make to their teaching.

Faculty Perceptions of Student Academic Challenges

Faculty commented on a number of challenges that they perceived that students face, including initial concerns about academic preparedness for university-level writing as well as ongoing challenges with academic reading and writing in terms of a lack of background knowledge, challenges with reading, and difficulties with disciplinary genres.

Many of the faculty talked about initial concerns about students' academic preparedness, especially their work ethic, study skills, priorities, and level of maturity and independence, but also their previous experience with writing. One faculty said that "a lot of the students coming out of the local school system are missing a solid foundation and basic skill set" (Professor H, Spring 2010). In terms of writing, this resonates with some of the students' reports of limited previous experience with writing:

> In high school we only wrote 100 to 250 words in English class. [The teachers] give you the topic. The students write paragraphs for each topic and memorize each paragraph without thinking. (Dima, Fall 2009)

As students progressed through their undergraduate studies, some of these concerns diminished; by the second or third year, the faculty reported that the students worked more independently and took more ownership of and responsibility over their own learning.

Some faculty described students' difficulties with writing as arising from a cultural emphasis on oral rather than written communication. Faculty described students as having stronger oral than written skills, despite the value that writing has for learning:

> For the students here, in some ways they are much better at expressing themselves orally. But writing itself is a way of kind of thinking through something by having to formulate sentences that string one after another, you actually have to think about what you are saying in ways that you don't when you are speaking. (Professor R, Spring 2013)

Professor R pointed out that writing is a much different skill from speaking, and that the act of writing can help students to learn, a perspective that is supported by research on writing-to-learn (see, e.g., Hirvela, 2011; Williams, 2012).

Many of the faculty discussed students' challenges with reading. In many courses, students' writing was based on assigned readings, and so these challenges with reading also directly affected students' writing. According to one history professor, "[many] students have trouble with vocabulary in primary sources" and "students also have trouble understanding the historical context, as it is unfamiliar to them" (Professor B, Fall 2009), indicating that students' difficulty reading source texts was not only linguistic but also due to a lack of background knowledge.

Some faculty who came from the university's main campus commented that students at the IBC read more slowly and were not used to the amount of reading that would typically be assigned at the main campus. Professor M stated that "I came here and . . . I realized they just they read a lot slower than the students [at the main campus]" (Fall 2012). Similarly, Professor K stated, "I think the other thing that I've noticed here compared to students [at the main campus] is the amount of time that it takes them to be able to read and comprehend and formulate a long answer . . . and actually write it out, and so that makes it really difficult." On the main campus, he said, students "have 50 minutes and it's fine" but at the IBC students "don't even get to the last couple of questions" (Spring 2013). The need for more time not only to complete individual exams and assignments, but also additional class time to "catch up" on background knowledge were common issues discussed by the faculty.

Reading challenges and lack of background knowledge made it difficult for students to interpret texts sufficiently in order to write about them. This was particularly challenging in a course that demanded the reading of literary and cultural theory, which was new to many students. Thus, students' coping strategy to understand and write about the texts was to rely heavily on the professor, as explained by Professor E:

> I think these students rock. It's simply that they don't have this experience of talking to anyone . . . about what the texts mean. They, like, look at me . . . and they take notes like crazy . . . I'm the source of wisdom and knowledge. So it's like no textbooks work, nothing really matters to them as much as what I say. So it's how it works here. It's like the oral culture of knowledge . . . [On the main campus] you just give them one idea [and] they do the rest themselves (Spring 2013)

As this professor explains, many of the students in this institution are academically strong, but they have little background in interpreting theory-heavy texts, leading to reading struggles. Furthermore, Professor E relates students' coping strategy of relying on in-class explanations to the oral nature of the local culture, as described earlier.

Some professors commented that students' challenges with reading and writing were related to their wanting to find the right answer rather than, or in addition to, a lack of understanding and appreciation for complexity and application of ideas. In this regard, Professor S commented that:

> [The students] are too busy looking for the "right" answer. Part of what I have to educate them out of is that I am not concerned about "right" answers . . . Some [students answer] yes; some say no; and they both get full credit. And it starts to sink in. Then they can stop looking for the right answer and look for developing a thoughtful and theoretically rounded paper (Fall 2010).

The focus on finding the right answer rather than complexity and application of concepts may also be related to students' focus on memorization. Describing students' pre-college experiences, Professor J commented:

> I think a lot of the curriculum that they come out of in high schools here is very memorization based. It's very based on, you know, not applying those concepts to various situations, but much more regurgitation of the information, and so when you force students in any discipline to do problem solving . . . they really hate that. (Spring 2013)

A number of faculty commented on students' challenges with the types of analysis, application, and critical thinking skills that are expected at the IBC, and attributed these to the focus on memorization and "regurgitation" in students' pre-college education. Another professor related students' focus on finding the right answer in their pre-college education to a lack of motivation to write in college:

> And they went through this schooling where people tell them "this is wrong" and "that is wrong" and "[you] just can't write." They are not writers and they don't love it. If you don't love it you will never get better and you will never become that person who writes. (Professor E, Spring 2013)

Weak reading, analytical, and critical thinking skills, as well as unfamiliarity with the demands and expectations of academic writing, led to challenges in students' meeting their professors' writing expectations. The students' unfamiliarity with academic and professional writing norms was also observed in students' inadequate formatting of papers as well as challenges with rhetorical modes and genres, as commented on by Professor P:

> The letter of application for a job is like a five-paragraph essay. When I teach it on [the main campus], it seems elementary because the students know this structure. But, here, they don't, so students struggle making functional paragraphs for the application letter. Students also have trouble deconstructing business arguments. New product proposals were broken into paragraph-size sections, but they weren't paragraphs—no sense of beginning or end. Business communicators need to be able to break complicated ideas into manageable ones (Spring 2011)

As did other professors, this professor compared his students on the branch campus to those on the main campus, speaking of his concern about the students' unfamiliarity with the five-paragraph essay and the students' ability to effectively construct paragraphs. Although constructing arguments in an organized manner and organizing ideas in manageable, clear paragraphs is something that is heavily discussed in the students' two first-year academic writing courses and in other writing-intensive courses such as history, students struggle applying these concepts to professional and disciplinary writing.

Other faculty also discussed students' challenges with reading and writing as arising from a lack of genre knowledge rather than a lack of linguistic knowledge, such as Professor M who commented that "if you are bouncing from textbooks to technical things to doing research on the web to a Harvard business review article, they have a hard time." "I don't think it's the language issues anymore," she said, "I really think that the genre switching is a bigger problem than the language issues" (Fall 2012). On the main campus, the students may be more familiar with these genres and may be better able to navigate the variety of disciplinary genres they encounter. This genre knowledge also affects writing instruction, as Professor T explained, "You're really not teaching exactly the same genre here that you teach [on the main campus]."

When the genre is unfamiliar to students and the content is more challenging, it is also likely that the students' language abilities and writing skills will break down. For example, when students had to write a literature review for the first time in a computer science course, Professor D was quite disappointed with the outcome, commenting that:

> In a literature review, [the] writing [was] terrible. Everything was wrong: introducing [the] topic, organizing [the] topic, transitioning between sections, run-on sentences, punctuation, content, incorrect words. Both individual and group assignments were terrible (Spring 2011).

Although Professor D describes students' poor performance in this writing task in terms of organization, grammar, and punctuation, writing a literature review is a complex task that can be daunting for any writer, particularly to second-year undergraduate students with no previous experience with this genre. As a result, when feeling overwhelmed by such a task, students are likely to make mistakes in language and structure.

The faculty described students' challenges with reading and writing as resulting from a number of factors, including students' lack of extensive writing practice during their pre-college education, a cultural emphasis on oral communication, students' tendency toward memorization and retelling of facts rather than analysis and application, and students' lack of background and genre knowledge. Given these challenges, faculty have to make informed decisions about their teaching practices to meet students' needs, which may include adapting their pedagogical practices to the teaching context.

Curricular Adaptations to Meet Students' Needs

As mentioned earlier, some faculty continue teaching at the IBC in the same way as they have at the university's main campus or at other (non-IBC) institutions. They continue to assign the same amount and types of reading and the same writing assignments. Others do away with having a reading and writing-focused course, while others become very strategic about the amount and kinds of scaffolding they provide students to enhance their learning. Holding students at the branch campus to the same standards as the students on the main campus is what drives some of the professors' decisions to keep their requirements the same. However, others argue that by adapting their requirements, they are enhancing student learning.

For example, to reduce the complexity of the writing of business case analyses, Professor S completely did away with having students read business cases in his courses and instead uses television shows and films as cases. Students analyze these visual cases in the form of a written case analysis using the relevant business theories discussed in class. Professor S explains that with this innovative and motivating teaching practice, he aims to reduce the cognitive demands of the task by using content that is more familiar to students, both in content and modality:

> The television shows lend themselves to discussion. [The students already] watch their favorite American shows and discuss them with their family. They say "did you see Friends last night?" or whatever. [I am] leveraging what they [already] do, which is making compelling content then relatively easy to get people talking about it, laugh and then ground them in the context of the theory. I think . . . talking comes naturally, and then [I frame] the discussion, so that it is more than just descriptive or opinion. . . . I can see the output of it and I am pleased (Fall 2010).

Although this professor may be criticized for not exposing students to authentic, written business cases, he argues that this innovative approach to case analysis makes it more accessible to students, as the vocabulary and background knowledge are more familiar. This, in turn, allows students to focus on in-class discussion and the written case analysis separately from comprehending the case itself.

Instead of eliminating readings entirely, after a year of teaching in Qatar and realizing students' reading challenges, Professor M made strategic decisions to assign less reading and focus more on scaffolding the reading he did assign. Reflecting on this adaptation, Professor M commented:

> It's much more difficult to read in a second or a third language . . . I cut the total pages but I wanted to make sure that the topics were covered. So one thing was I [did not assign] readings that I felt didn't really add that much, and the other was I've worked on a variety of ways to provide guidance to the students when they sit down to read so that they are doing directed reading instead of just kind of reading and pulling out the main topics [on their own] . . . Initially when I started out as a professor I was, "I'm just going to give you a bunch of stuff and you need to figure it out on your own." Eventually that is something that you should develop as a professional, but it's not necessarily fair to expect that from a junior in college, I don't think. (Fall 2012).

Given the positive results of this adaption that Professor M saw at the IBC, he continued these practices when he returned to the main campus, where he found that the adaptations were equally as effective:

> So I was here for a semester and then I went back to [the main campus], and guess what? I did the same things I did here when I went to [the main campus] and some students liked the readings a lot more and . . . the students were getting more out of the readings. It's just good teaching . . . It required me to change my thinking and approach [away] from "you are an upper class student at [this institution], you should already know how to do this." [to an approach where] if you are not there yet, I need to meet you where you are and show you how to get there. (Fall 2012)

The adaptations that Professor M made as a result of his experiences at the IBC seem not only to be accommodations for a different context with a different student population, but also strategies for scaffolding student learning more generally. He found that although some people might consider adaptations that reduce the amount of work students are assigned to be "watering down" the curriculum, he feels that these adaptations are just examples of good teaching:

> The goal was not to water [the curriculum] down at all. The goal was [to] think thoughtfully . . . I could get away with being sloppy on the [main] campus in a way that I couldn't here. . . . And I give these directions and these guidelines and this scaffolding, and a number of people on the main campus when I tell them that [say] "you are watering down the education." And the reality is that I'm really not. To the contrary, it's making me be a better teacher. (Fall 2012)

"Watering down" the curriculum is a common concern at IBCs, who want to hold the students to the same standards as the students on the main campus. However, what we see from Professor M is that adaptations that need to be made in an IBC are not necessarily decreasing the standards but can be considered a fine-tuning of curriculum and pedagogy.

Like Professor M, a number of faculty discussed scaffolding. When it comes to writing, as with reading, one way to help students meet the expectations of professors, the program, and the university is to offer appropriate scaffolding for students, as many professors in this institution do. For example, the two first-year English courses include multiple-draft writing with extensive written feedback from the professors as well as individual conferences with the students for each paper. In courses in the students' majors, the students are also encouraged to submit drafts for which they obtain written feedback from their professors. Students are also encouraged to visit the writing center to get help with their linguistic choices to strengthen their ideas and make them clearer for the final version of an assignment.

Perhaps the most scaffolding that students receive in courses in their major comes from Professor X who carefully guides students in the writing of case analysis assignments, from helping students comprehend the case to providing samples and guiding questions for students to effectively write a case analysis, as explained by the professor:

> The biggest obstacle our students have is that . . . most of them are not able to read a five-page case description and understand it. So, essentially, . . . I am reading with them. I am being like a parent reading with a kid. They need that. . . . What I do is I take the case and I show them how to read the case, and that helps because they do not know how to read the case . . . I highlight and I say "hey see this sentence, interesting sentence. This is how you should do it." (Fall 2013).

Clearly, providing this amount of scaffolding requires a great deal of commitment, effort and time by the faculty, and the recognition that this amount of guiding and scaffolding will eventually pay off in the end. Not all professors are willing to put in this effort and not all can, given the amount of material that needs to be covered in a course and the time constraints of the semester. Recognizing that his students needed the extra help, this professor offers extra sessions outside of class time to scaffold students' reading and writing. Although the students indicate that they find his help valuable, according to Professor X, he feels that students do not take full advantage of it. While most students come to the extra session he offers, many fail to start their assignments early enough to be able to obtain feedback from the professor on early drafts, resulting in writing assignments with various flaws.

Providing scaffolding and additional help may not always be productive if students do not take advantage of what is offered. Recognizing the weaknesses in student writing, some faculty continue to have the same requirements and demands, but change their expectations in terms of language. For example, Professor C commented that:

> In short answer writing, I look to make sure the concepts are there, not necessarily how they are connected on the paper

> [linguistically]. [On the main campus], I graded down for grammar more, as I felt that it showed a lack of precision, but I don't do this here because otherwise most students would get low grades. (Fall 2011)

Like this professor, other professors tend to focus on the "concepts" and ideas in students' texts, with less focus on how the ideas are connected linguistically, and without holding students as responsible for writing coherent, organized responses in standard English as they might do on the main campus.

Similar to changing language expectations, some professors give value to the varieties of World Englishes used by students, and become more tolerant of the influence of the students' mother tongues in their writing. While some professors push their Arabic-speaking students to be more direct in their writing and do away with the indirect and "flowery" (Professor W, Spring 2012) language valued in Arabic (see also Hall, 1976), some professors are concerned with the imperialistic overtone of such demands, as explained by Professor S:

> I'm reading something [a student] wrote, and I said, "[student's name], I don't understand what this means. This sounds to me like it's a translation in your mind from Arabic to English." She said, "Oh, yeah, that's what it is. This is what we say in Arabic." And for me, I had to stop for a second and [think], you form your identity by this language. And here I'm saying, "No, this is wrong." What kind of ramifications does it have? How imperialist must I sound at the moment to this poor student? (Spring 2010).

While Professor S struggles with having his students write academic texts that meet the expectations of writing in the American academy without being imperialistic in his demands, he, like others, finds ways to communicate his expectations while still valuing students' mother tongues.

While some professors provided support for student writing by offering scaffolding or adaptations to writing assignments, given students' writing challenges, other professors decided to assign less writing. When we asked faculty about their writing practices in their courses, some faculty described feeling limited in their ability to help students with writing. Professor N stated that writing is "not something I feel I should teach" because it "isn't my job" (Spring 2013). As a result, some faculty focused less on writing in their courses, and some assigned no writing at all, as explained by Professor G:

[Now,] I use only short readings and reporting on quizzes because many very bright students have difficulty expressing themselves in English. I'm not so concerned with writing, though . . . I have them write only a sentence or two. I don't assign essays demanding full paragraphs. I taught in [a country in Asia], where there were lots of [Asian language]-speaking students. Months or years would go by before I saw a full paragraph produced by any of [the students]. Students [here] have many grammatical errors, limited vocabulary, have trouble with subtle nuances. I don't think that students necessarily have to be good at expository writing. (Spring 2012)

Instead of offering more opportunities and appropriate scaffolding for students to practice their writing, this professor has his students do minimal writing, as he feels the students are not good at writing effective and clear paragraphs with accurate grammar, something he claims is not so important for business students who will likely write reports which will then be edited by a professional business or technical writer.

Conclusions and Recommendations

The results reported above lead to a number of conclusions and recommendations for teaching writing at IBCs. In addition, given the rapid increase of IBCs and other English-medium institutions across the MENA region, as well the perception that oral rather than written communication may have greater cultural emphasis in this region, we note that many of our conclusions and recommendations may be applicable to writing instruction in the MENA region in general.

We first suggest that minimizing reading and writing requirements or doing away with them completely, as some faculty in the present study reported doing, are not optimal solutions. Doing so may be detrimental to student learning and development because it limits students' exposure to academic literacies. Academic literacy development is a difficult task that takes many years and requires practice, instruction, and imitation (Sommers, 2008). Reading and writing disciplinary genres is an important part of becoming a full-fledged member of a discipline (Canagarajah, 2002; Duff, 2001; Johns, 1997), and limiting students' opportunities to developing their academic literacy skills to only English or humanities does not give students the opportunity to practice the disciplinary genres that they will likely encounter after they graduate.

Adapting reading and writing assignments to the context does not "water down" the curriculum, and such adaptations can enrich and improve teaching and learning, as Professor M points out when he says that the adaptations he made in his teaching at this IBC forced him to "be a better teacher."

Because of the benefits for students and teachers, we advocate for a focus on writing and reading across the curriculum, with learning scaffolded to enhance students' literacy skills. While we recognize that scaffolding student learning, particularly in writing, is not an easy task and requires commitment, time, and effort as well as a clear understanding of the writing demands of a discipline in order to make them explicit to students, we have found that there are committed teachers at this IBC who understand the importance of helping students develop their academic literacy skills, such as Professor X, who offers optional extra sessions outside of class time. However, a number of faculty in our study noted that because students at the IBC required additional time to complete readings or complete assignments, more class time would be useful to help students acquire the background knowledge that might be lacking. More time may mean extending the four-year curriculum to a five-year curriculum, giving students more time to complete exams, or having enough time in a course to properly scaffold student learning by, for example, having fewer students in each class, or dividing a course into two semesters that might typically be taught in one. Having enough time to focus on individual students and make certain writing practices standard, such as multiple draft writing (which occurred in English courses, but few other courses in the present study), is likely to enhance student writing.

While faculty may have the motivation and commitment to help students develop their writing skills, some may not have the knowledge or tools to teach writing, and some might feel, as Professor N did, that teaching writing "isn't my job." However, we argue that teachers who assign writing in their courses are, to an extent, responsible for making sure students understand how to write those assignments. Thus, we recommend that professors who embark on the journey of teaching at a branch campus abroad are equipped with the fundamental skills needed to teach writing (and reading) to linguistically and culturally diverse students. This can be done by engaging in faculty development around these and other teaching practices through collaborations with English faculty and other learning and writing specialists who can help faculty deconstruct sample texts in their fields so that faculty can better understand and make more explicit to students the features of disciplinary genres as well as faculty's expectations of writing (see, for example, the Teaching and Learning Cycle: Humphrey & Hao, 2013; Mahboob & Devrim, 2013; Martin & Rose, 2005; Rothery, 1994). Faculty development around teaching with writing is especially important, given that students' lack of familiarity with specific genres was brought up often by our study participants in terms of challenges students had with reading and writing but was seldom mentioned in terms of strategies that faculty have for addressing students' difficulties.

Our current work on this branch campus is moving us toward more explicit instruction of disciplinary genres. Our four-year longitudinal study of academic writing development has allowed us to understand the writing demands of various disciplines and analyze how students met those demands and expectations longitudinally and what challenges they have. Now we are in a position to work together with the faculty to help them better understand the writing expectations of their discipline and of the genres they assign. We hope that, as a result, faculty across the curriculum will be better able to design writing assignments and develop the tools to make their expectations explicit to students, enhancing both the teaching and learning of writing.

As a part of our advocacy of faculty across the curriculum playing an important role in students' writing development, we also urge faculty to hold students to high standards while being reasonable about their expectations for students who are still developing academic literacies. In our data, we saw that some faculty reduce their expectations of students in terms of writing and language use. From interviews with students, we also found that students quickly learn what the expectations of different professors are: when the expectations are low, students tend to be less careful about their work, and when expectations are high, students tend to be more careful. While we believe that a focus on content is important and that faculty should recognize the challenges of writing in a second language, we also feel that completely disregarding attention to language is not an appropriate solution. Doing so may lead students to think that linguistic accuracy is not important, and as the findings of our study indicate, holding students accountable for both the content and accuracy of their written work will contribute to their development as writers and English language users in their courses across the curriculum and beyond.

Note

1. This publication was made possible by NPRP grant # 5-1320-6-040 from the Qatar National Research Fund (a member of Qatar Foundation). The statements made herein are solely the responsibility of the authors.

References

Altbach, P. G. (2007). Twinning and branch campuses: The professorial obstacle. *International Higher Education, 48*, 2–3.

Armstrong, L. (2007). Competing in the global higher education marketplace: Outsourcing, twinning, and franchising. *New Directions for Higher Education*, 2007(140), 131–138. doi:10.1002/he.287.

Becker, R. F. (2009). *International branch campuses: Markets and strategies*. London: Observatory on Borderless Higher Education.

C-BERT. (2014). *Branch campus listing (Updated May 29, 2014)*. SUNY Albany. Retrieved from http://www.globalhighered.org/.

Canagarajah, A. S. (2002). *A geopolitics of academic writing*. Pittsburgh: University of Pittsburgh Press.

Coleman, J. A. (2006). English-medium teaching in European higher education. *Language Teaching*, 39, 1. doi:10.1017/S026144480600320X.

Crabtree, R. D. & Sapp, D. A. (2004). Your culture, my classroom, whose pedagogy? Negotiating effective teaching and learning in Brazil. *Journal of Studies in International Education*, 8, 105–132. doi:10.1177/1028315303260826.

Debowski, S. (2005). Across the divide: teaching a transnational MBA in a second language. *Higher Education Research & Development*, 24, 265–280. doi:10.1080/07294360500153992.

Dobos, K. (2011). "Serving two masters"—Academics' perspectives on working at an offshore campus in Malaysia. *Educational Review*, 63, 19–35. doi:10.1080/00131911003748035.

Doiz, A., Lasagabaster, D., and Sierra J. M. (2013). *English-medium instruction at universities: Global challenges*. Bristol, UK: Multilingual Matters.

Duff, P. A. (2001). Learning English for academic and occupational purposes. *TESOL Quarterly*, 35, 606–607.

Duff, P. A. (2008). *Case study research in applied linguistics*. New York: Lawrence Erlbaum.

Dunn, L. & Wallace, M. (2004). Australian academics teaching in Singapore: Striving for cultural empathy. *Innovations in Education and Teaching International*, 41, 291–304. doi:10.1080/14703290410001733285.

Dunn, L. & Wallace, M. (2006). Australian academics and transnational teaching: An exploratory study of their preparedness and experiences. *Higher Education Research & Development*, 25, 357–369. doi:10.1080/07294360600947343.

Eaves, M. (2011). The relevance of learning styles for international pedagogy in higher education. *Teachers and Teaching: Theory and Practice*, 17, 677–692.

Evans, S. & Morrison, B. (2011). Meeting the challenges of English-medium higher education: The first-year experience in Hong Kong. *English for Specific Purposes*, 30, 198–208. doi:10.1016/j.esp.2011.01.001.

General Secretariat for Development Planning. (2008). *Qatar national vision 2030*. Doha, Qatar. Retrieved from http://www.qdb.qa/English/Documents/QNV 2030_English.pdf.

Gribble, K. & Ziguras, C. (2003). Learning to Teach Offshore: Pre-Departure training for lecturers in transnational programs. *Higher Education Research & Development*, 22, 205–216. doi:10.1080/07294360304115.

Hall, E .T. (1976). *Beyond Culture*. Garden City, NY: Anchor Books.

Hefferman, T., Morrison, M., Basu, P. & Sweeney, A. (2010). Cultural differences, learning styles and transnational education. *Journal of Higher Education Policy and Management*, *32*, 27–39. doi:10.1080/13600800903440535.

Hirvela, A. (2011). Writing to learn in content areas: Research insights. In R. Manchón (Ed.), *Learning-to-write and writing-to-learn in an additional language* (pp. 37–60). Philadelphia: John Benjamins.

Hoare, L. (2012). Transnational student voices: Reflections on a second chance. *Journal of Studies in International Education*, *16*, 271–286. doi:10.1177/1028315311398045.

Hughes, R. (2008). Internationalisation of higher education and language policy: Questions of quality and equity. *Higher Education Management and Policy*, *20*, 102–119.

Humphrey, S. & Hao, J. (2012). Deconstructing written genres in undergraduate biology. *Linguistics and the Human Sciences*, *7*, 29–53.

Johns, A. M. (1997). *Text, role, and context*. London: Cambridge University Press.

Khondker, H. H. (2004). Globalization as glocalization: Evolution of a sociological concept. *Bangladesh E-Journal of Sociology*, *1*(2), 1–9.

Lane, J. E. (2011). Importing private higher education: International branch campuses. *Journal of Comparative Policy Analysis: Research and Practice*, *13*, 367–381. doi:10.1080/13876988.2011.583106.

Lane, J. & Kinser, K. (2014). Transnational education: A maturing phenomenon. *European Association for International Education Forum, Summer*, 8–10.

Leask, B. (2008). Teaching for learning in the transnational classroom. In L. Dunn & M. Wallace (Eds.), *Teaching in transnational higher education: Enhancing learning for offshore international students* (pp. 120–132). New York: Routledge.

Mahboob, A. & Devrim, D. Y. (2013). Supporting independent construction online: Feedback in the SLATE project. *Linguistics and the Human Sciences*, *7*, 101–123.

Martin, J. R. (2013). Genre-based literacy programs: Contextualising the SLATE project. *Linguistics and the Human Sciences*, *7*(1–3). doi:10.1558/lhs.v7i1-3.5.

Martin, J. R. & Rose, D. (2005). Designing literacy pedagogy: Scaffolding democracy in the classroom. In J. Webster, C. M. I. M. Matthiesen & R. Hasan (Eds.), *Continuing discourse on language: A functional perspective* (pp. 251–280). London: Continuum.

McBurnie, G. & Ziguras, C. (2007). *Transnational education: Issues and trends in offshore higher education*. London: Routledge.

Meleis, A. I. (1982). Arab students in Western universities: Social properties and dilemmas. *Journal of Higher Education*, *53*, 439–447. doi:10.2307/1981609.

Miliszewska, I. & Sztendur, E. M. (2011). Australian transnational education programmes in South East Asia: Student satisfaction with the learning environment. *Australian Universities' Review*, *54*, 12–21.

Miller-Idriss, C. & Hanauer, E. (2011). Transnational higher education: Offshore campuses in the Middle East. *Comparative Education*, *47*, 181–207. doi:10.1080/03050068.2011.553935.

Naidoo, V. (2009). Transnational higher education: A stock take of current activity. *Journal of Studies in International Education*, *13*, 310–330. doi:10.1177/1028315308317938.

Noori, N. & Anderson, P. K. (2013). Globalization, governance, and the diffusion of the American model of education: Accreditation agencies and American-style universities in the Middle East. *International Journal of Politics, Culture, and Society, 26*, 159–172. doi:10.1007/s10767-013-9131-1.

O'Neill, M. (2012). Transnational education: A case study of one professional doctorate. *Higher Education Studies, 2*, 14–30. doi:10.5539/hes.v2n4p14.

Organisation for Economic Co-operation and Developmant. (2005). Guidelines for quality provision in cross-border higher education. Retrieved from http://www.oecd.org/education/innovation-education/35779480.pdf.

Ormond, B. (2011). Shifts in knowledge teaching: The unexpected consequences of assessment practices on secondary history. *Pacific-Asian Education, 23*, 5–22.

Ortega, L. (2009). Studying writing across EFL contexts: Looking back and moving forward. In R. Manchón (Ed.), *Writing in foreign language contexts: Teaching and research* (pp. 232–255). Clevedon, UK: Multilingual Matters.

Pessoa, S., Miller, R. T. & Kaufer, D. (2014). Student challenges and development in the transition to college literacy at an English-medium university in Qatar. *International Review of Applied Linguistics, 52*(2), 127–156. doi:10.1515/iral-2014-0006.

Poon-McBrayer, K. F. (2011). Quality assurance challenges of transnational higher education in Hong Kong. *Pacific-Asian Education, 23*, 43–56.

Pyvis, D. (2011). The need for context-sensitive measures of educational quality in transnational higher education. *Teaching in Higher Education, 16*, 733–744. doi:10.1080/13562517.2011.570436.

Richie, J., Spencer, L. & O'Connor, W. (2003). Carrying out qualitative analysis. In J. Richie & J. Lewis (Eds.), *Qualitative research practice: A guide for social science students and researchers.* London: SAGE.

Rothery, J. (1994). *Exploring literacy in school English (Write it right resources for literacy and learning).* Sydney: Metropolitan East Disadvantaged Schools Program.

Shams, F. & Huisman, J. (2012). Managing offshore branch campuses: An analytical framework for institutional strategies. *Journal of Studies in International Education, 16*, 106–127. doi:10.1177/1028315311413470.

Smith, K. (2010). Assuring quality in transnational higher education: A matter of collaboration or control? *Studies in Higher Education, 35*, 793–806. doi:10.1080/03075070903340559.

Sommers, N. (2008). The call of research—A longitudinal view of writing development. *CCCC Studies in Writing and Rhetoric, 60*, 152–164.

Sonleitner, N. & Khelifa, M. (2005). Western-educated faculty challenges in a Gulf classroom. *Learning and Teaching in Higher Education: Gulf Perspectives, 2*, 1–21.

Wang, T. (2008). Intercultural dialogue and understanding: Implications for teachers. In L. Dunn & M. Wallace (Eds.), *Teaching in transnational higher education: Enhancing learning for offshore international students* (pp. 57–66). New York: Routledge.

Waterval, D. G. J., Frambach, J. M., Driessen, E. W. & Scherpbier, A.J.J.A. (2015). Copy but not paste: A literature review of crossborder curricu-

lum partnerships. *Journal of Studies in International Education, 19*(1), 65–85. doi:10.1177/1028315314533608.
Wilhelm, I. (2011, September 14). Carnegie Mellon U. to open campus in Rwanda, a milestone for Africa. *The Chronicle of Higher Education*. Retrieved from http://chronicle.com/article/Carnegie-Mellon-U-to-Open/128991/.
Wilkins, S. (2001). Management development in the Arab Gulf states: The influence of language and culture. *Industrial and Commercial Training, 33*, 260–265.
Wilkins, S. & Huisman, J. (2012). The international branch campus as transnational strategy in higher education. *Higher Education, 64*, 627–645. doi:10.1007/s10734-012-9516-5.
Wilkins, S. & Urbanovic, J. (2014). English as the lingua franca in transnational higher education: Motives and prospects of institutions that teach in languages other than English. *Journal of Studies in International Education, 18*(5), 405–425. doi:10.1177/1028315313517267.
Wilkinson, R. & Yussof, I. (2005). Public and private provision of higher education in Malaysia: A comparative analysis. *Higher Education, 50*, 361–386. doi:10.1007/s10734-004-6354-0.
Williams, J. (2012). The potential role (s) of writing in second language development. *Journal of Second Language Writing, 21*, 321–331. doi:10.1016/j.jslw.2012.09.007.
Willis, M. (2004). Looking East—looking West: Exploring the views of Hong Kong university students about traditional Chinese cultural values in terms of the delivery of foreign programs. *Journal of Marketing for Higher Education, 13*, 159–177. doi:10.1300/J050v13n01_09.
Ziguras, C. (2008). The cultural politics of transnational education: Ideological and pedagogical issues for teaching staff. In L. Dunn & M. Wallace (Eds.), *Teaching in transnational higher education: Enhancing learning for offshore international students* (pp. 44–54). New York: Routledge.
Zimitat, C. (2008). Student perceptions of the internationalisation of the undergraduate curriculum. In L. Dunn & M. Wallace (Eds.), *Teaching in transnational higher education: Enhancing learning for offshore international students* (pp. 135–147). New York: Routledge.

Appendix: Faculty Interview Protocol

Background & Discipline

1. Please tell me about your background and how you ended up here.
2. Please describe your discipline. What do [business administration, computer science, or information systems] experts do?
3. What is the role of language (reading, writing, jargon) in your discipline?
4. How important is it to be a good communicator in your discipline?

The Course(s) Taught

5. Please describe the course(s) you teach to the class of 2013 this semester. What are the objectives and outcomes of the course(s)?

Perception of Students

6. What is your general impression of these students?
7. How are the students doing in your course(s)? To what extent are they meeting your expectations?
8. How prepared or unprepared do you find these students? What are their major strengths and challenges?
9. What factors contribute to your students' success in your class? What do successful students in your class do?

Reading in Your Course(s)

10. What is the role of reading in your course(s)? Are there required reading materials? Do students have to read course material before class and show their understanding?
11. To what students do you know if students do the reading? Do you check if students completed the reading? And if so how?
12. To what extent do your students show an adequate understanding of the reading material?
13. How would you rate your students' reading abilities?
14. Do you do anything in particular to help your students with their understanding of the reading material?
15. Do you know come to you for help with the reading materials? Do you know if they seek help from our resources such as teaching assistant, the Academic Resource Center, or friends?

Writing in Your Course(s)

16. What is the role of writing in your course(s)? Do you have writing assignments in your course(s)? If so, what kinds of writing assignments? Do students submit work individually or in groups?
17. Why do you have students write in your course(s)?
18. How do you prepare students for your assignments? Written guidelines, explanation in class, draft writing, written feedback, sample papers, revisions based on feedback?
19. If you provide written feedback on student writing, what do you focus on?

20. How do you grade your students writing? Is there anything you focus on the most?
21. What are the qualities of an A written product in your course(s)?
22. How do your students perform in the writing assignments? What are their strengths and weaknesses?
23. To what extent do you see improvement from draft to draft, from assignment to assignment?
24. Do your students come to you for help with their writing assignments? Do you know if they also use other resources such as teaching assistants, the academic resource center, friends?

Teaching Adaptations

25. Since you have come here, have you made any changes to the way you teach to address the needs and interest of the students here? If so, what have you done?
26. How effective to student learning are your adaptations?
27. Do you see any drawbacks with these changes you have made?

9

Hybrid Writing Positions within WAC/WID Initiatives: Connecting Faculty Writing Expectations and MENA Cultures

Amy Hodges
TEXAS A&M UNIVERSITY (QATAR)

Brenda Kent
TEXAS A&M UNIVERSITY (QATAR)

> Writing-intensive courses for engineers at Texas A&M University at Qatar provide a unique view into the efficacy of writing-in-the-disciplines (WID) policies and practices in the Middle East. In this chapter, the authors draw upon qualitative data from faculty interviews to examine their perceptions surrounding the teaching and learning of writing. The authors argue that hybrid writing consultants—staff positions with the combined roles of tutor, teacher, and writing fellow—are a locally relevant way to help mediate between engineering faculty members' expectations and multilingual students' development as writers.
>
> Keywords: WAC/WID; writing support; multilingual writers; engineering; international branch campus

After being invited to open an international branch campus (IBC) by the Qatar Foundation, the Texas A&M University at Qatar (TAM-Q) undergraduate engineering programs began admitting students in 2003. TAM-Q students major in one of four areas of engineering: petroleum, mechanical, chemical, or electrical and computer engineering. They take the same courses and meet the same requirements as students in the engineering department on the main campus, and, as the main campus writing-across-the-curriculum (WAC)/*writing-in-the-disciplines* (WID) initiatives transferred as well, their course load includes writing-intensive (WI) courses. Although not an uncommon sight in the Arabian Gulf region today, most IBCs in the area have been operating for fewer than 15 years. In 2011, Miller-Idriss and Hanauer classified over half—34 out of 57—of "transnational" universities in the Middle East as IBCs like ours (p. 183). They also observed that a majority of these IBCs provided degrees in technical and professional fields, such as business, information technology, and engineering (Miller-Idriss & Hanauer, 2011, p. 188). In addition to adding new options for tertiary education, as Miller-Idriss and Hanauer (2011) have noted, IBCs have spearheaded a larger shift in technical education in the Gulf "away from rote learning and fixed curricula toward an emphasis on learning-by-doing and on-the-job learning" (p. 193). (See Miller & Pessoa, this volume, for extensive description on IBCs; see also Telafici & Rudd, this volume, for further IBC challenges.)

Although the curriculum and degree are exactly the same as our home campus in the US, almost all of our students at our IBC are multilingual; around half are Qatari, and the rest are from other areas in the MENA region and Southeast Asia. As such, not only do our students have to become familiar with the discourse of western academic English (and, in some cases, while they are still acquiring aspects of everyday spoken and written English), they are also adopting the secondary discourse of writing as an engineer.

Our engineering faculty members are expatriate residents (not citizens) of Qatar, and most have terminal degrees from the US, Canada, or UK. Several are fluent in Arabic—although not always the local Qatari dialect—but others are not; for all, the bulk of their academic and industry work is conducted in English. Further discussion of our interview population can be found in the methodology section, but for now it is worth observing that our engineering faculty members tend to have two significant commonalities in addition to their disciplinary knowledge: they have achieved success—an undergraduate or terminal degree—in a western educational institution, and much of their national, ethnic, and cultural background is not shared with over half of their students. Thus, our IBC is a complicated location where, on the one hand, power differences between expatriate faculty and local students can resemble a kind of cultural imperialism (Tomlinson, 1991), and, on the other, the institution provides our students with a space to "reconstruct their languages, cultures, and identities to their advantage" (Canagarajah, 1999, p. 2). In this context, we want to consider how a WAC/WID initiative with a WI course requirement impacts the relationship between MENA cultures and disciplinary writing in the English language.

We are sensitive to the perception voiced by critics such as Altbach (2004), that the combined forces of globalization and higher education result in "the loss of intellectual and cultural autonomy by those who are less powerful" (p. 9). Others have written about IBCs' complicated sociopolitical effects on

Gulf Arab educational institutions (Witte, 2010) and indigenous forms and conditions of knowledge-making (Donn & Al Manthri, 2010). These broader questions about transnational education inform how we understand the relationships between faculty and students in our institution's classrooms, and in particular, how we interpret faculty and student perceptions of WI courses. Previous research has suggested that students in the Gulf region view western education and the English language with a "simultaneously imitative and resistant" attitude (Findlow, 2006, p. 31; see also O'Neill, 2014). Primary and secondary education in the Gulf and wider MENA region has been criticized in western scholarship for its emphasis on rote learning, where "the book itself acts as the sole source of information" (Heyneman, 1997, p. 452; see also Steer, Ghanem & Jalbout, 2014, for statistics on student retention in the MENA region). Others have indicated that MENA students "are not used to interrogating texts and are not familiar with the western convention of writing with the audience in mind" (Golkowska, 2013, p. 340) and "are graduating [secondary school] without the basic skills needed to succeed at the university level" (Borger, 2007, para. 1). If these descriptions of the region's student population are true, we decided that it would be worthwhile to explore how our faculty members perceive their roles in a transnational WAC/WID initiative. Their experiences of both broadening access to and serving as gatekeepers of disciplinary writing would help us decide how to support the work done in engineering courses.

Our experiences at our IBC, particularly one of the co-author Kent's experience as a writing consultant for an Ethics and Engineering course, led us to raise an important question for other IBCs and institutions with diverse student bodies: How do engineering faculty members perceive the roles of writing and the teaching of writing in their engineering courses that serve a predominantly multilingual student population? To answer this question, this chapter examines qualitative data from IRB-approved interviews conducted with engineering faculty members who taught writing-intensive (WI) courses at our university. In our analysis, we reflect on themes that emerged from the interviews, and we conclude by arguing for the efficacy of hybrid writing positions, like the one held by Kent, who works to fill gaps between faculty expectations and multilingual students' development as writers.

Writing as an Engineer and WAC/WID Initiatives

Winsor's (1990) research introduced the idea of working engineers "writing themselves as engineers," that is, using writing both to generate knowledge and establish themselves as members of the professional engineering world

(p. 66). This complex understanding of writing, rhetoric, and identity can be difficult for engineering students to comprehend and apply to their WI courses. Leydens (2008) has suggested that the integration of writing identities and engineering identities, as well as an understanding of rhetoric as an important part of engineering practice, may not develop in engineering students until after graduation and more on-the-job experience.

Studies have shown that engineers on the job appreciate and seek out peer review and constructive feedback on their writing (Steiner, 2011), and that they find writing engaging when they "know their texts will be acted upon by others in the development of the design," or, in other words, when engineers write for real, active audiences (Sales, 2009, p. 90). Winsor's 1996 book, *Writing Like an Engineer: A Rhetorical Education*, advocates for an adjustment in the way that workplace writing courses teach audience by highlighting the ways in which engineers see writing as a social activity, a perspective echoed in the requirements from the Accreditation Board for Engineering and Technology (ABET). ABET educational objectives stress students' ability to identify, formulate, and solve engineering problems in writing; to function on multidisciplinary teams and to communicate effectively with team members; and to engage with knowledge of contemporary issues in engineering. These requirements for accreditation and the research on the engineering workplace have been helpful justification for writing-intensive courses, but such courses can involve teaching technical and workplace communication in ways that are new or uncomfortable for engineering educators and writing specialists (Leydens, 2012).

In this chapter, we examine these issues from our particular positions in our IBC. Co-author Brenda Kent, a staff member supporting an Ethics and Engineering course described later in this section, collaborated with co-author Amy Hodges, an instructional assistant professor with a background in writing centers, to investigate what engineering faculty members think about the teaching of writing in their engineering courses and to consider what our university could do to better support faculty and students. We wanted to know about "flaws in our assumptions about the universality of writing programs" (Anson & Donahue, 2015, p. 33) and consider the context of our students' previous and current literacy learning.

Kent's position as writing consultant was created to serve one WI course required of all engineering students at our IBC. Ethics and Engineering is co-taught by a professor from an engineering discipline and a professor from a liberal arts discipline. On our home campus in the US, those professors are assisted by graduate student teaching assistants (TAs) who lead discussions and provide feedback on writing assignments. Since our campus mainly serves undergraduate students, the Ethics and Engineering professors did not have access to TAs and hired Kent in 2010 to supplement their writing instruction and feedback. In interviews, these professors expressed their feelings that, given their "unique situation" with a majority of multilingual students, hiring professional staff members for the role of writing consultant would provide more continuity and a better quality of teaching experience for the students.

Prior to working at our IBC, Kent earned a BA in teaching, taught writing in public and homeschool settings in the US, and worked in business writing and editing. At first, she was hired part-time as a professional tutor in our writing center, and soon her duties shifted to working with only students in the Ethics and Engineering course as a full-time writing specialist. Over the past four years working with this course, her role has encompassed duties held by writing faculty members, teaching assistants, and writing fellows. During the semester, Kent provides lessons on critical reading, organizing, and argumentation, and she guides 50–60 students through peer reviews of all six writing assignments. She estimates that she holds at least 200 tutorials per semester. Kent is not quite what we would traditionally call a TA—she is not working on and does not hold a graduate degree in either engineering or ethics—but neither is she a writing fellow, since she has already completed an undergraduate degree. Instead, she fulfills a hybrid role somewhere in between these models for writing support, coaching students through writing assignments while also taking authority for the teaching of writing within the course.

Neither of the professors who hired Kent had specialized knowledge of WAC/WID initiatives. In the rapidly changing and expanding world of IBCs, Kent had few previous models for her position in the Middle East, much less at an engineering IBC in a similar situation. We were curious about how her hybrid writing position mediated some of the conflicts among writing-intensive course goals, TAM-Q faculty writing expectations and TAM-Q students' cultural and educational backgrounds.

Methods

In order to determine what our diverse group of engineering faculty expected from their student writers and what perceptions about disciplinary writing guided their choices as teachers, in the spring semester of 2014 we interviewed 10 current or recent instructors of engineering courses designated as a WI course. In the case of Electrical and Computer Engineering, our recruitment included teaching and lab staff members. The Electrical Engineering WI course is the first half of students' senior design course series, in which students complete a major project that is the capstone of their engineering knowledge. Although the lead instructor is a faculty member, we interviewed the lab TAs who had the most frequent and sustained contact with the students' writing. An additional interviewee (Dr. Tareq) was contacted because his sophomore-level course was well known to be writing intensive, even if it did not have the official designation from the university. All of our interviewees are identified by pseudonyms, and more information on their roles at the university can be found in the Appendix.

One interviewee (Dr. Holly) identified as a native English speaker, and the rest identified their mother tongue as other than English. Most had postgraduate degrees from the US and the UK, so they considered their English language skills to be above average for their professional tasks. Two of our ten faculty interviewees (Dr. Holly and Dr. Sharifa) were female, and two male interviewees also served as administrators at the university.

As we conducted our interviews, we came to understand that the number of credit hours assigned to the WI course was an important part of our interviewees' perspective on writing in their courses (see Appendix). Our home campus, and thus our Qatar campus as well, requires two WI courses in the major; although each of our engineering programs required Kent's three credit-hour Ethics and Engineering course, the credit hours of the other WI courses varied. As mentioned above, Electrical and Computer Engineering combined their senior design courses with the WI course requirements, but the other programs did not.

Many of our interviewees were well known to us as friends and members of our small academic community. Thus, our research methodology was informed by the perspective of Selfe and Hawisher (2012), who have viewed interviews "more like conversations that involved participants in a joint project of inquiry" (p. 38). Several of our interviewees were aware that Kent provided writing support, and they were curious about what she did and how their course fit into the larger scheme of WI courses at our IBC. We collected our interview data as a team, approaching our interviews as a "less-structured conversation in which meaning is made, negotiated, and interpreted collaboratively" (p. 45). Thus, our semi-structured interviews included some of the following questions, but we also allowed the conversation to flow and fit the narrative that the interviewee wanted to tell about his or her course.

- What kinds of writing do you do professionally? What kinds of writing are you training your students for?
- How often (in class hours per week or class periods per semester) do you spend in class on writing instruction?

- How much time per week or per semester would you estimate that you spend preparing lessons on writing? Consulting with students on writing? Grading or evaluating writing?
- What assignments do you give? How did you develop these assignments?
- How do you evaluate the students' writing? How did you come up with this method?

These interviews lasted approximately 30 minutes each. Additionally, we collected relevant documents from our interviewees, such as syllabus materials, assignment prompts, and sample student writing. These documents helped us understand the context of our interviewees' perceptions of teaching disciplinary writing.

After transcribing these interviews, we coded them according to theme (Merriam, 2009). The following sections describe some of our major themes and point to our initial findings about the role of writing support in WAC/WID programs in the MENA region. This is a small study in a specific context, but some findings may be transferable to other contexts, including other IBCs in technical fields and universities with significant numbers of students from the MENA region.

Results

WI Requirement: Faculty Attitudes and Student Reactions

Professors reported a wide variety of assigned writing in their courses, including lab reports, technical reports, resumes, reflective writing, film reviews, informative reports, memos, proposals, literature reviews, market surveys, progress reports, argument-driven academic essays, and several different kinds of presentations, both in class and on video. Most interviewees, particularly those who taught one-credit-hour WI courses, expressed concern that the amount of writing weighed heavily on their students' already challenging course load. Dr. Sharifa reported that her students "always complain every end of semester . . . 'too much work, too much work for a one credit course.' And it is too much work." Dr. Holly told her students on the first day of class, "Look, I am going to tell you right now. I can't do anything about this. This is a university requirement. You need to do this." The perception that the standards and expectations for the course were high placed the instructors in a defensive mode; Dr. Tareq, for instance, felt like he needed to justify his writing assignments: "I am not asking them to write a lot. I am asking them to write enough, but to them it is very, very much."

Even as the professors reported large amounts of writing and high standards for their courses, they did not think that many of the students met their expectations. Dr. Burhan summed up the perspective of many of our interviewees: "We have been surprised and we have been disappointed quite frequently." While all of the faculty and staff members saw the value of the skills, practices, and products they were teaching, few were comfortable with how well their knowledge about writing as an engineer was being transmitted to the students. Dr. Sharifa was disappointed in one of her classes, saying that they were "smart but they did not put any effort in the lab. . . . They totally neglected [the lab reports] for the other courses, so they would hand in their reports late. They would give it in a sloppy way. You could tell that they [didn't] care." Dr. Rahmat saw a "big gap. The basic[s of writing] are not really good. They have difficulty to write." Several traced this disconnect to the students' heavy workload—did they really have time to complete all of the requirements of a WI course while working on their other engineering courses?—but others thought that the students' educational background played a significant role. As the instructor of a required WI course connecting issues in the humanities and in engineering, Dr. Burhan felt that the students "did not have any training in humanities, so we had to take a few steps back and start where one would start at grade 7" in the US or another western educational system.

We can identify in these responses a frustration voiced in departmental meetings around the world, as Dr. Burhan phrased it: "we have tried our best to bring the horse to the water." Even as professors validated the relevance and importance of WI courses, they struggled to reconcile their expectations for the students and the students' performance on their writing assignments. On the one hand, they saw themselves and their students as powerless before the abstract expectations of the university system and the engineering discipline at large, but on the other hand, they positioned themselves as the standard-bearers and gatekeepers of student writing expertise and work ethic.

Professional Identity and Definitions of Writing

Overwhelmingly, our interviewees, like many of their counterparts elsewhere, viewed "writing" in terms of surface features of student texts, such as grammatical and mechanical usage, formatting, use of technical vocabulary, and labeling of figures and tables. Mr. Samir explained that "the first stuff they submit is usually disastrous. . . . They don't put page numbering. They don't number their sections. Fonts are chosen randomly and are not consistent with the whole report. They don't number figures." Dr. Holly told us that she has students who "don't know when to capitalize, when to end a sentence and start a new one. This is simple." In his lectures on writing, Dr. Tareq said that he taught about some of the common mistakes that "students are making grammar wise . . . affect and effect, like this. . . . I assume these are the common things that they learn in their English courses anyway." On the one hand, we were impressed by faculty members' willingness to closely critique students' work and provide substantial feedback. On the other, we wondered what role they saw writing support staff members playing other than a grammatical fix-it service.

Moreover, the interviewees often considered "writing" to be disconnected from the "technical" or content features of texts, also not an uncommon view among disciplinary faculty. Mr. Ahmed felt like his job "is not to check on their English writing. The intention here is to look on the technical material. It is not on how they are writing English, [or] is the grammar correct. Sometimes, if we find something misspelled, we underline that, but the intention here is the technical part." Dr. Sharifa told us that she mostly grades the "technical point of view and the format." Dr. Burhan felt that teaching a writing-intensive course in his field was "almost like teaching two courses at one time. . . . So they may write a beautiful sentence, but it makes no sense in ethical terms." Dr. Holly, who reported spending time in her office instructing students on the finer points of sentence boundaries, questioned how to evaluate student writing with her knowledge of engineering: "It could have been great sort of content-wise, but really awful grammar. How do I grade that? What do I do?" Dr. Rahmat wondered why his students misspelled words because the "simple things [writing] are supposed to be straight from the beginning."

This view of writing informed their identities as professors and teachers, as several of our interviewees told us they "[didn't] know how to teach writing, and . . . how to teach grammar," or that they "don't teach them English or that sort of thing." Dr. Miraj felt that faculty resistance to integrating writing in their courses was caused by a lack of training:

> [Engineering professors] resist to do it because they are not trained to do it. They don't see it as their job to do it, and maybe they don't appreciate how important it is. . . . Some of the professors are brilliant technically, but maybe they never learned professional, technical writing. So how do you expect them to teach it if they were not comfortable with it? They can write very well, but they are not instructing [the students].

Dr. Sharifa also expressed interest in further training in the teaching of writing, explaining that she "would like to have some ammunition.... I admit that I am not a perfect writer." However receptive our interviewees were to more knowledge about *writing* pedagogy, their perception of what is or is not writing concerned us.

Carter (2007) has argued that the perceived divide between writing and the disciplines needs to be bridged by "conceptualiz[ing] writing in the disciplines in a way that is grounded in the disciplines themselves, a viable alternative to an understanding of writing as universally generalizable" (p. 387). By situating disciplinary ways of knowing and writing within metagenres, or similar ways of doing, Carter (2007) places faculty members in the disciplines in a position of authority over writing "on their own turf" (p. 408). Despite the implementation of the home campus' WAC/WID requirements, our interviewees persisted in separating "technical" aspects of texts from the "writing" of texts; they absolved themselves of responsibility over writing by not worrying about it or leaving it for others to "fix." Kent's role was created to fill such a need; overwhelmed by the needs of their multilingual student writers, the professors in charge of the Ethics and Engineering course assigned all of the course duties related to writing to her. Our interviewees were very interested to hear about the services Kent provided to the course's students and faculty, and many expressed a desire to hire someone to take over the teaching and tutoring of writing in their own courses.

We see these findings as a call to continue to negotiate definitions and practices of writing with our disciplinary faculty and, as we explain in the next section, we feel that hybrid writing positions like Kent's provide a chance to, in Dr. Miraj's words, "make the professor like [integrating writing into a course] because it [does] not put him into a stressful place."

Discussion

Our interviews showed us that our faculty members in the STEM fields—even those who speak multiple languages and have lived in the same regions of the world as their students—have perspectives that challenge some of the current ideology on teaching discipline-specific writing. These findings add to the rich literature on faculty constructions of their role in a WAC/WID program with a significant L2 population (Ives, Leahy, Leming, Pierce & Schwartz, 2014; Zawacki & Habib, 2014). Much like other disciplinary faculty members depicted in the research, our interviewees expressed views along a spectrum that encompasses both engaged, passionate teaching and careful (although occasionally problematic) attention to surface-level features of texts. They illustrate the "gap between faculty fantasies about writing and the reality of students struggling to make sense of academic literacy" (Carroll, 2012, p. 8). Further ethnographic research might help us understand how the sociopolitical context of the Arab Gulf region has impacted these stances.

However, we wanted to use these interviews as "mirrors for our own perspectives and belief systems, and thus help us examine more critically what we ourselves think and do, both within our own classrooms and with respect to the larger institutional contexts in which we teach" (Zamel, 1995, p. 507). While these findings might reflect universal faculty perceptions, our response had to consider the context of an engineering IBC in Qatar. Given what we knew from these interviews, how might we work towards mediating faculty expectations for student writing and also promoting writing pedagogy that would be beneficial to our multilingual student population?

As might be expected, we found in the interviews various constructions of a writing teacher's role. Some faculty members took on this role themselves through direct instruction in one-on-one conferences with students, but all implied or stated that a writing teacher would use more authoritative methods to pass on knowledge; in some instances, faculty reported giving lectures on writing or asking others to come in and instruct students on grammatical or mechanical norms. Kent's status as a teacher-figure in the Ethics and Engineering course addressed faculty members' desire for direct teaching of western academic and professional writing conventions, and many of her one-on-one consultations helped students understand the grammatical and mechanical expectations of their instructors. Because of their previous educational experience in the MENA region, TAM-Q students tend to be familiar with a more teacher-centered learning environment than those in the US. Canagarajah (1999) has questioned writing pedagogy and institutional structures for assuming that learning styles translate across cultures, as for some students, "it seems likely that they would prefer a more formal, product-oriented, teacher-centered pedagogy, of the sort now denigrated by center professional circles" (p. 14). Our experience observing local secondary school classes has suggested to us that this is also the case for many of our students. In this light, we argue that Kent's course meetings, which cover critical reading, organizing, and argumentation strategies, mediate faculty expectations that a writing teacher will act as an authority and student expectations formed from their previous experience with other teachers in the MENA region.

The other issue we reflected on after completing the interviews was how our faculty members conceptualized the role of a writer. Even though faculty were often published writers in their own discipline, they did not often position themselves as writers to their students and saw writing as something different from technical work. Kent's hybrid role—somewhere in between a teaching assistant and a writing fellow—complicated this binary. As both an outsider to the engineering discipline and, because of her years of experience with one class, a growing expertise in issues related to ethics and engineering, Kent blurred the boundaries of the technical/writing divide that faculty perceived as important. Her use of peer reviews and other indirect methods of teaching promoted a different view of writers—one that is less authority-based and more democratic. The teaching part of Kent's role helped our initiative adapt to faculty expectations and pedagogical methods that students were familiar with, and the tutoring part of her role pushed both parties towards understanding new ways of learning. As we work towards LeCourt's (2012) vision of a critical WAC program, one that "redefines thinking and learning through writing in terms that recognize the viability of the students' discourses as much as the disciplinary ones" (p. 82), hybrid positions like Kent's provide a promising way to bring disciplinary faculty and students into conversation over how to develop expertise as a writer and an engineer.

The Potential for Hybrid Writing Positions in the MENA Region

We recognize that others, in the Gulf region and out of it, see similar attitudes in their faculty members, and perhaps, even see some of themselves in the interviews analyzed in this chapter. We also recognize that our perceived acquiescence to some of these attitudes may strike some of our readers as problematic—after all, shouldn't we correct some of these statements and implement more WAC/WID programming that forces disciplinary faculty to meet us on our own terms, the terms of mainstream western writing pedagogy? At our IBC, we have taken the advice of Lyon (2009) to heart: "While overseas teachers may nod to the community values inherent in . . . local pedagogies, *true understanding requires risking their own foundations*" (p. 234, emphasis in original). We took a risk by adapting our WAC/WID initiative to the findings from our interviews and what we understood about our MENA context. Exporting WI courses and WAC/WID initiatives to universities in the Middle East does not guarantee their success, just as integrating writing into engineering courses may not change faculty members' minds about how to teach their subject. Our institution's WAC/WID initiative, like those of many others, continues to negotiate and mediate faculty expectations for student writing in order to provide a cohesive, transformative experience for the students who walk our hallways.

Our study started with a very practical question: what did our disciplinary faculty think about our WAC/WID initiative, and more specifically, how did they perceive their own role within that initiative? We concluded that hybrid writing positions like Kent's could help students come to terms with the conflicting expectations their engineering instructors held about writing, their experiences with traditional Gulf pedagogy (teacher-centered, product-oriented), and their exposure to writing and engineering pedagogy common to American institutions (student-centered, problem-based). Additionally, our IBC's focus on engineering allowed us to provide specialized support, a strategy also advocated by Strang (2006), who used professional tutors to provide "consistently high quality of one-on-one tutoring that results from their profound knowledge about writing" and, in some cases, their discipline (p. 295). Yet this inquiry also opened up new questions about the future of WAC/WID programs in the MENA region. Recent scholarship on translingual approaches to writing (Horner, Lu, Royster & Trimbur, 2011) offers exciting possibilities for faculty development programs, particularly programs in the region which serve a diverse population of faculty and students. Such professional development could focus on all faculty members' hybrid roles and the ways we all move between and beyond boundaries, such as those between technical knowledge and writing knowledge, or between the titles of teacher and tutor.

References

Altbach, P. G. (2004). Globalization and the university: Myths and realities in an unequal world. *Tertiary Education and Management, 10*(1), 3–25.

Anson, C. M. & Donahue, C. (2015). Deconstructing "Writing Program Administration" in an international context. In D. S. Martin (Ed.), *Transnational writing program administration* (pp. 21–47). Logan, UT: Utah State University Press.

Borger, M. (2007). Teaching cross-cultural perspectives in the Arabian Gulf: Academic bridge program, Doha, Qatar. Paper presented at the Society for Intercultural Education Training and Research conference. Retrieved from http://www.sietar-europa.org/.

Canagarajah, S. (1999). *Resisting linguistic imperialism in English teaching*. New York: Oxford University Press.

Carroll, L. A. (2012). *Rehearsing new roles: How college students develop as writers*. Carbondale, IL: Southern Illionis University Press.

Carter, M. (2007). Ways of knowing, doing, and writing in the disciplines. *College Composition and Communication, 58*(3), 385–418.

Donn, G. & Al Manthri, Y. (2010). *Globalization and higher education in the Arab Gulf States*. Didcot, UK: Symposium Books.

Findlow, S. (2006). Higher education and linguistic dualism in the Arab Gulf. *British Journal of Sociology of Education, 27*(1), 19–36.

Golkowska, K. U. (2013). Voice and dialogue in teaching reading/writing to Qatari students. *Journal of International Education Research, 9*(4), 339–344.

Heyneman, S. P. (1997). The quality of education in the Middle East and North Africa. *International Journal of Educational Development, 17*(4), 449–466.

Horner, B., Lu, M., Royster, J. J. & Trimbur, J. (2011). Language difference in writing: Toward a translingual approach. *College English, 73*(3), 303–321.

Ives, L., Leahy, E., Leming, A., Pierce, T. & Schwartz, M. (2014). "I don't know if that was the right thing to do": Cross-disciplinary/cross-institutional faculty respond to L2 writing. In T.M. Zawacki & M. Cox (Eds.), *WAC and second language writers: Research towards linguistically and culturally inclusive programs and practices* (pp. 211–240). Fort Collins, CO: The WAC Clearinghouse and Parlor Press. Retrieved from http://wac.colostate.edu/books/l2/.

LeCourt, D. (2012). WAC as critical pedagogy: The third stage? In T. M. Zawacki & P.M. Rogers (Eds.), *Writing across the curriculum: A critical sourcebook* (pp. 69–84). Boston: Bedford/St. Martin's.

Leydens, J. A. (2008). Novice and insider perspectives on academic and workplace writing: Toward a continuum of rhetorical awareness. *IEEE Transactions on Professional Communication, 51*(3), 242–263.

Leydens, J. A. (2012). Sociotechnical communication in engineering: An exploration and unveiling of common myths. *Engineering Studies, 4*(1), 1–9.

Lyon, A. (2009). "You fail": Plagiarism, the ownership of writing, and transnational conflicts. *College Composition and Communication, 61*(2), 222–239.

Matsuda, P. K. & Jablonski, J. (2009). Beyond the L2 metaphor: Towards a mutually transformative model of ESL/WAC collaboration. *Academic Writing.* Retrieved from http://wac.colostate.edu/aw/articles/matsuda_jablonski2000.htm.

Merriam, S. B. (2009). *Qualitative research: A guide to design and implementation.* San Francisco: Jossey-Bass.

Miller-Idriss, C. & Hanauer, E. (2011). Transnational higher education: Offshore campuses in the Middle East. *Comparative Education, 47*(2), 181–207.

O'Neill, G. T. (2014). "Just a natural move towards English": Gulf youth attitudes towards Arabic and English literacy. *Learning and Teaching in Higher Education: Gulf Perspectives, 11*(1). Retrieved from http://lthe.zu.ac.ae/index.php/lthehome/article/view/160.

Sales, H. E. (2009). *Professional communication in engineering.* New York: Palgrave Macmillan.

Selfe, C. & Hawisher, G. E. (2012). Exceeding the bounds of the interview: Feminism, mediation, narrative, and conversations about digital literacy. In L. Nickoson & M. P. Sheridan (Eds.), *Writing studies research in practice: Methods and methodologies* (pp. 36–50). Carbondale, IL: Southern Illinois University Press.

Steer, L., Ghanem, H. & Jalbout, M. (2014). Arab youth: Missing educational foundations for a productive life? Retrieved from https://www.brookings.edu/research/arab-youth-missing-educational-foundations-for-a-productive-life/.

Steiner, D. G. (2011). The communication habits of engineers: A study of how composition style and time affect the production of oral and written communication of engineers. *Journal of Technical Writing and Communication, 41*(1), 33–58.

Strang, S. (2006). Staffing a writing center with professional tutors. In C. Murphy & B. L. Stay (Eds.), *The writing center director's resource book* (pp. 291–299). New York: Routledge.

Tomlinson, J. (1991). *Cultural imperialism: A critical introduction*. Baltimore, MD: Johns Hopkins University Press.

Winsor, D. A. (1990). Engineering writing / writing engineering. *College Composition and Communication, 41*(1), 58–70.

Winsor, D. A. (1996). *Writing like an engineer: A rhetorical education*. Mahwah, NJ: Lawrence Erlbaum Associates.

Witte, S. (2010). Gulf State branch campuses: Global student recruitment. *International Higher Education, 58*, 5–6.

Zamel, V. (1995). Strangers in academia: The experiences of faculty and ESL students across the curriculum. *College Composition and Communication, 46*(4), 506–521.

Zawacki, T. M. & Habib, A. S. (2014). Negotiating "errors" in L2 writing: Faculty dispositions and language difference. In T. M. Zawacki & M. Cox (Eds.), *WAC and second language writers: Research towards linguistically and culturally inclusive programs and practices* (pp. 183–210). Fort Collins, CO: The WAC Clearinghouse and Parlor Press. Retrieved from http://wac.colostate.edu/books/l2/.

Appendix: Interviewees

Name	Engineering Discipline	Faculty/ Staff	Course Description	Credit Hours of Course
Dr. Holly	Mechanical	Faculty	Senior Seminar	1
Dr. Sharifa	Chemical	Faculty	Engineering Lab	1
Dr. Miraj	Mechanical	Faculty	Ethics and Engineering	3
Dr. Burhan	Liberal Arts	Faculty	Ethics and Engineering	3
Dr. Rahmat	Petroleum	Faculty	Technical Presentations	1
Mr. Ahmed	Electrical and Computer	Staff	Senior Design Seminar	3
Mr. Mustafa	Electrical and Computer	Staff	Senior Design Seminar	3
Mr. Samir	Electrical and Computer	Staff	Senior Design Seminar	3
Dr. Pouyan	Mechanical/ Industrial	Faculty	Senior Design Seminar	1
Dr. Tareq	Mechanical	Faculty	Engineering Lab	3

Section 4: Creating Student Space(s)

10 Literacy Narratives Across Borders: Beirut and Dearborn as Twenty-First Century Transnational Spaces

Lisa R. Arnold
NORTH DAKOTA STATE UNIVERSITY (US)

William DeGenaro
UNIVERSITY OF MICHIGAN-DEARBORN (US)

Rima Iskandarani
AMERICAN UNIVERSITY OF BEIRUT (LEBANON)

Malakeh Khoury
AMERICAN UNIVERSITY OF BEIRUT (LEBANON)

Zane Sinno
AMERICAN UNIVERSITY OF BEIRUT (LEBANON)

Margaret Willard-Traub
UNIVERSITY OF MICHIGAN-DEARBORN (US)

This chapter reports on a research and teaching collaboration among students and faculty at American University of Beirut and University of Michigan-Dearborn and suggests some of the paradoxes about the transnational spaces we and our students inhabit. The authors posit the locations of Beirut and Dearborn as representative of broader trends and as particularly "transnational" locales. Introductory writing students interviewed partners overseas via technologies such as Skype and then composed literacy narratives based on those interviews. The corpus for the analysis includes the literacy narratives and reflective writings of approximately 150 undergraduates at the two universities.

Keywords: transnational; first-year writing; literacy narratives; empathy; multilingual writing; global-local

In higher education, context is everything; the world beyond the classroom shapes research agendas, methods, teaching, and student learning. In recent decades, the global migrations of students and the proliferation of new communication technologies have opened up students' perspectives and complicated their backgrounds, increasing dramatically the cultural and linguistic diversity of our classrooms. Shifts in higher educational policies and practices worldwide—the rapid growth of new institutions of higher education and international branch campuses (IBCs); regional "harmonization" initiatives such as the Bologna Process aimed at fostering international student and faculty movement across national borders; and the surge in online programs—comprise a response to and consequence of higher education as an increasingly transcultural and transnational space (for more information about IBCs, see Hodges & Kent; Miller & Pessoa; and Rudd & Telafici, this volume). This chapter describes a pedagogical project that takes into account this larger picture of itinerant student bodies, changing subjectivities, and institutional flux, situating it in the context of the global turn in writing studies. This project suggests that writing and the exchange of ideas in transnational contexts are meaningful to students, and it considers what scholars might learn from students as a result of these exchanges. This chapter also suggests some of the paradoxes about the transnational spaces we and our students inhabit (for a faculty perspective on transnational exchange, see Theado, Johnson, Highly & Omar, this volume).

This chapter reports on a pedagogical partnership among four faculty members at the American University of Beirut (AUB) and four at the University of Michigan-Dearborn (UMD), wherein students in eight first-year writing sections were partnered with overseas peers to conduct interviews and write literacy profiles and follow-up reflective essays. In creating this partnership, we wanted to give students the opportunity to investigate one another's literacy practices as they lived, studied, worked, and socialized in Beirut (Lebanon) and Dearborn, Michigan (US).

Beirut and Dearborn are representative of broader, global trends and are uniquely "transnational" in terms of their linguistic, cultural and national diversity. Lebanon's capital city confounds and defies easy categorization due to religious, ethnic, economic, and linguistic pluralism. In the *Hamra* neighborhood surrounding the American University of Beirut, for example, one finds western fast food chains alongside family-run bakeries specializing in *man'oushe*. Dearborn, Michigan, the home of Ford Motor Company and, for much of the twentieth century, a segregated, white residential community, has become home to large diaspora communities from many countries, including Lebanon, Iraq, and Yemen. Like the area around AUB, the immediate environs of the University of Michigan-Dearborn are multilingual (Lebanese-dialect Arabic in particular is commonplace), and commuter students can find a pre-class *man'oushe with zaatar* as easily as an Egg McMuffin. These two very different places are, at the same time, linked by the migration of residents as well as business and economic ties. In short, we posit these two locations, Beirut and Dearborn, as at once particularly "transnational" locales—for example, in terms of linguistic, cultural and national diversity among students—and at the same time as representative of demographic and socio-cultural trends in increasingly globalized, higher education contexts more broadly.

Beirut has historically been viewed as a meeting place of cultures. Many of the AUB students claim membership in diverse communities simultaneously. Often they have more than one nationality and have lived parts of their lives in different countries. They belong to privileged classes not only economically but also symbolically in terms of their knowledge of different languages, their ability to travel abroad, and their access to an elite, private institution of higher learning. Many of the Dearborn students come from lower-middle or working-class backgrounds, and many also have various "hyphenated" identities and labels (Arab-American, first-generation college student, Muslim-American, non-traditional), arguably placing themselves on the margins of dominant North American academic culture. This atypical situation of an encounter between the West, which has some roots in the East, and the East, which has claims on the West and its way of life, challenges conventional definitions of the local and the global and makes the distinction difficult and uncertain. Putting the local and global in contact and dialogue with one another moves the emerging context away from static and homogeneous notions of tightly bound context or community, as Canagarajah (2002) puts it.

University students require rhetorical dexterities and sensitivities to navigate increasingly postmodern, global contexts—contexts where identity and culture are dynamic and shifting, and where linguistic, racial, and ethnic differences are everyday realities. Further, as institutions of higher education respond to imperatives to provide critical and contextual literacy training, we believe they also (paradoxically perhaps) ought to consider local attributes, literacy practices, and material conditions as resources to provide these types of critical, literacy lessons (see also Nebel; Ronesi, this volume).

Background and Methods

The idea for the transnational collaboration described in this chapter initially emerged from an extended collaboration between Willard-Traub's classes at UMD and classes at a French university, which in turn led to the establishment of "cross-cultural" writing sections at UMD. When DeGenaro subsequently was appointed as a Fulbright scholar at the American University of Beirut during 2010–11, he and Willard-Traub established a "pilot" collaboration that joined their writing classes across institutions in doing literacy narratives of overseas partners. While working at AUB, DeGenaro met AUB co-authors Khoury, Sinno, Iskandarani, and Arnold. During the 2011–12 academic year, we, the co-authors of this piece, along with two additional faculty members at UMD (who later opted out of the data analysis for this project) collaborated to develop an IRB-approved joint pedagogical project called the "Beirut-Dearborn Writing and Learning Collaborative" (BDWLC).

Specifically, in this project we paired students across institutions and asked them to conduct interviews with one another using Skype, Facebook, or another form of social media, to learn more about one another's literacy practices. We asked students to find out about the types of reading, writing, school, and social media activities that occupied each other's lives on a daily basis. Students then composed literacy narratives based on these interviews—profiles of the literate activities of their peers abroad. The corpus for the present analysis includes the literacy narratives and reflective writings of approximately 150 undergraduates at the two universities who, working in English during the Winter/Spring semester of 2012, conducted interviews of overseas partners, wrote literacy profiles about their partners, and reflected in writing on their experiences.

Methodologically, the faculty participating in this project received IRB approval for their project at their respective institutions in Fall 2011, and a third party collected informed consent in early Spring 2012 from students enrolled in the faculty members' respective sections of first-year writing. After the conclusion of the Spring 2012 semester, the co-authors anonymized the data, attaching pseudonyms to all student writing, and worked individually and then together to rhetorically analyze texts produced out of eight sections of first-year writing courses (four at AUB, four at UMD). During this collaboration the authors communicated electronically via Skype, email, and an online discussion forum in order to generate initial impressions about the data.

In formulating these initial impressions, each collaborator identified key themes in the writing and areas of pedagogical concern. We decided methodologically on a close, rhetorical analysis of the student writing in large part because the literacy narrative assignment itself was an inherently rhetorical task, one that required students to take into account in their writing and their own data collection (i.e., in their interviews) an initially unfamiliar "audience" (though many students came to know their partners very well, and even reported maintaining close ties after the conclusion of the assignment). We compared our first impressions in order to identify overlaps and potentially to reconcile any conflicting interpretations (though we did not encounter these). Collectively, our analysis was informed by the work of scholars in rhetoric and composition, literacy studies and applied linguistics, especially those who have advocated for research and teaching that consider the consequences of composing in transnational and global-local contexts, such as Suresh Canagarajah and Alastair Pennycook (linguistics), Christiane Donahue, Bruce Horner, and Min-Zhan Lu (rhetoric and composition), Deborah Brandt (literacy studies), and Cynthia Selfe, Gail Hawisher, and Patrick Berry (technology and literacy).

Through this analysis, we identified the following themes and areas of pedagogical concern discussed in this chapter (N.B.: pseudonyms used throughout): students' conceptions about literacy development; the role of empathy in students' emerging sense of themselves as writers and critical users of language; students' attitudes toward language and the value they attached to multilingualism; and students' tendency to rely on overgeneralizations or simplifications about their overseas partners' experiences in ways suggestive of the material effects of globalization.

In our analysis of the student writing, we kept in mind admonitions by U.S. scholars Christiane Donahue, Chris Anson, and others against adopting a hegemonic, "import-export" model of U.S.-based writing instruction (see Donahue, 2009). We also hope that this transnational project will go beyond a neo-liberal "accommodation" model of writing instruction geared primarily to "equip[ping] students as 'global citizens' who are at ease with transnational structures of employment, residency, and commerce" through developing skills with intercultural and technologically mediated communication (Payne, 2012, p. 2)—alternately conceiving of our work as a pedagogy of "intervention" (Horner, 2012) that acknowledges pragmatic needs while foregrounding context and students' awareness of their own subjectivities and perspectives.

By encouraging students, as they generated complex definitions of "literacy," to consider the flux of contexts and their own shifting, hybrid, and dynamic identities, loyalties, and language practices (Starke-Meyerring, 2005, p. 476–477) this project ultimately challenged the usefulness of a notion of borders as rigidly "fixed" and supported Lebanese sociologist Samir Khalaf's (2006) emphasis on the importance of open exchange in a diverse public sphere among multiple, complex and shifting perspectives across national contexts. At the same time, informed as it was by U.S. writing studies, conducted only in English, and comprising a required assignment for students, this project was never free from ideology or cultural influence (an irony not lost on some students). We continue to be attracted nevertheless to the ways in which the contours of a collaborative assignment, along with the unique sites of our institutions, have the potential for illustrating borders and contexts in flux, and to the ways in which such a project is generative of unique, transnational narratives of students, institutions, and geographic places.

Students' Conceptions of Literacy and Writing

Email discussions, reflections, Skype conversations, and drafts culminated in the literacy narratives. In examining these literacy narratives, AUB and UMD investigators noticed that student attitudes about literacy and writing evolved, both cognitively and affectively. We theorize that this maturation came about for two reasons: First, students engaged in discussions about the concept of literacy, in which traditional and non-traditional literate practices were explicitly considered. Second, students were involved in a transnational exchange that challenged their assumptions about the "other." In short, the particular demands of the assignment not only helped students come to terms with a theoretical understanding of literacy, but also encouraged them to recognize and articulate similarities, differences, opinions, and competing values as they examined the question of literacy together.

During their interactions, partnered peers negotiated their definitions of literacy, which ranged from a perception of literacy as the simple ability to read and write to a more elaborate awareness of literacy as intricate and multimodal. Some students equated literacy with awareness of context, "a way of life and without it, people can't live and function properly because they lack one of the most important necessities of life." Definitions also included "backgrounds[,] . . . parental support as well as childhood reading material." Students also discerned different types of literacies, including digital, social, and legal.

Student definitions or descriptions of literacy in their narratives assumed that literacy was rooted in education, but what constituted "education" varied for AUB and UMD students; discussions of literacy led to the realization that literacy was complex and composite, a sum total of diverse skills and resources in addition to those provided by formal education. For example, students identified interpersonal skills as part of literacy education, writing that "developing social skills at university, in a new environment, and meeting new people can also be defined as literacy." Adapting one's qualifications and skills to the context, being socially dexterous, as well as interviewing a stranger, became for students components of literacy.

Analysis of the literacy narratives and reflections also revealed students' conception of writing. Having an audience in a different national context helped illustrate what adapting to a new reader really entails for students. Reviews completed by peers at their home institutions were especially helpful for making students more aware of the potential for disconnect between writers and readers. Advice received from peers refined their conceptions of academic writing to include validating claims and including sufficient detail to satisfy readers' needs.

The differences between personal, creative writing and academic, standardized writing was a central concern that came up frequently in the literacy narratives. To some AUB and UMD students, "creative" writing was seen as an expression of emotions and inner self, as a way to deal with life and its challenges. One student wrote, ". . . I came to the conclusion that . . . expressive writing, varies depending on culture, the social constraints in academia put in place to standardize writing created distance between the writer and their audience." Thus, in this student's narrative at least, academic writing was seen as constrained and externally imposed whereas creative writing was perceived as more enjoyable and inspired. Creative and free-writing came to be a way to "work through the multitude of emotions [students were] facing." One student pointed out, "writing can be a way to escape solitude . . . a type of anger management, but also a place to express myself. . . . Like a diary with character."

Writing was also clearly seen as performative, a way to get good grades by following the prescribed conventions. Many AUB students seemed to learn from the example of their UMD peers to include more detail, examples from personal experience (which could be said to be more discouraged in the Arab world) and integration of authoritative sources. Thus AUB and UMD students had to negotiate the cultural dimensions of writing conventions and the institutional differences between, for instance, how much "the personal" was accepted in academic essays.

Further, AUB and UMD students sometimes incorporated classroom jargon, co-opting terms like *rhetorical situation, discourse community,* and similar disciplinary terms into their writing. That these are largely terms from U.S. writing studies suggests perhaps a hegemonic force at work, despite the best intentions of this transnational, global exchange. At times these terms also have a rote feel in students' literacy narratives, something the students themselves picked up on and wrote about. One student decried the "structural limits put into place by authority figures," finding them stifling and leading to the student's dislike of academic writing.

Nonetheless, AUB and UMD students alike felt that academic writing should please the teacher and meet with the assignment's predetermined criteria. This was also noted in the peer review process (again, a peer review completed by local or overseas peers) that followed the interview and first draft of the literacy narrative. Although a systematic analysis of peer review comments was not a part of this study, we noted anecdotally that some peer reviewers seemed to replicate the teacher's role, while nevertheless seeming also to challenge their partners to think more metacognitively.

Differing levels of formality in format, style, tone and even content also allowed students to think more deeply about cultural dimensions of audience. Some UMD students expressed surprise at the level of formality of their AUB peers' texts, noting that the tone in their peer's emails was more appropriate for communication with teachers. The inclusion of formal components such as a salutation and complimentary closing, as well as formal tone, sentence structure and paragraphing, were surprising for UMD students who expected less formality in communication with overseas peers. Such encounters seemed to bring with them increased awareness of audience and content in a mediated context.

Empathy and Transnational Literacy Narratives

The long distance one-on-one conversations between AUB and UMD partners about their feelings revealed moments of empathy. Mead (1993, p. 27) defines empathy as the "capacity to take the role of the other and to adopt alternative perspectives vis-á-vis oneself." His definition highlights the cognitive component of empathy where the empathizer is actually able, through understanding the object of empathy, to actually put himself/herself in the role of the other. Rogers (1969) states that emphatic understanding "means temporarily living in [the other person's] life" (p. 4). Clearly, a reflective interaction between the self and the other is essential in the development of empathy among individuals. The current viewpoint that this generation's seemingly increased social connectedness and involvement is often only superficial was frequently challenged in our globally connected courses.

An analysis of the narratives revealed that the most dominant layers of connectedness among students were Davis' (1983; 1996) perspective taking and empathic concern. Though it may not be surprising to find incidents reflecting empathy on the surface level, instances in literacy narratives based solely on online exchanges that show closer connectedness and more involved empathy seem significant. For example, Lina, an AUB student, speaks of her illiterate grandfather. Janice, her UMD partner, intrigued by this fact, concludes her paper saying, "Maybe I will write a book and I'll have it made into an audio book for all those who might not be 'literate.'" This student's emphatic concern that motivates her to want to take action to help others shows what West (1993) describes as a "capacity to get in touch with the anxieties and frustrations of others. . . . The moment of connection means never losing sight of the humanity of others" (cited in Schneider, 2005, p. 206).

Indeed, some students demonstrated an attitude of receptiveness, understanding, humility, and ultimately empathy. Karim, an AUB student describes the process through which he learned about "himself" through his talks with his UMD peer, Gina:

> When I first started talking to Gina, I was surprised that she was very nice and very helpful, but what truly shocked me is that Gina didn't think that American people are better than others. It was then that I realized that it wasn't Gina that was ethnocentric; it was me.

Talking to his peer allowed Karim to revisit his preconceptions about Americans. He was guided by the responses to interview questions he received from his partner and was able for the time being to lay aside the views and values he held for himself in order to enter Gina's world without prejudice (Rogers, 1969). More importantly, he was able to adopt alternative perspectives vis-a-vis oneself (Mead, 1993), for he learned more about himself through the process of getting to know his partner, and in the process he and "the other" juxtaposed their positions by discovering that he might be the source of prejudice, and his partner a victim of it. In this sense, Karim entered Gina's world through a mirroring process (Bloom, 2013) and realized that what separates the self from the other has become fuzzy and blurry.

Another example of the adoption of an alternative perspective, vis-à-vis oneself, is an AUB student, Yousef, who described his UMD peer in empathic terms:

> Even though he doesn't have to pay for college, he works 35 hours per week at a grocery store. When he told me this, I was stunned and embarrassed because I have never worked in my life and always relied on my parents. I believe this experience not only made me realize how lucky I am but also broadened my mind because it let me see a real example of the American way of life, not the one we see in movies or read in books, far from preconceptions, far from the single story of the US aka the American dream.

Again, students had the chance to think about the literate lives and material lives of their partners, as Yousef in the above quotation comes to a realization about the socio-economic realities of his partner David. The ethnographic and personal nature of the exchange allowed the students to go beyond simple us/them dichotomies. This sometimes resulted in clichés of homogeneity in their writing, but sometimes fostered very concrete specificity as they described one another's lived experiences around reading, writing, and living in the global twenty-first century.

In an even stronger instance of empathic involvement, another AUB student reached the point where he was reflecting on his own priorities:

> [My partner] has put her priorities straight; work and education go first, and then goes leisure and fun afterwards. She is a non-stop worker. She barely has the time to enjoy her weekends or even her vacations. On a Sunday morning in Michigan, she was forced to cancel our Skype session because she was called into work. It made me sad. I wasn't sad because she canceled the interview, but I thought it was too much for a 17 years old girl. I remember that Sunday, I had nothing to do, I was lying on the couch watching TV after a tiring week, and she was still working. I told her every time we talked "I'm not going to pressure you, consider it part of your free time."

Thus, it could be argued that these exchanges not only precipitated peer empathy but, through this empathy, facilitated a better understanding of the self and other cultures.

Another AUB student compared her experience with bullying in middle school to her partner's experience:

> Since I had myself been rejected during that time, I immediately related to his story. I couldn't believe that a guy like him would be categorized as a "weirdo" and he couldn't believe that a girl like me didn't have friends. This brought us closer, and I think that what I've learned from working with him is that, no matter how different we think we are, how our perceptions of the world can be divergent, we all face the same obstacles: having a blurred identity as teenagers, always trying to fit in, being judged by others and afraid of standing up for ourselves.

The AUB student analytically compounded both experiences into the universal narrative of being bullied, where the self is reflected in the mirror of the other. This is likely an example where our own assignments needed to encourage students to go beyond the imperative to homogenize, connect, and empathize via signifiers like "bullying." In this instance, students may have had the rewarding experience of connection but may also have lost an opportunity to articulate and grapple with nuance and difference.

Effectively, the transnational exchange gave students the chance to hear stories and share their experiences, thereby creating a dynamic interaction among voice, identity, and context. It is this interaction that helped them showcase their feelings of empathy and integrate the experience of the other into the story of the self. Not every experience was positive—or empathic. One AUB student, who happened to be Muslim, wrote that she was "disappointed about how little people in the West know of our lifestyle, religion, and traditions. I discovered this when my partner called the mosques 'Muslim churches.'" The UMD student may have connected with the AUB student by linking the mosque with "the church" in her own background. However, this "connectedness" remained one-sided for it was not recognized as such by the partner, reflecting a one-dimensional perspective. Of course, the UMD student was an anomaly in many ways—studying (and perhaps living) in a city full of mosques and not being familiar with the term—but her lack of familiarity created a negative impression that her partner generalized ("people in the West"). However, across these varied moments of connection, it may be argued that the virtual journeys and communication mostly fostered transnational empathy with other individuals and contexts, the "unothering" of the other. In many instances, the journey turned out to be one of self-discovery where learning about the other was often a vehicle to unfolding the self or at times even an ingredient in knowing oneself.

Students' Attitudes to Language and Multilingualism

Our purpose was for students to develop a more critical and sensitive relationship not only to others, but also to language. While our primary concerns as teachers of English-language writing courses tend to focus on rhetorical situations in English, students' attitudes towards multilingualism may in fact be important considerations that closely relate to conceptions of "self" and "other" (for a description of other students' attitudes about multilingualism, see Ronesi, this volume). The transnational dialogue among our students elicited explicit writing and reflection about multilingual language practices. The literacy narratives therefore offer an important place to begin analyzing what attitudes about language(s) can tell us about literacy and learning as well as the ways in which transnational collaborations can benefit both students and teachers who are negotiating monolingual contexts and expectations. It should be noted that these exchanges among students were not always English monolingual, even though students were enrolled in English-medium institutions. In several instances where the UMD student spoke Arabic, partners chose to communicate in a combination of English and Arabic.

For some UMD students the language practices of their peers in Beirut appear to have been central to their understanding of AUB students' identities—at least according to the titles of their literacy profiles: "A Language Beside One's Own," "Tongues of the World," "Fluencies," "An Outburst of Miscommunication," "The English Language," and "The Language of Lebanon." Often UMD students were fascinated by AUB students' multilingual lives: Beirut students' knowledge of multiple languages really distinguished them in the eyes of their American counterparts, though occasionally UMD students used diction ("outburst of miscommunication") suggesting a negative connotation for these same skills.

Students' actual discussions about language practices in the literacy narratives reveal a set of assumptions and stereotypes about what languages mean in context, particularly as they are used by "foreigners." For example, some UMD students expressed surprise about their partners' fluency in English, revealing no knowledge of Lebanon's multilingualism, sometimes juxtaposing this with admiration for their multilingualism. Of course, given the background of many Dearborn students, linguistic realities in Beirut were not unknown to many of them and in fact, many Dearborn students are also multilingual. However, this knowledge and personal capability did not keep students from commenting on their AUB partners' use of English in particular. For example, a UMD student points out that her AUB partner, whose "father is Lebanese and mother is German," "speak[s] to [her] mother in French and Arabic to [her] father." She then writes that "Listening to [her partner] answer my questions and speak in English was cool to me because I felt as if I was speaking to someone attending . . . [UMD]. Her English was really good and the more we talked, the more we figured that we are pretty similar." Even though this UMD student had the ability to speak in Arabic with her partner, she seemed to feel more comfortable communicating in English for this project and she felt a certain familiarity in doing so, perhaps because she considers English to be the most appropriate language for school or educational purposes. Other possible explanations are that because she and her partner were communicating across a social media platform, English seemed most appropriate, or that they associated English with youth culture (both students mentioned communicating with their parents in Arabic). Or, perhaps a variety of reasons—conscious or unconscious—prompted the students to use English. Regardless, the exchange itself gave the students agency to make a choice about what language they preferred, or perhaps an opportunity to engage in code-meshing if they chose, and, later, to reflect on those choices.

UMD students frequently commented on the perceived, practical value of the multilingualism of their AUB peers, noting, for example, the professional possibilities language skills represent. Others focused on the educational and cultural use-values of English for their overseas peers. One UMD student (mis)characterized the study of English at AUB as the study of a foreign language, when in fact most Lebanese students grow up learning English from a very early age, synchronously with other languages. Drawing on her own experience as a monolingual student studying in the US, the student wrote of her partner's literacy: "I was intrigued by her wanting to pursue an advanced comprehension of English since I thought that a foreign language, in general, would be less focused upon overseas, as it is in the United States." This student's ready assumption about English's use-value, her assumptions about her partner's capabilities in the language, and her North American frame of reference led her to characterize other subjects as "more demanding" and the learning of languages, in general, as a "useless" pursuit. As with most facets of literacy, attitudes toward multilingualism among UMD students were varied and informed by lived (sometimes limited) experience.

For their part, AUB students also seemed interested in making connections with their peers' language capabilities or attempts to learn other languages. In the connections that they made, however, AUB students tended to suggest implicitly (and perhaps accurately) that they were the experts vis-á-vis multilingualism. For example, one AUB student noted that her partner "just speaks English, but he took one Spanish course at school . . . I took English and Spanish courses at school, but moreover, I can speak French and Arabic. The fact that he doesn't travel that much can be the cause of his lack of second language. He never traveled outside USA, he didn't need to use another language than English." Again, the subject of literacy allowed the students to explore each other's material lives—in this case, including contrasting exposure to language study and contrasting socio-economic status as well. On one hand, the UMD student is positioned (perhaps accurately) as being in a privileged position because he doesn't "need" to speak any other language, which, of course, might be an anachronistic observation if one believes that in the era of globalization we all "need" multilingual and multicultural skills. Paradoxically, this observation about the student also reveals that despite speaking a global lingua franca he still does not have access to international travel—suggesting, perhaps, a certain irony regarding elements of western hegemony.

Another student found her partner's interest in French "intriguing" but also problematic. In response to her UMD partner's explanation that "I wanted to major in French because I find it so interesting that one person can just switch languages and it is not gibberish," the AUB student offered a soft critique, writing that, "His remark was very acute, yet it overlooked an important aspect of being multilingual: one does not simply 'switch' between two languages. In fact, the transition between two tongues is often paved with struggles." Again, the AUB student is in the position of speaking from experience and authority.

Some AUB students articulated similar assumptions connected to the monolingualism of their UMD partners. One AUB student, for example, was surprised by her monolingual partner's perceived imperfections with written English, writing that "As I was expecting, Denise was fluent when it came to speaking English. It's the main and only language that she speaks. However, I was amazed how she never got the hang of writing!" Another AUB student, however, offered a telling anecdote: She asked her UMD partner what languages she speaks and was told, "It is funny to ask such a question, because it is uncommon for Americans to know more than one language." The AUB student reflected, "I think maybe their language is the worldwide used language so they are not in need to know another one." In this case, the AUB student did not belittle her partner's lack of languages other than English but rather understood her partner's monolingualism as evidence or consequence of English's global value. Further, her words at the same time offer a subtle (or perhaps not-so-subtle) critique of the hegemony of English, suggesting her coming to a tentative conclusion that monolingualism might itself represent privilege.

Challenges and Limitations of the Project

As our collective experience attests, and as some of the examples above illustrate, the integration of a transnational exchange within a writing class—while certainly providing students with an innovative and engaging learning experience—does not mean that students' writing will achieve the level of richness or complexity we know, or hope, is possible during an opportunity such as this. Ultimately, we realize that our students are still practicing writing: in writing classes, students are attempting to find a voice that will be legible within academic contexts (for a discussion on students' struggles to achieve authorial voice, see Jarkas & Fakhreddine, this volume); they are often negotiating the social, educational, and cultural differences between high school and college; and more practically, they are struggling to understand and meet the expectations of their teachers. It is not a surprise, therefore, that we found our collaboration not only rewarding, but also challenging and limiting. We articulate some of these limitations here and consider some revisions we have undertaken in subsequent collaborations.

As we have already noted, students on both sides of this exchange expressed surprise and often delight at finding that their partners were so much "like" them. For example, they felt they shared a sense of the importance of relationships with family, and some shared affinity for European and U.S. literature and music. This identification at times led to expressions of empathy and concern for each other, with some students reporting they planned in the future to stay in touch over Facebook or hoped to meet some day when traveling abroad. Such reflections, taking place outside the assignment proper, exemplify the potential materiality (Bleich, 2013) of transnational language exchanges. That this exchange was, itself, focused on the uses of language in students' lives—on their own experiences with literacy—perhaps made for an even more profound experience of this materiality.

As has been pointed out, however, students tended also at times to over-generalize about their own and others' experiences: presenting (or at least being perceived by their partners as presenting) their own individual experiences as representative of either the US or Lebanon (or the Levant more generally), and then generalizing yet again about how their peers' experiences were like or were different than their own. Ironically, perhaps, feelings of empathy in students could increase a tendency to over-generalize: in such a transnational exchange and collaboration, over-identification with partners' experiences may be as problematic for students' critical reflection about how literacy, schooling, and culture are complex within and across geographic, national and institutional boundaries, changing over time and as individuals and contexts change. In other words, a "simple" kind of empathy or over-identification could well undercut the exchange's potential for promoting a strong, material agency on the part of students for whom the conclusion, "Well, we're so much more alike than I ever would have imagined," neglects important differences.

We are not suggesting, of course, that we would want to discount our students' discoveries about similarities or discourage their feelings of empathy in favor, conversely, of overstating the scope or significance of difference (which would be just as inaccurate). Still, with such projects it is important to keep in mind, as feminist rhetoricians Wendy Hesford and Wendy Kozol (2005, 2011) also have suggested, that western representations of o/Others may serve uncritical, globalized discourses and political hegemonies (even when those representations purport to serve purposes of advocacy) if— in attempting to prompt western audiences to connect or empathize with o/Others—they elide important (material) differences in lieu of newfound "understandings" and feelings of empathy, or take on a "paternal," "maternal," or "rescuer" orientation.

This outcome—the ability to recognize commonalities without defaulting to uncritical, "universal" understandings—requires time built in to the assignment for the kind of reflection that Jacqueline Royster and Gesa Kirsch (2012) call "strategic contemplation" (p. 84). Relatively early on in her literacy profile, for example, one UMD student reported that even though her AUB partner very much enjoyed writing, including writing for pleasure outside of school, her partner had decided not to pursue writing as a career. Mary quotes her partner first as giving this reason for not pursuing a career as a writer: "'Becoming a writer is one of my dreams but in this digitized world, I believe there isn't a place for writers anymore. In Lebanon and even in other countries people don't tend to read like before. These days people are on the internet 24/7.'"

The generalization made by Mary's partner that there is no "place for writers" in a digitized world is one that appears to have stood briefly without challenge in the interview/conversation though not, ultimately, in Mary's essay. Mary further goes on to quote her partner as identifying yet a different (and perhaps more compelling) reason for setting particular career goals: "'I'd love to become a writer but unfortunately writers don't make money these days and you know what a big role money plays these days.... Despite that I have to tell you, something changed my mind a little bit and gave me some hope. I watched a video called Chimamanda Adichie: The danger of a single story. Please try to find this video on YouTube and watch it. Because of this video now, I believe that if I have the will to deliver my words to people, I will find a way to do so one day.'"

In this example, Mary's partner reflected upon Adichie's TED talk, which had been shown to her class, as an opportunity for strategic contemplation trained on her own generalizations about literacy. Mary, on the other hand, ended her essay by coming to two conclusions, both generalizations unsupported either by her own or her partner's experience, or by other data: Mary concluded first that U.S. students see writing as a more viable career option than do students in Lebanon; and second, she concluded that this was true because of the relative, greater freedom of expression that exists in the US compared to Lebanon. Further, Mary came to these generalizations despite also saying she believed that "all college students" everywhere have been "brainwashed" to think they must choose careers based on how much money they stand to make in the future. While she says in her essay that she is struck by her partner's mentioning a few times having "hope" for a less circumscribed future, Mary fails to follow up on how or why such hope might exist for her partner—losing an opportunity to reflect critically on the limits of her own generalizations.

Once our study was completed, two team members (Willard-Traub at UMD and Iskandarani at AUB) continued to engage our students in the transnational exchange during four additional semesters, through Fall 2015. The extended collaboration/interview/literacy narrative was again assigned to students, but with three major changes designed to increase the opportunities for all students to engage in strategic reflection and revision. First, the student exchange was preceded with a required writing task that formed a shared basis for exploring notions of literacy. This task also focused students' attention on a nuanced argument about generalizations based on cultural difference. Specifically, the assignment asked students to summarize the main points and respond personally to Adichie's TED talk entitled "The Danger of the Single Story" mentioned in Mary's essay. In the talk, Adichie speaks directly to how single "stories" that generalize the experiences of those who are culturally and/or linguistically the "Others" function, and how these stories have material consequences on their lifestyles, literacies, and career opportunities.

Secondly, the two collaborating team members involved themselves in the large group dialogue with all of their students, each Skyping into full class meetings with each other's students to talk a little about themselves and answer questions about the aims of the assignment. During these Skype sessions, the two team members introduced themselves and opened the floor to student questions that often paralleled the sample interview questions that were an integral part of the interview process. Students asked about their professors' lifestyles, their literacy habits, and they often ended up sharing with them little vignettes from their lives. In effect, they modeled a collaborative interview, with whole classes participating in the exercise.

And finally, the two team members used reflection as a critical intervention strategy, asking students to send copies of the revised essays to their partners who, after reading what was written about them, reflected on those texts. Specifically, they asked them to respond to the following questions:

> How does it feel when others have written about you? Were you surprised while reading your partner's paper? Did your partner present a new perspective about your culture? What do you have to say about "seeing yourself through your partner's eyes"?

Through this opportunity for critical reflection about their own and their partners' observations and values, and the differences among these, students repositioned themselves as emerging writers who could analyze and generalize the experiences of those coming from another cultural and/or linguistic background, and who also could interpret the impact of these narratives on their own material lives.

In Fall 2014, the assignment was further enhanced through the addition of another opportunity for strategic contemplation—and for accountability—on the part of students. Indeed, once the students had exchanged their final drafts with overseas partners, they filled out peer review forms which required elaborate feedback in the form of comments, criticism, and suggestions. In this way, students were involved in a more focused type of reflection while maintaining some level of control as well. These transnational peer reviews allowed students not only to correct mistakes of fact, but also to negotiate the meanings and limits of generalizations about experiences.

Even with these revisions in place, we acknowledge that improvement in critical thinking and writing practices takes time; no single assignment or assignment sequence should be understood as a "magic bullet" that can resolve the difficulty every writer experiences as he or she navigates the numerous rhetorical choices involved in composing for a variety of audiences. With this caveat in mind, we see the transnational exchange required in our assignment as particularly fruitful in that it encourages students to consider perspectives and lives other than their own. The exchange required students to listen and respond to a peer, leading them to identify commonalities and differences toward a better understanding of themselves and others. Even when these commonalities and differences are expressed in stereotypical or simplistic fashion, we believe the process of engagement and dialogue—and the moments of empathy and recognition that students experienced as a result—suggest that they are primed to think in new ways about the world and the people who live in it. We argue that such priming represents a positive consequence of the exchange, in that it may inform future ways of writing and will certainly last far beyond any given semester.

Conclusion

The transnational exchange fostered an awareness of what Eileen Schell (2006) has termed "rhetorical location" (p. 168), an awareness that forging an effective relationship with a particular audience also must involve articulating a relationship to the culture(s) and language(s) of the communication context. As students communicated with their partners and gained more understanding of their peers' ideas, circumstances, experiences and context, they not only gained more understanding of themselves and their situations as writers, but also entered and constructed a mediated, transnational community. All of this made them more aware and hopefully more critical of their role and position as writers, of expectations and conventions, and of possible alternatives for communicating their ideas, helping them to realize that as writers they make choices about strategies. They could contest, negotiate and or adapt as they practiced their agency (Bourdieu, 1986).

Part of the appeal for students which they expressed in their reflections was that the subject matter meshed with the reader, and inevitably with the writer him- or herself. Writing about their partners became a way to write also about themselves, as they reflected on how their and their peer's experience, ideas, values, and understandings compared. This Russian-doll situation fascinated students and made the assignment appealing in spite of the difficulties AUB and UMD students faced with logistics like conflicting time zones and very different university calendars. Students in academic writing courses do not always have opportunities for writing about themselves and/or their peers as literate agents but, in this instance, they had the chance to at once analyze literacy practices and take part in those practices as well. Students experienced a sense of satisfaction because in the context and community of an academic writing course they practiced agency in giving a voice to a subject which is usually alienated, to borrow Foucault's notion (Rabinow, 1991). The context in which students' writing was created was the most notable aspect of the transnational exchange. Though the students were composing in a supposedly global context, they were creating through their exchange their own local context, or perhaps more accurately, a local-global context that contradicted stereotypes about Orient and Occident.

A consideration of students' individual reflections, both contained within their literacy profiles and as commentaries upon reading the profiles others had written of them, offer insights about a larger institutional ethos for such projects—an ethos centered not simply on preparing students for living and working in globalized economies but rather (or also) centered on students' ongoing development as language users and as critical thinkers about language use within contexts that are both local and global simultaneously. When we think then of larger, institutional ethos, we might also consider how projects such as these both communicate and help shape an institutional awareness about rhetorical location, especially on the part of universities which are notoriously slow to change despite the fact they serve students coming from increasingly diverse socio-economic, cultural and geographic backgrounds—students who themselves are already (or soon will be) moving into and out of complicated transnational and transcultural spaces. Such transnational pedagogies challenge programs and institutions more broadly to conceive of their mission also as interventionist, as not simply preparing students for jobs and careers within a global marketplace but as preparing them also to act within those contexts in ways they ordinarily might not, perhaps ways that even subvert widely held values or practices of the marketplace. In short, transnational projects such as these model for students the agency they purport to teach; that they model that change over time is a necessary condition for such agency.

For programs and institutions as well, such opportunities for critical reflection about shared values and differences in mission are important to initiating and evolving partnerships. What does each program/institution have at stake in any given project? In what ways (if any) do students have the opportunities to examine their home—and partner—university's "stake"? An analysis of our collaboration, for example, might also profit from a consideration of how being at "American-style," English-language universities affected the outcomes of the exchange. An analysis also might profit from considering how differences in students' socio-economic status—in addition to national and cultural backgrounds—affected the exchange. Many students at UMD for example were in awe of AUB students' relatively extensive experience with private secondary schools and travel abroad, and AUB students were in equal amazement about the number of hours a week students at UMD work at outside jobs. It's fair to ask the question whether students' differences socio-economically, even more than culturally or linguistically, weren't some of the most important differences in this exchange, especially given the realities of the globalized economy in which all of them find (and will continue to find) themselves living and working.

Projects such as ours have the potential for turning institutions "inside out" in ways that can drive other changes. These changes might include new programs and courses, such as the "cross-cultural writing" sections now offered in the writing program at UMD, as well as broader, institutional changes such as a greater appreciation and integration of translingual approaches to language difference advocated by many scholars (e.g., Canagarajah; Horner, Lu, Royster & Trimbur; Tardy). Such projects also might be expanded as part of signature efforts in the first year. In *Developing and Sustaining Successful First-Year Programs* (2013), Greenfield, Keup, and Gardner describe programs and the "high-impact" pedagogies attached to them which are designed to promote student engagement and help ensure success and retention in the all-important first year—optimally on any one campus a constellation of programs, curricular and co-curricular. Often, however, such programs necessitate a change in institutional culture, in particular because they require collaboration with a range of constituencies on campus and involve significant faculty development. Having said this, what would a project like ours look like were it to be expanded to include faculty and students working in courses in the social or natural sciences, or professional schools? How might beginning students in engineering, for example, benefit from a collaborative exchange about professional aspirations within globalized, corporate contexts? What would be the benefit for students new to a pre-med major, or to a major in education or business, of a transnational exchange that emphasized collaborating with diverse others? Projects such as ours raise many exciting questions and possibilities.

References

Berry, P. W., Hawisher, G. E. & Selfe, C. L. (2012). *Transnational literate lives in digital times.* Logan, UT: Computers and Composition Digital Press/Utah State University Press.

Bleich, D. (2013). *The materiality of language: Gender, politics, and the university.* Bloomington, IN: Indiana University Press.

Bloom, P. (2013, May 20). The baby in the well. *The New Yorker.* Retrieved from http://www.newyorker.com/arts/critics/atlarge/2013/05/20/130520crat_atlarge_bloom.

Bourdieu, P. (1986). The forms of capital. In J. Richardson (Ed.), *Handbook of theory and research for the sociology of education* (pp. 241–258). New York: Greenwood. Retrieved from http://www.marxists.org/reference/subject/philosophy/works/fr/bourdieu-forms-capital.htm.

Canagarajah, S. (2002). Multilingual writers and the academic community: Towards a critical relationship. *Journal of English for Academic Purposes, 1*(1), 29–44.

Canagarajah, S. (2013). *Translingual practice: Global Englishes and cosmopolitan relations.* New York: Routledge.

Davis, M. H. (1996). *Empathy: A social psychological approach.* Boulder, CO: Westview Press.

Davis, M. H. (1983). Measuring individual differences in empathy: Evidence for a multidimensional approach. *Journal of Personality and Social Psychology, 44*(1), 113–126.

Donahue, C. (2008). Cross-cultural analysis of student writing: Beyond discourses of difference. *Written Communication, 25*(3), 319–352.

Greenfield, G., Keup, J. & Gardner, J. (2013). *Developing and sustaining successful first-year programs.* San Francisco: Jossey Bass.

Hesford, W. (2011). *Spectacular rhetorics: Human rights visions, recognitions, feminisms.* Durham, NC: Duke University Press.

Hesford, W. & Kozol, W. (2005). *Just advocacy? Women's human rights, transnational feminisms, and the politics of representation.* New Brunswick, NJ: Rutgers University Press.

Horner, B. (2012). The WPA as broker: Globalization and the composition program. In D. Payne & D. Desser (Eds.), *Teaching writing in globalization: Remapping disciplinary work* (pp. 57–78). New York: Lexington.

Horner, B. & Lu, M. (2011). The logic of listening to global Englishes. In V. A. Young & A. Y. Martinez (Eds.), *Code-meshing as world English: Pedagogy, policy, performance* (pp. 99–114). Urbana, IL: National Council of Teachers of English.

Horner, B., Lu, M., Royster, J. J. & Trimbur, J. (2011). Language difference in writing: Toward a translingual approach. *College English, 73*(3), 303–321.

Khalaf, S. (2006). *Heart of Beirut: Reclaiming the Bourj.* London: Saqi.

Mead, G. H. (1993). *Mind, self, and society.* Chicago: University of Chicago Press.

Payne, D. (2012). Pedagogies of the globalized: Education as a practice of intervention. In D. Payne & D. Desser (Eds.), *Teaching writing in globalization: Remapping disciplinary work* (pp. 1–16). New York: Lexington.

Pennycook, A. (2010). *Language as local practice.* Oxford, UK: Routledge.

Rabinow, P. (Ed.). (1991). *The Foucault reader: An introduction to Foucault's thought.* London: Penguin.

Rogers, C. R. (1969). The interpersonal relationship in the facilitation of learning. In C. Rodgers (Ed.), *Freedom to learn* (pp. 102–127). Columbus, OH: Merrill Publishing Co.

Royster, J. & Kirsch, G. (2012). *Feminist rhetorical practices: New horizons for rhetoric, composition, and literacy studies.* Carbondale, IL: Southern Illinois University Press.

Schell, E. (2006). Gender, rhetorics, and globalization: Re-thinking the spaces and locations of women's rhetorics. In K. Ronald & J. Ritchie (Eds.), *Teaching rhetorica: Theory, pedagogy, practice* (pp. 160–73). Portsmouth, NH: Boynton/Cook.

Schneider, B. (2005). Uncommon ground: narcissistic reading and material racism. *Pedagogy: Critical Approaches to Teaching Literature, Language, Composition, and Culture, 5*(2), 195–212.

Starke-Meyerring, D. (2005). Meeting the challenges of globalization: A framework for global literacies in professional communication programs. *Journal of Business and Technical Communication, 19*(4), 468–499.

Tardy, C. M. (2011). Enacting and transforming local language policies. *College Composition and Communication, 62*(4), 624–661.

11 The Dance of Voices: A Study on Academic Writing at AUB

Najla Jarkas
AMERICAN UNIVERSITY OF BEIRUT (LEBANON)

Juheina Fakhreddine
AMERICAN UNIVERSITY OF BEIRUT (LEBANON)

In this chapter, the authors hypothesize that first-year composition students benefit from explicit instruction in developing what we call "authorial voice." To study this hypothesis, the authors analyzed the academic, personal, and reflective writing of 44 students taking Advanced Academic English courses at the American University of Beirut. This study showcases the impact of multi-leveled explicit instructions that have been developed in assignments that emphasize the rhetorical moves that students can make when incorporating internal and external sources/voices into their writing. The authors then trace to what extent students were able to achieve an "authorial voice," distinguishing between an array of voices across a variety of writing genres in their reflective and academic writing assignments. The chapter's findings suggest that although L2/3 students coming from the MENA region gradually learn to incorporate external voices into their texts, they struggle with maintaining and interweaving their "authorial voice" with the other voices they refer to in their academic argumentative writing.

Keywords: authorial voice; writing pedagogy; positioning; L2 writing; rhetorical moves

Context and Motivation

Although voice is "one of the most frequent metaphors employed in rhetoric and composition" (Yancey, 1994, p. vii), scholars who have written about and debated the importance of the concept of voice in writing have used the term in such various ways that the metaphor of voice seems "to mean almost anything" (Elbow, 1994, p. 2). A look at the literature demonstrates what Zhao (2012) refers to as the "elusive nature" (p. 217) of the concept of voice, resulting in its emergence as a controversial concept (Elbow, 1994; Hirvela & Belcher, 2001).

As such, it has also been difficult for critics to assess studies written on voice because they fail to address what scholars initially meant by the term (Stapleton, 2002; see responses by Atkinson, 2001; Elbow, 1999; Matsuda & Tardy, 2008).

Despite the fact that some critics from second-language writing feel that voice has been overstated in the literature and that more emphasis should be put on ideas and arguments in L2 writing than on voice (Stapleton, 2002), the literature shows that considerable attention continues to be given to voice as an integral element in academic writing and an essential component of writing pedagogy. Researchers who have attempted to measure voice in their students' writing (Macalister, 2010; Zhao, 2012) seem to place little emphasis on how to specifically train L2 students to acquire appropriate voices in their writing. Yet, this is an approach that we find imperative in our writing pedagogy so that students can learn how to distinguish and maintain their own voices (Hyland, 2005) while interweaving their voices with the voices of other authors (for additional studies on student writing in this volume, refer to Arnold, DeGenaro, Iskandarani, Khoury, Sinno & Willard-Traub; and Ronesi, this volume).

We believe that by empowering L2/3 writers—for whom English could be their second or third language (if they were French educated)—to acquire what we call an "authorial voice," their arguments and ideas will become clearer and more persuasive in their academic writing. We define authorial voice as the use of language that articulates the author's position clearly, particularly in relation to other voices or texts. As teachers at the American University of Beirut (AUB), we find that authorial voice in the first-year composition (FYC) classroom is illustrated well in personal and reflective writing; our goal in this study was to understand whether, and how, explicit instruction of three rhetorical moves—what Joseph Harris (2006) calls "coming to terms," "forwarding," and "countering"—might improve FYC students' ability to develop an authorial voice in academic writing contexts. By "rhetorical moves," we refer to Harris' notion, explained in *Rewriting: How to do Things with Texts*, that when incorporating external sources, voices, or texts into our own research writing and thought, we enter a dialogue and use a set of writing strategies to push the conversation forward. We refer explicitly to the rhetorical moves described in *Rewriting* because they offer students practical rhetorical strategies through which texts can be incorporated into students' academic writing as they develop and maintain an authorial voice.

Our Study

The purpose of our research was to study the effectiveness of our assignments in the second of a two-semester FYC sequence at AUB in helping students develop an authorial voice. Our assignments, as well as in-class instruction, specifically focus on the three rhetorical moves noted above. In our analysis, we consider whether, and to what extent, students achieve an authorial voice in their academic writing after being given explicit instruction in these moves. We ground our research questions in the notion that it is writing teachers' responsibility to embrace the concept of authorial voice in their pedagogy and explicitly train students to make the appropriate rhetorical moves to develop their own authorial voices. We find inspiration in Harris' *Rewriting* (2006), Elbow's "Voice in Writing Again: Embracing Contraries" (2007), and Bazerman's "Creating Identities in an Intertextual World" (2015).

Our study investigates the following questions:

1. To what extent does explicit instruction of "coming to terms," "forwarding," and "countering," as described in Harris (2006), help students develop an authorial voice in their academic writing?
2. How do FYC students reflect on the notion of authorial voice in the activities they do in academic writing courses?

Research on teaching voice indicates that it is a problematic issue (Cadman, 1997; Fox, 1994; Hinkel, 1999; Ramanathan & Atkinson, 1999; Ramanathan & Kaplan, 1996; Stapleton, 2002; Wu & Rubin, 2000) in the context that certain social practices of the L2 learner's culture operate as inhibitors against promoting the individualized voice, authorial identity and presence required when writing in English. Linguists have argued that interdependent or hierarchical values may either prevent L2 learners from projecting a strong voice in their writing or diminish their presence as authors (Helms-Park & Stapleton, 2003). However, these studies have dealt primarily with students in East Asia or Latin America.

Our study extends this list to include L2/3 students in the MENA region, mostly from Lebanon, Syria, and Palestine, for whom individualism as a concept is not so foreign, although they may belong to collectivist cultures. As this study shows, these students are neither "voiceless" nor "devoid of a writerly identity" (Hirvela & Belcher, 2001, p. 84) upon entrance to the university. As L2/3 writing teachers ourselves, we see that "voice is not necessarily tied to the ideology of individualism," nor is it "necessarily foreign to students who come from so-called collectivist cultures" (Matsuda, 2001, p. 140).

The challenge our students face, as L2/3 writers, is in developing an authorial voice, in which they position themselves in writing, where they need to clearly "adopt a point of view to both the issues discussed in the text[s] [they use] and to others who hold points of view on those issues" (Hyland, 2008, p.

5). Hence, we adopt Elbow's (2007) notion of voice as a powerful metaphor that allows writing teachers to support students, and we endorse Bazerman's (2015) advice that we, as writing teachers, need to create appropriate tasks and nurture a suitable environment for students to create and reinvent their authorial voices and identities. We believe that students should be capable of creating their own "authorial identity" (Pittam, Elander, Lusher, Fox & Payne, 2009, p. 154) in their writing, a task that is difficult for novice writers in English to achieve. We want students to gain practice articulating an authorial voice, establishing a position within what we call a "dance of voices," where students learn to interweave their voices with those of other authors, orchestrating those other voices to support an argument and push the academic conversation in new directions.

In other words, we argue that students can better control this "dance of voices" with explicit instruction on rhetorical moves that develop an authorial voice. This practice, in turn, enables L2/3 FYC students to more easily come to terms with the intertextual nature of writing (see Bazerman, 2015). We believe all college students need to receive explicit training in how to write about the "sea" of scholarly texts available (Bazerman, 2003, p. 83) and to integrate the ideas of others to support their own "authorial voices," rather than eclipsing them.

Research Design and Methods

Our action-research study was conducted with three sections of Advanced Academic English (English 204) at AUB, during the seven-week summer semester of 2014, after having piloted it with two sections during spring 2014. We obtained IRB approval from AUB and presented consent forms to each other's students after they had submitted their final research papers. We assured students that we would not open the consent forms until all final grades had been formally released, to protect them from undue pressure. Students were asked to insert their signed consent forms in sealed envelopes and drop them off at the English department's main office to further protect them. Seventeen students signed the consent forms and provided pseudonyms. All excerpts from students' writing reproduced in this chapter use the pseudonyms they suggested in their consent documents. It is imperative to mention here that we did not inform students of the purpose of our study at the beginning of the semester, because we wanted them to work on their assignments with no undue pressure and to trace the process of development of their authorial voices without imposing our own hypothesis that, with the support of explicit instruction in three of Harris' rhetorical moves, they would be able to invent and cultivate an authorial voice as they took a position in their academic writing.

For the study, we selected representative samples from a variety of writing assignments. Our pedagogy in English 204 is process-oriented and mainly designed to offer L2/3 student writers "training in academic critique, argumentation, and research," as stated in the course syllabus. In English 204, students write informally in addition to composing rough drafts to produce approximately 30 pages of formal writing. The course focuses on the development of students' critical thinking, reading, and writing, and the development of analyzing, critiquing, and synthesizing ideas from a variety of texts. The course outcomes, in turn, require attention to positioning and the development of an authorial voice in academic writing. To meet these goals, we designed a number of reflective and personal (informal) and academic (formal) assignments throughout the semester that would emphasize the rhetorical move(s) commensurate with the specific assignment and level of difficulty for our students. In order to create a suitable environment to "nurture the students' invention of themselves as powerful academic writers" and acquire an authorial voice (Bazerman, 2015, p. 45), we engaged students in a number of activities, including oral presentations, and assigned them a variety of written genres throughout the period of study. The assignments were ordered so that students would gain the skills needed to develop a longer argumentative essay. Some of these assignments called for personal and reflective voices, while others initiated their entry into research writing within their learning communities and encouraged them to experiment with different authorial voices and rhetorical practices. For the latter, students accessed academic articles, which they learned to "come to terms" with through paraphrase, quotation, and summary. Then, they learned to use academic texts to "forward" ideas, or evidence, in agreement with their arguments. Finally, they learned to "counter," in which they presented counter arguments and traced the limitations of academic arguments.

In order to analyze students' assignments, we developed two checklists adopted from Ivanič & Camps (2001) and Whitney (2011) (see Appendix). The first checklist directed our assessment of students' informal reflective writing, while the second checklist guided our assessment of their formal academic assignments. We used the first checklist to measure the extent to which students were able to position themselves in the context of their assignments, and take a position of authority or control over their own writing. The first checklist also guided us in measuring students' ability to clearly convey a message, engage the reader using a unique personal voice, and use appropriate evidence to illustrate their own ideas. We also wanted to analyze the extent to which students were able to control their own writing by speaking their own mind and pulling away from mere repetition of others' ideas. We used the second checklist to analyze the extent to which students could incorporate textual examples and creatively interweave other writers' ideas into their own texts while maintaining a strong authorial voice in their argumentative academic writing (Ivanič & Camps, 2001; Harris, 2006; Whitney, 2011).

AUB Students

The FYC student cohort at AUB has a complex language background. In the case of the Lebanese students who form the majority in our classes, the National Lebanese High School Curriculum does not stipulate that all instruction be taught in their first language (L1), standard Arabic. Sciences and math are taught in a foreign language L2/3 (English or French), while social studies is taught in standard Arabic, the L1. In addition, all students are required to learn a third language (L3), French or English, in grades 7–12. As such, students who enroll at AUB could have Arabic as their L1, alongside French and English as their L2 and L3. In some private schools, foreign languages might be taught in other arrangements (for example, some students may grow up with French as their L1, English as their L2, and Arabic as a third required language). Besides the complicated nature of government-stipulated language requirements, there is a clear discrepancy in the language level among students coming from public and private schools, where there is more emphasis on the first foreign language (English/French) in the private schools than state-owned public schools. More importantly, in the context of writing, while students in some private schools, including those in the International Baccalaureate Program, are required to write documented research papers using APA or MLA style, students who follow the National Lebanese Curriculum are not trained to write more than 250–300 word personal opinion essays in English.

The majority of FYC students at AUB enroll in English 203 (Academic English) upon entry and then move on to English 204 (Advanced Academic English). We chose to carry out action research with students enrolled in English 204 because it is the final required writing course for most AUB students. Moreover, these students are expected to acquire transferable skills that enable them "to use information ethically, develop critical approaches to discourse, design research projects, and produce oral and written accounts of their research" (English 204 course syllabus). As writing teachers working with these groups, we also regard it as our responsibility to introduce these students to the concept of entering the "Burkean parlor" (as quoted in Harris,

2006, p. 34) in academic writing, to teach them how to appropriately position themselves as writers in their discourse communities and become lifelong learners able to act on "worldwide stages mediated by texts" (Bazerman, 2015, p. 45). For this reason, we developed explicit instruction about rhetorical moves students should make when they incorporate other voices into their own academic writing.

Results and Analysis

The sequence of assignments in this study was designed to allow students to identify and gradually develop their authorial voice through at least three phases in different contexts. First, students were asked to articulate an authorial voice in personal writing through an introductory letter (what we'll call a "cover letter") and personal narrative; then, in the next few assignments, students were asked to apply explicit instruction in three of Harris' rhetorical moves to argumentative research-based writing. The final assignments—peer review and final reflection—asked students to demonstrate meta-awareness of authorial voice.

Building on the concept of the "architecture of voice" (Hirvela & Belcher, 2001, p. 84) we traced and analyzed the level to which the novice writers were able to distinguish among an array of voices across a variety of genres as they worked on the sequenced assignments. We also wanted to see to what extent our explicit instruction in the three rhetorical moves enabled them to acquire an authorial voice as they "forwarded" or "countered" other authors' ideas in their academic writing (Harris, 2006).

Authorial Voice in Personal Writing

The notion of authorial voice as an expressive medium was called upon early on in the semester. We started with low-stakes personal and informal tasks that asked students to articulate an authorial voice in genres they were likely already comfortable with, such as the cover letter and the personal narrative. In the cover letter, students were asked to create a personal profile in which they introduced themselves to their writing community, and determined a writing goal they might set for themselves to achieve upon taking the course. In the second assignment, the personal narrative, we introduced the "Burkean parlor" metaphor, which is one of the prominent steering concepts in the course. The metaphor allows students to experiment with positioning their own voice within a writing/learning community where they could participate in a conversation and reflect on what they did in order to be able to effectively participate in a debate. They were instructed to refer to the source(s) they had read to be able to better participate in the debate and add value to the conversation on the topic; in addition, they had to reflect on their participation in that discussion to assess their experience and show how they could distinguish their own "voice" among the other voices participating in the conversation.

Both assignments were designed in a way to enable students to express their authorial voice before being "appropriated by specialized discourse" (Bartholomae, 1986, p. 9), and before being exposed to academic writing conventions of the argumentative synthesis. These informal assignments were analyzed based on the first checklist we developed (see Appendix) to examine how they were able to position themselves in a writing context, engage the reader in a conversation on the ideas being discussed, and express a unique voice while maintaining control over their own writing.

Students shared their cover letters on an online forum on Moodle (the official learning management system at AUB) and were encouraged to read other postings by peers and comment informally on them, creating, as such, a communal sense of a writing discourse community (Ivanič & Camps, 2001). Students assessed strengths and weaknesses in their writing, and expressed expectations using the first-person pronoun which allowed them to "insert themselves into texts" (Lores-Sanz, 2011, p. 173) and display a "high level of authority" (Tang & John, 1999, p. S26) and ownership of their first written text in the course. For example, Marita wrote: "If I had to define myself in just a few words, I'd say free-spirited, ambitious, sociable and a little (too much) stubborn . . . open minded person [who has] strong opinions on almost every matter." This statement reflects the student's ability to strongly represent her opinion and engage the reader by using a unique voice to serve the purpose of the assignment. Marita continued to establish a context for her writing and said that "[her] dream is to become a psychiatrist, and provide people with the assistance they need, especially in a country such as Lebanon, where psychiatric disorders are not given enough care and attention."

However, most students' writing goals in this first writing assignment were centered on writing skills and how to improve their language needs with an eye on future academic goals and career requirements. One student, Sam, wrote: "I have all the ideas in my head but find it difficult to start writing." His expectations from the course were to "enhance his writing skills and be able to use proper citation methods to avoid plagiarism."

Expressive writing in the cover letter was revisited in the personal narrative and gradually worked its way to the proposal and final reflection. In the personal narrative, authorial voice was regarded by some students as something heard and as "an idea defended or logically growing to persuade another speaker or audience" (Marita). Marita said she felt "proud," "empowered," and more "organized" as she got the support of other texts to defend her own ideas and win a debate.

Sarah, too, like many other students, felt that using what she perceived as reliable information would help her win the debate and distinguish her voice as a writer. She said that "[i]n the discussion I felt that there was something that distinguishes my voice from the others, and I think that it was . . . the trustful resources from which I got my information."

Others talked more about the need to go through a process of writing, starting with what one student, Habib, termed a "personal voice" to win a debate:

> I then decided to take my own pathway to support my thesis . . . I discovered the thoughts of famous atheists like Richard Dawkins and Stephen Hawking . . . I tried my best to use a logical . . . approach to support my argument, by starting with my own personal voice and supporting it by famous scholars' voice [sic].

Hassan, however, seemed more cautious while entering a debate. He said he preferred to "stay silent" and "listen to different opinions" before he intervened in a debate. James was also hesitant to argue on a topic at this early stage of the course. He wrote: "One thing that I do know is that I do have ideas on my own, but sometimes prefer to keep them to myself; sometimes it's easier to listen and accept things than to argue endlessly."

To sum up, while some students were able to articulate a position clearly when they were working in their comfort zone, others like Habib, Hassan, and James, who were still hesitant about proclaiming a clear position on a specific topic, needed training on how to express their opinions when they had to argue for or against a topic. However, we felt their voices generally seemed individualistic and persuasive, which served the context and purpose of the assignments, and their choice of words represented the set of values they adhered to.

Authorial Voice and Harris' Rhetorical Moves

One main principle in our pedagogy is that, after allowing our students to express their personal goals and experiences, they can be moved to academic writing genres where they need to incorporate scholarly texts by other authors into their own writing. Moreover, we insist that students do not merely "recite or ventriloquize" (Harris, 2006, p. 2) resources in "bipolar oppositions" (pro or con) (Harris, 2006, p. 25)—that is, we do not want students to totally agree or disagree with everything an author says in a text. Hence, the second phase of assignments engaged students in a more academic context, where their tasks required a more formal authorial voice through the rhetorical practices in a more formal academic context. As we noted above, we borrowed from Harris (2006) the notions of "coming to terms," "forwarding," and "countering," and designed tasks that required students to articulate an authorial voice in argumentative and research-based genres they might be uncomfortable with, which would enable them to create a new research space for their thinking to develop.

The assignments in this phase of the study were meant to substantiate students' authorial voice with appropriate support while incorporating external sources into their academic writing. The guidelines we offered for each assignment asked students to pull away from a reliance on quotations and excerpts, and to focus instead on using their own "authorial voice." The papers were assessed based on the students' abilities to position themselves in the writing context and represent their claims strongly and clearly, while at the same time engaging themselves in the discussion of specific topics. We looked into how students could incorporate external sources, invoke the expertise of other authors, and creatively borrow or extend the ideas and arguments of other authors while they maintained control over their own writing (see Appendix). In short, we wanted to assess whether explicit instructions and training students on such rhetorical moves would help them articulate their position clearly in relation to other authors' voices/texts.

To prepare students for the first formal assignment in the semester, which marked students' entry into research, we trained students on how to "come to terms" with a text. Our instructions required students to think intentionally about a text, mark key terms and passages, and write an account of the author's aims, methods and materials. In their account of a given text, students were encouraged to summarize, paraphrase and use direct quotations, and to incorporate the text into their own writing. They were asked to identify what a text sees and does "well," and suggest what it "stumble[s] over or occlude[s]" (Harris, 2006, p. 25). Hence, "the key questions to ask [had] to do not with correctness but use" (Harris, 2006, p. 25). In this assignment, students learned to look at texts in ways they might not have done before, in the sense that they identified what ideas in the texts they could make use of in a new context and what they could see as gaps or limitations in the texts that would allow them to open new research space for their own writing.

Since texts and scholarly conversations build on previous texts and conversations, students need to fully grasp and dissect texts before they are able to incorporate any excerpts into their own writing or take an informed position on any topic in the conversation. Hence, identifying what they needed from a text and whether a text could fulfill that need or not opened novice writers' minds to the world of research writing and their ability to enter the conversation, while articulating a clear authorial voice.

For this first assignment of "coming to terms," we selected moderately easy texts, yet very few students managed to successfully grapple with the concept of coming to terms and express themselves adequately. Marita, one of the very few students who could identify the author's background and grasp the main aim behind the text, could see that:

> ... in her article for *The Times*: "Bombs and Botox in Beirut: How do you cope with living in Lebanon? Get a nose job" the young British journalist [was discussing] an opinion piece that offers a rather unique point of view concerning the contrast under which the city of Beirut is drowning. It is the contrast between people's behavior and the alarming political situation that [she] ... wrote about ...

However, Marita's attempts to assess the text's limitations fell short of noting the text's context as an opinion piece in a popular journal; she stated that there were no in-text citations, and that "the author didn't use any website."

The text was too subtle for some students to come to terms with, and many of the students felt the author was too cynical rather than appreciative of the complex nature of the situation in Lebanon. The fact that most students struggled with recognizing the author's main aims and goals warned us that more training on critical reading along with "attentiveness and intention to writing" (Blumner, 2007, p. 72) was required and which was, therefore, given at this stage of the course.

Another problem arose when students had to assess uses and limitations of the text "Brain drain or brain gain? A Lebanese perspective" (Safieddine, Jamali & Daouk, 2004). Most students' assessments were rather brief, lacked appropriate interrogation of the authors' claims, and fell short of substantial attempts to examine the reliability of the external resources. For example, one student, with the pseudonym of SWRM, wrote: "Since Safieddine, Jamali, and Daouk (2004) are experts on this subject . . . their views . . . are credible along with the extensive use of percentages and examples . . . [that] back up all the information and thesis that they are trying to prove." We might relate this to cultural practices among students in the MENA region, where authors are mostly considered to be infallibly credible and reliable; hence, students lent total authority in their writing to the authors of the texts we assigned without being able to appropriately and objectively identify limitations.

Another student, Farah, who attempted to identify a limitation in the text and follow our instructions to take the conversation in a different direction, said that the authors "were unable to trace some positive aspects of emigration"; yet she couldn't back up her ideas with substantial support, writing that "emigration may be sometimes positive in a way where it may result in diminishing unemployment in a society by offering 'the middle class' work opportunities . . . [and] provide our country with investments and capital money received by the emigrant's family."

After students worked on identifying the author(s)' purpose in a text, they were moved to another level of engagement with texts where they had to show how a text could be useful for them as researchers with their own authorial voice, and, more importantly, how a text that falls short of offering them the needed support could still allow them to create their own research space for future work and investigation. As such, the "forwarding" and "countering" assignments called on students to show how they could use authors' ideas in order to "push [the discussion] forward" (Harris, 2006, p. 25).

One main principle in our pedagogy is that argumentative practice does not call for ventriloquizing resources in a "bipolar" way, in the sense that students should not approach writers' arguments in their texts as "simple antitheses (either x or not-x)" (Harris, 2006, p. 25). In order to train students how to make use of what they read in different texts, they were given a text, asked to "come to terms" with it, "forward" two ideas they were in agreement with, and support their thesis statement with evidence from two other articles that they found on their own and that were related to the theme. They had to summarize, paraphrase, or use direct quotations and include in-text citations and a bibliography for the assignment. Prior to that and within their small groups, students practiced selecting ideas, evaluating, concluding, and reporting them using the appropriate strategy. Emphasis at this stage in the course was on the strategies for citation rather than on documentation styles.

Some students were able to state a clear argumentative thesis statement but fluctuated between their own authorial voice and those of other authors as they were trying to synthesize external texts in their writing. They became invisible when they referred to external sources to validate their arguments and lent authority to the other authors, allowing voices other than their own to take over their writing. This trend could be seen when one student's idea ventriloquized the main points of the assigned text rather than her own stance toward the research topic. Farah, for example, wrote: "[the author] covers how individuals are able to impact their job opportunities by being 'special, specialized, anchored or adaptable' (Friedman, 2005) and finally tries to discuss uncontrollable conditions." Instead of invoking the expertise of another author to support her own argument, she just reiterated what the author was arguing and, we believe, lost her authority over her writing.

Sam, like most of the students, was unable to unable to creatively engage in extending the ideas/arguments of other authors to advance his/her own ideas in his own research project. Although he managed to construct an argumentative thesis statement, he was unable to develop his own arguments and seemed to waver between summarizing, paraphrasing, or quoting external sources to "forward" his own ideas. He started his first body paragraph with his own idea: "The job market is no longer like it used to be, after the industrial revolution in the 1900s the competition for well-paid and stable jobs has been increasing . . ." Then, as he tried to support that idea, he resorted completely to the external source and became invisible by lending full authority to the author:

> Knowledge workers . . . won't be outsourced (Friedman, 2005, p. 238). If you can't be specialized then you have to acquire new knowledge, skills, and expertise in order to become adaptable and add value to your work. "The people who are losing out are those with solid technical skills" (Friedman, 2005, p. 239). One example provided by Friedman was about his childhood friend Bill Greer . . . a freelance artist and graphic designer . . ."I had to look for work that not everyone else could do." (Sam)

Sam continued by offering a synopsis of Friedman's account of his childhood friend and ended his paragraph without pulling out of the example to make his own point. We regarded this as the student's invisibility in his own writing and his struggle with how to adequately "put in his oar" (to use the Burkean parlor metaphor) at this stage. Students like Sam also alerted us to the fact that more rigorous training and emphasis on how to create and maintain an authorial voice (Whitney, 2011), and how to forward other authors' ideas in support of the writer's own, was still needed.

However, students' authorial voice gained momentum as they gradually proceeded in the course, and especially when they wrote the proposal assignment, in which they had the freedom to choose their own topics. Students again used the first-person to signal their personal stance in their writing, and the task allowed students to gain authority over their writing, express a strong stance towards their experience, and uniquely relate themselves to their contexts (Brooke, 1987) as students in their majors. Their use of the first-person also helped them establish a sense of credibility and commitment toward their readers (Hyland, 2002). Individualism and "textual ownership" (Elbow, 1999, p. 327), which some linguists, such as Ramanathan and Atkinson (1999), may not have expected from L2 writers, were evident in some of our students' choices of topics that dealt with taboos and went against traditional notions of animal use or sex education. We regarded this as an individualistic notion in the sense that the students chose topics that were not normally discussed in conservative cultures likes those in the MENA region. One student, Yasmine, who opted to work on sex education was conscious of her individualistic and personal purpose:

> I chose this topic because I consider sex education an important issue that isn't discussed the way it should be. I will be defending the importance of this education, and I will prove that the society as a whole is responsible [for] this "ignorance." *My purpose* is to draw attention to the danger we are facing just because we consider sex a taboo. In my paper I'll be focusing on the youth because these young people are the real victims . . . I will be treating the subject *in my way adding my opinion* towards [those] responsible or my *own interpretation* when it comes to our "*conservative societies.*" (emphasis added)

By allowing students to see purposes for writing beyond taking good grades and to regard themselves as writers first and students second, they engaged, according to Brooke (1987) in an "underlife behavior" (p. 141), which allowed them to subvert their role as passive learners. Students could now position themselves as novice researchers in their learning communities, a concept central to our writing pedagogy. Annotations, which provided short statements about how student writers intended to use each source, allowed students to further see themselves as the primary authors navigating external texts in an academic writing project.

After students learned models of argumentation and how to trace logical fallacies in authors' arguments, we introduced the "countering" move. The general guidelines to this assignment reminded students to keep in mind that they needed to "highlight the unseen," "suggest a different way of thinking," and respond to the position an author takes by constructing their "own position," and they were asked to use one of the following three strategies: "arguing the other side," "uncovering values," or "dissenting" (Harris, 2006, pp. 56–63). Students were asked to situate their ideas in a new context and take the discussion in a new direction while supporting their ideas and arguments with other credible sources.

In most of the samples in the countering assignment, students assessed what they thought were biases, unjustified observations, extremism, irrelevance of some findings, and shortcomings of the text; however, they were not as successful in adding something new to the topic or substantiating their ideas with further evidence or support. For example, one student, Sam, located a limitation in one of his sources and found proof from another in his attempt to push the discussion forward, but he failed to extend the idea with appropriate evidence and support. In his assignment on genetically modified food, Sam described Henry I. Miller as a "a physician and molecular biologist at Stanford University (2013) who contends that genetic engineering is actually making food safer rather than making it more dangerous." Sam then explained how such a presumption should be considered erroneous because although "Miller believes that genetically modified food has [fewer] contaminants such as fungus and mold that can prove to be dangerous for human consumption . . . many health problems can take decades before they surface." Sam invoked the expertise of an epidemiologist to support his argument by saying that "HIV/AIDS epidemic went unnoticed for decades . . . even though there were by then thousands of HIV/AIDS cases worldwide."

But Sam cuts his discussion at this point without giving further evidence and without moving the conversation forward. This shows students struggled, at this stage of the course, with how to interpret an argument, negotiate it, or provide an alternative that would be convincing enough to the audience. This struggle suggests that more training on how to counter a text is required before students can appropriately contribute to a debatable topic and add value to it. So we emphasized these rhetorical moves in the instructions to the research paper and offered more training as they worked on their forthcoming assignment.

The instructions for the final argumentative paper in this course highlighted the different learning outcomes that should be met by the assignment, along with the expected rhetorical moves students should be making. By recounting these moves in the prompt, we meant to have students purposefully build on the previous training. Students were reminded of the context of the Burkean parlor metaphor and the added value that "putting in their oar" (Harris, 2006, p. 34) and maintaining their authorial voice would give to the ongoing conversation. In this context, students were expected to start a journey of negotiating all the different voices in their writing, interacting with their resources, and showing how they were relevant to each other in relation to the research paper and the topic they have chosen to defend. The students were expected to orchestrate their stances in relation to the sources and the ideas within them.

A student who chose the pseudonym SWRM, for example, wrote:

> The first major factor behind marijuana legalization is economic, which was shown as one of the biggest factors behind voters legalizing marijuana in Washington State and Colorado in 2012 (Shane, 2014) . . . most of the focus is on the United States. The two main economic benefits of marijuana legalization are the ability to tax marijuana sales and the savings in law enforcement (Dighe, 2014), so even though the data is western-oriented, we can easily apply these principles to Lebanon.

This student could contextualize evidence and maintain her own authorial voice as she related the main ideas in the text to a local problem in Lebanon. She pushed the conversation forward by citing a number of external sources in parentheses without losing authorship. However, very few students managed to take the main ideas of their sources in new directions.

While many of the students in our classes accessed external source and referred to well-researched facts and statistics as they integrated a range of substantial data in support of specific arguments, counter-arguments, and rebuttals, we believe what is missing is the ability to situate the resources intertextually, conversing with each other. Students needed more training on holding a bird's eye view and developing control over a "dance of voices" with their resources, where they could participate in a conversation with the authors they researched for their project.

Authorial Voice, Revision, and Reflection

The last phase of the course allowed students to demonstrate meta-awareness of authorial voice through peer reviews and final reflections on the course. By self-assessing their learning experience in the course, we expected that student writers would be able to move beyond task-specific practices and position themselves in the larger context of academic writing in a specific learning community.

Instructions for the peer review required that students read critically at least two of the first drafts of their peers' research reports that were posted on Moodle. We created online discussion forums that were sometimes designed for small research groups, and, at other times, for the whole class to participate in as one learning community. Students were expected to comment on how their peers had formulated claims and communicated the purpose behind writing; had drawn relationships between the different documents; had chosen evidence or information from various sources to support the arguments; and had integrated the summaries, paraphrases and/or quotes and developed them appropriately within the paper.

We wanted students' comments to be given in the form of advice on how to make their peer's texts achieve an A on the assignment. Highlighting strengths rather than weaknesses in their peers' assignments and offering advice rather than "corrections" were crucial strategies in our work, given that students belong to a culture where negative criticism, which might be constructive, is generally avoided. So our instructions allowed students to speak freely in the context of offering guidance without the threat of intruding on the positive face of their peers, a point which Ramanathan & Atkinson (1999) also found problematic for L2 learners. We thought that such instructions would indirectly reinforce the idea of authorial voice and help students assess how a writer could engage in extending the ideas of other authors to advance their own ideas and use texts for their own purpose rather than simply recounting them (see Appendix). In other words, we wanted to assess whether students were able to demonstrate a kind of meta-awareness of authorial voice in relation to their peers and their own writing.

Despite the instructions provided, some of the peer reviews showed that students were still occupied with language mechanics, rather than voice and positioning. One student commented, for example, that:

> If this was my draft, I would pay more attention to things such as grammar and links . . . that could lead to a useless loss of points. Also, despite the introduction of many ideas that back up the thesis, the ideas are not linked in a way that shows synchronization in between. (Siba)

Even though some students referred to organization of ideas, they hesitated to give clear and substantial advice to help their peers. For example, Farah wrote: "Personally, I would rather distribute each component in a different paragraph to make it clearer. Also, I might add two sentences in the beginning of each paragraph to assure the continuity of ideas and link my arguments." The fact that Farah said she would "add sentences" to show how her arguments link to each other suggest that at this stage she was aware of the need to pull away from the words and ideas of other authors to create space for her own thought; however, she did not provide her peer with further hints on how to show a clear authorial voice or better develop the writing. Another question that specifically asked them to trace and comment on whether their peers were able to infer or draw relationships between their external sources—in other words, "engage in a dance of voices"—was not addressed to a certain extent.

Although peer reviews might seem unsubstantial in terms of the added value they offered to the writers being reviewed, the reflection component of the assignment provided a glimpse of what students perceived to be good writing. A question that was included in the guidelines for the peer review required that students comment on what they have learnt when doing this peer review and how they thought they could make use of the strategies they learnt to improve their own papers. In response to that question, Yasmine wrote:

> I was searching for what weakened some arguments, and how the strong arguments were built. I will certainly use this critical reading to correct my first draft . . . to identify the weak points . . . and strengthen my argument. I will also try to quote less from my sources.

Although this student, like most of the students in our study, did have an eye on some of the basics of argumentation, she still needed more training on what to do with quotations from external sources other than look at frequency of use. Our question that specifically asked them to trace and comment on whether their peers were able to infer relationships between their external sources was not fully addressed, either.

The students' comments on what they had learned from peer reviewing, on the other hand, demonstrated a strong authorial stance. Sam, for example said, "I've learnt from the experience that we can highlight some points that [my] peer has not seen and at the same time accept others to criticize you." We regard this as a progress on the part of the student, who, after some practice, and with the guidance of our instructions and assignments, was able to take criticism openly and offered guidance to his peers without worrying about any resentment on their part.

In their final reflections, students were asked to briefly self-assess their experience in the course. We wanted to probe more into their perceptions of rhetorical moves and authorial voice. We asked students to reflect on what they had learned about knowledge construction and how much the training on rhetorical moves had helped them position themselves as novice writers in their academic learning communities. They were also asked to assess the development of their own authorial voices in their academic assignments.

Sarah felt that her positions in her writing developed from being shy to becoming more confident and traced this happening mainly in her second peer review. On the other hand, Marita found "countering" as the most difficult rhetorical move despite the fact that she reported she had been "unconsciously using the 'forwarding' or the 'countering' methods [she] had learned in the previous weeks." Moreover, Habib found that the course mostly helped him develop his position as an author, and changed [his] way of reading texts and analyzing them." He said that "small assignments . . . dealing with one aspect of writing such as 'countering,' 'forwarding,' [and] 'coming to terms'. . . helped [him] to focus on one purpose at [a] time, learning progressively how to employ these methods in any coming essays." He added that "the most important thing [he] learned . . . was how to distinguish [his] voice from other authors' voices."

Students reported that the course created a space for them to progress in research writing. Starting with "coming to terms," then moving to arguments in agreement with their thesis, to addressing counter arguments and the need to rebut them, students practiced research in an organized and linear way. They traced a development beyond what they had anticipated in their cover letters, yet almost none referred to the nonlinear stance of the "dance of voices" with their sources in their papers. Moreover, they could not offer an insight into the reflections to demonstrate how they have internalized the strategies being discussed.

Discussion and Conclusion

Amid the debates in the literature around the level of emphasis voice should be given in L2 writing pedagogical practices, our primary interest in this chapter is to demonstrate to what extent explicit instruction in Harris' rhetorical moves can assist L2/3 writers to acquire an "authorial voice," which can in turn allow their arguments and ideas to become clearer and more persuasive. Our study shows how certain social practices of L2/3 learners' MENA culture may operate as inhibitors against capturing the individualized voice, the authorial identity, and presence required when writing in English. For example, when our students tried to incorporate external sources, they rarely justified what each borrowed idea meant; very few noted degrees of agreement or disagreement with authors' ideas or articulated their ideas as extending or building on other authors.

In answer to our first research question, "How does explicit instruction of rhetorical moves allow students to invent and cultivate an intellectual and authorial voice as they take a stance in their academic discourse communities?" we found that, to a certain extent, some students have developed an authorial voice and accessed external resources for support and evidence in their responses to the first two argumentative/research-based writing assignments: "coming to terms" and "forwarding." Our findings strongly suggest that although L2/3 students coming from the MENA region gradually learn to incorporate external voices into their texts, they struggle with maintaining and interweaving their authorial voice with the other voices they refer to in their academic argumentative writing, a rhetorical strategy that we refer to as a "dance of voices," which Harris explains:

> You *move* in tandem with or in response to others, as part of a game or dance or performance or conversation—sometimes toward a goal and sometimes just to keep the ball in play or the talk going, sometimes to win and sometimes to contribute to the work of a group. (Harris, 2006, p. 4)

Moreover, in their countering assignment, students hardly moved beyond the one-dimensional stance of totally agreeing or disagreeing with all that an author said. Because students did not move beyond this stance, we believe that more training should be given to make sure students acquire more rhetorical strategies and practice when noting limitations in other texts. We believe, in other words, that they should be able to engage in a bird's-eye view of their sources so as to dance with these voices in their academic argumentative writing.

The answer to our second research question "How do FYC students reflect on the notion of authorial voice in the activities they do in academic writing courses?" can be traced in students' proposals, peer reviews, and mostly in their final reflections on the course, all of which fall within the category of informal writing activities. Students' use of the first-person pronoun allowed them to express ownership of their texts, and their annotations of references allowed them to see how it could be possible to navigate external sources in their writing. Moreover, being able to reflect on their choice of topics, which might go against students' collectivist conservative cultures, demonstrated authorial voice and individualist positioning in such assignments. In their peer reviews, students developed self confidence in critiquing others and accepting criticism on their work. In their final reflections, although some students revisited concerns about language proficiency that they had mentioned earlier in their introductory cover letters, many of them were content with their growth as writers and their ability to acquire an authorial voice while taking a position with or against an argumentative topic in their final papers.

To sum up, while we note that many of our students were able to project their authorial voice when they engaged in informal writing, the journey to develop an authorial voice in argumentative research-based writing was not smooth for many. Despite the training our students received and the progress reflected by some of them in their final papers, where their writing became clearer and persuasive, other students remained reluctant to "engage voice in meaningful ways" (Hirvela & Belcher, 2001, p. 84). Each rhetorical move was significant to student writers in the context of the individual assignments; however, combining all the moves at a more developed level in their own writing is an area where these novice writers need more training.

Our recommendation for a future research project is to conduct a longitudinal study covering English academic writing courses and a number of content courses at the university level in order to trace students' development in using an authorial voice. We believe that coming to terms with a text, which requires more training on critical reading along with "attentiveness and intention to writing" (Blumner, 2007), should be the focal and entry point in writing assignments across the curriculum in order to enable students to "come to terms" with what they read before they can "put in their oar" and "forward" or counter an idea. Moreover, L2/3 students need to internalize the process of acquiring and maintaining an authorial voice as a transferable skill to all college writing. Thus, as writing teachers, we have to incorporate training on rhetorical strategies into our writing pedagogy and to embrace the term "authorial voice" in our class discussions and especially when giving feedback on student writing, in order to empower students to orchestrate their *dance* with other authors.

References

Atkinson, D. (2001). Reflections and refractions on the *JSLW* special issue on voice. *Journal of Second Language Writing, 10*, 107–124.

Bartholomae, D. (1986). Inventing the university. *Journal of Basic Writing, 5*(1), 4–23.

Bazerman, C. (2003). Intertexuality: How texts rely on other texts. In C. Bazerman & P. Prior (Eds.), *What writing does and how it does it: An introduction to analyzing texts and textual practices* (pp. 83–96). London: Routledge.

Bazerman, C. (2012). Writing with concepts: Communal, internalized, and externalized. *Mind, Culture, and Activity, 19*, 259–272.

Bazerman, C. (2015). Creating identities in an intertextual world. In A. Chik, T. Costley & M. C. Pennington (Eds.), *Creativity and discovery in the university writing class: A teacher's guide* (pp. 45–60). Sheffield, UK: Equinox.

Blumner, J. S. (2007). A host at a parlor: A review of *Rewriting: How to do things with texts*. *The WAC Journal, 18*, 69–72. Retrieved from http://wac.colostate.edu/journal/vol18/blumner.pdf.

Brooke, R. (1987). Underlife and writing instruction. *College Composition and Communication, 38*(2), 141–153.

Cadman, K. (1997). Thesis writing for international students: A question of identity? *English for Specific Purposes, 16*, 3–14.

Elbow, P. (1981). *Writing with power.* New York: Oxford University Press.
Elbow, P. (1994). What do we mean when we talk about voice in texts? In K. B. Yancey (Ed.), *Voices on voice: Perspectives, definitions, inquiry* (pp. 1–35). Urbana, IL: National Council of Teachers of English.
Elbow, P. (1999). Individualism and the teaching of writing: Response to Vai Ramanathan & Dwight Atkinson. *Journal of Second Language Writing, 8*(3), 327–338.
Elbow, P. (2007). Voice in writing again: Embracing contraries. *College English, 70*(2), 168–188.
Harris, J. (2006). *Rewriting: How to do things with texts.* Logan, UT: Utah State University Press.
Helms-Park, R. & Stapleton, P. (2003). Questioning the importance of individualized voice in undergraduate L2 argumentative writing: An empirical study with pedagogical implications. *Journal of Second Language Writing, 12*(3), 245–265. Retrieved from http://dx.doi.org/10.1016/j.jslw.2003.08.001.
Hinkel, E. (1999). Objectivity and credibility in L1 and L2 academic writing. In E. Hinkel (Ed.), *Culture in second language teaching and learning,* (pp. 90–108). Cambridge, UK: Cambridge University Press.
Hirvela, A. & Belcher, D. (2001). Coming back to voice: The multiple voices and identities of mature multilingual writers. *Journal of Second Language Writing, 10*(1–2), 83–106. Retrieved from http://dx.doi.org/10.1016/S1060-3743%2800%2900038-2.
Hyland, K. (2002). Authority and invisibility: Authorial identity in academic writing. *Journal of Pragmatics, 34*, 1091–1112.
Hyland, K. (2005). Stance and engagement: A model of interaction in academic discourse. *Discourse Studies, 7*(2), 173–192.
Hyland, K. (2008). Persuasion, interaction and the construction of knowledge: Representing self and others in research writing. *International Journal of English Studies, 8*(2), 1–23.
Ivanič, R. & Camps, D. (2001). I am how I sound: Voice as self-representation in L2 writing. *Journal of Second Language Writing, 10*(1–2). Retrieved from http://dx.doi.org/10.1016/S1060-3743%2801%2900034-0.
Lores-Sanz, R. (2011). The construction of the author's voice in academic writing: The interplay of cultural and disciplinary factors. *Text & Talk, 31*(2), 173–193.
Macalister, J. (2012). Giving "voice" a voice in the academic writing class. *The English Teacher, XLI*(1), 1–12.
Matsuda, P. K. (2001). Voice in Japanese written discourse: Implications for second language writing. *Journal of Second Language Writing, 10*(1–2), 35–53. Retrieved from http://dx.doi.org/10.1016/S1060-3743%2800%2900036-9.
Pittam, G., Elander, J., Lusher, J., Fox, P. & Payne, N. (March 2009). Student beliefs and attitudes about authorial identity in academic writing. *Studies in Higher Education, 34*(2), 153–170.
Ramanathan, V. & Atkinson, D. (1999). Individualism, academic writing, and ESL writers. *Journal of Second Language Writing, 8*(1), 45–75.

Safieddine, A., Jamal, D. & Daouk, M. (2004). Brain drain or brain gain? A Lebanese perspective. *The Daily Star*. Retrieved from http://www.lebanonwire.com/0402/04022304DS.asp.

Stapleton, P. (2002). Critiquing voice as a viable pedagogical tool in L2 writing: Returning the spotlight to ideas. *Journal of Second Language Writing, 11*, 177–190. doi:10.1016/S1060-3743%2802%2900070-X.

Tang, R. & John, S. (1999). The "I" in identity: Exploring writer identity in student academic writing through the first person pronoun. *English for Specific Purposes, 18*, S23-S39.

Whitney, A. E. (2011). I just turned in what I thought: Authority and voice in student writing. *Teaching English in the Two-Year College, 39*(2), 184–193.

Wu, S. & Rubin, D. (2000). Evaluating the impact of collectivism and individualism on argumentative writing by Chinese and North American college students, *Research in the Teaching of English, 35*, 148–178.

Yancey, K. B. (1994). Introduction: Definition, intersection, and difference—mapping the landscape of voice. In K. B. Yancey (Ed.), *Voices on voice: Perspectives, definitions, inquiry* (pp. vii-xxiv). Urbana, IL: National Council of Teachers of English.

Zhao, C. G. (2012). Measuring authorial voice strength in L2 argumentative writing: The development and validation of an analytic rubric. *Language Testing, 30*(2), 201–230. doi: 10.1177/0265532212456965.

Appendix: Checklists

Checklist to assess voice in Reflective writing, based on Ivanič & Camps (2001) and Whitney (2011)

- ✓ Positioning oneself in the Writing Context
- ✓ The student writer strongly represents his/her opinion in establishing a context for the journal.
- ✓ A clear message is conveyed throughout the reflection.
- ✓ The student writer is able to engage the reader in a conversation on the ideas being discussed.
- ✓ The choice of words represents a set of values the student writer adheres to.
- ✓ The student voice is unique to serve the context and purpose of the assignment.
- ✓ The student writer appropriately selects evidence from his/her own assignments to illustrate his/her own ideas.
- ✓ Ability to take a stance of authority/control over one's own writing
- ✓ The student writer is sure to explain and justify his/her ideas.
- ✓ The student writer offers an insight into the reflections to demonstrate how he/she has internalized the strategies being discussed.

- ✓ The student writer creatively engages in extending the ideas/arguments that reflect control over his/her own ideas.
- ✓ The student writer successfully transfers strategies used in assignments to other contexts/situations.

Checklist to assess voice in academic writing, based on Harris (2006), Ivanič & Camps (2001), and Whitney (2011)

- ✓ Positioning oneself in the Writing Context
- ✓ The student writer strongly represents his/her opinion in the thesis statement/claim.
- ✓ A clear message is conveyed throughout the text.
- ✓ The student writer is able to engage in a conversation on the topic being discussed.
- ✓ The choice of words represents a set of values the student writer adheres to.
- ✓ The student voice is unique to serve the context and purpose of the assignment.
- ✓ Reference to sources (summary/paraphrasing/quoting)
- ✓ The student writer appropriately selects evidence from other authors' texts to illustrate his/her own ideas.
- ✓ The student writer is selective in borrowing other authors' ideas/arguments.
- ✓ The student writer appropriately invokes the expertise of other authors in support of his/her own ideas.
- ✓ The student writer creatively weaves/recombines other authors' ideas/arguments into his/her own writing.
- ✓ Ability to take a stance of authority/control over one's own writing
- ✓ The student writer explains and justifies what each borrowed idea/excerpt means.
- ✓ The student writer offers ideas/arguments that other readings referred to in the context fail to address.
- ✓ The student writer creatively engages in extending the ideas/arguments of other authors to advance his/her own ideas.
- ✓ The student articulates his/her ideas as an alternative to other authors' opinions.
- ✓ The student writer successfully pulls away from the words and ideas of other authors noting degrees of agreement and points of departure.
- ✓ The student writer uses texts for his/her own purpose rather than simply recounting them.

12 Students Running the Show: Performance Poetry Night

Lynne Ronesi
AMERICAN UNIVERSITY OF SHARJAH (UAE)

This chapter chronicles a student-initiated performance poetry event at the American University of Sharjah (AUS) in the United Arab Emirates. The data suggest that performance poetry evening, as a student-driven initiative, was situated in the cultural context and literacy strengths of the student poet population at AUS. The students turned these evenings into opportunities for multi-vocalic expression that built community and good will across differences, and indeed, highlighted translingual strengths of "synergy" and "serendipity." The accommodating nature of performance poetry—adjustable to local parameters and context—was suited to the participants' affinity-space approach to negotiating an environment which was accessible, participatory, learning-filled, and evolving. Faculty encouragement of and interest in extracurricular student literacy practices can support multilingual literacy development, even when—as is often the case in English-medium institutions in multilingual contexts—the writing curriculum focuses strictly on academic English writing.

Keywords: performance poetry; extracurricular; participatory literacies; translingual; affinity space

One spring evening in 2012, I made my way to a campus lecture hall to attend a performance poetry event organized by a group of four friends. The four, my former students, were on the stage experimenting with stage lighting variations, debating the placement of the lectern, and decorating the venue's white board. As students tentatively began to enter the hall, some with paper in hand, lured by emails and posters announcing a poetry slam, an expectant energy pervaded the room. One of students—referred to as Omar in this chapter—shared his initial reaction to the event in an interview in my office a few months later:

> So I walk into the place a bit early because I'm, like, "I might as well go and see," and I see the organizers setting up, and

> I'm [thinking] "This is so exciting." And I find out then that 20 poets [had signed up], and I'm ... "oh wow" ... picturing it. The organizers [told me] they weren't expecting [many students] to come. But then people start coming in. I start kind of getting nervous, and I sit in the front row, because I am, I think, the tenth [poet], maybe? So when [it is my turn], I get up, and I turn, and I look, and I am ... I am totally taken aback. This is a *full* room. (Omar, a student poet)

Omar's account echoes the surprise of the other interviewed poets and event organizers at the popularity of the first performance poetry event at the American University of Sharjah (AUS), an English-medium, co-educational university in the United Arab Emirates (UAE). His description highlights an evidently erroneous perception that was shared by many of the event's participants—including myself—that few AUS students share an interest in, or are even familiar with, performance poetry, or spoken word—poetry written to be performed. As I observed the full lecture hall and the participants' enthusiastic response to the event, and later, listened to the poets and the audience members animatedly discussing the poems and requesting a second event, I could understand that the four organizers had located and drawn to campus a literacy practice that was a quiet interest of many.

My own initial surprise at the success of the event hinged on two notions of mine that I felt warranted examination. Perhaps because I am less digitally-oriented than my students, one element of my surprise concerned how much impact digital life has on students. As performance poetry had had a fairly limited scope in the UAE and no known presence at UAE postsecondary institutions—unlike its presence at colleges and universities in the US—I, like the organizers, thought there would be fairly limited interest in the event. Although well-aware that numerous websites, forums, and YouTube channels are devoted to performance poetry performances and competitions, I was still intrigued to learn that evening that student poets had developed their interest and capacity solely via digital means and embraced this first opportunity of a poetry performance night to make their pastime "live."

The second element of my surprise was more in line with that expressed by the students; like Omar and others, I was excited at the breadth of enthusiasm demonstrated that night. While AUS has its English majors and its share of excellent student writers, it was obvious to me, as I observed and interacted with the group of students that evening, that performance poetry was an interest that cut across majors, nationalities, heritage languages, or academic English proficiencies. This enthusiasm ran counter to an unfortunate perception of "deficit" that exists on campus—that students generally dislike or are not proficient at writing—a perception about writing in English that seems perpetuated by students' struggle with first year composition (FYC). This "deficit" label that accompanies students' English academic writing fails to acknowledge the extent of AUS students' linguistic abilities. In moments between classes, AUS student expression is linguistically rich; they chat or text on their phones, and joke and debate with their friends in languages and dialects from over 80 countries. AUS students transition easily between their languages and English, employing both almost simultaneously—switching between English and another language, perhaps Farsi, Urdu, or Arabic, or shifting from one of the many Arabic dialects to another—to accommodate the speaking patterns or preferences of whomever has joined them. This is a campus characterized by super-diversity (see Nebel, this volume) and linguistic multi-competencies, yet this richness seems overshadowed by the pervasive deficit attitude noted above. Because of that attitude, the enthusiastic and communal celebration of poetry in English during that evening seemed astonishing.

As I began to evaluate both my and the students' reaction to the events of the evening, it struck me that performance poetry night constituted the type of emerging literacy phenomena that New Literacy scholars Lankshear and Knobel (2013) identify as an opportunity for "Let's See" research, a practice: "with the primary aim of understanding in depth a "new" social practice and the literacies associated with or mobilized within this practice. . . . [that] encourages researchers to get as close as possible to viewing a new practice from the perspectives and sensibilities of 'insiders'" (p. 9).

To apply a "Let's See" approach to investigating the development of performance poetry night, I decided to undertake a naturalistic study to learn more about students' interest and involvement in this participatory literacy event. This study was approved by the AUS IRB and funded by a small AUS seed grant. While the nationalities of the student poets and organizers ranged from Egyptian, Emirati, Lebanese, Pakistani, Syrian, to Yemeni, I have changed their names and omitted identifying details in the text to protect their anonymity. None of the informants were my students during this study. I conducted this research over several months during which I interviewed all four organizers—Jamal, Ahmad, Khalil, and Haris—and five poets—Sakina, Badr, Omar, Samir, and Amal—in two roughly hour-long semi-structured interviews after the first and the second performance poetry events. These interviews were digitally audio recorded, then transcribed. In addition, I engaged as a participant-observer—attending meetings run by the organizers—and I reviewed related documents—email exchanges between the organizers, publicity emails, posters, and online event sign-up pages. Ultimately, my initial "Let's See" approach evolved into the following research question: How did the student organizers and the poets situate the concept of performance poetry—a participatory literacy practice that participants were exposed to purely through digital media—to accommodate the AUS context?

As my interviews with participants commenced, I also began exploring performance poetry through the New Literacies framework. New Literacy scholarship acknowledges the dynamic, technological, and multimodal nature of contemporary literacy practices, highlights the role of identity and social context in an individual's determination to engage in them (Gee, 2004; Low, 2008; Selfe, 2009; Weinstein, 2010), and advocates drawing on student out-of-classroom literacy practices for classroom content. A fair amount of New Literacies scholarship treats integrating performance poetry into the language arts classroom (Camangian, 2008; Dyson, 2005; Fisher, 2005; Low, 2008; Reyes, 2006). Kinloch (2005) and Smith (2010) identify spoken word curriculum as beneficial for multicultural students and those struggling with academic English and writing.

In particular, the New Literacies construct of "affinity space," theorized by literacy scholar James Gee (2004, 2005), seemed suitable for examining the development of the AUS performance poetry night. Gee describes affinity spaces as sites—either virtual or physical—where individuals informally engage in literacy practices that interest them. In coining this term, Gee deliberately sought to emphasize the primary role of affinity or common endeavor in drawing participants together, as opposed to the usual social characteristics around which learning communities are often based—even knowledge or ability. As such, there is great potential with affinity spaces for engaged learning and expression without interference from the usual barriers inherent in educational communities. Participant accessibility is another significant characteristic, and Gee refers to the inroads of accessibility as "portals"—"giv[ing] access to the content and to ways of interacting with that content, by oneself or with other people" (Gee, 2007, p. 94). In an interview with St. Clair and Phipps (2008), Gee elaborates on participant accessibility:

> The play with real and virtual identities, the many different routes to participation and status, the recruitment of diverse skill sets, the ways in which "ordinary" people can be producers and not just consumers, and the porousness and flexibility of "membership" that these new digital (and often partly virtual, partly real) spaces allow holds out, for me, real prom-

ise of new practices for equity and a sense of belonging and agency for people. (p. 94)

Due to the equivalent status of the participants, the rules of the affinity space tend to emerge through synergy rather than from imposition by leadership (Gee, 2004, 2005, 2007; St. Clair & Phipps, 2008). Context also plays a significant role in the development and maintenance of literacy practice, and particular emphasis is placed on the synergy between participants and their context:

> Gee argues that the contexts in which literacy events take place are too often imagined in a way that is overly static. "Situations (contexts) do not just exist," he writes. "Situations are rarely static or uniform, they are actively created, sustained, negotiated, resisted, and transformed moment-by-moment through ongoing work" (2000, p. 190). By insisting on the dynamism of the context, Gee advocates for a more active conception of composers. (Zenger, 201, p. 41)

Affinity space thinking is also useful for conceptualizing performance poetry as a literacy practice. As an art form, performance poetry is characterized by a sense of accessibility and as authentic expression of its context. Performance poetry and its competitive form known as "slam" have a populist appeal, with proponents asserting that the nature of poetry written for the "stage" rather than the "page"—approachability, audience response, community building—has drawn poetry out of the ivory tower and returned it to the people (Somers-Willet, 2007). Transnational research concerning the effects of performance poetry and slam competitions in the UK, South Africa, and Barbados (see Gregory, 2008a; Mnensa, 2010; Nanton, 2009) on the native oral poetry conclude that these forms have been accommodated alongside—rather than in lieu of—native oral poetry, the resulting "hybrid nature allow[ing] for people from varied backgrounds of different ages, who are on the margins of society, to find a platform to be heard" (Mnensa, 2010, p. 1). Gregory asserts that performance poetry is "re-created to fit with local concerns and existing culturally contextualized art worlds" (2008a, p. 205).

Translingual scholarship offers an additional way to theorize poetry performance night—a way that is compatible with New Literacies work and which resonates with the linguistic strengths of the AUS students. Work in translingualism (Canagarajah, 2007, 2013a, 2013b; Hall & Navarro, 2011; Horner, Donahue & NeCamp, 2011; Zenger, Mullins & Haviland, 2014), in line with the New Literacies scholarship discussed earlier, calls for pedagogical approaches that allow students to "bring into the classroom the dispositions and the competencies which they have richly developed outside the classroom" (Canagarajah, 2013a, p. 184). In particular, a translingual approach "push[es] compositionists toward greater recognition, appreciation, and use of the heterogeneity of students' language resources" (Horner, Donahue & NeCamp, 2011, p. 291). Translingual thinking rejects the "deficit" label—referred to earlier in my discussion of AUS student writing—as the limitation of a monolingual orientation.

Another area of compatibility between translingualism and the New Literacies scholarship highlighted above is the emphasis on the interaction of context and composers. Theorizing participatory events in a linguistically diverse setting, Canagarajah (2013) underscores not only the multiple linguistic negotiations that take place in day-to-day encounters in translinguals' (composers') lives but also the disposition that accompanies their interactions in this multicultural contact zone. This disposition, which Canagarajah terms "dialogical cosmopolitanism" (2013, p. 196), posits that, given the variety of ethics and norms in linguistically and culturally diverse environments, translinguals tend to establish community around collaborative practices rather than shared values. This tendency requires translinguals to rely on their flexibility, sensitivity, and creativity to negotiate linguistically rich contexts. Further, Canagarajah (2013), drawing on the work of Khubchandani, highlights the dynamic of synergy and serendipity in these contexts:

> "Synergy" captures the creative agency subjects must exert in order to work jointly with the other participant to accomplish intersubjective meaning.... "Serendipity" involves an attitudinal readiness to "accept deviations as the norm." To adopt this attitude, one must display "positive attitudes to variation" and be "open to unexpectedness." Subjects have to be radically other-centered. They have to be imaginative and alert to make on-the-spot decisions in relation to the forms and conventions employed by the other. (p. 41)

Indeed, the translingual attributes of "synergy" and "serendipity" also aptly characterize composer/context aspects of performance poetry and affinity space thinking.

Informed by the scholarship on New Literacies, performance poetry, and translingualism, I situate the development of performance poetry night as well as the data from this study at the intersection of affinity space and translingual orientation. The following depictions of context and participant perceptions over the period of several months showcase the performance poetry night event as a cohesive accommodation of different and sometimes unexpected elements—often, synergy and serendipity—working in concert: affinity spaces' porous parameters and flexibility in line with organic development; performance poetry's participatory and adaptive nature; and translingual participants' negotiation of diversity through collaboration and accommodation.

Because I want to underscore the intricate interactions between affinity space and translingual thinking in the development of performance poetry night, my findings appear below in two major sections. The first section is a recounting of the synergy and serendipity that led up to the emergence of the first performance poetry night as an affinity space, and the second presents the synergy between the participants and the translingual context that negotiated and sustained the poetry night's position as an affinity space.

Synergy and Serendipity: The Emergence of Performance Poetry Night as Affinity Space

Affinity space endeavors evolve more organically than artificially; such was the case with poetry night, whose first-night success could be certainly be understood as the consequence of student organizers responding to perceived needs for informal and shared learning at their university—synergy—and the chain of events which were characterized by a bit of coincidence, happenstance, and even misnomer—serendipity. As such, background into the origin of performance poetry night attests to the serendipitous and synergistic connections that were to become meaningful to its development.

While the performance poetry night developed outside the classroom, it had its origins in the training class for the AUS Writing Center tutors. As part of a small unit on World Englishes, tutor trainees watch a YouTube video of renowned Jamaican-born dub poet, Linton Kwesi Johnson, perform a poem entitled "If I Woz a Tap Natch Poet" in Jamaican Creole (The Guardian, 2009). Johnson's intense delivery, the ensuing discussions on "Arabizi," "Hinglish," or "Nigerian Pidgin" (English and local language "mixes" that are spoken by some of the students in the training class) make this activity one of the highlights of the semester. This video was the impetus for Jamal, then a tutor trainee in the class, to consider planning—with his friends—a staged poetry event at AUS:

> I wanted so much for us to organize this because I remember, when I first saw Linton Kwesi Johnson [perform his poem], thinking how amazing it was to write something like that,

you know, something that's meaningful and cool, and perform it.

By happenstance, Jamal and three friends—Ahmad, Haris, and Khalil—had recently begun to discuss holding events on the AUS campus that would attract like-minded students interested in exchanging knowledge, particularly about their own various intellectual or creative sidelines. In his first interview with me, Khalil expressed the group's hope that the activities planned by the group would make "make a space [on campus] for learning for the love of learning, separate from learning for the sake of grades, degrees, or career." Ahmad, who spearheaded this endeavor, did so in response to student interactions that he perceived as insularly academic-focused and to extracurricular activities that largely revolved around "career and making money and putting stuff on your CV."

The group approached the AUS International Exchange Office (IEO) for sponsorship and support. While the Writing or English departments might have seemed more appropriate prospects for supporting a literacy event, Jamal had befriended some of the student workers and younger staff at the IEO that semester while applying to the semester-abroad program. As Jamal shared his new interest with the staff, some of them introduced Jamal to their favorite poetry performances on the internet and were enthused at the prospect of hosting such an event. Most importantly, the IEO director readily agreed to sponsor a performance poetry evening, reasoning that spoken word events were popular activities on the American campuses that partnered with AUS and that the event would provide a venue for publicizing the IEO.

Within the next few weeks, email announcements—sent out to AUS students, staff, and faculty—invited "poets, aspiring poets, poetry lovers, and performers [who were] willing to share an original poem, or to interpret/recite/perform a poem of their choosing, in any language, 3–5 minutes in length" to a "poetry slam." Two links appeared in the posting: a link to an online sign-up sheet and another to a video of spoken word artist Sarah Kay performing one of her most popular poems, "Point B" at a TEDx conference. The organizers' familiarity with the TED Talks format led to the inclusion of what the organizers and poet participants would later agree was a significant part of the evening—refreshments in the lobby immediately after the show. Jamal explained their decision:

> For instance, a big part of TED Talks is not only when the [presenters] go on stage, but, also the lunches and the general breaks they have, [so attendees can meet] a lot of people and

make friends and connections and share ideas. So, I thought we should do the same thing for the poets.

Rounding out the event's marketing was Ahmad's poster, which, like the email announcement, invited students to a poetry slam: dramatic and edgy—like much slam imagery—it featured a young man behind a microphone, enveloped in wings of fire.

The Big Night

As suggested by Omar's account at the beginning of the chapter, the poet and audience response to the poetry event was striking. The 20 poets Omar referred to included students, professors, and staff. In fact, there were so many attendees that students sat on the stairs and lined the back wall. A handful of poets who were obviously familiar with the conventions of spoken word performed their poems, but, poignantly, many more students announced that this event constituted the first time they had gone public with their poetry, some hands visibly shaking as their owners read their poems from papers and from phone screens, and in one case, from a laptop precariously perched on the lectern. Audience members called out words of encouragement, and warmly applauded each poet. Despite the fact that "any language" was specified in the announcement, every poem was delivered in English except one—a poem in Arabic. However, this poem became a notable part of the evening, as Omar explained:

> [The poet] was talking about the woman that he loves, and he was, like, using lovely metaphors to describe her, but with every verse he would describe her in an Emirati dialect and then repeat [the sentiment by] switching to, like, Palestinian, then to Jordanian, then to Iraqi, then to Egyptian dialect—showing that we can say the same thing in six different ways. To hear someone perform it in, like, six different Arabic dialects was just something to hear.

While logistically, the first poetry performance event went off without a hitch, it was brought to the organizers' attention that the event was labeled in a confusing way. Indeed, despite the reference to a "poetry slam" both on the poster and in the email announcement, this event could not be called a poetry slam—poets in competition with an audience awarding points—but was instead a spoken-word event accommodating a wide range of interpretations of "performed" poetry. This contradiction was made clear to the organizers after the event during refreshment time in the lobby—the refreshment-time concept that they had "borrowed" from TED Talks. Some students who were unfamiliar with the term "poetry slam" questioned its meaning, while a few students who were more knowledgeable asked organizers "why" the event was called a poetry slam.

Later, in his interview, Jamal admitted that the organizers had not thought very pointedly about the distinction between "poetry slam" and "performance poetry" when drafting the announcements. Yet, despite this misnomer in the email and the fact that the event's poster, both in title and in image, was strongly evocative of slam poetry as portrayed in digital media, the rhetoric of the emails suggested a wide scope of interpretation for the night. This email announcement still opened a number of "portals,"—in Gee's (2007) words—or access points for participation in this first performance poetry night; students could read or recite or perform their own poem or the poem of another author, and in any language. Indeed, from an affinity-space perspective, the organizers' confusion regarding the performance/slam distinction seems to have provided this initial poetry night the condition of accessibility, as the lack of specificity allowed AUS poets at all levels of spoken-word ability and interest to consider participating.

Another portal to accessibility was the sponsorship of the IEO, an example which provides a clear example of the interplay between serendipity and synergy. Sponsorship of the event by the IEO would likely not have been considered by the four as an option but for Jamal's new connection with the program and its staff. While his involvement with IEO could be understood as serendipitous, the group's decision to seek sponsorship for this activity was largely synergistic—based on their understanding that IEO was a student-focused program that, because of its interaction with universities abroad, might welcome the opportunity to sponsor the event. As a portal, IEO sponsorship likely opened the door to more participants. On a campus that is largely described by faculty, staff, students, and alumni as "culturally diverse" (American University of Sharjah, 2010), a poetry event sponsored by the IEO is potentially more appealing to wider group of students than a poetry event sponsored by the Departments of English or Writing.

Given the accessibility afforded by the portals that first evening, participants came away with a sense of the potential of the event: the organizers could ascertain poets' level of interest and range of abilities; poets had the opportunity to perform their poetry to an audience and to learn from others; would-be performance poets seated in the audience could be inspired and motivated. Khalil, even in his capacity as an organizer, expressed surprise at the potentiality of the evening:

I think some of poets didn't think they were good at all or they had any sort of talent and then from the response they got, they were like "You know, I can do this." And it was really cool when, like, the poets were standing around [during refreshment time after the event] and then, one person would really like something about a poet's poem and they'd talk about it. That was really cool. And, another cool thing was—well, I didn't really think about it before—but I didn't expect that I'd remember someone's poem a month later.

While this may seem a mundane account of events, I argue that it is actually a complex interplay of synergy and serendipity, one that—partly by participant disposition and partly by happenstance—resulted in an accessible space for performance-poetry fans from all corners of the university, and it provided potentiality for further meaningful and enjoyable learning. While some of connections have already been made explicit above, analyzing the dynamics of its development expose the intricacies involved. I can assert, for example, that it was serendipitous that Jamal was exposed to performance poetry in his peer-tutoring in writing class. Yet, what was the disposition of the professor (me) who sought to introduce the class to the idea of World Englishes by showing a video of a Jamaican dub poet engaged in a participatory literacy act? This is an example of synergy. What were the dispositions of the students, like Jamal, Khalil, and Ahmad, who had at different times enrolled in peer-tutoring class to become tutors in the Writing Center? This is also synergy. That Jamal and his group of friends decided to become involved with informal learning opportunities is synergy. That Jamal became interested in performance poetry at the same time that he and his friends made that decision seems serendipitous.

The next section illustrates how, with the potential for an affinity space established, performance poetry night participants—both the organizers and the students—negotiated and sustained this affinity space to accommodate their diverse and translingual context.

At the Intersection of Participatory Literacy and Translingualism (Or "We Don't Know What This Is, But We Like It")

Once Jamal, Ahmad, Khalil, and Haris reconvened the following semester, the group decided to be more deliberate and clear in their second event planning, as this excerpt from Ahmad's email update to the organizers suggests:

> I had coffee with Jamal yesterday and we were of the opinion that we should probably start moving away from the title of "slam poetry" and redesign the poster with a sense of the actual event we hosted last time.

To help them "get a sense of the actual event" before proceeding with plans, the group decided to interview the poets for their insights on the first event. Jamal, Ahmad, Khalil, and Haris worked with the IEO office to contact and request group interviews with the poets. While the organizers' interview protocol addressed a number of logistical aspects, the focus of the interview concerned the structure and content of the event—particularly, the poets' perspectives on whether parameters should be set on the performance style of the poems. The interviewers sought to determine poets' thoughts about planning for an actual slam, or if not for a slam specifically, about incorporating elements of competition or evaluation.

The five student poets who showed up for the organizers' interviews were invested performers who sought to improve their performance styles for the following event; even so, they all favored maintaining an inclusive spirit rather than insisting on "performance over reading" or gravitating toward a slam model. Even as the poets admitted enjoying the excitement of slam competitions, they all believed that adopting a slam format was inappropriate for this event. To these student poets, it was more important to offer a venue to poets of all abilities and retain the warm, supportive environment of the first event—in short, to build a community for aspiring AUS poets. Evaluation—or being rated, poetry-slam style—was understood as a stratifying element that would drive away novices and remind the students too much of being graded. "I'm really only interested in critique [I might receive informally during the refreshment time after the event] or later when I see poets on campus," noted Omar. To that end, the term "poetry slam" was removed from all reference to the second event.

Elaborating on the organizers' question about performance styles in a subsequent interview with me, Sakina recounted what she told the organizers: that the first event's accessible approach promoted a relaxed atmosphere and relief from the "oppression" associated with being a student—lectures, deadlines, assessment—and highlighted how the event created an opportunity for important informal learning. She explained:

> For example, I wouldn't go [if I saw a poster announcing] a seminar on racism. I mean, [my response would be] "I know about racism. Okay. Finished. I'm not a racist." Whatever. You [respond] with these preconceived ideas. Whereas if [a

topic is presented with poetry] it's someone's experience, and it means more to the person who's listening to it, who gets to unwrap, or, like, unravel the layers with the poet who's speaking, as he's going along. You're like, you know, engaging in the presentation. You really feel that [the poets are] coming from somewhere, like maybe this has happened to them, so, you know, you take it personally. [Poets] need to be able to efficiently communicate if [the topic] is something serious like racism because people are more willing to learn this way than when put in a classroom setting.

Another poet, Badr, pointed out that an open and unrestricted poetry night offers a space where the multi-vocalic nature of their translingual community can be enacted, allowing for modes of expression not formally validated on campus:

The poetry slam should have come a long time ago, because there are a lot of poets here, and they never got a chance [until poetry night]. So, I don't want to interfere with that [by adding more parameters], because it's very nice, because we get a different flavor from everybody. And we can perform in different languages. I know it's going to be hard for non-Arabic speakers and everything, but it's also kind of an initiative, like, "Learn Arabic," you know? We Arabs know Arabic and English, you know, [so] non-Arabic speakers should also learn Arabic. And we should also learn Urdu for people who are going to be performing poems in Urdu. So if poets want to present their poems in Urdu, we'd be listening. We'd understand. So I think it's a very good idea that all of this [can be contained in] one event.

While learning Urdu to understand peers' poetry may sound excessive or exaggerated in a monolingual context, Badr's suggestion expresses a reality in the context of the UAE. Lots of languages, particularly Urdu, which is spoken by many of the Pakistani and Indian expatriates, are present in the UAE. Individuals here often "pick up" languages for trade reasons, or from watching entertainment media, or in the houses of friends. For these students, to acquire enough Urdu to appreciate the gist of a poem is not an unrealistic goal.

Even as the creation of a poetry community trumped the evaluation and competition the poets associated with slam, poets expressed in their interviews that improving for the next performance was definitely a goal. To that end, the organizers invited a faculty member from the English Department, a spoken-word poet who performs internationally, to present a workshop on performance poetry. This event, offered a few weeks before the second poetry night, was attended by many of the first-event poets and provided an overview of oral poetry and its different forms and techniques. Contemplating the organizers' decision to host the workshop, Khalil referred to an affinity-space experience—his role as a tutor in the writing center:

> It seems like we are drawing all these students in, even if they don't know what performance poetry is, and then helping them to bring [the event] up to a performance level, which is, I think, what we're doing this semester with the workshop, sort of addressing all those questions that the poets had, especially on performing their poems. It's the same way we do things at the writing center. You don't want to give too much content input; you want to guide [students] to learn on their own.

Ahmad, too, understood the poets' request for open and unconstrained learning, in line as they were with the organizers' earlier stated goals of promoting gatherings of like-minded individuals interested in exchanging knowledge. Like Khalil, Ahmad drew from an affinity-space experience as he discussed supporting the poets.

> Sometimes you don't want to be part of a competition. You just want to present your stuff and get other people's opinions on it, and see. You know, I used to do my graphics work just as a hobby and I posted my work on the internet to get other people's opinions on it, and it was a good experience. There are a couple of good forums where you can post your images and people comment and critique and discuss them and [suggest] ways in which you can make them better. You know, I think that's a crucial part of developing your talent or your skill. So, [poetry night] is something similar to that, I guess.

To reflect the new understanding of performance poetry night, Jamal, Ahmad, Khalil, and Haris spent some time re-imagining the poster. Their debates about the poster frustrated the group a bit but also served to highlight the importance they assigned to getting the right message across. After speaking with the poets, designating the event as "Performance Poetry Night" was an easy decision; however, the group sought a motto to set an appropriate tone for the event. Finally, a joke made by Khalil half in frustration, half in jest—"We don't know what this is, but we like it"—was identified as conveying the sense of the evolving event that had emerged serendipitously. That decided, Ahmad changed the poster design from what he joked "looked like an ad for a gritty, low-budget crime movie" to a whimsical look the group had decided on—a stylized graphic of green, blue and purple. The event name and motto encircled a sketch of a bird nestled in clouds—a simple bird sketch that Haris and Ahmad had drawn on the white board for the first poetry event. Appreciated by several poets and audience members that evening, the bird had become the event's mascot. The words "lofty," "soar," "untitled," "imagery," "transcend," "precipice," "whisper," and "stance" in quirky and fanciful fonts filled the background amidst purple curlicues. The new poster suggested imagination, growth, and potential.

Like the organizers, the poets also drew upon informal learning and affinity space practices for their role in the event. In the absence of a spoken-word community on campus and lack of easy access to the few events taking place in the UAE, the poet participants had resorted to honing their poetry and performance techniques through digital media. Sakina, Omar, and Samir engaged in watching poetry slams and spoken-word events on YouTube and learned about the occasional spoken word event through Facebook. Badr posted his poems on the site *PoetrySoup.com*, where he both provided and benefited from poet feedback. Amal had a blog in which she posted her poems and remained in contact with other poets through discussion groups and her Twitter account. However, as she pointed out, online engagement was, in this case, a poor substitute:

> I want to see likeminded people gathered in one place, and, for once, feel like, okay, there are people who like poetry and, no, they're not, like, 1,000 miles away, or a Twitter follower, or, you know, a person who likes my blog post, but that there's someone that's sitting right in front of me and we're discussing poetry [face-to-face].

While spoken word is, as Low (2008) points out, "awash in contemporary communication technologies" (p. 102), its attraction is the poet-audience and poet-poet interaction. While digital media could bring performances to these student poets, it could not provide a space for the skill development or the social interaction they desired. Indeed, this first AUS event prompted Samir and Omar to search other UAE venues to perform. For Omar, this event brought him into the realm of "imagined communities" (Norton, 2001;

Norton & Kamal, 2003; Pavlenko & Norton, 2005), as he perceived this experience as a step toward membership in the community of the spoken word performers he had admired online:

> After the first poetry night, I wanted to perform again. Like, I needed to do it again, so I was Googling for places in Dubai, you know, open-mic nights, what I could find. And I found this place in Dubai called Global Youth Empowerment Movement, and, as it happens, like, a month later they were going to have an open-mic night. I went and I performed a poem there, and I loved it. Actually, someone there took a picture of me and just put it on Facebook and I found it recently, and I was so happy, because I felt like I looked how [my favourite performance poets, Shihan, Black Ice, and Gemineye] do, when they perform.

"Yes, Let's Get This On": Going Translingual and Forgetting Differences

Indeed, Omar was not the only poet who came to the second poetry performance much better prepared. It appeared the various efforts on the parts of the participants—the more deliberate planning and publicity by the organizers, the oral poetry workshop, and the opportunity of several months for poets to practice and plan—led to a second poetry night that retained the enthusiasm of the first, but included more linguistic variety and more skilful deliveries. Samir compared the two evenings:

> We still got a lot of people, but [this time] a lot of people, like, knew what to expect. Because last time we were, like, okay, "We're not sure what we're really doing, but let's give this a try." But now it's more like "Yes, let's get this on, you know. Let's make this the best night of our lives and stuff." Even though I had an exam at eight AM the next morning, I still came. I was planning to, like, perform and watch a couple of my friends and then leave, but I just couldn't leave. I sat through the entire night. And even we socialised afterwards for, like, another hour. And, this time, a lot of exchange students came. Like, there was Amy and she's from Chicago, and she was telling us, "You guys are really good." It was really good.

Students Running the Show 281

Sakina observed "a lot of poets who did it last time were a lot more confident than before—you could tell from their body language. They were like, 'We'll ditch the paper. We'll perform it.'" As an Urdu and English speaker with a grasp of primary-school Arabic, Sakina felt that the performance of the poems minimized the need for the language to be understood:

> Yes, you could enjoy them, the feeling and the performance aspect, you know? Even if you didn't understand it all. I think that's the main thing about it being the performance poetry. I mean, you may not, like, have to dwell on the content all the time, and if it's not in your language, you can focus on how it's delivered, because these poets [performed] really well.

For this second event, "open-mic" time was added after the scheduled performances. The organizers added this component on the advice of poets who knew attendees who had brought poems with them to the first event "just in case," but received no invitation to perform. Open mic added another portal to the event, giving an opportunity to those would-be performance poets who might decide they want to join in, even if they had been too intimidated to sign up. One of the poets who took advantage of this opportunity was Badr, who volunteered during open-mic time to perform a hilarious but classic Arabic poem "Sawt Safeeral Bulbulee," ("The Song of the Nightingale") attributed to the renowned Arab poet Al-Asma'i, who performed the poem during the eighth century for the Abbasid Caliph Abu Ja'far Al Mansour. This difficult piece, a real tongue-twister, was appreciated by audience members, many of whom were familiar with the poem from their studies in Arab history. Badr, who had memorized it as a child along with his siblings at the request of their father, felt comfortable performing it in view of the number of Arabic poems that evening:

> Poetry night was amazing, because poets came and they said what they wanted to say. It was just like "come with your poetry." All [possibilities were] there. That was the beauty of the night. People came, speaking in Arabic, English. People talked about love, talked about personal topics, talked about their countries, talked about society in general. People talked about their happy days. And there was even the kid who had the dark, the very dark poetry. Even that.

Another aspect that added to, in Badr's words, "the beauty of the night" was the event's effect on students' willingness to overlook, for the evening, those statuses or characteristics that to him appeared to be salient on campus and divisive to student unity. Badr reflected on those unique to AUS:

> Now, in university, everyone has their own corner. Like, you know, everything divides. For example, if you're not a party person, if you're not a clubbing person, if, let's say, you're one of the EMO people. Then you have the jocks. And then you have, let's say, the preps. And the thing is, here's the major clash in AUS: you have people who are strictly Arab, and you have people who are strictly Western, and you have people in the middle, and each one of them is even subcategorised into different groups. . . . and, it's bad, because these [members of these different groups] would never meet. And [at performance poetry night], we kind of broke these subcategories that I am talking about and we all united in one, under one flag, kind of thing. That was the beauty of it.

Sakina noted that interest in performance poetry seemed to cut across students' gender and major:

> There were guys who were students in my lab, and I never thought that they would like poetry—and you know, like, that's the thing, it's like this weird perception [that] guys . . . and engineers . . . don't like poetry, which is just nonsense—but they were there, and they really enjoyed it. And they told me that they really liked my poem and that I should [continue performing]. So I asked, "Will you guys come if it's held again? They're like, yes, you know, we're even thinking that next time we will take part.

Samir appreciated the event's potential for community building:

> I like the positive energy. I mean, other than coming to listen to good poetry, I like the whole fact that there's like social acceptance. You know? It doesn't matter who you are, what you are, what you look like, you're a human being in front of us, you're reading something which we know has value, or depth, or whatever. And like, you know, we're there with you. Like the girl who got up and she read the poem about her late grandfather, like, we could all relate. You know? It didn't matter if the poem was good or bad. We were there for her, and we clapped and we screamed. Every time now on campus I see her, we wave or talk a bit.

While events leading to the second poetry evening seemed less serendipitous, clearly the organizers and the poets engaged in synergy with the context—they sought to negotiate a learning community that was supportive, flexible, unstratified, and accommodating to each participants' level of proficiency. The AUS performance poetry evening, as a student-driven initiative, was situated in the cultural context and literacy strengths of the student poet population at AUS. The participants turned these evenings into opportunities for multi-vocalic expression that built community and good will across differences, and, indeed, highlighted translingual strengths of "synergy" and "serendipity" (Canagarajah, 2013, p. 41). The accommodating nature of performance poetry—adjustable to local parameters and context—was suited to the participants' affinity-space approach to negotiating an environment that was accessible, participatory, learning-filled, and evolving.

Performance Poetry Night: Still Evolving

Performance poetry night is an evolving story. The original organizers have graduated, and currently, IEO student staff have taken on the planning, demonstrating the same inclusive spirit the founding organizers and poets established. During the refreshment break after the most recent event—the fifth performance poetry night, in which poems were delivered in English, Arabic, Farsi, and Urdu—my discussion with a new organizer-poet who had assisted the IEO staff in planning the event revealed a proposed change for future poetry nights. He envisioned starting the evening "as per tradition" with sign-up spoken word performances and open-mic opportunities, followed by a "proper" slam for poets who wanted to compete. I was excited by his ideas—AUS poetry night is evolving with continued emphasis on making room for all poets and abilities.

There is another new development. Some of the poets—including Omar, Amal, and Badr—have participated in the performance poetry events sponsored monthly by the Rooftops Rhythms group in Abu Dhabi. In fact, there is a synergy developing between the two performance venues. AUS participants who had attended the Rooftops Rhythm events introduced a new Rooftops Rhythm practice into the fifth AUS performance poetry night—a mid-performance challenge to create a poem using audience-brainstormed words. This component resulted in a richer sense of poet-audience engagement and community. At the same time, "seasoned" AUS performance poets were encouraging novices to investigate Rooftops Rhythms as another venue for their creativity. At this point, I am pleased to state that "a culture of performance poetry" has formed in the UAE, and some of those poets got their start at AUS.

Implications for Writing Programs

Many chapters in this book have addressed the level to which our MENA students are not considered prepared for English-medium, university-level writing. They cite the variety of educational models which comprised our students' secondary education, the lack of emphasis on learner independence or critical thinking in the curriculum, and the varying degrees to which English in general, and English academic writing in particular, are addressed (see Annous, Nicolas & Townsend; Hodges & Kent; Jarkas & Fakhreddine; Miller & Pessoa; and Rudd & Telafici; , this volume). As such, there is a daunting sense that students have a lot of "catching up" to do which must be accomplished as quickly as possible because writing assignments in their other courses require students to have already assimilated these skills.

To respond to this need, my Department of Writing—whose purview covers only the first-year writing requirements—has, over the past few years, steadily refined writing course content to a strict focus on argument and source-based writing. However, this focus may have come at a price, where students perceive writing at university as stripped of creativity and self-expression. While there are a few opportunities for creative writing in upper-level English department courses, many students do not consider those as options; indeed, four out of the five poet participants in this research were engineering students who felt the rigors of their coursework would not permit enrolling in creative writing classes. Yet, a significant number of AUS students have poems tucked away in their laptops or phones, or even spiral-bound notebooks—and many of these students would not be characterized as "strong" academic writers, even as their poems reveal that they can be wry and insightful, even skilful, commentators on life in English and other languages.

In our limited capacity as a first-year writing program with a strictly academic writing focus, how can the Department of Writing—and other departments like it in the MENA region—display an openness to and support for students' out-of-classroom use of English or translingual practices? How can we provide a platform for students who want to share literacy and linguistic practices that are different from the types of writing we require in our classes? And, significantly, how can we invite affinity spaces on the campus, which put the reins in the students' hands, empowering them to drive their own learning, which was certainly the strength of performance poetry night? This last point is especially important, as developing learner independence is a need of MENA-region students; many have come from largely authoritarian or regimented educational backgrounds and would benefit from opportunities where they are responsible for their learning.

As such, it appears necessary to broaden our approach in different ways. In view of the endeavor under study—the student-driven poetry night—it seems appropriate to look to the extracurricular realm, a place where, for many students, academic and personal interests meet with limited guidance from faculty. Supporting a student activity or club can translate into service for writing faculty who are expected to fulfill such requirements. Of course, a logical spring-board for encouraging similar extracurricular endeavors is the writing center, especially if it is staffed by undergraduate tutors who can take responsibility for organizing the activities. Writing centers are known sites of innovation, and their status as spaces for writing-across-the-curriculum easily opens doors to undertakings with different units and departments on campus; this is particularly so if the tutors represent a variety of majors and are cognizant of the variety of literacy activities that their peers engage in. Keeping in mind the role of the IEO in lending an international, cross-cultural legitimacy to performance poetry night, writing-center-sponsored activities that are pointedly interdisciplinary—for example, collaborating with computer engineering students on a "code poetry" event—would make such undertakings more relevant, and thus, more interesting to students.

While our writing courses may be standardized in terms of goals and outcomes, faculty may be able to drive at least some of the courses' content. Introducing a unit—with readings, an assignment, and perhaps presentations—on popular out-of-classroom literacy practices like blogging, fan fiction, and spoken word, to name a few, would help elicit discussions on the literacy acts students engage in outside of class. This kind of a unit could perhaps also generate interest on the part of some students to interact with peers to learn more about writing. Basing writing assignments on the topic of participatory literacy practices in English or in other languages may also compensate for the little room allotted to free or creative writing by validating, as a topic worthy of class attention, the practices students engage in on their own time. These topics may also mitigate the "deficit atmosphere" in the writing classroom if students understood their professors as valuing their own literacy practices, which will, in the MENA region, almost certainly cross languages. Moreover, the ensuing class discussion and the inherent learning can create inroads for student exploration with like-minded classmates and lead to activities similar to that of performance poetry night. As explained earlier in the chapter, Jamal's interest in spoken word—the driving force behind the event—was sparked by his exposure to a spoken-word performance in his tutor-training class; that half-hour classroom exercise played an undeniable role in the student-driven chain of events that ensued.

Supporting out-of-classroom literacy development in our rich translingual environments is becoming increasingly important even as we in the MENA region may find our resources to that extent limited for a variety of reasons. In response to those limitations, we should seek creative ways to engage our students in this undertaking. MENA students need to be encouraged to participate in their own learning, as Haris, one of the organizers noted:

> There's only so much the university can do; then it's up to the students. It's a two-way road: The university provides us with good professors, good auditoriums, a good library; we have good rooms to hold events. So now it's up to us [students] to actually take a step, and do our part.

Indeed, there is a great deal to be learned by letting students run the show.

References

American University of Sharjah. (2010). Chancellor's Snapshot.
Camangian, P. (2008). Untempered tongues: Teaching performance poetry for social justice. *English Teaching: Practice and Critique, 7*(2), 35–55. Retrieved from http://education.waikato.ac.nz/research/files/etpc/2008v7n2art2.pdf.
Canagarajah, A. S. (2007). Lingua franca English, multilingual communities, and language acquisition. *The Modern Language Journal, 91,* 923–939.
Canagarajah, A. S. (2013a). Negotiating translingual literacy: An enactment. *Research in the Teaching of English, 48*(1), 40–67.
Canagarajah, A. S. (2013b). *Translingual practice: Global Englishes and cosmopolitan relations.* New York: Routledge.
Dyson, A. H. (2005). Crafting "the humble prose of living": Rethinking oral/written relations in the echoes of spoken word. *English Education, 37,* 149–164.
Fisher, M. T. (2005). From the coffee house to the school house: The promise and potential of spoken word poetry in school contexts. *English Education, 37*(2), 115–131.
Gee, J. P. (2000). The New Literacy studies: From "socially situated" to the work of the social. In D. Barton, M. Hamilton & R. Ivanič, R. (Eds.), *Situated literacies: Reading and writing in context* (pp. 180–196). London: Routledge.
Gee, J. P. (2004). *Situated language and learning: A critique of traditional schooling.* New York: Routledge.
Gee, J. P. (2005). *Language, learning, and gaming: A critique of traditional schooling.* New York: Routledge.
Gee, J. P. (2007). *Good video games and good learning: Collected essays on video games, learning, and literacy.* New York: Peter Lang.

Gregory, H. (2008a). (Re)presenting ourselves: Art, identity, and status in U.K. Poetry Slam. *Oral Tradition, 23*(2), 201–217.

Gregory, H. (2008b). The quiet revolution of poetry slam: The sustainability of cultural capital in the light of changing artistic conventions. *Ethnography and Education, 3*(1), 63–80.

Hall, J. & Navarro, N. (2011, December 21). Lessons for WAC/WID from language learning research: Multicompetence, register acquisition, and the college writing student. *Across the Disciplines, 8*(4). Retrieved from http://wac.colostate.edu/atd/ell/hall-navarro.cfm.

Horner, B., Donahue, C. & NeCamp, S. (2011). Toward a multilingual composition scholarship: From English only to a translingual norm. *College Composition and Communication, 63*, 269–300.

Kinloch, V. (2005). Poetry, literacy, and creativity: Fostering effective learning strategies in an urban classroom. *English Education, 37*(2), 96–114.

Lankshear, C. & Knobel, M. (Eds.). (2013). *A new literacies reader: Educational perspectives*. New York: Peter Lang.

Low, B. E. (2008). Slammin' school: Performance poetry and the urban school. In M. Hoechsmann & B. E. Low (Eds.), *Reading youth writing: "New" literacies, cultural studies & education* (pp. 99–127). New York: Peter Lang.

Mnensa, M. T. (2010). Speaking out: African orality and post-colonial preoccupations in selected examples of contemporary performance poetry (Unpublished master's thesis). Nelson Mandela Metropolitan University, South Africa.

Nanton, P. (2008–2009). Protest and performance: New orality in Barbados. *Shibboleths: A Journal of Theory and Criticism, 3*(2), 97–104.

Norton, B. (2001). Non-participation, imagined communities and the language classroom. In M. Breen (Ed.), *Learner contributions to language learning: New directions in research* (pp. 159–171). Harlow, UK: Pearson Education.

Norton, B. & Kamal, F. (2003). The imagined communities of Pakistani school children. *Journal of Language, Identity & Education, 3*(4), 301–317.

Pavlenko, A. & Norton, B. (2005). Imagined communities, identity, and English language teaching. In J. Cummins & C. Davison (Eds.), *Kluwer handbook of English language teaching*. Dordrecht, NL: Kluwer Academic Publishers.

Reyes, G. T. (2006). Finding the poetic high: Building a spoken word poetry community and culture of creative, caring, and critical intellectuals. *Multicultural Education, 14*(2), 10–15.

Selfe, C. L. (2009). The movement of air, the breath of meaning: Aurality and multimodal composing. *College Composition and Communication, 60*(4), 616–63.

Smith, A. M. (2010). Poetry performances and academic identity negotiations in the literacy experiences of seventh grade language arts students. *Reading Improvement, 47*(4), 202–218.

Somers-Willet, S. B. A. (2007). Can slam poetry matter? *Rattle: Poetry for the 21st Century Issue #27, 13*(1), 85–90.

St. Clair, R. & Phipps, A. (2008). Ludic literacies at the intersections of cultures: An interview with James Paul Gee. *Language and Intercultural Communication, 8*(2), 91–100. doi:10. 1080/14708470802270950.

The Guardian. (2009, January 6). Linton Kwesi Johnson performs If I Woz a Tap Natch Poet [Video file]. Retrieved from https://www.youtube.com/watch?v =WmijkaVztqY.

Weinstein, S. (2010). "A unified poet alliance": The personal and social outcomes of youth spoken word poetry programming. *International Journal of Education & the Arts, 11*(2), 1–24. Retrieved from http://www.ijea. org/v11n2/.

Zenger, A. A. (2012). Constructing local context in Beirut: Students' literacy practices outside of class. In B. T. Williams & A. A. Zenger (Eds.), *New media literacies and participatory popular cultures across borders* (pp. 33–43). New York: Routledge.

Zenger, A., Mullin, J. & Haviland, C. (2014). Reconstructing teacher roles through a transnational lens: Learning with/in the American University of Beirut. In T. M. Zawcki & M. Cox (Eds.), *WAC and second language writers: Research toward linguistically and culturally inclusive programs and practices* (pp. 415–438). Fort Collins, CO: The WAC Clearinghouse and Parlor Press. Retrieved from http://wac.colostate.edu/books/l2/.

Afterword

Michele Eodice
UNIVERSITY OF OKLAHOMA (US)

> While the interest and activity in writing research is global, the responses are local.
> —*Bazerman, et al., 2009, p. ix*

I want to say a few words about what I think are the three main strengths of this collection. First, the collection follows a trajectory set up and supported by some of the best researchers in the world; second, it does not take lightly the implications for English-language dominance in global contexts; third, all of these chapters honor those global contexts in admirable ways, even when collaborating across continents.

Following the International Writing Centers Association (IWCA) Summer Institute at Stanford University (US) in 2006, Cecelia Hawkins, who was then posted at the Texas A&M writing center in Doha, Qatar, invited me to visit Education City. While I was there, Hawkins hosted writing teachers and writing center/learning center directors from the region; the outcome, after spending two days talking together, was the start of the Middle East–North Africa Writing Center Alliance (MENAWCA). While president of IWCA in 2007, I was privileged to recognize MENAWCA as an official regional organization within IWCA. This moment opened up opportunities for many of us to join groups from all over the world, not as the writing center experts from the United States, but as true partners in an effort to create a global community of writing center leaders. Terry Zawacki's keynote address at the MENAWCA conference in 2012 is described in this book's introduction as another such moment of opportunity and awareness, moving us toward developing more intentional research and publication and thus nurturing a global writing studies movement. At the same time, researchers like Charles Bazerman and others were creating a larger space for this larger conversation through conferences such as Writing Research Across Borders and through collections of research, such as Traditions of Writing Research (2010) and International Advances in Writing Research: Cultures, Places, Measures (2012). Granted, this summary is based on my experiences with these places and people, conferences and texts; I am sure hundreds of researchers are right now contributing to the growing literature on teaching writing in "global contexts" (Lillis & Curry, 2010).

One productive result of all the work outlined above is found in the book you are reading, where a particular research stance has emerged, one grounded in valuing all the varied linguistic skills student writers come with, first and foremost, and one that regards language negotiation as pedagogical, not problematic. Included in this stance is deeper engagement with methods and participants, preventing, as Christiane Donahue (2009) warned, "'internationalizing' efforts that remain stuck in a-historical, a-contextual, and highly partial modes of intellectual tourism" (p. 236). The researchers here have acted as responsible global citizens, embodying a "rhetoric of respect" (Rousculp, 2014) as they engage with communities of writers in the Middle East–North Africa region. Perhaps some have even achieved a level of engagement Suresh Canagarajah (2013) calls "radically other-centered" (p. 41).

The researchers here (clearly following the lead of the editors' sensibilities) avoid colonizing moves in their interactions by foregrounding over a dozen different contexts and acknowledging that the "imposition of English on non-native speakers of English has raised the issues of linguistic and cultural hegemony" (Uysal, Chapter 2, this volume). So while we will learn about new classroom strategies or new language policies, this collection emphasizes that making knowledge through interaction with this text and then in our own communities requires that we not lose sight of context. In *Decolonizing Educational Research*, Leigh Patel (2016) explains this responsibility:

> In addition to being answerable to learning and knowledge, educational research is answerable to context. . . . However, being answerable to context does not only mean attending to the historical and ongoing destruction of colonialism. Additionally, it means attending to the ways that humans . . . engage in learning. . . . Being answerable to context dynamically helps to illuminate what kinds of knowledges are important. Projects of systemic social change cannot pursue knowledge without regard to the context they are trying to change. (p. 78)

Most writing centers and composition classrooms in the US share something in common: the staff and students are predominately white English speakers. In some cases, it matters little to an institution that this scene prevails in spite of amazing diversity within our student populations. Unfortunately, in the US many see "non-native" speakers as a growing problem and not a linguistic gift. In the MENA region, writing specialists have moved way beyond U.S. discussions of EFL, EAP, ESL, and the like. This recursive discussion in the US "keeps us stuck in old thinking that is tied to an ideology few sociolinguistic scholars would still espouse" (Nebel, Chapter 1, this volume). Those who work most often with student writers (in classrooms or writing centers) need to cultivate superdiversity if we are not already right smack in the middle of it.

> Among the new social formations are contexts of learning in higher education where there is now a mixing of people who geographically, socioeconomically, and linguistically might otherwise never have come together. Recognizing the challenges and opportunities of this phenomenon allows us to explore previously held constructs in a new and fluid space that should necessarily invite a shift in thinking to meet the complex characteristics of context and time. (Nebel, Chapter 1, this volume)

Nebel's message is an important one for us to hear, especially in U.S. higher education. Uysal pushes us even further, beyond classroom teaching, to consider the impact of a global English imperative on scholarly writers from the MENA region. As more and more writing specialists work with faculty writers, we will need a fuller understanding of the evolving publishing demands and markets and what those markets are saying about language in this "post-monolingual world" (Nebel, Chapter 1, this volume). The extent of co-researching/co-authoring in this collection is remarkable too, and I can only imagine the impact each individual researcher made on their research teams in terms of language exchanges and sharing diverse ways of knowing. In the midst of research collaboration, Theado, Johnson, Highly, and Omar uncovered hidden assets by working across institutions: "Merging pedagogical preferences and practices produced new instructional approaches that better suit [our] teaching contexts" (Chapter 7, this volume). Many researchers in this collection have taken admirable risks in crossing transnational borders to improve curriculum and pedagogy. They have designed studies to learn directly from faculty and students how the tension between teaching content and teaching language (especially in those English-medium universities) influences the perceptions of academic challenge (Miller & Pessoa). It may surprise some that the very same issues we talk about in the U.S. context are being studied in the MENA region: student preparedness for academic literacy, plagiarism, the value of creative and reflective writing, and more.

How will this collection impact me, someone who has visited the region and has some understanding of the contexts and issues? What I am now noticing, as an editor of *The Writing Center Journal* and as a professor who is developing a new graduate seminar called Composing Leadership, is that I need to take this book into that work. The writing center folks who read the journal and the graduate students who take the seminar will benefit from seeing the scope of research projects undertaken by the authors in this collection. They need to see how integrative the thinking is about writing in multiple settings; and they need to see how collaboration across institutions and continents works. And I realized that while thinking about possible readings for the seminar (designed to prepare future writing program administrators, writing-across-the-curriculum program directors, and writing center directors), I had been eagerly waiting for the moment when the first big wave of research from this region would hit our shores. In addition, the faculty fellows who work on our Writing Enriched Curriculum project will be reading several chapters from this collection to inform their understandings of WAC/WID models in very different settings.

Finally, what I have been most impressed with is that each chapter contextualizes its own political landscape, from the locations where language policy and language-learning pedagogies are mediated, to the curricular, where critiques of aims and practices are designed to respond to particular contexts. Communities of writers are always communities in context; I have come to believe all writing *is* community writing. Collective efforts, such as this edited edition, have contributed to supporting and recognizing writing researchers from all over the world while furthering a stance that seems especially important for those of us working from the west to take—that resisting the western, Americentric, Anglocentric, or Anglophone influence is achieved through understanding global communities in context. Based on the evidence presented by these researchers, I believe we do share these commonplaces: that writing research is educational research; that writing is potentially transformative for student writers (as well as for writers of research); and that we study writers and writing to acknowledge and ultimately improve the contexts in which writing is taught and produced. In *Emerging Writing Research from the Middle East–North Africa Region*, readers can find evidence that these shared commonplaces, as valued within contexts, will bring us closer to knowing each other.

References

Bazerman, C., Krut, R., Lunsford, K., McLeod, S., Null, S., Rogers, P. & Stansell, A. (Eds.). (2009). *Traditions of writing research*. London: Routledge.

Canagarajah, A. S. (2013). Negotiating translingual literacy: An enactment. *Research in the Teaching of English, 48*(1), 40–67.

Donahue, C. (2009). "Internationalization" and composition studies: Reorienting the discourse. *College Composition and Communication, 61*(2), 212–243.

Lillis, T. M. & Curry, M. J. (2010). *Academic writing in global context*. London: Routledge.

Patel, L. (2016). *Decolonizing Educational Research*. New York: Routledge.

Rousculp, T. (2014). *Rhetoric of respect: Recognizing change at a community writing center*. Urbana, IL: NCTE.

Contributors

Samer A. Annous is Assistant Professor of English and Coordinator of the graduate program in the Department of English at the University of Balamand (Lebanon). His research interests include English as a Medium of Instruction (EMI) policy in the MENA region and Lebanese identity and language learning.

Lisa R. Arnold, Director of First-Year Writing and Assistant Professor of English at North Dakota State University, was previously an Assistant Professor of English and Director of Communication Skills at the American University of Beirut. She has been published in *College Composition and Communication*, *College English*, *JAC*, and *Pedagogy*. She is currently drafting a book titled *An Imagined America: Writing Policies and Practices at the Syrian Protestant College, 1866–1920*.

James P. Austin is Assistant Professor of English at Fort Hays State University and holds a doctorate in Education from the University of California, Santa Barbara. Prior to this, he lived in Egypt for four years and taught writing at the American University in Cairo.

William DeGenaro is Associate Professor/Writing Program Director at University of Michigan-Dearborn. He was a Fulbright Scholar to Lebanon in 2010–2011 and currently serves on the Executive Committee of the Conference on College Composition and Communication. He writes about basic writing, service learning pedagogies, and working-class studies.

Rula Diab is Associate Professor of English at the Lebanese American University (LAU) in Beirut, Lebanon. She is the founding director of the LAU Writing Center. Her research interests include learners' and teachers' beliefs about second/foreign language learning, particularly second language writing; writing centers; and writing across the curriculum.

Michele Eodice is Associate Provost and Director of the OU Writing Center at the University of Oklahoma. She is a past president of the International Writing Centers Association and a current co-director of The Meaningful Writing Project. Eodice has had the privilege of traveling to visit writing centers around the world, including in the MENA region.

Juheina Fakhreddine holds an MA in education with emphasis on TESOL. She teaches academic writing at AUB Lebanon. She has extensive experience in teaching English as an L_2 in high schools and universities across the country. She also co-authored a number of English language textbooks addressed to ESL/EFL students.

Aneta L Hayes is Lecturer in Education at Keele University. She is interested in educational transitions, socio-cultural theory, and international/transnational education. In her work, Aneta has explored teacher, student and institutional identities, as well as the role of higher education institutions in international students' experiences.

Tom Highley is an adjunct professor and doctoral candidate in literacy at the University of Cincinnati. His research focuses on digital literacies, discourse analysis, and international university partnerships. Tom has worked in the MENA region as an educator and grant worker, co-teaching at Salahaddin University and conducting workshops across Iraq.

Amy Hodges is a postdoctoral associate at the Massachusetts Institute of Technology with a joint appointment at Singapore University of Technology and Design's writing center. Her teaching and research interests include multilingual writers, WAC/WID, and community literacy.

Rima Iskandarani completed her MA in Teaching English as a Foreign Language at the American University of Beirut, Lebanon. An avid believer in the inherent power of storytelling, Rima thinks that there is a child in every one of us. She is currently incorporating social media technologies to enhance students' engagement in learning in her courses.

Najla Jarkas is a Senior Lecturer and Assistant Director to Writing in the Disciplines in the Department of English at the American University of Beirut. Her recent research interests are in the fields of action research in academic English courses, the Literary Fantastic and Digital Humanities.

Holly Johnson is Associate Professor in the Literacy and Second Language Studies Program at the University of Cincinnati. She has worked on international projects for the last five years in Iraq, India, and Pakistan and is a Returned Peace Corps Volunteer. Her scholarship focuses on adolescent literacy and disciplinary literacy. Her publications include both books and articles in the field of literacy and teacher education.

Brenda Kent taught the writing component of the Ethics and Engineering course for Texas A&M University at Qatar. She has been involved in education for 30 years. Brenda has also worked as an editor for consulting firms and as an aide to a U.S. Congressman.

Malakeh Raif Khoury-Khayat studied English Literature and language at the American University of Beirut, Lebanon, where she currently teaches composition classes. She completed coursework for an Ed.D. in TESOL with the University of Leicester, UK. She has worked and is interested in curricular assessment, creative writing, translation and Arabic literature and language.

Nasser Mansour is Senior Lecturer in Science Education and Director of MSc Educational Research at University of Exeter. He is interested in socio-cultural issues in education, scientific literacy, the relationship between religion and science education, learners' ideas, and misconceptions, and alternative frameworks for understanding education. His work explores teacher beliefs and practices and teacher professional development based on multi-cultural studies in science education.

Ryan T. Miller is Assistant Professor in the English Department at Kent State University. His research areas are second language reading and writing. His research investigates development of academic and discipline-specific writing skills and genre knowledge, and dual-language involvement and support of reading comprehension and reading sub-skills.

Anne Nebel is Senior Assistant Dean in the School of Foreign Service at Georgetown University Qatar. She teaches undergraduate writing courses and directs an academic support unit that includes the writing center. Her research interests focus on task-based language assessment, linguistic superdiversity, complexity theory and writing development, and critical discourse analysis.

Maureen O'Day Nicolas is Associate Professor at the University of Balamand in Lebanon. She has served as Chair of the Department of English at a time of comprehensive curriculum reform and Assistant Dean of the Faculty of Arts and Social Sciences. Her research interests include writing as a learning tool and teachers' professional development.

Saman Hussein Omar has a Ph.D. in the Modern American Novel and currently works as the Director of the Language Center at Salahaddin University-Erbil. He is interested in literary and pedagogic research. He also teaches Modern English Drama, Poetry, and the Novel at the English Department in Salahaddin University-Erbil.

Silvia Pessoa is Associate Teaching Professor of English at Carnegie Mellon University in Qatar. Her areas of interest are academic writing development and immigration. Her work informs pedagogical practices in writing in the disciplines and policy on immigration. She is currently involved in literacy intervention studies in various disciplines.

Lynne Ronesi is Assistant Professor in the Department of Writing Studies at the American University of Sharjah in the United Arab Emirates. Her research interests include participatory literacies, translingualism, peer tutor training, and WAC/WID. Her work has appeared in the *Journal of Language, Identity, and Education*, the *Writing Center Journal*, and *Across the Disciplines* as well as in several edited collections.

Mysti Rudd serves as the Director of the Academic Success Center as well as Assistant Professor of English at Texas A&M University at Qatar.

She earned her Ph.D. in Composition/TESOL from Indiana University of Pennsylvania, specializing in the impact of teaching practices on the retention and engagement of first-year students.

Zane Siraj Sinno is Lecturer at the American University of Beirut, Lebanon. In 2008, she earned her doctorate from the University of Leicester (UK). She teaches Communication Skills Program courses at AUB. Her research interests are mainly in language, globalization, and power in the Arab world; language and identity in the Arab world; e-language use; and digital reading.

Michael Telafici is Instructional Associate Professor at Texas A & M University at Qatar, and he currently teaches Foundation English, First-Year Composition, and Technical Business Writing classes. He previously spent nearly a decade as a technical and professional writer. His research interests include critical pedagogy, language and identity, technology in education, and motivation.

Connie Kendall Theado is Associate Professor and Director of Graduate Studies in the School of Education at the University of Cincinnati. Her work appears in *JAC*, *Classroom Discourse*, *Language & Literacy*, and *Open Words*. Most recently, she co-edited a special issue of *Composition Studies* focused on writing instruction in multilingual, translingual, and transnational contexts.

Martha A. Townsend is Professor Emerita of English at the University of Missouri and former director of its internationally renowned Campus Writing Program. Townsend's publications have played a central role in the conceptualization and development of writing-across-the-curriculum programs in the United States and abroad. She is a former literacy consultant to the Ford Foundation.

Hacer Hande Uysal is Associate Professor and Director of the Gazi Academic Writing & Research Center at Gazi University, Ankara, Turkey. She received her MA in English Education and her Ph.D. in Foreign Language/ESL Education from the University of Iowa. Her research interests are second language writing, intercultural rhetoric, academic discourse, early language teaching, and language planning and policy.

Margaret Willard-Traub is Associate Professor of Composition and Rhetoric and former Director of the Writing Program at the University of Michigan-Dearborn. Her research and teaching interests include transnational and translingual pedagogies, feminist composition, reflection, scholarly memoir, genre studies, writing assessment, and critical pedagogy. Her articles have appeared in *College English*, *Assessing Writing*, *Rhetoric Review*, *Feminist Studies* and *Pedagogy* as well as in a number of edited collections.

www.ingramcontent.com/pod-product-compliance
Lightning Source LLC
Chambersburg PA
CBHW070129080526
44586CB00015B/1611